Child Labour in Various Industries

Encyclopaedia of Child Development: Priorities for 21st Century - 3

Child Labour in Various Industries

Editor
S. Wal

SARUP & SONS
NEW DELHI

Published by
SARUP & SONS
4740/23, Ansari Road
Darya Ganj, New Delhi-110002
Ph. : 23281029, 23244664, 51010989
Fax : 011-23277098
email : sarupandsonsin@hotmail.com

Child Labour in Various Industries

ISBN : 81-7625-635-8

© Reserved

Edition 2006

Printed in India

Published by Prabhat Kumar Sharma for Sarup & Sons, Laser typesetting at Manas Typesetter, New Delhi Printed at Roshan Offset Press, Delhi.

Preface

The use of child labour in various industries is a big area of concern for our policy makers. In many developing countries a very large number of children work in sub human conditions and are payed very less for full work. It has been seen that a large number of children are surviving under great health and safety hazards. Above all the workplace trauma is widespread, stunting the growth of the children both physically and mentally.

Hence, considering the problem in its totality, an effort has been made to cover the diverse aspects of the subject.

Editor

Content

		Page Nos.
1.	Introduction	1
2.	Child Labour in India : Retrospect & Prospect	11
3.	Child Labour in Indian Industries	20
4.	Child Labour Dimensions : An Appraisal	30
5.	Innocents' Agony : Child Labour in India	37
6.	Child Labour at Work	44
7.	Children in the Glass Industry	52
8.	Migrant Child Labour in Orissa	63
9.	Child labour in Agriculture Sector	79
10.	The Child Potters of Khurja	109
11.	Traditional Crafts and Child Labour	126
12.	Child Labour in Chikan Industry	133
13.	Child Labour in Lock Industry	167
14.	Children Working in Agarbatti Industry	181
15.	Children Work in the Brass Ware Industry	192
16.	Moradabad Child Labour Project	220
17.	Child Labour in Nepal	228
18.	Child Labour in North America	237
19.	The Child Gem Polishers of Jaipur	284
20.	Annexure	302

1

INTRODUCTION

Child labour is not a new phenomenon. It existed in different from in its history. Children were given apprenticeship training in family based occupations like agriculture, crafts and trades from tender age so as to prepare them to take over future responsibilities. Learning of specific skills by participating in the family trade activities had a positive effect on developing of competence without imposing constraints on their overall development.

The evil of child labour is prevails not only in under develop countries but in many of the develop countries as well. The practice of child labour is more prevalent in poor countries which lack resources and infrastructural facilities for children, such educational institution, vocational training centres and the like. In many parts of the world child labour is preferred as it is cheaper and unorganized. Most of these countries are from Asia and Africa.

A major portion of western and southern part of Africa have a very high share of working children. (above 35 per 1000 population). Some of these countries have an exceptionally highly proportion of child labour (above 50 per 1000 population) are Rwanda (55.6). Berin (53.8), Botswana (53.8), Mali (53.3), Sri Lanka (53.0), Bhutan (31.2), and upper vilta (50.0). The countries from outside Africa. Which are included in this catagory are Haiti from the (Aribbean and Nepal, Bhutan, Bangladesh and Sri Lanka From Asia). In 17 countries, child labour is high (25-35 per 1000). Most of these countries are from the African continent. According to Moonis Raza (1984) twenty three countries, mostly from Asia and Africa belongs to the medium catetgory (15-25 pre 1000). The middle and south American countries which are included in this category are Gautemala, El Salvador, Nicaragua and Bolivia.

A low proportion of working children (5-15 per 1000 population) is found in the middle and south American countries and a few countries of Northern and Western Africa. Many of the Asian countries like Syria, Lebanon, Jordan, Saudi Arabia, Democratic Yemen and Malaysia are belong to this category.

A very low share of working children (less than 5 per 1000) is found in most of the countries from Europe. North America and Astralia. The countries from other continents which fall in this category are Cuba. Hondurar and Jamica from middle America, Surinam and Guyana from south America, Cyprus, Israel, Iraq, Kuwait, Singapore and Japan from Asia. In a number of countries, the share of working children is negligible (less than one per 1000 population) such as Sweeden, Finland, Denmark, Poland, Hungary, Bulgaria, Belgim, etc.

It will be surprise to know that according to latest available data there is no working child in the

USSR, New Zealand and Papua New Guinea.

Participation of children in work is not a phenomenon peculiear only to our age. It has been there is different forms in every society throughout history. Mendelievich has correctly observed:

"To a greater or lesser extent, children in every type of human society have always taken part, and still do take part in those economic activities which are necessary if the group to which they belong is to survive."

It has been pointed out in the Reported of the Committee on Child Labour that "Child Labour is not a new phenomenon to our age. It has existed in one form or other in all historical times."

Children in this country have been associated with work from immemorial time. The work that they were asked to undertake used to provide them an opportunity for direct fulfilment of their natural abilities and creative potentialities and thus was conducive to their healthy growth and development.

When the structure of society was not so complicated, various occupations used to be pursued on the caste lines within the framework of the joint family system in which the pleasures and pains, prosperity and poverty, and business and idleness used to be shared by all the members according to their capacity and needs of all members used to be fulfilled within the available family resources. The system was based on the principle of 'each for all and all for each', under this system elders used to ensure that opportunities for fullest development of children became available to them and all obstacles in the way of their proper development were timely removed. They used to see that the work done by children provided them creative opportunities equipping them with healthy experiences and that there was no adverse effect of work on the personality of children.

Children, in fact, were given apprenticeship training these family based occupations in the form of Chikan crafts to prepare them to gradually take up various adult roles. Menedeleivich has aptly remarked "in earlier times children used to work within their family circles. Little by little through almost unconscious observation, association and initiation they learnt the role they would be called upon as adults. During this process of socialisation, of which "on-the-job" training formed a part, the child grew to physical and intellectual maturity without ill-treatment and virtually without being exploited and was simultaneously prepared for adult life.

Children's participation in work is not always commercial. The effect of work, constructive and meaningful or otherwise, depends upon purpose for which it is sought to be undertaken by children and the nature or work that is performed as also the conditions under which it is done. Government of India have also admitted that:

"All forms of work by children cannot be considred deleterious. In fact, work plays an important role in development of child, if it involves purpose, plan and fredom. The function of work in childhood should be primarily developmental and not economic, and children's work as a social good is the direct anit-thesis of child labour as a social evil."

Today children are required to work individually without being given an personal and paternalistic guidance that they used to get in earlier time while working in family undetakings. They perform different types of repetitive, spontaneous, unpromising and hazardous and are a quite often maitreated and exploited. The net effect of the participation of children in work today is negative and harmful to their proper physical, mental and moral development. The work that children do today is characterised by "long hours of work, late hours or night employment. continuous standing. Sitting or use of single set of muscles, emphasis on the finer neuromuscular coordinations with attendant nervous strain, indoor confinement in noisy factories and dusty traders, carrying heavy loads under the arm, presssure of speed in the perfomance of simple mechanical acts, contact with industrial poisons exposure to inclement weather...harmful conditons for growing child peculiarly susceptible to certain deformation and diseases.

The condition of work and working conditons are often so bad that the various functions performed by children today have converted their work into labour. The children work on nominal wages for long hours without any rest, interval, educational or recreational facilities beyond their capacity and against their wishes.

It has been rightly pointed out. "Every child labourer is a child with all the needs of other children. He needs opportunity for growth not only physical, but in mind and personality, through all the activities and experiences, which properly belong to childhood, when the business of wage earning or of participation in self of family support, conflicts directly or indirectly with the business of growth and education the result is child labour. The function of work in childhood is primarily developmental and not economic. Children's work then a social good is direct anti-thesis of child labour as a social evil". Thus, in modern time, child labour is a social problem obstructing the normal development of children.

The protection and promotion of interests of working children has become a subject of paramout importance and any civilised society cannot afford to over look it. It has been correctly mentioned in the Preamble to the Children Act, 1960 "Children are the most vulnerable group in any population and in the need of the greatest social care. On account of their vulnerability and dependence, they can be exploited, ill-treated and directed into undesirable channels by anti-social elements in the community. The State has the duty of according proper care and protection to children at all times as it is on their physical and mental well-being that the future of the nation depends."

Recent development, physical and social, sciences, have unfolded many dimensions of the entire process of personality development. They have shed sufficient light on different aspects of the needs and problems of children as also their consequences from the standpoint of healthy growth if they are not properly tackled. Recognition of these developmental needs of children and various adverse effects of their non-fulfilment have made it more imperative for a society which, feels concerned about its future and wants to make it bright and prosperous, to take such positive measures as may be helpful in adequately by providing them sufficient opportunities for their development as healthy and resonsible members of tomorrow.

Thus, the recognition of various evil effects of child labour on the physical, mental and moral development of children, commitment of the State to safeguard its children from exploitation and the ensure them a healthy and satisfying life free from want and misery, and ever-growing realisation of the need for timely fulfilment of various developmental requirements during childhood which is the formative period, have significantly contributed to identification of child labour as a social problem in modern times.

Child Labour as a Social Evil

Compelled by the situation children accept roles, which turn them into the victims of a situation which is characterised by the fact that it one does not work, one has to option but to starve or adopt socially disapproved means for his survival. Children have no choice but to take the jobs at an age at which they would have gone to school. Through children think that they are taking decision to work fact is that it is not the children but the society, through its inability to provide adequate means for the subsistence of family, decides at the time of their birth itself that they are destined to take up employment at an early age. It is not only the children who are harmed due to their involvement in various kinds of work at an early age but the society also which has to suffer a great loss because of childrens emploment at an early age. This system employers who are always after gaining maximum profit with minimum investment.

The system of child labour adversely affects the society in two ways. It denies the employment opportunities to the young population of the society, forcing many of them to go out of work in the present age of wide-spread employment and under-employment. It also considerably lowers down the rates of the wages in the society. In fact, child labour is as much the cause as the consequence of adult unemployment and under-employment.

The terms 'child labour' is at times used as a synonym for 'employed child' or 'working child'. In this sense it is co-extensive with any work done by a child for economical gain. But more often than not, the term 'Child Labour' is used in a social sense. It suggests something which is harmful, unjust and full of exploitation. The term 'child' has been variously defined. "The Child Labour (Prohibition and Regulation) Act, 1986 has stated" Child is a peson who has not completed his fourteenth year of age. Operation Research Group at Baroda has defined the age group of child workers to be between five to fifteen years.

The term 'Child Labour' not only applies to the children working in organized industries but also to the children working in all forms of non-industrial and un-organized occupations, which are injurious to their normal physical, mental and social development.

In India, there is hardly any statutory 'provision' which defines the term 'Child Labour' in precise terms. Even those various legislative provisions which prescribe the minimum age for the admission to employment in different vocations do not fix uniform age for reasons of variations in the nature of the operations in which children are employed.

A generally valid definition of Child Labour is presently not available either in the national or international context. However, child labour can be defined as that segment of child population which participates in work which accrues to the economical and material benefits.

Helmer Folks, the Chairman of the National Child Labour Committee defined Child Labour as-
"...Any work of children that interferes with the full physical development of their opportunities for a desirable minimum of education."

V.V. Giri has used the term 'Child Labour' in quite analytical manner. According to him the term Child Labour is commonly interpreted in two different ways; first, as an economic practice and secondly, as a necessary social evil. In the first context, it signifies, employment of children in gainful occupations with a view to adding to the labour force of the family. It is in the second context which signifies Child Labour is now more generally used.

In assessing the nature and extent of the social evil, it is necessary to take into account the character of the jobs, in which the children are engaged, the dangers to which they are exposed, and the opportunities of development which they have been denied.

Thus three basic characteristics are included within the concept of child labour. These are:

First—The child should be employed in gainful occupation;

Secondly—The work to which he is exposed is dangerous; and Thirdly—it must deny to him, the opportunity of normal mental and physical development.

The term Child Labour is not only applied to children working in the industries, but also to the children working in all firms of un-organized non-industrial occupations which are injurious to their pysical, moral and social development.

'Mendelievich' has correctly observed, "To a greater or lesser extent, children in every type of human society have always taken part, and still do take part in those economic activities which are necessary it the group to which they belong is to service."

It has also been pointed out in the Report of the Committee on 'Child Labour' that "Child Labour is not a new phenomenon to our age. It has existed in one form or other in all historical times."

The Government of India has also admitted that "All forms of work by children can not be considered deleterious. In fact, work plays an important role development of a child, if it involves purpose, plan and freedom. The function of work in childhood should be primarily developmental and not economic, and childrens work as a social good is the direct anit-thesis of child labour as a social evil."

A distinction may be made between child labour and exploitation of child labour. Work when taken up as a means for the fulfilment of some other needs, becomes enslaving the character and deleterious in its impact.

The entrance of children into labour market reduces the employment opportunities for the adults and also lowers the bargaining power of adult workers. Childhood employment results in permanently weakened and damaged labour force. Child Labour involves the use of labour at its point of lowest productivity. Hence it is an inefficient utilization of labour power. Child Labour deprives children of educational opportunities, retards their physical growth, hampers their intellectual employment and brings them into the army of un-skilled labourers or depending on the low wages all their lives.

Magnitude of the Problem

Several estimates have been made about the magnitude of child workers in India, varying from as low as 10.74 million to 100 million (1971 census).
— According to global labour force estimates of the 'ILO' every fifth child in the age group of 10-14 years was part of the active labour force. The number of child workers in India was estimated as 15.1 million in 1975.
— 1971 census estimated child workers below the age of 15 years as 10.72 million.
— The 'NSS 32nd round' (1977-78) estimated child workers in the age group of 5-14 as 16.62 million as principal status workers and 3.40 million as subsidiary status workers. Five year later in 38th round (1983), the number increased by 15.95 million children as principal status workers and 4.51 million as subsidiary status workers.

According to '1981 Census', 13.6 million children are in the labour force, (11.2 million as main workers and 2.4 million as marginal workers).

In 1983, the National Planning Commission had projected the number of child workers at 17.36 million.

6 / Child Labour in Various Industries

Table 1 : Showing Children Working in Different Occupation in India, According to 1971 Census and 1981 Census

S. No.	Nature of activity	1971	%	1981	%
1.	Cultivation	3870	36.05	4013	35.95
2.	Agricultural Labour	4586	42.72	4774	42.16
3.	Livestock, Forestry, fishing, hunting, plantation, etc.	885	8.25	704	6.30
4.	Mining & quarring	24	0.22	27	0.23
5.	Manufacturing, Processing, serving, repairs, etc.	653	6.08	695	8.63
	(a) Hosing Industry	338	3.15	425	3.79
	(b) Others	315	2.93	540	4.84
6.	Construction	59	0.55	79	0.72
7.	Transport, Strong & Communication.	42	0.59	34	0.29
8.	Trade and Commerce	211	1.97	246	2.20
9.	Other services	405	3.77	326	2.92

(Number of child workers in age group 0-14 years)

The findings of Operations Reserach group, Baroda (published in 1983) came up with an estimate of 44 million working children in India. This figure is based on All India Child Labour Sample Survey conducted by the Operations Research Group in 1980-81.

In the 1971 census no distinction in made between "man" work and marginal" work. In the 1981 census "Main Workers" have been defined as those who have worked for more than six months. The 1981 census figures given above relate to "Main Workers" only.

In India work force is divided into—

ORGANISED : Those who are organised into trade unions, registered or un-registered.

UNIRGANISED : Those who have not been able to organise in pursuit of a common objective because of constraints. Such as casual nature of employment, ignorance and illiteracy, small size of establishments with low capital investment, per person employed, scattered nature of establishments and superior strength of the employer operating singly or in combination.

The Committee on Child Labour (1979) has observed that child workers are found in the following occupations :-
1. Agriculture,
2. Plantation,
3. Mining and quarrying,
4. Bids,
5. Glass and Bangles,
6. Handlooms and carpet weaving,
7. Zari and embroidery,

8. Gem cutting and polishing,
9. Match and fire works,
10. Cashew processing and manufacturing of coir products,
11. Machine tool repair shops and petrol pumps,
12. Domestic workers,
13. Helpers in hotels, restaurants, canteens, tea stalls, shops and way side establishments.
14. Rag picking,
15. Construction,
16. Howkers, vendors, newspaper sellers,
17. Cooli, etc.

This lilst covers only some of the known employments employing child labour.

Table 2 : Showing Statewise Distribution of Workers in the Age Group of 0-14 Years, According to 1971 Census and 1981 Census

S. No.	India/States/Union Territories	No. of workers in age group of 0-14 years	
		1971 census	1981 census
1.	Andhra Pradesh	1027	1754
2.	Assam	239	---
3.	Bihar	1059	893
4.	Gujarat	518	462
5.	Haryana	138	142
6.	Himanchal Pradesh	71	60
7.	Jammu and Kashmir	70	109
8.	Karnataka	309	966
9.	Kerala	112	68
10.	Madhya Pradesh	1112	1372
11.	Maharashtra	988	1263
12.	Manipur	15	17
13.	Meghalaya	30	39
14.	Nagaland	14	14
15.	Orissa	492	515
16.	Punjab	233	179
17.	Rajasthan	587	589
18.	Sikkim	--	7
19.	Tamil Nadu	713	871
20.	Tripura	17	19
21.	Uttar Pradesh	1327	1246
22.	West Bengal	511	573
23.	Andaman & Nicobar Islands	1	1
24.	Arunachal Pradesh	18	14

8 / Child Labour in Various Industries

25.	Chandigarh	1	1
26.	Dadra and Nagar Haveli	3	2
27.	Delhi	17	24
28.	Goa, Daman and Diu	7	6
29.	Lakshadweep	03	--
30.	Mizoram	4	31
31.	Pandicherry	4	3
	All INDIA	10734	11168

The Table 2 reveals that there has been a constant rise in the number of child labourers over the years from 1971 and 1981 in India. The States which have the highest number of child labours are Uttar Pradesh, Madhya Pradesh, Andhra Pradesh, Bihar and Karnataka in order while the States having lower number of child labourers have been the Nagaland, Manipur, Tripura and Arunachal Pradesh in the sequential order.

CAUSES OF CHILD LABOUR

The causes of child labour are numerous and varied. No single factor alone is responsible for the social problem. The various causes of child labour are all intrinsically interrelated. The various causes of child are as follow :

1. Poverty

The most important factor forcing children to taken up employment is poverty. In India, a developing country, where 60% of the population lives below the poverty line, parents are compelled by poverty to send their children to seek employment.. Children are forced to work with a view to supplementing the family income.

2. Increased Profits

Child Labour is seen by the employers as a much cheaper commodity. Employers feel that since children provide the same productivity as adults, and in several cases even more at a far lower costs, so it recognised as a means of lower overheads and increased profits. Very truly, Jerome Davis in his book 'Prokers Problem and Modern Industry' has made the following statement :
"Child labour exists not because children are more able workers but because they can be had for less money."

3. Easily Amenable

For a number of tasks, employers prefer children to adults as children have less developed ego and status consciousness. Becuase of this they can be put to ducaning jobs without much difficulty as children are more active and quick. Employers find them more amenable to discipline and control.

4. Lack of Educational Facilities

Inadequate and poor educational facilities as well the neglect of the enforcement of free and compulsory education for all children below the age of 14 years leads to child labour. Because of poverty their families are not able to afford the expenditure on education, however, less it may be. Education facilities were not available for girls beloging to traditional families having purdah among the families.

5. Illiteracy and Ignorance of Parents

In India the lower groups are iliterate. They think only of the present and not of the future. A seminar on 'Emoplyment of Children' had in December 1975 indicated that 'child labour' is prevalent extensively in lower series economic group because of lack of opportunities on their part of the role, that, education plays in improving life and living conditions of the people."

During the course of the Survey, it was found that the educational status of parents whose children were found doing Chikan Work was very poor. In most cases the mothers were totally illiterate. It was observed during the course of survey that although parents were totally illiterate, yet they knew the importance of educating their children. But due to economic pressure, they were compelled to send their children out for work.

6. Laxity in Enforcement of Protection Labour Legislation

Overwyears, various laws have been promulgated with the regard to Child Labour. The most recent enactment was the Child Labour (Prevention & Protection) Act 1986. This Act prohibits the employment of children below the age of 14 years. In certain industries while specifying their working conditions in other industries where their employment is not banned.

In the Chikan Industry which comes under the un-oranised sector, children are found to be working, as unoraganised sector is not covered within the perview of the Law.

7. The Unorganised Nature of Job

Child workers are not organised on lines of trade unions and hence they cannot fight for their demands.

The underlying causes of child labour cannot be attributed simply to one factor or the other but to combination of factors just revealed above. In the final analysis, child labour is infact a product of any society's economic and social conditions.

LEGISLATIVE PROVISION

The Indian Constitution, in keeping with its welfare approach, has promulgated various enactments over the years. India has also affirmed its commitment to the United Nation's Declaration of Rights of the child. Besides, there are at present thirteen major legislature enctments, which provide legal protection to children against exploitation. These legislations the minimum age, minimum wages certain working conditions and regulate their working hours. The legislation are:

1. Factories Act 1948,
2. Minimum Wages Act 1948,
3. Plantation Labour Act 1951,
4. Mines Act 1952,
5. Merchant Shipping Act 1958;
6. Shop and Commercial Establishment Act,
7. Motor Transport Workers Act 1961,
8. Apprentices Act 1961,
9. Employment of Children Act,
10. Children Pledging of Labour Act 1938,
11. The Beedi and Cigar worker (conditions of employment) Act 1966,
12. Atomic Energy Act 1972,
13. Child Labour (Prohibition and Prevention) Act 1986.

Almost all the developing countries of the world have various Children's laws in their land to safeguard their rights. But without a strong social mechinery to enforce them these laws are merely just like the "dead letter". Public will to enforce their laws is unfortunately lacking. There is no breathing room to encourage a debate on childhood with a view to developing and enforcing social and economic conditions which may guarantee the implementation of rights of the child for safety and protection in their working environment.

2

CHILD LABOUR IN INDIA : RETROSPECT & PROSPECT

Introduction

The significance and the importance of the child lies in the fact that the child is universe. If there was no child, there would be no humanity and there can not be a universe without humanity. Therefore, mankind owes to the child the best that it has to be given. If there is no proper growth of child today. The future of the country will be in dark. It is thus an obligation of every generation to bring up children who will be citizen of tomorrow in a proper way. Today's children will be the leader who will hold the country's banner high and maintain the prestige of the nation. If a child goes wrong for want of proper attention, training and quidance, it will indeed be a deficiency of the society and of government of the day. Every society must, therefore, devote full attention to ensure that children are properly cared for and brought up in a proper atmosphere where they would receive adequate training, education and guidance in order that they may be able to have their rightful place in society when they grew up.

Both at the national level and the international level great interest is being shown in the matter of welfare of children. Children need special protection because of there tender age, physique and mental facilities. They are a "supremely important national asset," and the future will-being of the nation depends as to how children grow and develop. They need special law to protect them from exploitation and fraud, to save them from certain liabilities and to develop their personality in view of them weak position. A study team of social welfare has rightly stated: "The importance of child welfare services lies in the consideration that the personality of man is built up in the formative years, and the physical and mental health of the nation is determined largely by the manner in which it is shapped in the early stages."

It is not an exaggeration to say that the children are the blooming flowers of the garden of society and so, it is our duty to protect these flowers from damaging effects of excessive exposure to heat, cold and rain. It is quite imperative to give vent to the thought of Hon ble Mr. Justice Suba Rao who has rightly observed: "Social justice must begin with children. Unless tender plant is properly tendered and nourished, it has little chace to growing into a strong and useful tree, So, first priority in the scale of social justice shall be given to the welface of children. Similarly, Gabrial, Mistral of Chile, Nobal prize winning poet, gas rightly highlighted:

"We are quilty of many faults, but our worst crime is abandoning the children, neglecting the fountain of life. Many of the things we need can wait. The child cannot. Right now is the time his bones are being formed, his blood is being made and his sense being developed. To him, we cannot answer, 'Tomorrow,' His name is 'Today.'

Today there are no two opinions that the children are the hope of parents and future of the nation and thus be given age-quate opportunities and facilities for developing themselves. The growth of the child into a mature and happy person with fully developed personality largely depends upon the support and attention he receives from the society. If a child does not get proper education, diet and other facilities, his very development into a self sustaining human being is dwarfed, the child because of his physical and mental immaturity needs special safeguards, it becomes, therefore, the duty of state of protect children's right by legislative and other means. The needs and requirements of the child, the primordial ground norm of this universe, the most innocent and helpless human being incapable of enforcing his legal rights, but to speak of demanding new rights obligate the state to secure him distributive justice. As distinguished from adults, children are peculiarly susceptible to certain harms. They cannot raise their voice against those who injure them or deprive them of their rights. The peculiar position of the child arising from his physical and mental disability and position of dependence recognizes the need for the special provisions in many matters and the law should take care of all this in the interest and general welfare of child. The protective arm of the law has, therefore, to be long and strong enough if distributive justice to the adults of tomorrow is to be secured.

However, the reality lies in the fact that child still has not been given proper attention and is being exploited by the people who achieve their selfish ends. This is quite evident from the Report of Director-General of International Labour Organization published in 1960, though the acute estimate of child labour, either from a qualitative or quantitative point of view, is not possible, yet the report discloses that:

> "Children and youth make up a fifth to a fourth or even a third of the total labour forces in many of the industrializing countries. Young people (between) 15 to 19 make up 20 percent of the labour force of the Egyptian Region of the United Arab Republic, and a higher percentage in many of less developed Asian and African countries, and it should be noted that in most of the less developed areas the great bulk or children seek to enter the labour force by the time they are 12, 13 or 14, if they have not begun to work at a much earlier age."

It is estimated that by 2000 A.D. 25 per cent of the world's population will be children and 40 per cent of the entire global labour force will be below the age of 15 years. In developing countries 40 per cent of the total population under 15 years and 75 per cent are employed as child labour. International Labour Organization in a study concluded that in Asian Countries 70 to 80 per cent of children are either working or "simply wasting their lives away." Employment of children has continued therefore to be a problem.

Nature of the Problem

Child labour is not a new phenomenon to our age. What is new, however, is its perception as a social problem the world over. There has been a distinct change in recent past in the values and attitudes of the legitimizing groups of society vis-a-vis child labour because of some new developments. In the pre-in dustrial agricultural society of Inda, children worked as helperrs and learners in hereditarily determined family occupations under the benign supervision of adult family members. The work place was an extension of the home and work was characterized by personal informal relationships. The tasks and technology that work involved were simple and non-hazardous which the child could learn smoothly, almost unconsciously, over the years through association and limitation.

The social scenario, however, changed radically with the advent of industrialization and unbanization under the impact of the newly generated centrifugal and centripetal forces, there was an unbroken stream of the rural poor migrating to unban centers in search of livelihood. The child had to work as an individual person either under an employer or independently. His work environment endangered his physical health and mental growth and led to his exploitation. The protection and welfare of these children, therefore, become an issue of paramount social significance.

Another sociological factor bearing on the problem of child labour was the emergence of welfare consciousness on a world scale. The industrial revolution in the west generated such vast demands for manpower that even children had to be pressed into service. Contemporary wirtings reveals under what atrocious conditions. These children had to work in coal mines and textile mills. However, once the West had built up its affluence and the baneful effects of child labour become out rageously manifest, the sate took appropriate measured to meet the evil. The welfare measures enunciated had a universal appeal to human conscience. In the more recent past they have been thoughtfully embodied in various resolutions of the ILO and other organs of the United Nations. Countries of the less developed world, after their exancipation from colonial domination, also accepted a number of these resoiutions even though their social and economic infrastructure was still inadequtae for fulfilling all the commitments. Free India has similarly embodied in its constitution many provisions eastablishing thereby the normative superiority of welfare considerations over the economic one and has endeavored to weed out the antagonism betwen child labour and child development.

Yet another factor highlighting the evil aspect of child labour is the recent advances in various sciences having a bearing on the child. Today, scientific knowledge has revolutionized our outlook on the care of child and his developmental imperatives. Diffusion on this knowlage has created a new awareness in the major institutions of society as to the relationship the child should have with his milieu, his need objects and his work, etc.

Child labour, of late, has evoked deep concern. However, we must make a distinction between child labour and exploitation of child labour. Both are a problem though of different orders. Child labour as distinguished from work experience has mostly negative attributes. It can now be asserted on scientific grounds that work as a direct fulfillment of the child's natural abilities and creative potentialites is always conducive to his healthy growth. But work when taken up as a means for the fulfillment of some other needs becomes enslaving in character and deleterious in its impact. Labour is work of the latter type irrespective of the degree of strain or exploitation involved in it. Labour in the case of child is especially harmful because the energy that should have been expanded on the nutriting of his latent poers is consumed for purposes of base survival.

Child labour is as much the cause as consequence of adult unemployment and under-employment. It at once supplements and depresses the family income. Child labour is not only a subsidy to industry but a inducement to the payment to low wages to adult workers. The entrance of the children into the labour market reduces the volume of employment for the adult the lowers he bargaining power of adult workers. Regions of childhood employment result in a permanently weekened and damaged labour force. Child labour involves the use of labour as its point of lowest productivity. Hence, it is an inefficient utilization of labour power. The argument that employment of children, increses the earnings of the family and keeps children away from mischief is misleading. It glasses over the fact that child labour deprives children of educational opportunites minimizes their chances for vocational training, stunts their physical growth, hampers their intellectual development and, of forcing them into the army of unskilled labourers or blind alley jobs, condemns them to low wages all their lives.

Compelled by the exigencies of situations children accept role which run them into both victims and involuntary accomplices of unjust situations. In many situation which is characterized by the fact that if one does not work. One has the option of either starving or adopting socially disapproved means for one's survival, children have no choice but to decide to take up jobs at an age which they should have gone to school. Though at the fact, of it, it appears that it is the children who take the decision to work but the fact remain that it is not the children but the society to which they belong which though its inability to provides adequate subsistence for their families decides at the time of their conception itself that they are destined to be forced to take up employment at an early age. Mendelievich has rightly maintained : "It is not the family that should carry the blame for the fact that the child has to work, since the courses of action open to the family are few in number. It is society as a whole that is at fault. It is not only the children who are harmed dut to their involvement in various kind of work at the tender age but society also which has to suffer a great loss because of children being employed by employer who always make their best efforts to export minimum benefits with minimum investment. The employment of children adversely affects not only employment opportunities of others forcing many to remain jobless in the present age but also considerably lowers the rates of their wages. In fact, it has been rightly maintained in the Report Committee on Child labour "Child Labour is as much as the the cause as consequence of adult umemployment and under employment. It at once supplements and depresses the family income." Mendelievich has correctly depicted the picture of various circles that exists between child labour and poverty in the society. There is in fact vicious circle here on the one hand, child labour increases unemployment among adults and reduces their income, on the other, the unemployment and low wages of adults force them to put their children to work in order to boost the family income. Thus child labour simultaneously increases and reduces the family income; but as is clear, it reduces rather than increases that income.

Meaning of Child Labour

A generally valid definition of child labour is presently not avilable either in the national or international context. Any definition upon the precise meaning we attach to two components of the term "child labour" i.e., "child" in terms of his chronological age, and "labour" in terms of its nature, quantum and income generation capacity. Child labour, however can broadly be defined as that segment of the child population which participates in work either paid or unpaid.

The definition of child labour varied from one fact to another depending upon the seriousness of the problems of the children working in a particular employment. The precise age of what constitute child labour has not been laid down anywhere because of variations in the age of child as given under different legislative enactments. Section 82 of the Indian Penal Code reads: "Nothing is an offense which is done by a child under 7 years of age. Section 83 of the Indian Penal code, provides, "Nothing is an offense which is done by a child above 7 years and under 12 who has not attained sufficient matruity of understanding to judge the nature and consequence of the conduct on the occasion. Section 105 of Indian Evidence Act, 1872, lays down, "When a person is accused of any offense, the burden of proving the existence of circumstances bringing the case within any of the general of special exception including that of childhood of the Indian Penal Code of any concerning law is upon him.

Under the Indian majority Act, 1874 the age of majority has been fixed at 18 years. Under the Vaccination Act, 1880, children have been defined as perosn, "who have not attained the age of 14 years in case of boys and 18 years in case of girls." Under the Reformatory School Act, 1887, "Youth Offender" means any boy who has been convicted of any offense punishable with imprisonment for life or death and who at the time of such conviction, was under the age of 15 years. "The child Marriage Restraint Act, 1929 (sharda Act) defines child as" a male below twenty-one years and a female below eighteen years of age.

According to Employment of children Act, 1938. "No child who has not completed his fifteen years shall be employed or permitted to work in any occuption...No child who has completed his fifteen years but has not completed his seventeenths year shall be employed or permitted to work in any occupation unless the period of work of such child for any day are so fixed as to allow an interval of rest for at least twelve consecutive hours which shall include at least seven consecutive hours between 10 p.m. and 7 a.m. as may be prescribed...No child who has not completed his forteenth year shall be employed or permitted to work in any workshop within any of the processes set forth in the schudule is carried on.

Under the Motor vehicles Act, 1939, child has been defined as a person under the age of 18 years. According to the U.P. Children Act, 1951, "Child" Means a person under the age of 16 years. As per the plantation of Labour Act, 1951 "Child" means a person who has not completed his fifteenth year." Section 24 of the Act lays down : "No child who has completed his twelfth year shall be required or allowed to work in any plantation. The young person as or a person under the age of 20 years. Under the Suppression of Immoral Traffic in Women and Girls Act, 1956, "girl" means a female who has not completed the age of 21 years." According to the Orphanages and Charitable Homes (Supervision and Control) Act, 1960. "child" means a boy or girl who has not completed the age of eighteen years. As per the provisions of the Children Act, 1960. "child" means a boy who has attained the age of 18 years.

In the Merchant Shopping Act. 1958, employment of children below fifteen years as seamen has ordinarily been prohibited. Persons below years cannot the employed as trimmer and stokers. According to the Motor Iransport Worker's Act, 1961, "child" means a person who has not completed his fifteen years. Section 21 of the Act provides : "No child shall be required or allowed to work in any capacity in any motor transport undertaking." Section 22 lays down : "No adolescent shall be required or allowed to work as a motor worker in any motor transport undertaking unless—(a) a certificate of fitness granted with reference to him...is in the custody of the employer, and (b) such adolescent carries with while hs is at work, a token giving a reference to such certificate." "Adolescent." according to Section 2 (a) of the Act, "means a person who has completed his fifteenth year but has not completed his eighteenth year."

Under the Radiation Protection Rules, 1971, farmed under the Atomic Energy Act, 1962, "A child has been defined as a person below eighteen years of age. "According to Section 2(2) of the U.P. Dooken Aur Vanijya Adhishthan, Adhiniyam, 1962, "child" means a person who has not completed his fourteenth years." Section 1 of the Act clearly says: "No child shall be required or allowed to work in any shop or commerical establishment except or allowed to work in any shop or commercial establishment except as an apprentice in such employment as may be notified by the state government in the gazette.

In shops and Commercial Establishment Acts passed by other states and union territories, child has been defined as a person between 12 and 14 years. It is because of this variation in age of child in different laws but the child labour have to be defined in the context of a vocation in which a child is employed. According Section 2(b) of othe Bidi and Cigar Workers (Conditions of Employment) Act 1966, "Child" means a person who has not completed fourteenth of age." Section 24 of the Act provides, "No child shall be required or allowed to work in any industrial premises."

The work 'child labour' has been differently defined in various studies. According to the committee on child labour, "child labour, however, can broadly as that segment of child population in work either paid or unpaid." In their study of working children in Bombay, Singh, and others have held a view : "child labour means a working child who is between 6 and 15 years of age," is not attending school during the day, is working under an employer or is learning some trade as an apprentice. "In the study titled as working childern as working childern in urban Delhi conducted by the Indian Council of Child Welfare. "Every child below 14 years, who contributed to the family income or was gainfully employed including those marginally working was treated as a worker."

Sri. V.V. Giri has expressed the view: The term "child labour is commonly interrupted in two different ways: first, as an economic practice and second, as a social evil. In the first context it signifies employment of children in gainful occuptions with a view to adding to the total income of the family. It is in the second sense that the term child labour is now more generally used. In assessing the nature and extent of social evil. It is necessary to take into account the character of the jobs on which children are engaged, the danger to which they are exposed and the opportunities of development of which they have been denied.

Hommerfolks, Chairman of the United Nation Child Labour Committee, has defined child labour as or any work by children that interferes with their full physical development, their opportunities for a desirable level of education of their needed recreation. Kulshreshtha is of the view that, child labour in a restricted sense means the employment of child in gainful occupations which are dangerous to their health and deny them the opportunities of development... The term child labour not only applies to the children working in the industries but also to the children in all forms of nonindustrial occupations which are injurious to their physical, mental, moral and social development." According to Alakh Narayan Sharma," child labour means the employment of children in gainful occupations (in industrial as well as non-industrial occupations) which are injurious to their physical, mental moral and social development. Thus, the term includes wage-labour as well as self-employed children working independently as well as in family enterprises. Child labour therefore, can be defined here as any work undertaken by children below 14 years in such works which are injurious to their health, and harmful to their proper development.

Magnitude of the problem of child labour

The problem of child labour in India is also of immense magnitude when one considers the number of children involved, According to the 1971 census, there were 10.74 million children working, representing 4.66 per cent of total population and 5.95 per cent of the total labour force. According to the 1981 census, workers in the age group below 14 years of age (excluding Assam) were 13.59 million. On the basis of the National Sample Survey (32nd Round) the number of child workers as on Ist March, 1983 was 17.36 million. The working children mainly belong to the age group 5-14 years. Nearly 93 per cent of the total child labour force works in the rural areas and the rest in urban areas. A great majority of these children work in agriculture and the unorganized sector like small commercial establishments and shops or quasi family undertakings. 79 per cent are employed as cultivators or agricultural labourers, 8 per cent in livestock, forestry plantations etc, 6 per cent in household and other services, the rest in trade, commerce and transport. Various surveys conducted by the labour bureau reveal that children are employed to do light job, such as helping in the field, in factories for packing, pasting of labels, etc, and in match factories, tea factories, tea estates, bidi manufacturing, printing, publishing, etc. Unorganized sector employs a large number of children as domestic servants, works in hotels, restaurants, canteen, wayside shops, newspaper selling, coolies, shoes-shine boys, vender, etc. Through Indian law does not prohibit the employment of children in cottage industries, family house-holds, restaurants, or in agriculture yet it is quite evident that the working conditions of the children in these small organizations is far inferior to those of large factories.

According to the report prepared by the India Social Institude on Child Labour, 80 per cent of all child labourers belong to the the scheduled castes and tribes that have been exploited and marginalized in India centries. A major consequence of this "is the deprival of the possibility of education and the consequent upward modality. Thus child labour has become a mode of perpetuating an unjust social system and of ensuring the continued availability of subservient, unskilled, illiterate labourers who do not have the bargaining power to question the system that marginalizes them and deprives them of their right to be human."

In the long list if dubious distinctions India is famous for, child labour comes on the top. The wholesale and unchecked exploitation of children of less than 14 years is a punishable crime under the Indian law. But a selfish and immoral political leadership corrupt bureaucracy, rampant poverty, growing unemployment and a society bareft of values gave all conspired to turn India into the "largest concentration of child labour in the world." In India every third child is working child and every fourth child in the age group 5-15 is employed. An estimate by the international labour organization puts the number of child workers in India at 44 million. But an un-offical survey estimates the number of working children at around 100 million. While 21 per cent of the child workers are urban-based, the rest are rural-based.

There is hardly any product in India that has no child labour behind it. Lock, carpet, bangle, brick, match box, cracker wood carvingor any other product has the invisible stamp of the tail put in by children caught in the web of poverty and an exploitative social system. Indeed, child labour in India is comes cheap and easy.

The magnitude of the child labour in India is quite evident form the depicted as per next page :

The study of Table 1, reveals that total population increased by 24.9 per cent in 1971 and 51.6 per cent in 1981 with 1961 as the base year. The table also shows the trends in total child population and child-labour. Child population increased by 27.9 per cent it 1971 and 46.1 per cent in 1981 as the

Table 1

Year	Total Population	Total labour force	Total child population	The child labour
	100.00	100.00	100.00	100.00
1961	438936918	188675500	180082782	14469774
	124.00	95.66	127.90	74.30
1971	548159652	180485006	230334822	10753982
	151.60	117.94	146.10	77.20
1981	665287832	222516568	263064491	11168819
1991	836605522	314903522	NA	NA

base year, which is slightly lower than the increase in total pupulation. Child labour decrease by 25.7 per cent in 1971 and 22.8 per cent in 1981 with 1961 as the base year. During 1971-81 the average child population was 22,44,97, 302 and average child was 1, 21, 30, 859, i.e. child labour was 5.66 per cent of total labour force and 2.31 per cent of tatal population on an average during the period from 1961 to 1981.

Similarly, Table 2 throws a flood of light on the different aspects of child labour in India. It shows the percentage change in child labour, total labour force and child population in respect of the total child population, total labour force and total population during 1961-1991.

Table 2

Year	Child labour in total child population	Child labor in total population	child labour in total labour force	child population in total population	total labour force in total population
1961	8.04	3.29	7.67	41.02	42.98
1971	4.69	1.96	5.96	42.02	32.93
1981	4.25	1.68	5.02	39.54	33.45
1991	NA	NA	NA	NA	NA
%age	-3.97	-1.61	-2.65	-1.48	-9.53

It is revealed from Table 2, that the share of child labour decreased by 3.79 per cent in total child population, 2.65 percant in total labour force and 1.61 per cent in total population. The share of total labour force in total population and total child population in total population decreased by 9.53 per cent and 1.40 per cant respectively. From the above analysis we find that the share of child labour is decreasing very slowly in the country, in spite of preventive and protective legislations and the government policy to prevent child employment. The percentage do not seem to be very alarming, but must be kept in mind that the percentage would be much larger. If we include shoe shine boys, vehicle clearners, domestic servants children who work in their own house to enable their parents to go out to work, etc. and excluding infants and children below the age of five years from the 0-14 years age group which we took for our analysis.

The high incidence of child labour in India is not only shocking from the moral point of view, but also represent a waste of waste resources, which instead of being improved upon through education and training is utilized in a most unproductive and wasteful manner.

A recent state-wise figure reveals that Andhra Pradesh topped the list with over 19 lakh child labour followed by Madhya Pardesh, Maharashtra, Utter Pradesh, Karnataka and Bihar, each accounting for over lakh. From this it is quite evident that the employment of chldren, which is a centuries-old phenomenon in India has given to a number of social, psychological economical and legal problems.

The social evils involves in the employment of children are widespread illiteracy resulting in lack of development of child's personality which may continue even in his adult life. The economic problem involved in the employment of children in agriculture and industrial sectors are in on way of less significance. The inadequacy of family income and desire to supplement family income has compelled children to work in agricultural and industrial sectors. However, employment in such establishments do not provide them adequate wages. The legal problem involved in the employment of children are: (1) what should be their minimum wages? (2) what should be the industries in which they may be employed? (3) what should be the number of their work? (4) what should be the direction of their work? What privilege should be afforded to them in the matter of leave and holidays? (6) what protection should be afforded to them in matter of health, safety and welface? (7) what securities should be allowed to them in case of their compulsory removal from their work?

It is true that the constitution of India provides that no child below the age of 14 years shall be employed to work in any hazardous employment. Article 15(3) children in the light of philosophy contained in Article 39 which states that the tender age of children shall not be abused and that the children are given proper opportunities and facilities to develop in a healthy manner youth are protected against exploitation and against moral and material abandoment. Our national charter further endeavors to provide, within a period of ten years from the commencement of the constitution, for free and compulsory education for all children until they complete the age of 14 years.

Keeping in view the constitutional commitment many legislations have been passed relating to the welfare and special protection of the children. Today we have more then 300 union and state statutes dealing with children on one way and other. In 1974, adopted a national policy for children which begins by saying that the children are supremely important assets of the nation the year 1979 have gone. The world has celebrated the year but the child labour remains. Thus the problem of child lebour welfare requires a considerable attention from social scientists, activists on the field and the government.

The problem is more acute particularly in under-developed and developing country like India. It is now a realized and accepted truth that protection of children against exploitation is essential to their mental and physical development and in the ultimate analysis to the development to nation as a whole. Thus the present work is a humble attempt to bring forth some of the legal aspects of this multi-dimensional problem and to give some suggestions for mitigating the acuteness and gravity of this evil.

3

CHILD LABOUR IN INDIAN INDUSTRIES

According to a recent ILO estimate, there ae 52 million working children in the world. Of these, approximately 29 million are from South Asia, 10 millon from Africa, 9 million from East Asia and 3 million from Latin America and only one million will originate from developed countries.

Out of the 29 million woking children in South Asia. 10.7 million child workers are estimated to be in India (1971 census). Out of total population of 548 million recorded in 1971 census, about 230 million were children below 15 years, i.e.. 42 % of the total population. The number of child workers according to the 1971 census was 10.7 million as against 14.5 million recorded in census. This step decline can be assigned to the conceptual differences in the definition of workers adopted in the 1971 census. Proceeding logically on the basis of the increase in population and the treands in the economy, the actual volume of child labour is likely to be much higher than the estimated 10.7 million from 1971 census. Children constitute 5.9 per cent of the total labour force of the economy.

The percentage of child labour to total population is as high as 9.24 in Andhra Pradesh whereas it is as low as 1.30 per cent in Kerala. Of the bluk of child labour in country, nearly 93 per cent are in rural areas and rest in urban areas. According to ILO estimate, 80 per cent of these working children would be classified as 'unpaid family workers.' The great majority of these children are in agriculture or in small scale industries in rural area and in workshops, petty shops and quasi-family undertakings in urban areas. Seventy-nine-per cent of the child workers are said to be employed as cultivators, agricultural labourers, all over the country. Eight per cent are engaged in live-stock, foresty, plantation, etc.. about 6 per cent manufacturing and processing in another 6 per cent in household and other services industries and the rest in trade, commerce and transport.

The first all India Agricultural Labour Enquiry conducted by the Ministry of Labour revaled that 4.9 per cent of the total agricultural labour force were children in 1950-51. It was 7.7 per cent in 1956-57, 7.4 million children are engaged in agriculture according to the 1971 census. The Rural Labour Enquiry conducted by the Ministry of Labour revealed that child agriculture labourers constitute 6 per cent of the total agricultural labour force in 1964-65.

Like most problems in India, child labour emerges out of the socio-economic conditions prevailing in the economy. Children are often forced to work due to economic needs and social conditions. Whatever, might be the conditions leading to the children seeking employment—for economic considerations or otherwise, it conditions detrimental to their health, welfare and development. Most of these children have never been to school or have dropped out of schools at some stage or the other. A working child is deprived of education, training and acquiring skills which are prerequisites for earning, sustaining and for economic development. The perception of child labour as a social problem has become an public, trade unions, welfare and social service organizations and the state.

Constitutional Provisions

Article 24 of the Indian Constitution lays down:
"No child below the age of 14 years shall be employed to work in any factory of nine or engaged in any other hazadous employment."
Article 39(c) lays down that the health, strength of workers-man, woman and the tender age of children are not abused and that citizens are not forced by economic necessity to enter avocation unsuited to their age or strength.
Article 39(c) proclaims:
"The childhood and youth are protected against exploitation and against moral and material abandonment."

Other Legislations

With a view to eradicate the problems of child labour the following legislations have been enacted regulating the employment of children:

The *Children (Pledging of Labour)* Act, 1933. The Act defines 'child' as person who is under the age of 15 years. The Act prohibits the making of agreements to pledge the labour of children and the employment of children whose labour has been pledyed. The Act also lays down that any agreements or contracts to pledge the labour of a child is void and imposes penalties on any such agreement or employment of a pledget child.

The second Act relates to the Employment of Children Act, 1938.

Section 3(1): No child who has not completed his fifteenth year shall be employed or permitted to work in any occupation-
  (a) connected with transport of passengers, goods or mails by railway, or
  (b) connected with a part authority within the limits or any part, or
  (c) connected with cinder picking, clearing of an ash pit or building operation, in the railway premises, or
  (d) connected with the work in a watering establishment, at a railway station, involving the management of a vendor or any other employeee of the establishment from one platform to another or into or out of a moving train, or
  (e) connected with the work relating to the construction of railway station or with other where such work is done in close proximity to or between the railway lines.

Section 3(3): No child who has not completed his fourteenth year shall be employed or permitted to work in any workshop where any of the process set in the schedule is carried on.

The Schedule

(1) bidi-making; (2) carpet weaving; (3) cement manufacturing, including bagging of cement; (4) cloth printing, dying and weaving; (5) manufactureing of matches, explosives and fire-works; (6)

mica-cutting and splitting; (7) shellac manufacture; (8) soap manufacture; (9) tanning; and (10) wool cleaning.

Several other legislations and Acts have laid down special provisions and clauses pertaining to the employment of children.

I. The child is defined as follows in the different Acts:
   1. Beedi & Cigar workers (Condeitions of Employment) Act, 1966, Sec. 2(b): 'Child' means a person who has not completed 14 years of age.
   2. Factories Act, 1948 and Minimum Wages Act, 1948, Sec. 2(c): 'Child' means a person who has not completed his fifteenth year of age.
   3. Mines Act, 1952, Sec. 'Child' means a person who has not completed his fifteenth year.
   4. Motor Transport Workers Act, 1961, Sec. 2(c): 'Child' means a person who has not completed his fifteenth year.
   5. Plantations Labour Act, 1951, Sec 2(c): 'Child' means a person who has not completed his fifteenth year.

II. The minimum age of employment of a child is given in various Acts as follows:
   1. Factories Act, 1948, Sec. 67: No child who has not completed his fourteenth year shall be required to or allowed to work in any factory.
   2. Mines Act, 1952, Sec. 45: No child shall be employed in any mines nor shall any child be allowed to be present in any part of mine which is below ground or in any (open cast working) in which any mining operation is carried on.
   3. Plantation Labour Act, 1951, Sec. 24: No child who has not completed his twelfth year shall be required or allowed to work in any plantation.
   4. Indian Marchant Shipping Act, 1958, Sec. 109: No person under fifteen years of age shall be engaged or carried to sea to work in any capacity in any ship, except
      (a) in a school ship or training ship, in accordance with the prescribed conditions; or
      (b) in a ship in which all person employed two hundred tones gross: or
      (c) in a home-made ship of less than two hundread tons gross: or
      (d) where such person is to be employed on nominal wages and will be in the charge of his father or other adult near male relative.
   5. Motor Transport Workers Act, 1961, Sec. 21: No child who has not completed to work in any capacity.
   6. Beedi and Cigar Workers (Conditions of Employment) Act, 1966, Sec. 24: No child who has not completed his fourteenth year shall be required or allowed to work in any industrial premises.
   7. State Shops and Commercial Establishment Acts

The minimum age of employment in shops and commercial establishments is 12 years in Bihar, Gujrat, J&K, Madhya Pradesh, Karnataka, Orissa, Rajasthan, Trupura, Uttar Pradesh, West Bengal, Goa, Daman and Diu and Manipur, and 14 years in Andhra Pradesh, Assam, Haryana, Himanchal Pradesh, Kerala, Tamil Nadu, Punjab, Delhi, Chandirgarh, Pondicherry and Meghalaya. The Minimum age of employment is 15 years in Maharashtra. There are no separate shops and commerical establishments Acts in Andaman & Nicabar, Arunachal Pradesh, Dadra & Nagar Haveli, Lakshdweep, Nagaland & Sikkim.

   8. Radiation protection Rules, 1971, Persons below 18 years cannot be employed under the

Radiation protection Rules, 1971.
9. Apprentices Act, 1961, Sec. 3 (a): A person shall not be qualified for being engaged as an apprentice to undergo apprenticeship training in any designated trade. Unless he is not less than 14 years of age.
10. The Children (Pledging of Labour) Act, 1933, Sec. 3: An agreement to pledge the labour of a child (below 15) shall be void.

III. Prohibition of allowing children to work in hazardous occupations under the Factories Act, 1948 is given below:

1. Factories Act, 1948 Sec. 22(2): No young person shall be allowed to clean, lubricate or adjust any part of prime mover or of any transmission machinery while the prime mover or transmission machinery is in motion, or to clean, lubricate or adjust any part of machine if the cleaning, lubrication or adjustment thereof would expose the young person to risk of injury from any moving part either of that machine or of any adjacent machinery.

Section 23(1): No young person shall work at any machine to which this section applies unless he has been fully instructed as to the dangers arising in connection with the machine and the precautions to be observed and—(a) he received sufficeint training in work at machine, or (b) is under adequate supervision by a person who has a through knowledge and experience of the machine.

Section 23(2) Sub-section (1) shall apply to such machines as may be prescribed by the (State) Government, being machines which in its opinion are of such a dengerous character that young person ought not to work at them unless the foregoing requirements are complied with.

Section 27: No child shall be employed in any part of a factory for pressing cotton in which a cotton-opener is at work:

Provided that if the feed-end of a cotton opener is in a room separated from the delivery end by a partition extending to the roof or to such height as the inspector may in any particular case specify in writing; children may be employed on the side of the partition where the feed-end is situated.

Section 34 (2): The (State) Government may make rules prescribing the maximum weights which may be lifted, carried or moved by children employed in factories or any class or description of factories or in carrying on any specified process.

IV. The hours of work for children are regulated as follows:

1. Factories Act, 1948, Sec. 7 (a) : No child shall be employed or permitted to work in any factory for more than 4 and 1/2 hours a day.
2. Minimum wages (Central) Rules, 1950, Sec. 24: The number of hours which shall constitute a normal working day shall be 4 and 1/2 hours in case of a child.
3. Plantation Labour Act, 1951, Sec. 19: No child shall be required or allowed to work on any plantation for more than 40 hours a week.
4. State Shops and Commercial Establishment Acts : The hours of work for young persons in shops and commercial establishment are 7 per day in Andhra Pradesh, Bihar, Tamil Nadu, Tripura, Pondicherry and West Bengal: 6 per day in Gujarat, Maharashtra, Jammu & Kashmir, Uttar Pradesh and Delhi: 5 per day in Himanchal Pradesh, Madhya Pradesh, Karnataka, Orissa an Punjab and 3 per day in Rajasthan.
5. Apprentices Rules, 1962, Sec. 8: The weekly hours of work of an apprentice while undergoing practical training shall be as follows:

(i) The total number of hours per week shall be 42 to 48 hours (including the time spent on related instructions):
(ii) Apprentices undergoing basic training shall ordinarily work for 42 hours per week including the time on the related instructions:
(iii) Apprentices during the second year of apprenticeship shall work for 42 to 45 hours per week including the time spent on related instructions:
(iv) Apprentices during the third and subsequent years of apprenticeship shall work for the same number of hours per week as the workers in trade in the establishments in which the apprentices is undergoing apprenticeship training: Provided however, that short-term apprentices may be engaged to work up to a limit hours per week.

V. Children are prohibited from working at night according to the following Acts:
1. Factories Act, 1948, Sec. 71 (b): No child shall be employed or permitted to work in any factory during night.
(For the purpose of this Section 'night' shall mean a period of at least twelve consecutive hours which shall include the interval between 10 p.m. to 6 a.m.)
2. Plantation Labour Act, 1951, Sec, 25: Except with the permission of the State Government, no child worker shall be employed in any plantation otherwise than between the hours of 6 am and 7 pm.
3. Beedi and Cigar Workers (Conditions of Employment) Act, 1966, Sec. 25: No young person shall be required or allowed to work in any industrial premises except between 6 a.m. and 7 p.m.
(Young person means a person who has completed 14 years of age but has not attained 18 years of age.)
4. State Shops and Commercial Establishments Acts. Night work for children and young person also prohibited under State laws relating to shops and commercial establishments. The childern and young persons are allowed to work between 6 a.m. and 7 p.m. in Andhra Pradesh, Gujarat, Maharashtra, Tamil Nadu, Pondicherry; 7 a.m. to 7 p.m. in Bihar and Kerala; 7 a.m. to 9 p.m. in Jammu & Kashmir and Madhya Pradesh; 6 a.m. to 8 p.m. in Karnataka; 6 a.m. to 10 p.m. in Orissa and Rajasthan and 8 p.m. during Winter and 7 a.m. to 9 p.m. during summer in Delhi. They cannot be employed after 8 p.m. in West Bengal and Tripura.
5. Apprentices Rules, 1962, Sec. 8(2): No apprentice. Other than a short term apprentice, shall be engaged in such training between the hours of 10 p.m. and 6 a.m. except with the prior approval of the Apprenticeship Adviser who also shall give his approval if he is satisfied it is in the interest of the training of the apprentice of the public interest.

International Organizations

The United Nations declaration of the rights of the child on November 20, 1959 lays down that the child shall enjoy special protection and shall be given opportunities and facilities by law and by other means to enable them to socially in a healthy and normal manner and in conditions of freedom and dignity. In the enactment of laws for this paramount consideration.

The Children's charter stipulates that for every child a community which recognizes and plans for his needs protectss him against physical dangers, moral hazards and diseases, provides him with safe and wholesome places for play and recreation and makes provision for his cultural and social needs.

Privisions in Ilo

In the interest of the working children all over the world, the International Labour Organization has adopted 18 conventions as follows:
1. Minimum Age (Industry) Convention (No. 5), 1919.
2. Minimum Age (Sea) Convention (No. 7), 1920.
3. Minimum Age (Agriculture) Conventions (No. 10). 1921.
4. Minimum Age (Trimmer and Stokers) Convetion (No. 15), 1921.
5. Minimum Age (Non-Industrial Employment) Convention (No. 33), 1932.
6. Minimum Age (Sea) Convention (Revised) (No. 58), 1936,
7. Minimum Age (Industry) Convention (Revised) (No. 59), 1937.
8. Minimum Age (Non-Industrial Employment) Convention (Revised) (No. 60), 1937.
9. Minimum Age (Underground Work) Convention (No. 123, 1973.
10. Minimum Age Convention (No. 138), 1973.
11. Medical Examination of Young Persons (Sea) Convention (No. 16), 1921.
12. Medical Examination (Sea fearers) Convention (No. 73), 1946.
13. Medical Examination of Young Persons (Industry) Convention (No. 77), 1946.
14. Medical Examination of Young Persons (Non-Industrial Occupation) Convention (No. 78), 1946.
15. Medical Examination of Young Persons (Underground Work) Convention (No. 124), 1965.
16. Night Work of Young Persons (Industry) Convention (No. 6), 1919.
17. Night Work of Young Persons (Non-Industrial Occupations) Convention (No. 79), 1946.
18. Night Work of Young Persons (Industry) Convention (Revised) (No. 90), 1948.

The Government of India have ratified 6 of the 18 conventions adopted by the ILO for children and young person. Following are the 6 conventions which have been ratified and implemented in the country:
1. Minimum Age (Industry) Convention (No. 5), 1919.
2. Minimum Age (Trimmer and Stokers) Convention (No. 15), 1921.
3. Minimum Age (Underground Work) Convention (No. 123), 1973.
4. Medical Examination of Young Persons (Sea) Convention (No. 16), 1921.
5. Night Work of Young Persons (Industry) Convention (No. 6), 1919.
6. Night Work of Young Persons (Industry) Convention (Revised No. 9), 1948.

One of the most important conventions is the Minimum Age Convention, 1973 which prescribed the minimum age as not less than 15 years for developed countries and 14 years for initial fixation by developing countries. For hazardous occupations, the minimum age fixed is 18. Fixing of minimum age for admission to employment needs to be preceded by creation of a suitable enforcement mechinery. To set up such a machinery, particularly for the unorganized sectors in agriculture, cottage and heavy industries, small scale industries, etc. becomes a difficult task in a developing country.

A Resolution was adopted in the International Labour Conference in its 65th Session in 1979 in the International Year of Child for the protection elimination of child Labour and for the Transitional measures to be adopted by the countries (Please see page 182).

Notwithstanding the constitutional provisions, Acts and legislations and documentary disapprovals, child labour is an empirical reality present in differential degree in almost all the sectors of our national economy, organized or unoganized, regulated or unregulated.

The National Commission or Labour has observed in its report that the employment of children is more of an economic problem than anything else. The Commission felt that the denial of opportunity to children for their proper physical development and for education is a serious issue keeping in view the larger interest of the society. The Commission has recommended that it is necessary to give the child education in his formative years and this can be ensured by fixing the employment hours of children so as to enable them to attend school. The Commission has also recommended that where the number of children is adequate, the employers, with the assistance of the State Governments, should make arrangements to combine work education.

The VIth Plan aims at universal primary education, increase in employment opportunities and improvement in family incomes. It is hoped that children will thus gradually be beaned away from work and sent to school.

Committee on Child Labour

With a view studving the problems of child labour and to suggest suitable measure for their protection and welfare, the Ministry of Labour, Government of India, has set up a Committee, in its Resolution dated 6/7th February, 1979. The following are the terms of reference of the Committee:
   (i) Examine Existing laws, their adequacy and implementation and suggest corrective action to be improve implementation and to remedy defects.
   (ii) Examine the dimensions of chiid labour, the occupations in which children are employed, etc.. and suggest new areas where laws abolishing/regulating the employment of children can be introduced.
   (iii) Suggest welfare measure, training and other facilities which would be introduced to benefit children in employment.

The Committee has been up a plan of action for making an in-depth and diagnostic study on the nature and extent of the problem adequacy of existing legal framework and the supportive measures. The Committee will be taking up case studies in different blocks in about eight selected states to study the rural conditions and right also be doing sectoral studies in the organized and unorganized sectors where the incidence of child labour is quite high. The Committee has also brought out a questionnaire to elicit information on child labour from the public, the politician, trade unions, social welfare and other institutions, employers, parents of children and Government organizations. The information received from the questionnaire will be tabulated and utilized in the report of the Committee.

The Committee on Child Labour is expected to make recommendations, inter alia, on the following main issues:
   (i) Prascribing a uniform minimum age for employment of children under all the Acts.
   (ii) Identify hazardous occupations and banning the employment of children in such occupations.

(iii) Recommending laws, rules, regulations, Acts and legislations for protecting children in employment and for progressive elimination of child labour, and
(iv) Suggesting labour welfare and social welfare measures to protect the working children from exploitation and suitable machinery for enforcement and implementation of provisions adopted for welfare of working children.

A child labour cell has set up to formulate, coordinate and to implement policies and programmes for the welfare of child labour. At present, the cell is assisting the committee on Child Labour. It is expected to take follow up action on the recommendations of the Committee on Child Labour.

Resolution

Concerning the International Year of the Child and the Progressive Elimination of Child Labour & Transitional Measures adopted by the International Labour Conference in its sixty-fifth Session (1979) at Geneva.

The General Conference of the International Labour Organization.

Recalling resolution 31/169 adopted by the United Nations General Assembly, proclaiming 1979 as the International year of the Child with general objectives of promoting the well-being of children, drawing attention to their special needs and encouraging national action on behalf of children, particularly for the least privileged and those who are at work.

Noting the activities that were undertaken at the national, regional and international levels in preparation for the International Year of the Child and the progress made since.

Convinced that the International Year of the Child provides for all member States an opportunity to review their economic and social policies concerning child welfare and to formulate guidelines in this sphere.

Considering that a new and fair international economic order would greatly contribute towards genuine economic and social development, primarily of benefit to children.

Recalling the endorsement by the ILO of the aims of the International Year of the Child and its pledge to make every effort and lend all support to member States for their earliest possible fulfillment.

Recalling the United Declaration of the Right of the Child, 1959, and particulary Principle 9. which stipulates that the child should be protected against all forms of neglect, cruelty and exploitation; that he should not be admitted to employment before an appropriate minimum age; and that he should in no case be caused or permitted to enagage in any occupation or employment which would prejudice his health or education, or interfare with his physical, mental or moral development.

Considering that since its foundation the International Labour Organization has sought to eliminate child labour and to provide protection for children.

Noting with approval the Director-General's Declaration on the International Year of the Child.

Deeply concerned that child labour still remins widespread in many parts of the world and that working children frequently work under conditions including those of exploitation detrimental to their age or strength.

Recognizing the need to ensure that the health and strength and the tender age of children are not abused and that children are not permitted to enter avocations unsuited to their age or strength.

Considering that the International Year of the Child should be an occasion to reaffirm with practical measures and deeds that the well-being of today's children is the concern of all people everywhere.

Recalling the decision of the Governing Body of the International Labour Office, taken at its 208th Session (November 1978) to request the Member States to supply a report in 1980 under Article 19 of the Constitution on the extent to which effect has been given or is proposed to be given to the Minimum age Convention (No. 138) and Recommendation (No. 146) of 1973.

1. Calls upon member States to strengthen effort for the elimination of child labour and for the protection of children, and in this context:
   (a) to implement the provision of the Minimum Age Convention, 1973 (No. 138) and, where they not already done so, to ratify this Convention as early as practicable:
   (b) to ensure in particular full recongnition of the principle that any work undertaken by children who have not completed their compulsory education shall not be such as would prejudice their education or development:
   (c) to apply the Minimum Age Recommendation, 1973 (No. 146), and the Minimum Age (Underground Work) Recommendation, 1965 (No. 124):
   (d) to report in detail in 1980 under the procedure of Article 19 of the Constitution on the progress reached in the implementation of the Minimum Age Convention (No. 138) and Recommendation (No. 146), 1973.
   (e) pending the elimination of child labour, to take all necessary social and legislative action for the progressive elimination of child labour and, during the transitional period until the elimination of child labour to regulate and humanize it and to give particular attention to the implementation of special standards of children relating to medical examination, night work, underground work, working hours, weekly rest, paid annual leave and certain types of hezardous and dangerous work embodied in a number of ILO instruments.
   (f) to make every effort to extend the provisions of appropriate educational facilities, in order fully to apply compulsory education and to introduce it where it does not exist and, where education is compulsory, to make it effective;
   (g) to ensure that appropriate protective labour legislation applies to all children at work in the sectors of activity in which they are employed;
   (h) to ensure that special attention is given to the provision of fair remuneration and to its protection for the benefit of the child;
   (i) to strengthen, where appropriate, labour inspection and to undertake all other measures conductive to the elimination of child labour;
      (i) to indentify the special needs of children to strengthen efforts to improve the general economy and social well-being of the family, and to lauch a national campaign aimed at creating awareness among the general public of the adverse effects of child labour on his/her development;
      (ii) to develop international solidarity and cooperation with the developing courtries and to activate efforts to establish a new and fair international economic order so as to respond more effectively to the basic measures undertaken by each State for better child protection.
2. Calls upon government and employer's and worker's, organizations to assess the situation of

child work and to assist the competent bodies and the ILO to strengthen their action programme for children.
3. Invites the Governing Body of the International Labour Office to instruct the Director-General to continue and reinforce the ILO's action through such means as factual survey of national situations and practices for the elimination of child labour and for the protection of children at work, and to make the necessary preparations for a global revision of the relavant ILO instruments.

4

CHILD LABOUR DIMENSIONS AN APPRAISAL

Introduction

Since ages, the prevalence of child labour phenomenon in common in India. But children rarely figures a 'special category' in the labour force considering their rights, activities, reactions and feelings. First, following the industrial revolution in Western Europe, the exploitative emergence of child labour factor received considerable public attention and widespread consciousness raised among the masses. Various measures were formulated to alleviate their problem. In India, particularly after the United Nations declaration 1979 as International Year of Child, the issue of child labour has gained impetus among academic circles, planners, policy makers and administrators. Since then a number of simple descriptive accounts on their living and working conditions in diverse sectors have been ushered in without any input into its cognition and notion. In fact, the crux of the emergence, growth and nature of dynamics of child labour intrinsically lies with the changing trends in production and reproduction of a given matrix and to its relation on the existing socio-economic structure of society. Like other Third World countries, in India, prior to the rise and consolidation of capitalism children were primarily assigned the status of helpers and learners in hereditable determined family occupations under the supervision of adult family members. The value of labour was taken thus as part of child's socialisation for reproduction of labour power (Lai Ah-Eng 1982) In short, work was considered as the central aspect of their socialisation and training (Kothari, S. 1983). Advent of capitalism rapidly transformed the scenario. The capitalist relations of production made redundant the traditional practice of family members working as a team. The child workers were thus forced out from the familial environment relationships, turned very formal in course of time and the child was gradually exposed towards hazardous environment. It is a double alienation-separation from the system of production and an expulsion from the family - (Sahoo 1986). As such, now child labour is viewed as a social problem.

Fxplanation of Child Labour

In last decade numerous explanations were put forth for the cause of acceleration of child labour force. The socio-economic backwardness followed by poverty, illiteracy, unemployment, demographic expansion and above all the government apathy are commonly considered as the most prominent causative factors for large scale employment fo children. These reasons, of course, are inbuilt in India's socio-economic formation.

Backwardness

Backwardness is historically specific phenomenon associated with the development of capitalism in the West and its relations of expropriations of the Third World like India (Brett 1973). Such ostencious situation is largely the product of colonial and imperial domination of over four centuries which have endangered the survival of the large masses of the people (Arrighi and Sau 1973; Fanon 1966). Expansion of colonialism and imperialism with technological and financial dependence along with the destruction indigenous knowledge, culture, etc. compounded the misery of masses. Even the post colonial situation has not altered the domination of imperialism. Now there is extraction of transformation of surplus through a series of metropolis satellite links on diverse sectors. This situation along with ineffective various Five Year Plans are adding to the continuation of backwardness in India. Even after four decades of independence, India has remained one of the poorest countries of the world both in terms of GNF and per capita income. An estimated 37.6 per cent of population live below poverty line. There has been increasing concentration of wealth on one hand and corresponding pauperisation, semi-proletarianization and unemployment on the other. As such, child labour is the product of such continual situation (Desai 1984). Again backwardness and stagnation as crucial factors for the intensity of child labour are also evident from the statistical world distribution figure of child labour. It shows that as much as 90 per cent of child labour is concentrated in the underdeveloped countries of the world (mendelievitt 1979). Incidentally, India possesses the highest child labour force in the world. According to 1981 Census figure about 17.36 million children were engaged in labour which constituted approximately 6 per cent of the Indian labour force (Govt. of India, 1981). Suffice it to mention that backwardness make a way for the emergence of the phenomenon of child labour.

Poverty

The issue of poverty is very relative and subjective concept. Though it is not sufficient condition for the phenomenon of child in India yet, quite essential in its essence on analyzing the issue (Horowitz 1969). In other words the association between child labour and the poverty in any given space and time is highly significant. But it has still remained as a cognition at an empirical, isolated and sectorial level. For instance in our country between 250 to 300 million people are in a condition of near starvation which has intrinsic relation with land and other productive assets of families involved in child labour (Raychoudhury 1985). It is a known fact that the bottom half of the rural households in India own only 4 per cent of the land, and 27 to 30 per cent are tenants and agricultural labourers (Govt. of India 1979). Approximately 70 per cent of our population live below the minimum level of income has raised the magnitude of child labour (Dacosta 1971). Similar is the factor of growth of child labour from among the families of Urban Poor. In India, a third of the total urban population live in object poverty. A factual evidence in Madras noticed that 98.8 per cent of the families of the working children have an income of less than Rs. 500/- per month (George 1975). The same is the case in Delhi and Bombay with 88 and 78 per cent respectively. This object poverty causes diseases or other forms of disabilities which very often cause imbalance in family budget and force the poor parents to send their children for work.

Bondage

Bondage is another dimension which is a product of such abject poverty. Pertinent to mention that almost 70 per cent of the total child labour force in rural areas and urban unorganised sectors are put under diverse form of bondage by the own parents and guardians (Juyal et al, 1985: 73; Ganguly 1984; and Singh et al 1982). The principal feature is the pledging of child against loan or an agreement between the employer and parents of child that child will work all the time in exchange of money or food. For instance, it has been found that in some villages of Medak district in A.P. landlords depend entirely on the labour of bonded children (Rural Wing NLI 1977: 539-545). Besides, due to the low level income in any emergency situation like medical treatment of some other cause force the parents to let the child to work without realising the harm of bondage of children to employer (Marla 1977: 424-430). Sometimes the child once bonded remains bonded till he or she is able to buy freedom by giving his or her offspring in bondage. Sometimes children are forced to sell themselves to repay the loan of parents (Mundle 1976: 653-656). The nature and character of bondage however vary depending upon the existing nature of agrarian structure. Similar grim incident is also seen in many urban unorganised sectors specially in match, bidi and textile industries (Daniel 1976: 6-9; Gangrade and Joseph 1983: Sarma 1979; 345-52). Thire meagre wages are often adjusted to their parents debts to the employer or the advances (Mehta 1983). This reflects not only the nature of informal sector but also the specific character of Indian capitalism which survives with the cheapest available labour.

Culture and Tradition

The peculiar restrictive tradition particularly on learning is another dimensions for the growth for child labour. Historically learning outside home has remained more or less confined to the privileged members of upper castes whereas children of the producing classes have learned the necessary skills from their parents for their respective hereditary occupations. Education has little relevance for their survival and development. Needless to say despite constitutional commitments and piecemeal efforts at the level of universalization of education, nearly two thirds of the people remain illiterate indicates continuity of the tradition. The children of the overwhelming majority of the country's population are committed to the culture of work from the beginning. For instance studies in the metropolitan city of Bombay found that 41 per cent of children were working in the manner as what was there family tradition (NIPC 1978).

Education

Child labour in another dimension it is observed that limited number of schools, their absence in several interior villages, the clash of school timings and agricultural operations, and the cost of schooling as well as its restricted nature of providing job opportunities facilitates the path of children of underprivileged classes to enter into the labour market. An estimated 90 per cent of children belong to the three lowest agrarian classes, namely agricultural labourers, poor and middle peasants (Acharya 1982: 18—20). Out of the 140 million rural children in the age group of 5 to 14, over 86 million are not enrolled in the school register. About 62 per cent of the children in the rural areas do not, attend the elementary school (OPS 1985). They can not but belong to the lower classes and below subsistence level families. In a broad sense, the denial of access to formal education ensures the reproduction of the unjust social system. Besides the low enrolment, the dropout rates are equally high. It increased with every higher grade. The dropouts mostly belong to marginal families in rural areas. For every 100 admitted to class-I, not more than 40 go upto class-V, and less than 25 upto class-VIII (Chakravarty 1972). Dropout rates are higher in backward states and this trend is found highest among the scheduled communities and women. This apart, Article 54 (directive principle of state policy) states that "the state shall endeavour to provide" within a period of ten years from the commencement of this constitution for free and compulsory education for all children until they complete the age fourteen years. Suffice it to say that in absolute terms illiteracy is accelerating. For instance it was 437 million in 1981 as against 300 million at the time of independence. India has the dubious distinction of housing nearly half of the total illiterates of the world. Indeed the growth rate of primary education has been falling from about 6 per cent at the beginning to a mere 2 per cent today. Expenditure on elementary education has declined form 56 per cent to 36 per cent of the total eudcational expenditure between the first and sixth plans. Small wonder that 40 per cent of the schools have no black board, 80 per cent have no bench or mat, 72 per cent have no books and 90 per cent have no building whatsoever. As against 7.2 per cent of the national expenditure during the first plan the share of education has declined to a mere 2.6 per cent in the sixth plan and come down to around 1 per cent in the first two years of the Seventh Plan. Compulsory schooling for children as a part of assimilative measure is however, found deceptive. (National Policy on Education 1986). As such, the phenomenon of child labour is the product of such indifference to education.

Unemployment

Since independence not only the population below the poverty line has been increasing at a faster rate but also unemployment is showing an unprecedented rate of growth. Leaving alone the disguised unemployment and underemployment the registered unemployed has increased from two million in 1966 to twenty four million today. Of those who are employed (268 million) only; per cent are working in the organised sector (Pathy 1985). The capacity of organised sector to absorb labour has in fact been steadily declining. On the other hand the informal unorganised sector is relatively expanding and that too in advanced regions. A significant part of the labour in this insecure informal market is either contractual or bonded, and most of the workers belong to the backward regions and lower castes and classes. Not only the backwardness but also progressive mechanization of agriculture has squeezed but a large number of farm lands and forced immigration to cities, had contributed to the acceleration of the growth of child labour (Khandekar 1970). Most of 16.5 million child workers, accounting for one-third of the total child work force sale their labour power in this petty commodity production. Surely the survival of this dependent and retarded capital rests primarily on the employment of large masses of people built in disunity in the recruitment of labour and open flouting of labour laws. The children are preferred to certain types of lobour where with less than half the adult wage, nearly the same quantum of adult work can be extracted from the child. In almost all the cases child workers are underpaid and work more hours than usual with lack of proper facilities in their working areas. Different empirical studies like match factories at Sivakasi state and pencil in Tamil Nadu, glass bangle industries at Firozabad, carpet weaving in Kashmir and Varansi etc, reveal the same facts. The hazards of the work result in chronic bronchitis, anemic etc. Kothari Smity 1983; Punekar

1975; 25-27). Children in rural areas particularly in mechanized farm are no way free from such hazards but there is little documentation on the subject and many incidents go unheeded. However, health problem of urban working children are more obvious. In addition the children also perform several household chores remain unrecognised.

Protective Legislation

Since independence numerous legislative had constitutional measures have been framed to curb the child employment in hazardous occupation. The legal history on the protection of child and his working conditions in India begin with the Indian Factories Act, 1881, which provided that the minimum age of employment in factories should be seven years, and the working hours restricted to nine hours, with at least four holidays per month. In 1891, the Act was revised in the sense that the minimum age was raised to nine years and the working hours reduced to seven hours. In 1901, the Mines Act prohibited employment of children below 12 years of age in mines and other dangerous employments. In 1911, the Factories Act prohibited employment of children during nights.

The period from 1921 to 1931 market some more progressive legislation. The formation of the International Labour Organisation in 1919, and the establishment of the All India Union Congress in 1920 gave an impetus to reform the law relating to the conditions of labour in general and as a part of those reforms certain measures relevant to child labour.

The International Labour Organisation since its inception had included among its primary objectives, the safeguarding and promoting the rights and welfare of child workers. It's constitution in the original form in article 41 declared it imperative for the organisation to promote the abolition of child labour. The Factories Amendment Act of 1922, passed to implement the ILO convention of 1919 contained that minimum age of employment should be 15 years, and the maximum working hours should be only six.

The period from 1931 to 1949 represented a comparatively more concerted effort to deal with the question of child labour. The comprehensive report of the Royal Commission of Labour (1931) recommended extensive reforms like abolition of recruitment of child labour through monetary advance, minimum employment age at 12, hours of work at 5 per day etc. Some of them were legalized through the Children Pleading Labour Act, 1933 and similar other enactments.

The twenty-third session of the ILO (1934) had adopted a convention in which a special article for India was inserted, fixing the minimum age at which children may be employed or may work certain occupations. It said, "children under the age of 13 years shall not be employed or work in the transport of passengers of goods or mails by rail or in the handling of goods of docks. Children under the age of 15 years shall not be employed or work... in occupations to which this article applies which are scheduled as dangerous ur unhealthy by the competent authority."

Further the Employment of Children Act 1938, prohibited the employment of children under 15 years and restricted the occupation in connection with transport of goods, passengers or mails or railways, and ruled out a procedure for certificate of age.

The period from 1950 may be described as the period progressive legal activity. The wide ranging provisions against exploitation, laid down in the Constitution (1950), gave further impetus to the protection of weaker sections of society. The Constitution of India recognises the need for granting special protection to children. The constitutional provisions are two-fold: (i) fundamental rights, (ii) directive principles. As regards to fundamental rights, specific provision have been made in part-III of the Constitution. While, in general the Constitution prohibits discrimination on certain ground; Act 15, clause (3) have the validity of laws making special for women and children. Act 24 provides categorically, no child below the age 14 years shall be employed to work in any factory or mines or engage in any other hazardous employment.

Though India piloted the resolution banning child labour at the Geneva Convention of International Labour Organisation, ironically the government now admits that it is not possible to put an end to child labour in the country. The reasons for laws not being implemented are economic backwardness of large number of families in India. Lack of educational facilities and the unorganised nature of the various economic sectors, like agriculture and smallness of the namufacturing units make the enforcement of the laws still difficult. In addition, there are many deficiencies in the laws as well.

Realising the inability to tackle the situation, the Ministry of Labour, Government of India, through its resolution, dated the 6/7th February 1979, on the occasion of International Year of the Child set up a committee to examine the existing laws and to suggest corrective action for their improvement. It would also examine the different occupational area and suggest the ways for proper implementation of laws, where it has not been introduced so far. Even the recetly passed Child Labour Regulation Act, 1986 adds nothing substantial to previous acts. As cheap source of labour their exploitation continues unabated. Ironically not a single case of enactment of these laws is observed till now. Again these ineffective legislation is applied only to less than 20 per cent of the child labourers. Nothing is done about the remaining 80 per cent working in the agricultural sector. Nearly 40 million child labourers do not come under the purview of the legislation. Paradoxically, in fact, prohibition of child labour make it harder to protect children from exploitation and diverse forces of oppression. The Constitution of India has abridged some of the rights it confers by not providing the minimm necessary conditions such as the right to live, right to education and a number of other socio-economic and cultural rights.

Conclusion

Invariably, backwardness and poverty are considered as the driving forces for the employment of children. Illiteracy, low social status, lack of schooling facilities and the like seem to reinforce and stimulate employment of children. It is no wonder than that the legislative measures have remained more or less ineffective, except perhaps in organized industries. Ultimately, all this shows that the "political will" is strongly biased in favour of the proprietary classes, and so long as the masses are inert and unorganised the ruling coalition will try to gain at their expenses.

References

Acharya, Poromesh 1982 "Child Labour", Seminar No. 275 July, pp. 18-21.
Arrighi, Giovanni and Saul, S. 1973 Essays on the Political Economy of Afric, New York; Montly Review Press.
Brett, E.A. 1973 Colonilism and Under-development in East Africa 1919-1938, London, Heinemann.
Chakravarty, Kumaresh 1972, "Education in the Fifth Five Year" Social Scientist Vol. I, No. 3.
Da, Costa 1971 "A Portrait of Indian Poverty in A.J.Fonseca (ed). Challenge of Indian Poverty, Delhi. Vikas Publishing.

Dannial Christopher 1976 "Child Worker has come to Stay" Social Welfare, XXII(8): 6-9.

Desai, A.R. 1984 Capitalist Path of Development, Bombay, Popular Prakasan.

Espenshade T.J.1972 "The Value and Cost of Children", Population Belletin, Population Reference Bureau, 32 (1).

Gangrade, K.D. and Joseph, Gathia A. 1983, Women and Child Workers in the Unorganised Sectors, New Delhi Concept Publishing Company.

Ganguly Piyus, 1984, "Child Labour Rules Fouled with Empunity". The Telegraph (16.04.84), Calcutta.

George, K.N. 1975 "Child Labour in the City of Madras". Paper presented in the National Seminar of Employment of Children in presented in National Seminar on Employment of Children in India, New Delhi.

Govt. of India. 1981, Census of India, New Delhi Census Commissioner and Registrar General Series 1, Part-II 15(1).

Govt. of India, 1979, Report of the Committee of Child Labour, Ministry of Labour.

Horowitz, David 1969. The Abolition of Poverty, New York, Prager.

Juyal, B.B. et. al, 1985 Child Labour; The Twice Exploited, Varansi: Gandhian Institute of Studies.

Khandekar, N. 1970. A Report on the Situtation of Children and Youth in Greater Bombay: Tata Institute of Social Science.

Kothari, S. 1983. "There is Blood on those Match Sticks, Child Labour in Sivakasi", Economic and Political Weekly. XVIII, 23, 2 July.

Lai Ah-Eng., 1982 "The Little Workers: A Study of Child Labour in the Small Scale Industries on Penang", Development and Change, Vol. 13, No. 4, Oct. p. 565.

Mamdani, M. 1972, The Myth of Population Control, London Monthly Review Press.

Marla, Sharm 1977 "Bondage in Medak District (A.P.) "NLI Bulletin, 30(10) Oct. pp 424-30.

Mehta, Manhabhai 1983 "How Children are Exploited in Socialist Indian "Organiser, Jan (Republic Any Number), 34(36).

Mendeldievitt, Elias 1979 "Child Labour" International Labour Review Vol. 18, No. 5. Sept. Oct.

Mundle, Sudipto, 1976 "The Bonded the Palama", Economic and Political Weekly, Vol. XI, .N. 18, pp 653-56.

NIP.C. 1978, Working Children in Bombay, New Delhi.

O.P.S. 1985 "High incidence of Child Labour", Economic Times, Nov. 10.

N.I.P.C. National Vol. 18, No. 5, Sept. Oct.

Pathy, J. 1985 "A Note on the Structure of Working Class in India". Paper presented in a Seminar on Industrial workers and Social Change in Centre for Social Studies, Surat.

Punekar, S.D. 1975 "Child Labour in Unorganised sed Industries "Paper presented at National Seminar on Employment of Children in India, New Delhi: November.

Raychoudhuri, Tapan 1985, "Historical Roots of Mass Poverty in South Asia: A Hypothesis" Economic and Political Weekly XX(18).

Rural Wing 1977 "The Dark World of Jeeta Gadus " National Labour Institute Bulletin, Dec. 539-545.

Sahoo, U.C. 1986 " Developing Informal sector and Child Labour: A Case Study of Surat" Vision Vol. VI, No. 1 & 2.

Sahoo, U.C 1900 "Child Labour and Legislation" Economic and Political Weekly, Vol. XXV, No. 46, November 17.

Sarma, A. N. 1979 "Child Labour in Indian Industries" The Indian Journal of Social Work, XI (3) 345-52.

Singh, B. et.al, 1982 "Impact of Technological Change in Farm Employment" Indian Journal of Labour Economics Vol. XXV, No.3.

5

INNOCENTS' AGONY : CHILD LABOUR IN INDIA

With a deep desire to discover its great socio-cultural heritage, when a foreign tourist visits. India, unfortunately he takes back home the memories of thousands of children he encountered with forlorn and helpless expressions on their faces, working in tiny restaurants, small scale industries and other forms of employment. Child labour continues to be a standing slur on our efforts to project India as a dynamic country on the move. As per the International Labour Organisation (ILO) reports, India suffers from the dubious distinction of having perhaps the largest child labour force in the world-some 16.5 million. Unofficial estimation gives a mind-boggling figure of 45 million of which arcund 20 per cent are in urban centres and the rest in rural areas. The high incidence of child labour in India alongwith some other developing countries has often attracted a lot of international attention-critical of course. Of late, an exploding interest has also been generated world wide on this heartening issue. In India it is reflected in the increasing emphasis of the government, burgeoning attention of the media and in some of the bold initiatives of the trade unions and some employers' organisations towards the progressive elimination of child labour.

Causes of Child Labour

Though it is not a difficult proposition to know what child labour is, the views of some social scientists on it can be taken into consideration. R.K. Maheswari, M.Karunakaran and B.D. Gupta defined child labour as any work done by the children in order to economically benefit their family or themselves directly, at the cost of their physical, mental or social development.[1]

In India well over 40.0% of the population is living in conditions of extreme poverty. This grim scenario obviates a socio-economic problem like child labour. Children work out of necessity in order to supplement the meagre income of their respective families. A large number of them do not even families or can not count on them for support in these conditions idleness, destitution or resorting to crime would be alternative for them, if they do not go for work.

The reasons for child labour in India are many. Employers submit their own justification for employing children to suppress their guilt feelings. Their explanation is that the work keeps children away from starvation. They are prevented from committing crimes and other anti-social activities which they would have indulged in if they had no jobs. The bureaucrats have their own justification. They admit that the total eradication of child labour is impractical because the government cannot provide substantial alternative employment of them. However, the social scientists hold that the main cause of child labour is poverty. The children either supplement their family's income (however meagre they may be) or are the only wage earners in the family. Apart from these views, cheap labour becomes one of the vital reasons for the employment of children in various works. Child labourers are often paid as little as Rs.3/- per day when the minimum wage law requires an adult to be paid an average of Rs. 1,400/-per month.[2]

The third reason forwarded for the existence of child labour is that they benefit industries in various ways. They can also be easily controlled and motivated. Children never organise and fight for their rights. They are meek and easily submissive. They would create less tension in comparison to their adult counterparts, for the employees. For this the carpet industry in Uttar Pradesh which employs 75,000/- children earns about Rs. 150/ crore a year in foreign exchange. In 1990, the export earnings were estimated to be about Rs. 300.- crores.[3]

Nature of Child Labour

Children are employed for various types of work and a majority of children work-force is concentrated in the rural areas. About 60% of the working children are below the age of ten. Business and trade absorb 23.0% while work in household covers 36.0%.[4] The number of working children of urban areas who are engaged in canteens and restaurants or in picking rags or hawking goods, is vast but unrecorded. Among the most unfortunate ones are those who are employed in hazardous industries. The data relating to nature and extend of child labour in India is simply mind boggling. Any citizen with an iota of conscience will be shocked at the prevailing situation as revealed in some select figures below:

i) Child labour has taken a more sinister form in big towns and metropolis. In Bombay and Goa, for example 'Pleasure-pack ages' or sex with children are available. An estimated 20% of the 1,00,000 prostitutes in Bombay alone are below 18 years of age.

ii) Around 50,000 child workers are employed in the highly hazardous gem and diamond polishing enterprises located in Surat in Gujarat.

ii) 30 lakh children work in the brocaded saree industry concentrated in and around Varanasi.

iv) In the highly hazardous small scalle match and fireworks factories of Sivakasi (im Tamil Nadu), around 50,000 children are employed.

v) More than 10 lakh children work in brick-pits, stone quarries and other hazardous industries on the banks of the Ganges.

vi) In the carpet belt of India (Mirzapur-Bhadohi in U.P) an estimated 1.5 lakh children work and hundreds of adolescent boys work in the shoe making industry in Agra.

vii) In Aligarh and Moradabad approximately one lakh young boys work in the metal and brass-ware industries.

viii) In the textile industries of Maharastra, thousands of young children between the age group of 7 and 17 work in the spinding and beaming process in the over 2 lakh power looms spread over the state.

ix) About 25 per cent of the one million workers employed in bangle factories in U.P are children of less than 15 years.

x) In the mining sector, 56% of workers are children below the age of 15. Children in this sector are preferred because their height allows to walk without bending in the tunnels.

Apart from this 19 lakhs of children are employed in the stone crushing and lime making units in the hilly interiors Uttar Pradesh, lock making units in Aligarh, Slate industry in Markapur (Andhra Pradesh) and Mandsaur (M.P), carpet industries in J & K, bidi rolling factories in Vellore (Tamil Nadu, woodcrafting units in U.P. and so on. Added to this are an unspecified number of children employed as domestic servants, hotel boys and agricultural labourers all over the country.

Child labour is also inextricably linked with bonded labour. In Andhra Pradesh, 21.0% of the bonded labourers are under 16. In Karnataka, 10.3% and in Tamil Nadu 8.7% belong to this age group. A study shows that at the time of entering bondage, many labourers are as young as five years old. In Orissa, one common way of clearing debt is to sell daughters, eight to ten years old, as maid servants to the creditor. In several parts of the country, bonded fathers, over 40 years old, free themselves by deputing their sons into bondage.[5]

Table-1 : Number of Working Children from 1971 to 2000 A.D.

Year	No. of working children
1	2
1971	10.7 Million
1981	13.5 "
1983	17.4 Million
1993	18.7 "
2000	20.2 " (Projected)

* K.N. Prakash, Civil Services Chronicle, Sept. 1995.

On the basis of the data of the previous years the figure of 20.2 million for the year 2000 A.D. has been calculated. However, the table shows the number of working children is steadily on the rise.

Working Conditions

Children are generally employed for highly hazardous job with extremely dangerous conditions. They work in polluted factories whose brick walls are scrapped with soot and strong odour in the air. They work near furnaces which burn at a temperature of 1400 degree centigrade. They even handle dangerous chemicals like arsenic and potossium.

In Sivakasi the children work in sheds rolling explosives into crackers or arranging match sticks in neat rows on collapsible wooden panels. The working day is ten hour long and seven days a week. Many child workers have been killed in accidents involving explosives in the firework units. Blasts and explosions in firework factories of Sivakasi are common.

A UNICEF survey reveals that children employed in the beedi making industries in villages around Vellor in Tamil Nadu are exposed to the danger of tuberculosis because they breathe the abnoxious smell of nicotine for several years on end.

The working condition of children working in the bangle factories of U.P. is more miserable.

They carry molten glass on iron rods from the furnace to the adult workers and back to the furnace. They have to run rapidly on a floor strewn with glass pieces so that the molton metal does not get cold before it reaches the adult workers who turn it into beautiful bangles.

In the textile sector, some of the loom owners are said to have gone to the extent of branding children with red hot iron rods, burning them with cigarette butts and handing them upside down for minor faults at work. The life of the child workers engaged in carpet weaving turns worse when they slog for 10-12 hours a day with little hope for future. Working as they do in dark dingy rooms clogged with woolen smog, many of these young boys develop diseases like tuberculosis and asthma.

Table-2 : Child Labour in India (Figures in 000's)

Industry	Location	No. of children employed.
Match & Fire Works	Sivakasi	50-80
Stone quarries	Kerala	
	Markapur (A.P)	20
	Mandsaur (M.P)	
Mines	Meghalaya	28
Fishing	Karala	28
Handloom	Trivandram	10
Hosiery	Tirupur	4
Lock Industry	Aligarh	7-10
Carpet weaving	J & K, U.P.	100-150
Glass	Ferozepur (U.P)	50
Gem Ploishing	Jaipur	13

Constitutional and Legislative Measures

The constitution of India has elaborate provisions concerning children. Article 24 states that no child shall be employed in any factory or mine, or engaged in any other hazardous employment. Further Article 39(e) of the Directive Principles of State policy state 'the tender age of children should not be abused and citizens should not be forced by economic necessity to enter vocations unsuited to their age and strength'. According to Article 39(f) the children should be provided with opportunities and facilities to develop in a healthy way and in condition of freedom and dignity. Apart from this Article 45 has also provisions that the state shall take steps to provide, within a period of 10 years from the commencement of the Constitution, free and compulsory education for all children until they complete the age of 14 years.

Thus the founding fathers of our Constitution had given much emphasis on the children, the future of our nation. Moreover their intention was not to allow the issue of child labour to be eclipsed or overtaken.

However, the government is of the belief that it is difficult to completely wipe out child labour. It, therefore, has only tried to improve their working conditions-reducing working hours, ensuring minimum wages and providing better facilities for health and education. Towards this end the national policy of education was adopted by the government in 1974. In 1986, the child labour (prohibition and regulation) Act was enacted will aims at prohibiting employment of children below 14 in certain hazardous employments. But, even after the act was passed, it took another seven years before a notification was issued on 26 May 1993. The 1986 Act legalized child labour, except in work relating to selling of crackers and fireworks with temporary licences or in processes like beedi making, carpet weaving, cloth printing, dying and weaving, manufacturing of matches etc. Also under the Act the hours and the period of work for working children are regulated. No child can work for a period that exceeds three hours at a stretch and every period of three hours will be followed by a break of one hour. In one day, a child should not work more than six hours and no child can work overtime or between 7 P.M. to 8 P.M. Every employer must send a notice to the imspector about the children employed. Register must be maintained and a notice regarding the 1986 Act must be prominently displayed. The penalties for the violation of the provisions of the Act have also been made more stringent. But, despite this is only in a very few cases in which the Act is actually enforced.

In 1994, the government formulated the ambitious Rs. 850 crore scheme to eliminate child labour in the manufacturing and services sector over a five year period. The scheme came into operation in April 1995. This scheme would concentrate on first 15 per cent of the estimated 17 million child labour population in the country. The reason for this is that children engaged in the agricultural sector are not subjected to exploitations as they mostly work in their families. The scheme follows an 'area intensive approach' and concentrates on the seven states of Andhra Pradesh, Bihar, Karnataka, Madhya Pradesh, Maharastra, Tamil Nadu and Uttar Pradesh whcih account among them for 73 per cent of the country's child labour.

Table-3 : Distribution of Child Labour Population in Eleven States of India

States	Percentage
Andhra Pradesh	14.30
Bihar	8.08
Gujarat	8.52
Karnataka	8.30
Madhya Pradesh	12.45
Maharastra	11.42
Orissa	5.15
Rajesthan	6.01
Tamil Nadu	7.15
Uttar Pradesh	10.52
West Bengal	4.44
Rest	7.67
Total	100.00

* Ministry of Labour.

Remedies

There is a direct co-relation between adult unemployment and child labour. This happens so when child workers are paid less and made to work even in hazardous situations. Obviously this results in low wages and adult unemployment. Besides this, according to the Gurupadeswamy Report of 1979. "Child labour assumes the character of a social problem in as much as it hinders, arrests or distorts the natural growth processes and prevents the child from attaining the full-blown manhood.[6]"

That children have to work is sad, but that they should work in conditions dangerous to their health and safety is totally unacceptable. It is indeed disheartening to note that inspite of a strong legal and constitutional backing to combat this menace, the problem continues to grow. Toiling long hours for a pittance, these little bread winners accept exploitation as a way of life. They only know their sorrows. Silent acceptance writ large on their face. Each day adds more to their growing numbers. "Though it is true that labour helps children in their survival, but should the children be made to pay for the governments inability to curb poverty? Should they be forced to inhabit an adult world, bear adult responsibilities, and suffer abysmal exploitations?" This is hightime that these questions are replied by suitable answers.

In this context, the policies which may not be specifically addressed to children but which try to alleviate poverty and inequality can have a significant and even decisive impact. Such policies may include agrarian reform, employment creation schemes, dissemination of improved technology among the poor, promotion of the informal sector and creation of co-operatives and social security programmes. Laws and regulations must be backed by the effective enforcement machinery. This calls for the strengthening of labour inspection and related services.

In order to facilitate the verification of ages, an effective system of birth registration should be maintained by the public authorities. It should be made mandatory for employees to maintain registers and documents indicating the names ages of all the employed children. Apart from this, the government must take stringent measures for punishment through legal means to those who violate child labour Act.

Conclusions

"The well known epigram in Rousseau's Social Contract echoes across the centuries. We exclaim in the same vein today and say that child is born free but very so often 'it' is in chains".[7] Child labour has become a blot on the conscience of society. It becomes a national humiliation that millions of children of our country spend a major part of their daily life in hazardous works while millions of youth and able bodied men go into oblivion without employment.

The problem of child labour is on the increase today inspite of the legal sanctions and Constitutional provisions against it. The most important reason behind the problem remains as it is—the poverty. Of course the government has taken a lot of steps towards poverty alleviation. However, complete eradication of poverty would remain only as a utopian idea. Thus child labour seems as indispensable social evil. To over-come the problem 'not only there is a pressing need to review and update the legislation and policy, there is equally an imperative need to integrate all child laws together and create the child code of India and the child labour code of India alongwith a comprehensive manual for administrators, social workers, citizens, social scientists, lawyers and judges.' However, in any case this must not be forgotten that a problem like child labour can never only be eradicated by laws alone. It has to be supplemented by comprehensive socio-economic programmes and measures for the educational upliftment of the under privileged sections of the society. Along with these an imperative need to mobilise public opinion against this social malady can not be under-scored. 'Child is the most lovely creation of nature to nurture in roses but when circumstances force them to hard labour, so as to earn livelihood from early childhood, disrupting their optimal development—the nation suffers a net loss of his capacity as a mature adult.' The budding personalities the back-bone of the nation, who will be useful adult citizens of tomorrow must not be allowed to decay. Because they are the stars, the hopes, the promises of the widening horizons for the tomorrow and the dayafters.

References

1. Dr. Narendra Prasad: 'Child Labour in India', 'Yojana', Vol. 34, No.8, May 15, 1990.
2. K.N. Prakash: 'The Tragedy of the Innocent', 'Civil Services Chronicle' Vol. VI, No. 3. Sept. 1995.
3. Ram Ahuja: 'Social Problems in India', p 207, Rawat Publications, New Delhi-1992
6. T. N. Kitchlu: 'Child Labour: Current Scenario', 'Yojana', Vol. 38, No.9. May 31, 1994.
7. L.M. Singhvi: "Redeeming the Rights of the Child", 'Yojana', Vol.35 No. 8, May 15, 1991.

6

CHILD LABOUR AT WORK

The institution of child labour in tea-stalls, sweet-shops and dhabas is not of recent origin. Its evidence has been found even in the earlier days of human civilization. The practice of engaging the labour of the children by the owners of the tea-stalls, sweet-shops and dhabas is the direct result of poverty and has thus become a chief source of the earning of the poorest elements of the society.

The mass exodus from Indian village is a well-known phenomenon. It is now a widely accepted proposition that influx of people migrating to the cities is increasing on an unprecedent scale day-by-day. The cross over to the opportunities in the village on the one hand and tremendous pressure on land on account of population exploitation of the other. Reduced to the state of penury, these poor creatures are left with no other choice than to be migrated to the cities in search of living. It is well established fact that majority of the people of the village being ignorant, poor, illiterate, and having no exposure to the formal education can only lay their hands upon mental jobs as are performed by the child workers in the tea-stalls, sweet-shops and dhabas, etc. This probably explains to the large number of people taking to this profession as a means of their livelihood. It is equally true with their children also. At present, it is well proved fact that the child workers inthe tea-stalls, sweet-shops and dhabas are not protected by any legislation. The result is that they are most exploited lot. In these establishments where the system of employing child labour is well established, the conditions of work and wages of these workers have not undergone any appreciable change over decades. Moreover, in the absence of any formal agreement between the child servant and his employer the term of employment are most arbitrary and exploitative and no job security is provided to them. They can be hired and fired on any flimsy pretext by their mightly employers. They have drudge right from early hours in the morning to late hours in the evening, with or without internattent rest pauses, for pitifully low wages. They have often to work right through the months and through the years. The child labour legislations appear to have made a little dent on their life and the employers of these establishments enjoy a long rope in regulating their conditions work and wages.

It is difficult to make an authentic estimate of number of such servants in the country because the mass exodus to the oftenly travel with the season. The Employment Exchanges (Compulsory Notification of Vacancies) Act, 1959 does not require notification of vacancies in these establishments. Nor is there such an obligation on the part of their employers to register the names fo their servants with the appropriate authorities. For the reasons mentioned above, it is thus difficult to put forth an estimated number of such child workers.

FINDINGS OF THE SURVEY

The survey of 55 establishments revealed that 212 workers were working in these establishments, carrying out all sorts of jobs which include cooking, cleaning, sweeping, serving, preparation of the tea and sweets, etc. It is revealed from the survey that 80 child workers were engaged in various services by the owners of the tea-stalls, sweet-shops and dhabas. It is evident from the Table 1.

Table 1

Sr. No.	Nature of Establishments	Number of Establishments	Total Employees	Adults	Children	%
1	2	3	4	5	6	7
1.	Tea-Stalls	12	34	19	15	44.11
2.	Sweet-Shops	16	67	44	23	34.32
3.	Dhabas	27	111	69	42	37.87
	Total	55	212	132	80	

The study of Table 1 show that out of 212 total workers, the number of children was 80. It constitutes 37.73 per cent of the total employment given to the workers in the 55 establishments. The number of adult was 132 which comes to 62.27 per cent when compared with the child workers in the establishments surveyed.

Further, the study of Table 2 reveals that the mode of employment followed by the owners of the establishments are of three kinds, viz, (i) employment through self, (ii) employment through relationship, (ii) other sources. Out of 80 child workers, 20 have stated to have got employment through self-pursuasions, 36 through their relationship and remaining 24 were induced by the owners through other sources.

Table 2 : Mode of Employment

Sr. No.	Mode of Employment	No. of children	Percentage
1.	Self	20	25
2.	Through Relations	36	45
3.	Others Sources	24	30

Similarly, the study of Table 3 (given below) discloses that the wage-range of child workers varies from Rs. 0-350 and above. Out of 80 child workers, 15 get their wages below Rs. 150, 44 child workers are given wages between Rs. 150-250, 19 get their wages between Rs. 250-350. There ae only two child workers who have stated their wages above Rs. 350. Thus, it is quite evident that only 2.5 per cent of working children get their salaries above Rs. 350 and remaining 97.5 per cent child workers draw their wages below Rs. 350. There are 23.75 per cent child-workers who have their wage between Rs. 250-350 and 18.75 per cent get a poor wage of Rs. 0-150 from their employers.

46 / Child Labour in Various Industries

Table 3 : Detail of Wages Earned by Children

Sr No.	Wage Range in Rs.	No. of Children	Percentage
1.	Upto 150	15	18.75
2.	150-250	44	55.00
3.	250-350	19	23.75
4.	Above 350	2	2.50

It is also very much clear from the survey that the child workers of these establishments belongs to different castes. Table 4 reveals that 68.75 per cent of the child workers are Rajput, 20 per cent Brahmin, 10 per cent scheduled caste and schedule tribe and 1.25 per cent Muslims. Thus, the study of Table 4 shows that 55 child labour belongs to Rajput families, 16 from the Brahamin, 8 from the scheduled caste and scheduled tribes and one from the Muslim.

Table 4 : Caste of Child Workers

Sr. No.	Caste of Children	No. of Children	Percentage
1.	Rajput	55	68.75
2.	Brahmin	16	20.00
3.	Scheduled Castes	8	10.00
4.	Muslim	1	1.25

Table 5 throws light on the age composition of the child workers in the 55 establishments surveyed by the researcher. During the survey it was found that 14 children were of 9 years of less than 9 years. It constitutes 17.5 per cent of the total child-workers interviewed, '38 children were between the age group of 9-12 years, it is 47.5 per cent, and 28 children were between the age group of 12-14 years which comes to 35 per cent of the total child workers in these establishments.

Table 5 : Age Composition of Child Workers

Sr. No.	Age range in years	No. of Children	Percentage
1.	Upto 9 years	14	17.5
2.	9-12	38	47.5
3.	12-14	28	35.0

The study of Table 6 shows the educational profile of child workers, in these establishments. It shows that 36 child workers, that is 45 per cent of the child workers, were totally elite, 35 child workers are those who had jointed the study but could not complete even fifth standard. The percentage of these child workers is 43.75 per cent. It is also found that 9 child-workers are those who though passed primary education but could not go beyond the middle standard. The percentage of these children is recroded as 11.25 per cent when compared with the total strength of the child workers of 55 establishments. However, none of the 80 child workers was matriculate or above. It is crystal elear from the educational profile of children given in Table 6.

Table 6 : Education Profile of Child Workers

Sr. No.	Education of Children	No. of Children	Percentage
1.	Not educated	36	45
2.	0-5th	35	43.75
3.	5th to 8th	9	11.25
4.	Above 8th	0	0

The study of Table 7 shows that out of 80 child workers 34 hail from Nepal, 10 from Bihar, 11 each from Shimla and Solan district, 4 each from Mandi and Sirmaur, 2 each from Hamirpur and Kangra, one each from Kullu and Una districts of Himanchal Pradesh. The study further shows that 55 per cent of the total child workers of these establishments belong to the place falling outside the Himanchal Pradesh. It is interesting to note that no child belongs to the neighbouring states of Punjab, Haryana, Jammu & Kashmir and Uttar Pradesh, Table 7 gives the detail of place of origin :

Table 7

Sr. No.	Name of Place	No. of Children	Percentage
1.	Shimla	11	13.75
2.	Solan	11	13.75
3.	Mandi	4	5.00
4.	mamirpur	2	2.50
5.	Kullu	1	1.25
6.	Una	1	1.25
7.	Sirmour	4	5.00
8.	Kangra	2	2.50
9.	Bihar	10	12.50
10.	Nepal	34	42.50

Table 8 deals with the nature of leave allowed by owner of these establishments to the child worker. 70 per cent of the total child workers have stated what no leave is allowed to them in any shape. However, one child worker has mentioned that his employer has allowed him 10 days as the leave period with full pay, 13. 75 per cent of child workers have mentioned that they are given 12 days as a leave period with full benefits annually. 4 child workers have stated that they evail annually 15 days as a leave period and get full wages for these days 2 workers out of 80 child workers have written in their response that they avail 24 days as leave period and their owners make full payment for the abve said days also, 3.75 per cent of the child workers of the sample units have mentioned 36 days as the leave period with full wages as agreed to by their owners. However, serial number 7 of Table 8 reveals that 3 child workers get days leave annually.

The clothing facilities availed by the child workers is depicted in Table 9. It is revealed that 48 children, that is 60 per cent of the total sample children interviewed, have mentioned that they do not avail the clothing facilities of interviewed have stated that they are given clothes by their employers in lieu of their wages. Besides, 12.5 per cent child workers have stated that they are given old clothes by their owners.

Table 8 : Detail of Leave Availed by Child Workers

Sr. No.	Annually leave	No. of Children	Percentage
1.	No leave	56	70
2.	10 days	1	1.25
3.	12 days	11	13.75
4.	15 days	4	5.0
5.	24 days	2	2.5
6.	36 days	3	3.75
7.	52 days	3	3.75

Table 9 : Detail of Clothing Facilities Availed

Sr. No.	Provision of Cloth	No. of Children	Percentage
1.	No provision	48	60
2.	Old clothes	10	12.5
3.	Yes	22	27.5

The study also shows that all the child workers interviwed by the author get the food and housing facilities. They have also mentioned that no recovery is made by their employers from their wages even if some breakage is done by them incidentally or accidently. They are also provided electricity facilities and water facilities for taking bath and washing clothes.

Similarly, the Data collected and tabulated under Table 10 speaks about the mode of entertainment provided to the child workers in these establishments. 58.75 per cent of the child workers have mentioned that there are not entertainment facilities to them. However, 25.0 per cent child workers have stated that they get enterainment through radio and tapes and 15 per cent have mentioned that they are given facilities of television by their employers. The child workers have made clear in their statements that they can reap the benefit of entertainment facilities only in the late hours of the evening and night when there is no rush of work for want of the customers.

Table 10 : Detail of Entertainment Facilities of Child Workers

Sr. No.	Made of Entertainment	No. of Children	Percentage
1.	No provision	47	58.75
2.	Radio	11	13.75
3.	Tape	10	12.5
4.	Television	12	15.0

So far as nature of their duties is concerned, they are: washing of utensils, preparation of tea and sweets, cleaning of table and chairs, sweeping of room, etc. Despite of large number in these establishments, they are not covered by any law or regulation and they are supposed to carry out jobs of mixed nature.

It is also evident from the statements of the child workers, that they are to work without intermittent rest pauses from morning till evening. It is revealed from the study of Table 11 all the child workers are to toil between 8-15 hours without any rest. 15 per cent of the total child workers have stated that they work for 8-12 hours a day, 72.5 per cent child workers have stated that their working hours vary between 12-15 hours, and 10 child workers, i.e. 12.5 per cent have mentioned that they are to work tirelessly for 15 hours or above every day. It is generally found from the statement made be child workers that their employers do not follow any child labour welfare legislation. As the child workers are whole-time servants and live in the premises provided by their employers, they usually work from early hours of the morning to late hours in the night without taking any rest.

Table 11 : Detail of the Working Hours of the Children

Sr. No.	Working Hours	No. of Children	Percentage
1.	0-8	0.00	0.00
2.	8-12	12	15.00
3.	12-15	58	72.5
4.	Above 15	10	12.5

CONCLUSION OF THE SURVEY

The data collected in the present survey presents a clear-cut picture of the working conditions of the child workers in the tea-stalls, sweet-shops and dhabas located in the periphery of Shimla City. The survey has shown that 37.83 per cent are still the child workers carrying out different types of occupations in these establishments. Out of 212 total employees in these establishments, 80 are child workers belonging to different castes. About 68.75 per cent child workers belong to Rajput families, 20 per cent are the Brahmins and 8 per cent fall in the category of the scheduled castes and scheduled tribs. There is only 1.25 per cent child workers who belong to the Muslim community.

The child workers have stated to have got the occupation through three different modes, viz., self, through relationship and other sources. It is seen from the survey that 25 per cent child workers got their occupations by their individual initiatives, 45 per cent through the media of their relaitonships, and 30 per cent could get their employment through other sources. The main reason for joining the occupation by these child workers is stateed as "poverty." It may be observed that caste has played a little role in the social evil of child labour. It is the poverty which seems to have been responsible to generate the evil of child labour in each and every establishment of country.

The survey has shown beyond the shadow of doubt that the working conditions of the children are far from satisfaction. The sruvey results reveal that the owners of these establishments do not adhere to laws made to regulate the hours of work as prescribed under the Child Labour (Prohibition and Regulation) Act, 1986. It has been observed that the daily working hours of children vary between 8 to 15 hours, as against 6 hours prescribed under Section 7, Clause (3) of the Child Labour (P &R) Act, 1986. To the surprise of the authors, 10 child workers have stated that they are forced to work even for more than 15 hours a day without any rest. The data collected reveals that the child workers are not allowed any rest during the whole course of their work in a day. Almost all the child workers interviewed have mentioned that there is no specific period given to them for the purpose of rest. This practice is highly in contravention to Section 7 (3) of the Child Labour (P & R) Act, 1986, where in every employer is under statutory obligation to arrange the period of work on each day in such a manner that no for more than 3 hours before he had interval for rest for at least one hour. It is also observed while the interview of the child workers that they are to work even in the late hours of the evening and there is no bar on the employers to restrain them as the employment of the children between 7 p.m. and 8 p.m. is totally prohibited under clause 4 of section 7 of the Act.

It is also quite evident that that child workers do not get any weekly holidays. 70 per cent of the children interviewed have stated that they are not entitled to any kind of leave. Only 30 per cent of the sampled units have mentioned that they get annual leave ranging between 10 to 52 days. The survey results. therefore, show that the mandate of Section8 of the Child Labour (P & R) Act, 1986, is not at all obeyed by the owners of tea-stalls, sweet-shops and dhabas.

So far as the health provision are concerned, the survey shows that the owners provide to the child workers a nominal type of medical facilities in case of their illness. All the 80 interviewed child workers have staged that they are provided with the house facilties, drinking water facilities, lighting facilitiecs, etc. by their employers. However, it is generally obsrved from the study that they are poorly paid and even get their wages between a poor range of Rs. 0-350. 97.5 per cent of the total child workers have staged that they get their wage between Rs. 0-350. There are only 2 children who have mentioned their wages above Rs. 350 per month. The survey, therefore, discloses that the poor child workers are not paid even the minimum wages by their employers which is sheerly in contravention to the decision of the Supreme Court given in M.C. Mehta vs. State of Tamil Nadu (AIR 1991 SC 417). The Honorable Court in this case has held that the child workers must get at least minimum wages which comes to 60 per cent of prescribed minimum wage for adult employees doing same job to be given to child in view of special adaptability of child's tender age to such work.

It is also observed from the survey that the educational profile of the child workers is very poor. None has stated his education above eighth standard. 45 per cent of the child workers have been found totally illiterate and there are only 55 per cent of the child workers whose education various between 5th-8th standards. It is observed that the majority of child workers have joined these occupations because they are basically poor and need waged as a source of their livelihood. There are hardly any night school for those who want to continue their studies. It is also revealed that there is lack of appreciation on the part of the their employers to give them education while serving in their establishments. The findings of the study therefore go against the spirit of the dicision of the Supreme Court in M.C. Mehta v. State of Tamil Nadu.

It is also equally clear that extreme poverty is the main reason for the wide prevalence of child labour. In Annexure-III, 79 child workers out of 80 have stated poverty as a reason for joining the establishments. Thus, it is revealed the that child labour could not be weeded out despite several welfare legislations enacted by the Government from time-to-time. It needs a change in social attitude. Social awareness is also needed to discourage the practice of child labour. Besides this, the tightening of laws and activising enforcement machinery are needed badly to weed out the child labour in its true perspective.

7

CHILDREN IN THE GLASS INDUSTRY

Vijay Pal, age sisteen of seventeen years: I started working at the age of six earning Rs. 5 for a six-hour shift. Today I make Rs 19 a day in a twelve-hour shift blowing glass. A blow glass worker can only work for ten years. Working for twelve to fourteen hours a shift means that the life of a worker is shortened by half. By the time a glass blower has reached thirty years of age, be the time a glass blower has reached thirty years of age, be cannot work much. Soon I will not be able to work as a glass blower. If I manage to save money, I'll start a shop; otherwise, when I have children, I will send them to work.

'I visited Ferozabad in July 1986, to study the glass indutry and the conditions of workers there. While the first part deals with the plight or workers in general, the second part addresses itself to child workers in particular. Visits to factories, interviews with factory owners and local government officials and lastly, discussions with some villagers of the area, built up a horrifying picture of the appalling conditions under which children and adults use up their lives in the glass factories of Ferozabad. This experinece of twentieth-century India does appear to be significantly different from what industrial workers in nineteenth-century England must have gone through. As we shall see later, some of Marx's observations about the predicament of workers in his time appear to be remarkably apposite.

THE ORGANIZATION OF THE GLASS INDUSTRY

Ferozabad is a tehsil (an administrative unit of the district) in Agra district of Uttar Pradesh (U.P.) It is also the home of the glass bangle and glassware indusrtry, which is a multicrore business. Out of 289 registered units (of which 133 units are registered as glass-blowing factories), approximately 70 per cent are not in fact working. However, they get their coal quot at controlled rates and sell it at a 100 per cent premium. The Labour Department certifies that on the day of inspection a particular number of workers were working at a particular unit. The Excise Department gives a certificate of production on the basis of which the Director of Industries recommends a coal quota. On record, even the temperature in the furnace is mentioned to prove that the factory was actually working (Chatterji 1986: 123: Pal 1986: and Barse 1986a). People say that the owners of bogus units can earn as much as Rs. 10 lakhs (Rs 1 lakh is equivalent to Rs 100.00) a year through the black marketing of coal without lifting a finger (Awasthi 1986:L 127). Workers cited the example of Som Glass Works where many of them were working. This unit had not functioned for five years but they had been getting a regular coal quota at the controlled rate. Any units which had permanent labourers have shut down their units in order to get rid of their permanent workers. Today, Labourers are recruited on a daily basis in the labour markers at Kotla Mohalla and Ghantaghar. They are, therefore, totally at the mercy of the employers.

The black-marketing of coal allows factory owners to keep their units closed and yet make money. Since 1974, the Uttar Pradesh government has stopped the setting up of new indstrial units which use coal as their main source of fuel. Bogus units established earlier can then sell their coal quota at a 100 per cent premium to units which are operating. In this way, they are able to earn money without the burden of running a factory.

Another common practice in Ferozabad is that units close for part of the year, ostensibly for furnace repairs. Workers, however, have a different story to tell. According to them, a tarkash (the man who threads hot glass on to a rolling pin) make 400-500 toras (strings of 312 bangles) in one shift which goes on for at least twelve hours. (Officially, there are supposed to be three, eight-hour shfits). However, for purposes of tax, they show that only 200 toras are made. The profits made on the side allow the factory owners to shut down the factories for part of the year while they live off their illegal profits and their coal quotas (Pal, 1986) This is also true of glassware production. Now that there is no exicise vertification on goods produced, the amount of black money made is even more and the effect on labour is obvious. The sum total of it all is that since factories remain closed for much of the time, where there should be a shortage of labour, there is in fact a surplus of labour.

Factory owners and government officials deny that there is any exploitation of workers in the glass industry. According to time; 'How can there be exploitation if workers come willingly to work? Yet many factory owners admit that they have dispensed with their permanent staff. According to the proprietor of the Saraswati Glass Works. Till 1965 they had only permanent workers. They were entitled to only three days leave with pay in a year. But in 1980-1, the rules changed and permanent workers were entitled to fourteen days leave with pay. It was therefore decided to do away with all permanent staff. In 1986, he gave forty workers about Rs. 2.75 lakhs and asked them to leave. Talking about the advantages of daily wage workers, he said quite candidly: the temporary worker knows he can be removed. It is easier then to get work out of him.

This was amply substantiated by what workers had to say. A Taarkash said:

Everyone says that a Taarkash gets Rs. 150 a shift and a belenwala gets Rs. 80 for working in one shift. But no one ever asks how many days in a week we get to work. In peak season, a taarkash or a belanwale gets work for three days a week and never for more than four of five months in the year.

A Jagaiya explained his helplessness and pointed out that he could not bring the same man for more than seven days to the factory. If he did so because he felt that the man needed the money, he would be in danger of losing his own job. In the same way, if the factory, owner feels that a particular worker is indulging in netagiri (politicking) or union-baji (unionizing), then the Jagaiya has no choice but to abide by the wishes of the factory owner and not to recruit the man. However, unfair the decision might be.

When work is scarce, workers are prepared to work on any terms. As one belanwala pointed out:

I have been unemployed for two weeks, I finally went to the Jagai and told him I would give a percentage of my wages to him.

It was settled that the Jagaiya would get Rs 80 from the factory but pay him only Rs 65. This apparently is the order of the day.

The local mafia (thugs and goons hired by factory owners) not only prevents labour trouble in Ferozabad but also prevents highly skilled Labourers from moving away from their factories, For example, if a man he mastered the art of blowing a particular type of fine glass for which the factory owner has got a big order, then it is virtually impossible for that worker to leave. It goes without saying that if the worker leaves, the order is lost. Many big companies like Air India, Oberois, IIDC (India Tourism Development Corporation) and Nestles order their glass-ware from Ferozabad. It is not unknown for a worker to be killed if he threatens to take business away. Thus while thugs prevent highly skilled workers form taking business away, they also ensure that other workers do not create union trouble and do not insist upon their rights do minimum wages and better conditions of work. In Ferozabad, workers are subject to severe exploition and their circumstances are akin to those of the labourers of nineteenth-century England. They have on choice but to work twelve to fourteen hours a day, if they refuse, there are always unemployed people waiting to take over their jobs.

DANGEROUS WORKING CONDITIONS

Workers in the glass industry are intimidated for a variety of reasons. One important reason why factory owners need a mafia it to hush up the many industrial accidents that take place because the working conditions are notably unsafe. The industry is technologically very primitive and the pressure on the workers is tremendous. There are two types of furnaces used the pot furnaces for making only bangles and the tank furnaces which make a variety of glassware as well as bangles. The pot furnace unit is smaller and can run only twelve hours and therefore there is only on shift. The temperature in these furnaces ranges between 700-800 C. The tank furnace units are much bigger and the temperature goes upto 1800 C. In the summer months, the temperature is so high that only the most tenacious workers can manage to work in the excruciationg heat. Combined with this heat, in factories where glasses are made in presses, the noise is deafening. The heat, noise and dust obviously have serious ill effects on the health of warkers (Chatterji 1986; Barse 1986 b, c). The net effect is that tuberculosis (TB) is widespread and the life of a worker is cut short by ten to fifteen years. But since there is not death of labour, to the factory owner it makes no difference what happens to the worker.

Marx pointed out that this was a result of the demands of capitalism which puts a tremendous pressure on the worker and which consequently leads to.. generations of stunted, short-lived and rapidly replaced human beings, plucked, so to speak, before they were ripe (Marx [1967] 1982: 380). Writing about the over-worked labourer in 1833, he observed that they 'die off with strange rapidity; but the places of those who perish are instantly filled, and a frequent change of persons make no alternation in the scene' (ibid.). This is also the case with glass workers in Ferozabad. At a *pakai bhatti* (a unit where bangles are baked in layers on metal sheets covered with silica sand) in village Chandwar, a worker had fainted due to heat exhaustion. This worker is a *pakaiwala* (the person who places trays of bangles into the furnace and also stokes it) and is thirty-six years old. The heat in the *pakai bhatti* is unbearable and it was not possible to stand even ten feet away from the furnace. This man started working at the age of eight and this summer he has fainted three times due to dehydration. He told me that he has only one more month of working life left in him. If he faints once more, he will tell the *thekedar* (contractor) to find another *pakaiwala* to replace him. According to this *pakaiwala*, there is an unwritten rule that a worker, when he is about to collepse, warns the *thekedar*.

No factory owner wants a labourer to die on the premises as there would be an inquiry and compensation would have to be paid. Workers said that in summer 200-400 glucose drips were given daily to workers who faint with dehydration and heat exhaustion. Private practice is flourishing in Ferozabad where there are almost 200.000 workers employed. Each glucose drip costs Rs. 65. Depending on how urgently the work needs to be done and how indispensable the worker is, the factory owner pays for the treatment. Otherwise, the worker borrows from others. The greatest fear of a worker is to collapse with heat exhaustion. He not only loses his day's wages but also has to borrow for expensive treatment (Pal, 1986). Factory owners, however, dent that serious industrial accidents take place. The proprietor of one of the biggest glass factories in Ferozabad, in fact said that except for the occasional case of heat exhaustion, workers did not suffer from any adverse effect of intense heat. In his factory, cut *nimmbu* (lemon) is freely available to workers if they feel the heat very acutely, he proudly added.

A noticeable feature in many factories is that workers in fact display few visible injuries and burn marks. The workers explanation for this state of affairs is that factory owners do not employ anybody other than a very healthy person. They not only cannot afford to have a death on their premises but the work involved is so strenuous and the conditions so appalling that only the healthiest survive. A mutha uthanewale (the man who removed the spring of hot bangles from the rolling Pin) said that factory owners and the supervisor decide how much a man can make in a day. If a worker produces less than the required quantity, he is dismissed without wages of with only half the wages. Since there are always plenty of desperate people who are unemployed, the Jagai looks around for somebody in very good health.

Glass bangles are being made illegally in tank furnaces since 1982 because the capacity of tank furnaces is greater and they run round the clock. Owners of tank furnaces openly make glass bangles because there is no excise duty on them. These bangles are of slightly inferior quality as the colour is put on them after the molten glass comes out of the tank furnace. These factories also make laboratory equipment, bulbs, chimney, glasswere, etc. Out of sixty glass manufacturing units, only twenty-one units are registered for purposes of excise. From the 1986-7 budget onwards, production verification has stopped. Whatever, the factory owners declare as shier production is accepted for purpose of Central excise. In 1985-86, the excise revenue was to the tune of Rs. one crore. In 1986-87 the estimated revenue was the supposed to be not than Rs 15 lakhs. On record the production of glassware has gone down by a third. There is absolutely no control now on what the factory makes and sells. 30 to 40 per cent of the total production of a tank furnace unit is in making bangles where the profit is as high as 50-60 per cent.

The story of Ferozabad is one of power, corruption, blackmail and exploitation. The inhuman conditions of work take their toll upon the health of workers. A man by the time he is thirty-five years old is almost finished and has to reply upon his children to save him from starvation and imminent

56 / Child Labour in Various Industries

death. There are almost 50.000 children below the age of fourteen years working in the glass industry making it one of the highest concentration of child labour in the world. If a person starts working at the age of eight or nine, he is burnt out by the time he is thirty-five. Poverty and ill-health force him to use his children and the vicious cycle continues inexorably.

In these conditons, what is the future of the workers of Ferozabad? Is there any hope that this vicious cycle will ever be broken? Workers in the glass industry have some suggestions which they feel will go a long way in improving their lives. They want that the Government of India Institute a high-level investigation into the black marketing of coal. If the government was able to stop the coal allotment to bogus units which have closed down on the pretext of seasonal repairs, it would force factory owners currently living off black money to reactivate their factories. If all the registered units were actually working, there would not be able to exploit the workers so easily. If there is full employment, the economic condition of workers will automatically improve.

Plight of Child Worker

The plight of child workers is indeed painful. As mentioned earlier, the two boys working in the glass industry were both left behind by their parents to pay off loans. They were lonely, homesick and had to live by themselves at the *pakai bhatti*, cook their food on sillica covered trays and work near furnaces whose temparatures went up to 800 c. The older boy was studying in school till a few a few months back, when his father had an accident working on a thresher and lost his arm and the boy was withdrawn from school and brought to Ferozabad. His father had taken an advance from the *thekedar* and the boy was to pay off the loan from his wages.

The other boy comes from Tundla village in Agro district; His father also took an advance of Rs. 500 from the *thekedar* and left his little boy behind. On being asked whether he had any brothers and sisters, the boy put his head down and began to cry. An old man sitting next to him explained that the boy was feeling homesick as his father had just come a few days previously to collect his wages and had gone back to the village without him.

Interviews with workers, factory owners and the local MLA revealed that there are almost 50.000 children below the age of fourteen year working in the glass industry at Ferozabad: the total labour force is estimated at 200.000.

A visit to any glass unit shows at a glance that at least 25 per cent of the workers present are children. The official figures reproted by the Labour Department estimate that there are 65,000-70.000 workers and that children constitute only 13 per cent of the total labour force. Official figures are considerably lower than what was reported in the field. Ferozabad would then appear to have one of the largest concentrations of child labour in India.

Participation of Children in the Work Force

Child labour is a touchy issue in the glass industry because of government's recent interest in the subject. In fact, according to factory owners and government officials, children are employed only to serve water to adult worker. But when faced with the facts, they present a complete volte-face and plead the case for the poor thus:

What can we do when fathers bring their children to us and beg us to employ them? If we did not help out, these poor people would starve.

While factory owners make out that they are in fact helping the poor to survive by employing their children, the arithmetic of glass manufacture tells a different tale. Child labour is so important for the glass industry that if factory owners did not employ children, their production would go down by 25 per cent. The owner of a big glass factory went to the extent of saying that the glass industry cannot function without children. They run much faster than adults and therefore production goes up.

Children perform a variety of jobs in the glass industry. There work is not very different from that of children in nineteenth centry England. A tour of four of the largest, glass-blowing units and one glass bangle unit (where only bangles are made) showed that children are involed in almost all the processes of bangle-making and glass-blowing and many of these processes are extremely hazardous for them.

Ashok, an eleven year-old glass factory worker, was interviewed by film maker Meera Dewan. He describes his first day at work when he did three shifts. He was new to the job and therefore made a small mistake and was beaten up for it.

I was so tired. I didn't do the work correctly, I made a mistake. This man next to me, he gave me a slap...it was such a hard slap that I couldn't ever forget the work now. (target 1996:54).

Children do all manner of jobs in glass factories. They were seen carrying molten glass on a seven-foot iron rod called labya from the furnace to the adult worker and back to the furnace. Nearly 85 per cent of the child labour force was engaged in the this activity and these are Labour Department figures.

Children sit in front of furnaces where the temperature is said to be about 700 c. In many of the factories where the children were drawing molten glass from tank furnaces in which the temperature was between 1500 c and 1800 c, the face of the child was within six to eight inches from the opening of the furnace. Since he was small in size, he had to put his arm right inside in order to draw adequate quantities of molten glass. As s result, his body was almost touching the furnace.

Most visitors to Ferozabad are taken on a conducted tour of some so-called model factories such a Advance Glass Works and Om Glass Works, who are makers of high-quality glassware for companies such as Air India. In these factories, child labour exists as well but one does not notice children so much because they are relatively specious; after the factory owners have told the visitor their human interest stories of poverty and child labour, one can actually leave the factory premises believing that factory owners are in fact doing the poor a good turn by employing their children. If however, one manages to visit factories other than the ones highly recommended, the conditions are well and truly horrifying.

One such factory is the General Traders (GT) Glass Works where the bulk of the glassware is made in automatic presses. Like other factories, they also make bengles and blow glassware. It is frighening to enter this factory where obviously labour inspections, have never taken place. The whole factory floor was strewn with broken glass and naked electric wires were to be seen everywhere. The noice in the factory was deafening and there was hardly any space to move without bumping into somebody or other. At least 30-40 per cent of the labour force in this factory seemed to be made up of children of the ages of eight of thirteen years (Barse 1986 a, b, c). They were carrying glasses made in presses on forks to the conveyor belt. They were sitting in front of small furnaces re-heating the loan (molten glass) on which colour had been applied. But mainly, they were engaged in carrying loam on labyas (the seven-foot iron rod used for carrying molten glass). There were children sitting on the ground in front of blow glass workers, closing the mould after the molten glass was put into it. Their job seemed to be to line the mould with paper and close it after the blow glass worker had put the blown glass into it. As soon as the child closed the mould, even before he had time to remove his hands, the mould would catch fire because of the paper inside it. The whole process taken a few seconds from the time the worker brings the molten glass on a labya to the glass blower and the blown glass is put into the mould. After that, children carry the product to another worker who cuts it and then it is taken away for further heating. While I was watching the children at work, about ten to fifteen young workers, including several children ran past me in a passage about three feet wide carrying molten glass. One worker bumped into another and part of the molten glass from his labya fell on inch away from my foot. There was on place to move because behind me were some loose wires and across this narrow passage, other children were sitting on the ground with their backs to the passage in front of small furnaces, re-heating the loam if the molten glass (the temperature of which I was told was nearly 1200 C) had not fallen near my foot, it would have fallen on a child's back. Under these working conditions, it is not surprising that industrial accidents are frequent though government officials and factory owners dent it. People even went to the extent of saying that fatal and near-fatal accident victims are thrown in to the furnaces to destroy evidence (Barse 1986 a, b, c).

Children are undoubtedly the most common victims of such industrial accidents because their bodies cannot take the trauma of such accidents easily. The interesting thing was that in spite of frequant burn injuries and accidents, I did not see any obviously injured worker in the factories. The reason for this was clear after a visit to neighbouring villages and conversations with workers.

Sriram, about nine years old, and thandibatiwala (the person who carries the molten glass after it is beaten into shape, back to the furnace) could not open his left eye which was very sore. A piece of hot glass flew into his eyes. He was being looked after by co-workers as his parents had left him there.

Grace, aged sixteen years, was wounded when he took the spring of glass bangles to show the supervisors. The man tried to break a piece by hitting it. Part of this flew into Grace's face and when I interviewed him, his face looked as if a hive of bees had attacked him.

While workers, including child workers, are paid on a time rate basis in the bigger factories, in the smaller units where bangles are joined in a process called *judai* (to join), all workers are paid on a piece-rate basis. In most these units, particularly the *takai addas* (unregistered units where designs are cut on bangles), children can be seen everywhere. The bangles are brought by the *thekedar* who as a unit in or hear his house. He enagages the labour and pays them according to the intricacy of the design. Breakage of bangles while cutting the design is adjusted against the wages of the workers. As it happens, children often end up by losing a whole day earnings for starts earning a reasonable wage.

The *judai addas* (unregistered small units where bangles are joined over acetylene flames), also have a very large number of child workers. At one adda (unregistered workshop). Out of twenty workers, at least three or four were very small children who were not quite eight. The room was so dark that only their eyes could be seen staring out of the inky blackness. It was lunch-time and the acetylene lamps had been switched off. The room was full of soot and there was no ventilation as the acetylene flames could be extinguished by the breeze. The workers in this unit came from Hallapur village, which is about four kilometers from Ferozabad town. on bicycles. The workers said that 50-60 per cent of this work was done by children and this led to tremendous eye-strain as the worker sat in front of the flames working continuously for twelve hours without removing his eyes from the flame. Many workers said that the high incidence of tuberculosis (T.B.) amongst *judai* workers was a result of inhaling kerosene fumes (Pal, 1986; Champakalakshmi n.d: 12).

Minimum Wages

Surprisingly, there are no minimum wages fixed for the glass bangle workers. Minimum wages were first introduced in 1974 for glass bangle and blow glass workers. In 1981, a revision of wages took place by a govenment order. In 1982, a high powered tripartite committee met and another government order was issued for revision of wages only for the bengle industry. The tripartite committee of labour leaders, union member's employers and government officials fixed the minimum wages and a govenment order (GO No. 4560(ST)0/36-1-637/ST/81 Lucknow dated November 12, 1982) was passed.

However, after the 1981 government order, the Glass Industrial Syndicate, Ferozabad, filled a writ pertition in the Allahabad High Court against minimum wages for bangle workers. It is said that the High Court slapped a contempt of court order on the UP Labour Secretary for insisting upon minimum wages glass bangle workers. The state government withdrew the GO of 1982 by GO No. 4195-36-3-55, dated 25-11-1983.

The Labour Department and its Views on Child Labour

Child labour is an indispensable part of the glass bangle and glass-blowing industry of Ferozabad because it is cheap (Chatterji 1986: 10; Barse 1986 a, b, c,). The Labour Department at Ferozabad had recommended to the higher authorities that child labour should not be banned because unless a child starts working at a very young age, he will not get acclimatized to the intense heat. They have even suggested that hostels be constructed where children who have to work on the night shift can stay. The argument is that children, who have to work back to the village at that hour and therefore they must have a place to stay. Since the glass industry cannot function without children and they have to run at night because otherwise factory owners will face losses through the heat in the furnaces going waste, children must work at night.

Night-work for children is forbidden under the Factories Act (63 of 1984) which, under Section 70, prohibits the employment even of adolescents below the age of seventeen years. But night work in the night shift. Factory owners today are not as honest as their counterparts in England in the nineteenth century who admitted that:

Great difficulty would be caused by preventing boys under eighteen form working at night. The Chief would be the increase of cost from employing men instead of boys (Marx [1867] 1982: 372)

In fact, this is the main reason why children are employed in the glass industry. Marx sarcastically explain the rationale for exploiting children by factory owners. He said that factory owners were not interested in discontinuing night-work because in industries which use furnaces, not only in there a loss form machinery lying idle but there would be a waste of fuel as well. The argument in favour of night-work was also that otherwise, time would be lost in heating up the furnaces and the furnaces themselves would suffer from changes in temperature.

Child Labour but Adult Unemployment

In India today, child labour is being justified on the grounds of pover. If the children of the poor do not work they will starve, it is argued. Another common argument is that will become vagabonds and anti-social elements. These young persons need to be harnessed for productive work. But a fact that is not being recognized is that child labour cannot be justified in a country where there is rampant adult unemployment and under employment. Ashok (referred to earlier) has an unemployed father. This man told Meera Dewan that he gets up at 4. a.m. to make morning tea for Ashok so that the boy can go to work. He feels bad about making his son go to work, so he helps out in his small way be making the morning tea and bringing Ashok's lunch to the factory (Target 1986:53).

Ashok describes his working day thus:

I pass on the iron rods with the melted glass on it to the blower, come back for a bite, and then go and give the next one (ibid.).

Marx's explanation for why glass manufaturers do not give regular, meal-times to children is that it would be time lost or 'wasted' (marx [1867] 1982: 374). Describing the lives of child labourers in the glass industry in England in 1965, he remarks:

A certain amount of heat beyond what is usual at present might also be going to waste, if meal-times were secured in these cases, but it seems likely not equal in money-value to the waste of animal power now going on in glass-houses throughout the kingdon growing boys not having enough quiet time to eat their meals at ease, with a little rest afterwards for digestion (ibid).

The exploitation of children in the glass industry is to be seen to be believed. Ashok's story is the story of every other boy in Ferozabad, some of them even younger than Ashok.

...I leave the house at four in the morning, after having some breakfast. Then it takes on hour to reach the factory site. I go from one to another, to find out where they need a person to carry the hot iron rods. Sometime, I sit in one factory waiting for the work. If I get it, that's fine. If not I have to go home without the work and money (Target 1986:53-4)-

Child labour is to be found everywhere in the glass factories and although children are engaged in the most dangerous of jobs described earlier, the Labour Department of the State Government in their recent report said that:

Compared to national standards, the above rates per thousand worker population are not alarming. Glass work is known to be less dangerous as compared to chemical works, power generation and basic metal industry (GOUP 1986 a: 6).

The Labour Department Committee was headed by the Deputy Labour Commissioner. Agra and the Assistant Director of Factories (Medical). The Committee, during the course of its inspection, found that:

Children as young as ten years of age were working but the processes in which they were engaged did not call for excessive strength or activity.

Labour laws are openly flouted in Ferozabad with the complete connivance of the local bureaucracy. The Labour Committee Report of April, 1986, Admits that while children under the age of fourteen years are prohibited from working under the Factories Act, yet they found that all the glass-blowing and glass bangle-making factories were employing children. Knowing that this was the case, when 125 factory inspections had taken place up to April 1986, only twelve employers had been prosecuted for violation of Section 67 of the Factories Act, which says that no child who has not completed his fourteenth year shall be required or allowed to work in any factory.

Owners of glass factories are aware that children cannot be employed under the Factories Act. This is why when government teams come to inspect factories, children just disapper. This is what happened when the Labour Department Committee went on its inspection tours. Accouding to its report. Shankar Novelties Glass Industries had violated Section 67: Emkay Glass works had only four children working because most of the children were removed from the premises as soon as the managment come to know about the visit of the Committee in neighbouring factory. This was also the case with the Om Glass Works from where most of the children has been removed before the Committee visited the factory. In the Refugee Glass Works and in Ashok Glass Works, illegal child labour was found.

When every single glass factory in Ferozabad employs children illegally, it is quite obvious from the figures given by the Committee on the number of prosecutions lauched under Section 67 of the Factories Act that they have only touched the tip of the iceberg. Instead of condemning child labour and prosecuting employers of child labour, the Labour Department justifies child labour on the grounds that:

* Child labour exists because of poverty.
* The children of the poor are not interested in conventional education.
* This is a hereditary occupation.
* Children need to work at an early age to get acclimatized to the intense heat.
* Most of the work that children do is non-hazardous.

It is undoubtedly true that the children in the glass factories of Ferozabad—like children elsewhere in India—work because their families are poor. But the argument that child labour is therefore necessary must be rejected. To blandly blame the abstract notion of poverty is to ignore the particular economic and social circumstances that constribute not the persistence of child labour. Once these circumstances are analyzed and understood, the possibility of changing them now arises rather than wait for that distant day when there is no more poverty. It is here that the exploitation of the worker by the glass factories of Ferozabad must be viewed as a means of ensuring the privileged position of factory owners. The obnoxious conditions of work shorten the productive life of the worker forcing him then to depend upon the labour of his children. During his productive period, since the gets employment for only a few days in a week and for not more than four of five months in the year, he cannot affort to educate his children; his children, then, are denied the option of breaking away form the rigours of their lives. For small sums of money, parents pledge their children to life-times of bondage. The area MLA and others contended that 90 per cent of the children are bonded slaves.

In the absence of althernative employment opportunities, the workers are dependent for their livelihood on the glass manufacturers. With low and uncertain wages, it is difficult for them to feed their children; the option of sending their children to school is simply not real (Burra 1986 b, c). Not surprisingly, illiteracy is widespread amongst these children. Nevertheless, there are a few examples of parents who have put their desperate economic straits. Said a worker in response to a question as to whether he would train his child in his avocation:

My life is virtually over at thirty-six. Do you think I want my son to suffer like this? It I can somehow see him through school, I'll try and keep him out of this industry. I don't want my son to die at the age of forty years which is bound to happen be someone working twelve to fourteen hours a day in this intense heat. But I know that I cannot work beyond another month; then how will I pay for his school clothes? If he doesn't have proper clothes, the teacher will not let him enter the classroom. Sooner or later, circumstances will force me to put him to work.

To justify child labour on the grounds that the children need to be acclimatized to the intense heat is only a reflection of our inhuman society which can even make such a suggestion. It has perhaps not even occurred to the Labour Department that such intense heat can in fact have very adverse effects upon the health of the child. Or does the department believe that with growing numbers, the children of the poor are an expendable commodity? And if this is the attitude of the bureaucracy to the plight of working children, then obviously for them the work that children do is in fact non-harardous.

The premise of the Child Labour (Prohibition and Regulation) Act, 1986, is that there can be no doing away with child labour as it is a consequence of peverty. Such an attitude does not bode well either for the families who are poor or their children who labour. Both Article 24 of the Constitution and Section 67 of the Factories Act explicitly direct that children below the age of fourteen years are not to work in Factories. Article 24 forbids the employment of children in hazardous occupations. Yet the Act does not make the glass industry out-of-bounds for children.

The Ministry of Labour has set up a Child Labour Technical Advisroy Committee to draw a line between hazardous and nonbazardous processes in hazardous industries: children will be banned from working in the former and allowed to work in the latter. Any attempt to carve out an area of non-hazardous children. This writer believes there can be no non-hazardous process in a hazardous industry. To illustrate, children in the glass factories are always exposed to hot, flying pieces of glass, whatever particular activity they are engaged in. Also, once children are allowed to work in a hazardous industry, who is to police the factory and ensure that they are doing only safe jobs? The answer cannot be a bureaucracy that is corrupt and amenable to power and influence; even assuming it to be conscientious, which bureaucracy can monitor what 50.000 children in the glass industry are doing? More fundamentally, the Committee will not even be able to find children when it visits such factories for they are whisked away whenever an inspection team is around.

What is the future of the chlidren of Ferozabad? They do not have much of past, steeped as they are in poverty, malnutrition and illiteracy. Their future depends in large part, on governmental response. Today, the prospects for these children are not at all bright. They can look forward to lives very similar to that of their parents, trapped in a web not of their own making. Can we not implement the Constitution of India and provide contitions for univeral primay education? Why should the State be so chary and coy in dealing with the vested interests of Ferozabad?

8

MIGRANT CHILD LABOUR IN ORISSA

Out of a host of serious menaces, India faces at the threshold of 21st century, the problem of Child Labour in general and the problems of migrant child labour in particular, is quite thought-provoking. The legislative enactment of 1986 namely the Child Labour Prevention and Regulation Act defines a child is one who is below the age of 14 years. The exertion of either body or mind undertaken partially or wholly by children aging below 14 years, with a view to getting some monetary remuneration is called child labour. Though, there are certain areas like parental agriculture, parental handicrafts etc. where a child along with his/her parents may be manifested as part-time labourer but if he/she becomes subject to a certain degree of exploitation by any type of social class having some vested interest, the scenario around them becomes horribly complex.

Alongwith the concept of child labour, the concept of migrant child labour is also concomitant. Child labourers are said to be migrant if their movements takes place from one geographical region to another geographical region with a view to getting some employment opportunity against some remuneration for a temporary period of time.

In fact, a singular cause can't be attributed for the concept of migrant child labour. Rather, there are plethora of reasons for the pervasiveness of this concept. Mainly geographical, social, and economic disadvantages of a particular region compel the parents to send their children to distant places with the objective of adding to their economic destiny.

Mostly, child labour in general and exclusively migrant child labour are found in some selected industries of our economy. Some of the occupational processes where child labourers are rampant phenomena which exist in agriculture, Brick-linking, Brassware, carpet weaving, Handlooms, Match and fire works, Glass and bangles, Diamond cutting and polishing, Gem Cutting, lock making, garage works, hotel works and a host of peripheral production processes like bidi industry, Zari and embroidery, stone quarries and slate quarries.

In all the above mentioned manufacturing Units, Child Labour appears both in the form of local child labour and migrant child labour. Again, migrant child labour happens either in the form of inter-state or intra-state migrant child labour as a sequel of mobility of parents from rural to rural, rural to urban or urban to rural. Whatever may be the case, certain factors are highly responsible for this situation. Some of the typical cases are explained subsequently.

The persistent and rude manifestation of nature in terms of flood and drought creates a sort of arena for the emergence of a labour class in terms of child labour. Due to the happenings of such natural catastrophes, the parental economic conditions are drastically ruined. Thus, they don't become hesitant to affiliate their children even in some hazardous work environments. It is not only a living fact but also a historical analysis. The worst such examples may be the Bengal famine of 1940's and the recent famine of Orissa is Kalahandi and Bolangir districts. In all these hitherto existing times, even a mother barters her minor son or minor daughter in the form of bonded labour, sex worker in a brothel or servant to some household.

Though, child labour persists in developed countries in certain pockets, but due to the absolute poverty, it is quite hydra-headed in developing countries like India. As per the planning commission report of the Export Group on Estimation of Proportion and number of poor through the percentage of total population, below poverty line are steadily declining during subsequent years. But there is no justification to believe that the fall is spectacular. It is clear from Table-1.

Table -1 : Percentage of People Living Below the Poverty Line-Expert Group Estimates

Area (1)	1973-74 (2)	1977-78 (3)	1983-84 (4)	1987-88 (5)
Rural	56.4	53.1	45.6	39.1
Urban	49.2	47.4	42.2	40.1
Combined	54.9	51.8	44.8	39.3

Source: Planning Commission Report of the expert Group; July 1993.

Thus, due to such an incidence of absolute poverty, it may be safely stated that nevertheless the parental irrationality nor the affairs of the Government, rather it is the pervasiveness of absolute poverty that lies at the crux of a mind-boggling child labour problem.

The third important cause of concern for child labour may be attributed to the existence of a larger tribal-belt in India. The tribal belt mostly comprises almost all the states like M.P., Orissa, Bihar, Rajasthan etc. except a few like Punjab, Haryana, Jammu & Kashmir, Sikim etc. The total tribal population is about 8.1 per cent of the lotal population as per 1991 census. The typical characteristic of such population are that due to their simple and innocent mentality, they are almost engaged in Primary sector for the sake of their livelihood. But in the grip of acute population pressure and overcrowdedness in agriculture, they are constrained to work as migrant labourers. Some selected communities likely ST, SC, OBCs, etc. become more prone towards such catastrophes. It is noteworthy here that due to hilly surroundings and other inconveniencies; infrastructural bottlenecks exist. As a matter of fact, other sectors of the economy don't flourish blissfully.

To add fuel to the fire, the failure of Govt. policy to provide adequate avenues of employment has been a compelling factor for the migrant workmen.

Magnitude of Child Labour

Attempts have been made by the various international and national agencies like the United Nations, ILO, The Red Cross Society, The Government Census, National Sample Survey and many other voluntary agencies to estimate the number of child labourers employed in India. Notwithstanding the series of efforts, the cross-section data in the sphere of agriculture and other peripheral activities are strictly not available.

The estimates of child labourers made by the census reports at two points of time or 1971 and 1981 are presented in Table-2.

Table-2 : Estimated Child Workers and Percentage of Child Workers to Total Child Population in Rural and Urban India

Census years	Estimated children (in million)	% of Child workers in rural areas	% of Child workers in urban areas	Total
(1)	(2)	(3)	(4)	(5)
1971	10.74	4.33	0.33	4.66
1981	14.50	4.77	0.44	5.17

Source: Data from Census Reports.

It is crystal clear from Table-2 that the number of child workers which was 10.74 million in 1971 has increased to 14.50 million in 1981. With the increase in the absolute number of child workers from 1971 to 1981, the percentage of child workers to that of the total child population has also increased from 4.66 to 5.17 over the same period of time.

In addition to the above mentioned date relating to the child labour force, ILO projects the same figure at 16.5 million, UNO puts it around 15 to 18 million and the Indian Red Cross establishes it 17.65 million during the year 1983. However, different unofficial sources point out it about 45 million, which is definitely a grim scenario.

Dimension

In the vast industrial landscape in India, involvement of child labourers are mostly found in some selected manufacturing units operating both in organised and non organised sectors. In those industries, child labourers belong to both local class and migrant class. Among the foremost causes for the employment of child labourers by the estimates made by different study groups, the wage rate varies from Rs. 2/- to Rs.15/- per day for child-workers. Another cause of concern in the absence of the spirit of trade-unionism among the child labour-force. Thus, employers feel it convenient that the child labour force will remain under their clutches. At the same time in certain works like tunnel works, carpet weaving etc; performance of child labourers are considered better. Thus, in the fitness of many variables, it is a better commercial thought on the part of the employers for the employment of child labour force.

The number of child workers employed in some selected manufacturing units are discussed in Table-3

Table-3 : No. of Child Labourers Employed in Different Manufacturing Units

Occupation processes	Area/No. of working children	Source of Information.
1	2	3
1. Agriculture	All India 8.8 million	1981 Census
2. Brassware	Moradabad (U.P.) 40,000-45,000	National Labour Institute, Noida (U.P.)
3. Carpet-Weaving	a) Mirzapur, Varanasi, U.P. 50,000 approx.	My name is today Jan. 94-Mar,94
	b) Kashmir Valley 27,000	-do-
	c) Rajasthan Carpet Industry-30,000	-do-
4. Handloom	a) Trivandrum 10,000	-do-
	b) Tirupur-8,000	-do-
5. Match & Fire Works	Sivakashi-50,000	Yojana, June, 95
6. Glass and Bangles	Firozabad-50,000	Yojana, June, 95
7. Diamond Cutting & Polishing	Surat-50,000	Yojana, June, 95
8. Gem Cutting	Jaipur-15,000	-do-
9. Lock Making	Aligarh, 8,000-10,000	-do-
10. Mines	Meghalaya 28,000	My name is today Jan. 94-Mar.94
11. Fishing	Quilon, Kerala	-do-
12. Bidi Industry	Tiruchirapalli (Tamilnadu-7,000)	-do-

The above table projects only a microscopic view on the employment of child labourers in some selected manufacturing units. But in reality, the number of manufacturing units under the banner of different categories of industries are too vast and varied that within a limited endeavour it is very difficult to provide a due picturization of child labour force. One thing is also clear from table-3 that, in all the discussed manufacturing units the involvement of child labour in each case happens in many thousands. Thus, if the figures are facts, as per the study of different institutions and researchers, the ILO estimation of child labour force at 45 million can't be repudiated.

Any discussion of child labour must remain incomplete, unless the real agony with them are discussed, thoroughly. In real terms, the agony of the child labourers in any type of employment opportunity are three-fold as the amount of opportunity cost, suffering from exploitation and suffering from health hazards.

Though, opportunity cost of a child labour are not studied in this paper in an exhaustive manner, but it is imperative to make a brief note of it. The foregone opportunity of using a productive resource somewhere else rather than in the present use is termed as opportunity cost. In fact, children are the most valuable assets. They are the brightest stars of the society and nation. Being employed at a very tiny age, their future dreams in terms of human capital are simply foregone. They could have been better utilized, if they were provided with better skills and education. At the tiny age, their mental faculties are not sound. Since they are employed, they nevertheless yield economically viable returns. Thus, in terms of opportunity cost, the employment of child labour makes a significant loss to the nation. To be more specific nipping of a bud denies the possibilities of a blossoming flower.

Another stigma associated with child labour is the continuous existence of exploitation around them by the employers. It is such a type of agony around them which never ends. Employers generally exploit the labourers mainly by offering extremely low wages, prolonging the work hours, inflicting physical tortures in the case of lower work performance and creating the possibilities of retrenchment. As per the study made by different groups, it has been found that the remuneration to the child workers are generally made on piece-wage basis. Since under piece-wage system, the remuneration is granted to the workers on the basis of amount of work performed by them, therefore, the employers fix a heavy work as the basis for wage payment. Thus, child workers perform their work from the dawn to the dusk with a view to enhancing the amount of total work. The fact will be ample clear if the point is studied in the context of some selected Industries. In the Bidi Industry of Tiruchirapalli (Tamilnadu), child workers are paid extremely low wage based upon piece rate system. During the calculation of total bidies rolled by a child labour, employer simply rejects 10%-20% of the total bidies. It is mainly done to deprive a child of his wage. Similarly, a study made by the author in the brick-klin manufacturing units of Ganjam district (Orissa), the child workers alongwith their parents get Rs. 50/- to Rs. 60/- for the manufacturing of 1000 rawbricks. On an average, a child worker contribute maximum 3,000 rawbricks/week. Thus maximum Rs. 150/- per week can be the amount of wage for him. Such a lower amount of wage is definitely due to the exploitative attitudes of the employers. Similarly in the lock industry of Aligarh, where children between 5-9 years work in the hand processes, polishing the buffering machines, electroplating spray, pointing, filling components, assembling and packing locks. They are paid hardly Rs. 70/- per month as their remuneration. At the same time, the child workers above 9 years get Rs. 150/- to Rs. 175/- as their monthly salary. Such type of wage payment is considerably lower and highlights the exploitative and cruel nature of the entrepreneur. Likewise the amount of wage of the boys working in tea-stalls, road-side restaurants, household servants, private garages etc. are hardly paid Rs. 30/- to Rs. 100/- as their monthly remuneration. Such type of dismal picture prevails invariably in all parts of India. Here, it is worth mentioning that such a large child labour force are mainly migrated from rural down-trodden families. With a desperate search of employment opportunities, they are scattered in different manufacturing units. Thus, to say about even in the face of sordid exploitation in their respective work environments, they chronically undertake the dehumanizing fight for survival.

Another ramification of exploitation in manufacturing units is about the stipulation of prolonged hours of work upon the child-labourers. If it is a piece-wage system, to raise the amount of total work and ultimately to get higher wage, the child workers undertake long hours of work. On the other hand, if it is a time-wage system, to obtain higher output from the productive contribution of child workers, the employers fix prolonged work-hours. To make the point more perceptible, some typical instances, may be studied with the help of Table-4

Table-4 : Work-hours in Some Selected Manufacturing Units

Manufacturing enterprises	Their location	Hours of work by child labourers
1. Fishing	Quilon (Kerlala)	4 PM to 3 a.m. (15 hours)
2. Handloom	Trivandrum	9-10 hours
3. Bidi Industry	Tirichirapalli (Tamilnadu)	11 hours.
4. Lock Industry	Aligarh	12-14 hours.
5. Brick Industry	Ganjam, Orissa	14-15 hours.
6. Textile Mills	Surat	18 hours.
7. Carpet weaving	Rajasthan, Mirzapur, U.P.	18-20 hours
8. Gem Polishing	Jaipur, (Rajasthan)	8 AM to 6 P.M. (10 hours)

Source : Compiled from different publishing and unpublished sources.

The Table-4 considers only some typical manufacturing units. There are thousands of such industries all over India, where the fixation of long hours of work is definitely a common practice. In those manufacturing units, normal hours of work and concentration of work by child labourers during day time are definitely myth.

Exploitation in the form of physical punishment by the employers is not uncommon. If the small children engaged in numerous chores of an enterprise, can't contribute towards to total output upto the satisfaction of the employers, they are being physically tortured. In usual practice, employers are not directly related with the works of the child labourers. There are a class of intermediaries called as Sardars who always act as a distinctive link between the child labourers and the employers. They are paid by the employers. At the same time, they also take some commission from the innocent child workers. So to say, they are such a class of person who are always performative towards some listed interests.

Although, there are provisions in the Factories Act, 1948 as regards health, hygiene, safety and welfare measures for workers and the child labour prevention and Regulation Act, 1986 categorically prohibits the employment of children in hazardous occupations, yet children in contravention to the existing rules and regulations are found largely in some selected manufacturing Units. Working in the hazardous occupations like carpet, matches, brassware, lock, pottery, brickklin, gems etc. the children contact various diseases like T.B., Fungal infections, Burn injuries, eye problems, asthama etc. Besides, children who work with dangerous machines, chemicals and furnaces with high temperature run the risk of getting involved in accidents.

Migrant Child Labour : A Case Study

After making a general survey of child labourers with a broader perspective at macro level, it has been decided to make a study of migrant child labour who are mainly from Bolangir district employed in the brick-klin manufacturing units of Ganjam district As has been stated earlier, child labourers are employed in a wide range of economic activities, however, for the purpose of study employment of child labourers in brick-klin manufacturing units have been selected. The author's long acquittance with such workers and easy accessibility to such activities prompt him to make an attempt to find out th e genesis, magnitude and the extent of exploitation of child labourers in this sector. Obviously, the study throws some light in identifying some factual data regarding the menacing problems of child labourers. So far as the identification of current economic problem and formulation of policies for their eradication are concerned, it may act as a touch-stone. Moreover, the study being the first of its kind in brick-klin sector, it is hoped that it can fell the research gap and add a new dimension to the existing literature.

Scope of the Study

The scope of the study is confined to brick-klin industry only. Again due to the constraint of time and cost, the study is confined to Sheragada, Hinjlicut and Dharakote blocks of Ganjam District. Thus, out of 22 blocks in Ganjam district only these three blocks have been selected for the purpose of study. Moreover, excluding traditional method of brick-production, only brick-manufacturing units involving modern method of production and employment of migrant labour including children have been studied in this paper.

Methodology

A rough survey has been made to estimate the number of brick industries employing migrant labourers. It has been estimated that about 300 modern brick industries employ migrant labourers mostly from Bolangir, Kalahandi and Sambalpur. The multistage sampling method has been adopted for the purpose of sampling. Here, it is worth mentioning that at the first stage only modern brick manufacturing units employing migrant labourers including children are listed. In the final stage migrant labourers including children from Bolangir District are studied. For the purpose of study a structured questionnaire has been prepared to collect data from the migrant child labourers. Out of the total child labourer households, 20% of the households have been studied. The head of the household has been interviewed during leisure hours. In this particular study, survey, personal interview and observation methods, have been adopted collectively. To ascertain the authenticity of data, in this study cross-examination and observation methods have been adopted.

Since our study is mainly concentrated on the migrant labour force including children from Bolangir district, therefore, it is quite legitimate on the part of the author to provide a brief profile as to this district.

The district of Bolangir lies between 20° 9' and 21° 11' north latitude and 82° 41' and 84° 16' east longitudes. It is bounded on the north by the district Sambalpur, on the east by the district of Baudh, on the north-east by the district Sonepur, on the south by the district Kalahandi and on the west by the Nawapara subdivision of the district Kalahandi.

According to Directorate of Economics and Statistics, Orissa, the district Bolangir covers an area of 6551.5 Sq. kms. It has a total population of 12,31,000 out of 50.45% (6,21,000) constitutes the total male population and 49.55% (6,10,000) constitutes the total female population, according to 1991 census. Again rural and urban population are 89.52% (11,02,000), 10.48% (1,29,000) of the total population respectively. SC and ST population constitute 15.35% (1,89,000) and 22% (2,71,000) of the total population of Bolangir as per 1991 census.

The district Bolangir covers a forest area of 11.08 square kms, which is 16.10% of the total land area of Orissa. The total cultivated area of the district in the year 1993-94, is 3,48,000 hectares, which is about 6% of the total cultivated areas of the State. The literary rate of the district is 38.63 per cent to be specific, 55.64 per cent of the total males, 21.30% of the total females are literates.

As the study is concentrated on the migrant labour force including children from Bolangir towards the brick-klin manufacturing units of Ganjam district, with the help of the structured questionnaires, it has been obverved that, these labourers mostly originate from four blocks as Patnagada, Belpare, Khaparakhol & Tunikela. Patnagarh, Belpara and Khaparakhol belong to Palnagade sub-division. Since Patnagarh, Belpara and Khaparakhol are the only three important locations (PSs) of this sub-division, therefore, from the study it is evident that vast masses of migrant labourers are heavily concentrated in this sub-division. From Turukela and Kantabanji blocks of Titlagarh sub-division people are also migrated towards the brick-klin manufacturing units, as revealed from the study. The main causes of their migration are the chronic failure of agriculture at their original place, failure of triokle-down policy and the rampant existence of absolute poverty, which is evident fromt the study.

People from all social classes are migrated during agricultural-off seasons. The percentage share of people from different social classes in the migratory labour is discussed in Table-5

Table-5 : Caste Composition of Migrant Labourers

Social Group (1)	Total No. of families (2)	Percentage of people migrated (3)
SC	8	18
ST	16	42
OBC	12	30
General	8	10
Total	40	100

From the table, it is found that out of the total migratory labour force, 42% belong to ST, 30% belong to OBC, 18% to SC and 10% belong to General category. Thus, it is demonstrated from the study most of the migrant labourers as well as migrant child labourers belong to ST, SC and Weaker Sections of the community.

In our study all the migrant families, out of 40 sample households, have been divided under four groups. 1-4 membered families are small families. 5-8 membered families are moderate families. 9-11 membered families are big families and more than 12 membered families are very big families. The distribution of different migrant households under different family sizes is shown Table-6.

Table-6 : Distribution of Migrant Household Under Different Family Sizes

Family size (1)	Total No. of families (2)	Migrant households (in percentage) (3)
1-4	11	27.5
5-8	19	47.5
9-11	10	25.0
12 and above	NIL	NIL
Total	40	100

Table-6 suggests that very big families don't exist. It is due to the division of big families into unclear families and pursuit for independent economic activities. Even after the division of big families most of the families fall in 5-8 membered families. This occurs heavily due to improper family planning. However, it is inferred from the study that migration mostly takes place from among 5-8 membered families due to economic compulsions.

Mode and Frequency of Migration

From the study, it is clean that people include children are mostly migrated after the harvest of the crop at their original place and they remain migratory towards different states and districts within Orissa upto the transplantation of paddy crop at their original place. That means from Dec., Jan. May, June they remain migratory. Though, for different activities people are migrated towards different parts of India, but specially for brick-klin manufacturing units, they are driven towards Madhya Pradesh, Andhra Pradesh and Assam on the basis of inter-state migration. There are certain labourers who traditionally follow intra-state migration, their migratory points are mainly Ganjam, Puri, Cuttack, Sambalpur and Bargarh District. In this context the percentage of Bonangir migrant labour class has been studies under two heads, which is clear from table-7.

Table-7 : Mode and Frequency of Migration

Mode of Migration	No. of household	Followers (in percentage)
Intra-state	19	47.5
Inter-state	21	52.5
Total	40	100

Sources of Income of the Labour Class Including Children

From our study, it is clear that the labourers who are migrated, they own some amount of land at their place of origin. It has been estimated from the study that yield rate/Acre in physical terms is 2.25 quintal and yield rate/Acre in money terms is Rs. 810/-. From this data, it is evident that due to extremely low productivity in this sector, agriculture remains completely an unremunerative way of life as a result of which they can't take out a living with their meagre agricultural income. Thus, the people suffer from indebtedness at their original place. Due to this fact, they are compelled to be migrated along with their children during agricultural off seasons. The percentage share of different agricultural classes in the total migrant labour of Bolangir district has been calculated and shown in Table-8.

Table-8 : Classification of land Holdings Among the Migrant Labourers

Different agricultural classes (1)	Families (2)	Percentage share in Migratory labour class (3)
Landless agricultural Labourers (0 Acres)	15	37.5
Marginal Farmers (0-5 Acres)	18	45.0
Small Farmers (5-10 Acres)	6	15.0
Big Farmers 10 Acres and above	1	2.5
Total	40	100

Table-8 exhibits that a large portion of migratory labour belongs to landless agricultural class and marginal farmer class. Due to chronic agricultural failures and ultimately extremely low agricultural productivity, even the small farmers and to a minute extent the big farmers also become prone towards migration. It is a traditional practice among these groups of persons that along with their families they are migrated towards different manufacturing units during agricultural off seasons. Following chronic agricultural failures and poor-availability of government works programmes they always do remain in the vicious trap of poverty. In this backdrop, the families including children are compelled to be migrated in search of some work for their existence.

Income Pattern at their Destination Place

As this study has been made in the context of brick-klim manufacturing units, therefore it is imperative to know the average money income of a labour including children in those manufacturing units.

As per the direct observation of the author, the total works performed by the migrant labourers occur in four different phases. In percentage terms, each phase involves 25% of the total works contributed by migrant labourers.

Four Phases

1st Phase : This phase involves making paste like clay from suitable soil and suitable earthern balls as required for a single brick. At this phase, adult females of the family and children are employed. Thus, to the Ist phase the contribution of adult females and children is 12.5: 12.5.

2nd Phase : This phase involves making raw bricks. Only adult males are employed in this phase. Therefore, the contribution to the total work made by adult migrant labourers is 25%. Due to the disadvantage of height, children become unfit for this work.

3rd phase : This phase involves carrying of raw bricks from the place of manufacturing to the drying-pit, where raw bricks are allowed to dry in sun-stroke. In this stage again the adult females and children are employed. Thus, again to the third phase the contributions made by adult females and children are 12.5: 12.5.

In the light of above 4 stages, the contribution of all labourers with respect to sex and age has been explained in Table-9.

Table-9 : Work Participation of Migrant Labourers in Various Operations

Types of labour	Percentage of total work contributed				Total
	1st	2nd	3rd	4th	
Adult-Males	-	25	-	12.5	37.5
Adult-Males	12.5	-	12.5	-	25.0
Child Workers	12.5	-	12.5	12.5	37.5
Total works					100.0

From Table-9, a mind boggling conclusion in drawn. As per the study the contribution to total work process by child workers and adult males remains same in percentage terms. Thus, a pitiable picture of child workers has definitely been studied.

Usually piece-wage system prevails in all the brick-klin manufacturing units. From the sample study it has been found that on an average Rs. 55/- is given per 1,000 dried raw bricks. In this study, estimates have also been made about the average monthly income of child labourers, female adult workers and male adult workers at Rs. 605/-, Rs.338/- Rs. 403/- respectively. From these figures, it is evident that, particularly families engaged in brick-klin manufacturing units, child labourers are the major players in determining the economic destiny of the family.

Consumption Pattern of Migrant Households

Their consumption pattern includes food items and non-food items. Their staple food is rice. As per the estimates of this study about 60% of their current income are spent for the consumption of food at the destination place. Another 20% of their income are spent for the consumption of non-food items. The non-food items mostly include conventional necessaries like tea, bidi, bhang, snuff, wine and minimum cosmetics and fashionable commodities. This type of consumption pattern represents backwardness. As the basket of items consumed by the migrant households comprised of basic necessities, it can be stated that they are under low standards of living.

In this context, it is pertinent to note that most of the migrant households are paid some advance (Rs. 1,000/- Rs.2,000/-) from the brick-klin owners through the contractors of sardars. A substantial portion of their income is spent at the destination point and they carry with themselves a very limited income. The advance money received in the beginning are partly or fully paid back towards the clearance of debt of money lender or locally known as gountia.

Hours of Work

Their income-generating process is subject to 12-14 hours of work. The work hours consist of two sessions daily. First session begins from 4 A.M. to 11 P.M. and noon. The second session begins from 3 P.M., 4 P.M., - 11 P.M. and Midnight. Thus, definitely they undertake prolonged hours of work in the desparate bid of increasing the level of income. And, due to the existence of piece wage rate, they are chronically incalculated towards prolonged hours of work. Since the first three phases of total works in these brick manufacturing units are simultaneous, thus children are also bound to be involved in the long hours of work. In the back drop of long hours of work over a period of time, labourers in general, and women and children in particular become the victims of manifold diseases. Besides, a large number of diseases like fever, diarrahoea, few particular health problems like chest-pain, body-sprain, rheumatism, tuberculosis, gastric, colic pain, asthma, etc. are largely found among the labourers in these manufacturing units. Child labourers due to nimble fingers become more prone towards fungal infection including palm-cracking and nail septic etc. It has also been observed that the pregnant female workers suffer a lot from malnutrition and delivery problems. Some instances of miscarriages have also been reported at our interview with them. As per the study, child workers and adult females carry raw bricks from the place of manufacturing to the drying pit which is approximately 100 meters away from the place of manufacturing. As per the calculation, the child workers carry about 300 raw bricks daily and at a time, they take only 3 bricks which require 4 minutes of time. Therefore, this process requires about 7 hours of work and more than 20 kms of walk daily. Thus, it is obvious that child workers suffers from extreme physical agony and torture.

Illiteracy is an indicator which explains the cause of migration towards brick-klin manufacturing units. In other words, migration of labour is always conditional upon the level of education. Thus, there is a positive co-relation between their level of income and migration, to brick-klin manufacturing units.

For the sake of this study, out of 40 sample households comprising 155 workers have been identified. Out of 155 workers, 115, 30, 4, 6 workers belong to illiteracy, primary, middle and secondary level of education respectively.

Table-10 : Level of Education of Migrant Labourers

Level of education (1)	No. of people migrated. (2)	Percentage of people migrated (3)
Illiteracy	115	74.20
Primary	30	19.35
Middle	4	2.58
Secondary	6	3.87
Total	155	100

Table-10 indicates that about 74% of the total workers in brick-klin manufacturing units are illiterates and 19% of the workers have their level of education at primary classes. Workers processing middle and secondary level of education are found minimum at about 3 per cent and 4 per cent respectively. From the study, it has also been observed that in the case of child labourers, the level of education remains below the primary standard. It is due to the characteristic of seasonal migration of their respective families during the months from Dec., Jan-May, June. Thus, there occur heavy dropouts of the children at this stage of education. Some child workers are also reported that they don't have any education due to object poverty of their families and their engagement in different household activities.

Work-Environment

A good and congenial work environment boosts the efficiency of labourers and raises the productivity. In this light, it is highly imperative to focus light on work-environment of migrant labourers.

It has been observed that the work-environment of Brick-klin manufacturing units are not proper and congenial. So far as drinking water is concerned, it is always arranged through temporary wells by the workers at the expense of their own labour which is never parted by the employer. In rare cases, water facilities are given which is quite insufficient for all types of uses by the workers. Latrine and lavatory facilities are never arranged by the employers for the workers. Employer-employee relationship is never emotional. If the employer finds insufficient work with a worker due to some health problem, the former retrenches the later and sends him to later's original place. Though minor diseases of the worker are treated at the expense of the employer major and chronic diseases are never taken into consideration. Since the majority of migrant labourers belong to ST and SC community, due to the taboos of caste system, they remain neglected subject to some degree of hatred and antagonism by the local workers and the employers. Thus, even in the absence of sympathy and pleasure in their work environment, desperately they continue their struggle for their bare survival.

Findings

In the light of the aforesaid study, the following findings are emerged.

1. It is inferred from the study that most of the migrant labourers comprise from scheduled caste, scheduled tribe and other backward communities.
2. The labourers with their family migrated during agricultural off seasons. Because of non-availability of work at their place of origin as well as due to their acute poverty, most of the families belong to 5-8 membered families.
3. The labourers follow both inter-state and intra-state migration. The proportionate share in both cases remains at best equal, though there is some marginal difference.
4. The people who follow migration to Brick-klin manufacturing units are mostly landless labourers and marginal farmers which constitute 82.5% of the total migrant labour force.
5. The average productivity of land per acre is only 2.25 quintals, which is significantly lower.
6. The contribution of child workers to the total income of the family is maximum in Brick-klin manufacturing units.
7. The consumption pattern of migrant labourers are mostly confined to the necessary food and non-food items mainly habitual necessaries. As the bulk portion of their income are spent for the basic necessities, they are in the grip of poverty and sub-human living.
8. Majority of the migrant-unskilled labour force employed in Brick-klin manufacturing units are illiterates.
9. Congenial work-environment doesn't exist in brick-klin manufacturing units coupled with insufficient medical and sanitary facilities.
10. Education for children either in a formal way or non-formal way is definitely of myth in these manufacturing units.
11. In terms of commission to the labour brokers called as sardars, they are exploited. The sardars take Rs. 5/- to Rs. 7/- as a matter of commission per 1000 raw bricks manufactured by them.
12. Workers including children undertake very long hours of work. They perform their work even at late-night, which is definitely illegitimate and illegal.

Legal Perspective

Though, there are huge constitutional provisions and a number of legislative enactments from time to time the pernicious problem of child labour rampantly exists. Since this study is categorically concerned with the genesis of child-labour in brick-klin manufacturing units, therefore, the discussion must be made with reference to different legal perspectives, which are violated in a planned manner. Some of them are discussed.

According to Article 24 of the Constitution children below the age of 14 are not to be employed in any factory or mine or engaged in any other hazardous employment.

The Directive Principles of State Policy, while not enforceable in the court of law are mandatory to the state in governing the country and it is incumbent upon the state of follow these principles while formulating legislation.

Article 39 (e) directs the state to see that the tender age of children is not abused and that citizens are not compelled by economic circumstances to do work that is unsuited to their age and strength.

Further Article 39 (f) emphasizes the need to see that childhood and youth are protected against exploitation and against moral and material abandonment.

Legislative Enactments

There are plethora of laws for the protection of child workers. Some of the important and respected legislative enactments which are catetgrically failed to be implemented by the employers in the brick-klin manufacturing units are discussed in this study.

(a) The Factories Act, 1948; The Mines Act, 1952; and Plantation Labour Act, 1951:

These Acts prohibit the employment of children between 7 P.M. and 6 A.M. in factories, mines and plantations; regulate the working hours and contain provisions for their safety and welfare.

(b) The employees State Insurance Act, 1948:

The benefits provided under this Act include sickness benefit, maternity benefit, disablement benefit, dependent benefit, medical and funeral benefit to the women and child labourers.

(c) The Minimum Wages Act, 1948:

This Act has been enacted to secure the welfare of the workers by fixing the minimum limit of wages in certain employments.

(d) The contract labour (Regulation & Abolition) Act, 1978:

This Act regulates the working conditions of contract labour (which includes children), payment of wages and provides for welfare facilities and creches for the children of working women engaged in construction work.

(e) The Child Labour (Prevention and Regulation) Act, 1986:

This Act specifically prohibits employment of children in hazardous occupations.

Besides, the above constitutional provisions and legislative enactments, the National Policy for Children Resolution, adopted in August 1974 sets out a Policy framework and measures aimed at providing adequate services for children. The National Policy for children emphasizes the importance of free and compulsory education for all children upto the age of 14, provisions of health and nutritional programmes and services, providing alternatives forms of education for children unable to take full advantage of formal school education and measures for protecting children against neglect, cruelty and exploitation.

In pursuance of constitutional directives and legal provisions, the Govt. of India formulates a National Child Labour Policy in 1987. The basic thrust of the policy is to co-ordinate and intensify on-going developmental programmes for income generation and employment in areas prone to child labour.

Merely, all the constitutional provisions, legislative enactments and different government policies remain as the paper-tigers only. They are practicable to the organised sector. Child labourers are mostly confined to the non-organised sectors. Thus, they are more prone towards exploitation. As if the agony of child labour never ends. On the basis of foregoing study, following recommendations may be forwarded:

1. Poverty alleviation programmes like JRY, IRDP, DWACRA, EAS, PMRY must be effectively implemented in the child labour prone regions. The bureaucrats must change their appetite towards this social evil and try to mitigate the problem by proper implementation of different programmes.
2. Adequate infrastructural facilities like irrigationl, education and health care should be made available in different area, which are suffering from chronic drought situations.

3. Universalization on Primary education should be accompanied with special emphasis for economically backward communities.
4. Schemes for non-formal education should be initiated to cover the drop-outs and adult bodies in the tribal areas. To compensate the loss of income due to non-employment of child labour, the parents should be provided adequate employment opportunities under different employment generating schemes.

Since approximately 80 per cent of child labour force belong to the rural areas, therefore, the objectives or rural development should encompass improved productivity, increased employment and higher incomes as well as minimum acceptable food, clothing, shelter, education and health for the people. The loopholes in the planning process must be identified and suitable development strategy should be evolved targeting benefit to the migrant households employing children. Effective and strong administration, suitable planning at the grassroot level, universalization of education, welfare schemes for the drought prone villages, honesty and sincerities of workers, people's participation in the development process-can go a long way in combating the problem of migrant child labour.

References

1. Informal Women Labour in India by S.N. Tripathy & Soudamini Das. Discovery. Publishing House, 1991.
2. Agricultural Labour in India by S. N. Tripathy & K.C. Pradhan. Discovery Publishing House, 1996.
3. Orissa District Gazetters: Bolangir.

9
CHILD LABOUR IN AGRICULTURE SECTOR

The child work force constitutes 6 per cent of the total work force in the country and as many as 92 per cent of child workers are enaged in agricultural and allied structures (Naravan, 1980). Abour 8 per cent are employed in allied activites like hunting, fishing, livestock breeding, plantation labour, etc (Kulshreshtha, 1978). According to an International Labour Organization report (1979), as many as one-third of the rural children aged between 10 and 14 years and one-eight of urban children are at work in India. They contribute about 14 per cent of the income and largely belong to lower income groups of families (Gupta, 1979). This indicates the significance of child labour force in the production and reproduction processes. The changes that have appeared since mid-1960s in the Indian agriculture, marked by enhanced commercial farming and green revolution, made the rural rich richer and poor poorer (Pattnaik, 1987). While this experience is, by and large, shared throughout Indian, the greatest inequality and class differentiation have occurred in the fastest growing areas. This however did not give the labourers the much talked about freedom from obligations under capitalism. Massive unemoloyment and underemployment, highly uneven capitalist growth, discovery of profitable uses of pre-capitalist relations of production, contributed to the growth of primitive accumulation of capital. Informal and unorganized labour market has grown phenomenally, so also the contrast and seasonally migrant labour. The employment of children too has increased and they are indeed preferred in certain agricultural and industrial operations.

One of the study carried out in Orissa by Sahoo (1995), in the two villages, there are 301 child workers, below the age of 15. distributed among 252 households. In other words, nearly half of the families have child workers. About 82 per cent of these families have a single child worker each. These include 12 girls of Chhadadiapalli who are actively enagaged in agricultural operation along with their mothers. Footy families contain two child farm workers each and five families have three child labourers and none more than that. For the purpose of the study, four girls and 248 boys belonging to 252 families were selected. That means one each from a family containing child farm labour was chosen for detailed investigation. A few of them work in their onw family only (1.9%). While others both in own fields as well as others fields (71.8%) or only in others field (26.2%). Besides, children also perform a wide spectrum of domestic chores. Though such labour is never meaused in economic terms. In fact, even in the analysis of agrarian structure the contribution of children and the possibilities of mobilizing their underutillzed labour for economic development are generally overlooked.

Socio-Economic Background

Generally, the prevalence of child labour is attributed to the poverty of the individual households and backwardness of the regional society. Indeed, almost all studies on child labour in India have axiomatized that poverty coupled with illiteracy and unemployment compel the families to send their beloyed children into the vortex of unjust labour market. There is after all a considerable body of factual and qualitative information to support. Nonetheless, the correlation, based on just two indicators and seperated from the total socio-historical context conceals more than what it really reveals. This is more pertinent especially when poverty is a very relative term bound by a given time and space. As both poverty and illiteracy change with changes in socio-economic configurations, any scientific work demands analysis of social formations for the comprehension of the nature and extent of employment of children.

In Chhadiapalli and Kulanda, there are 164 and 137 child workers respectively. The 128 child workers from the former village and 124 from the latter were selected. In other words, 49.5 per cent of households in the two selected villages have at least one child worker each. Except the Brahmins, all castes and tribes have child workers. But there is a significant difference in the nature of employment of the children belonging to enterprising peasant castes and other castes and communities. Children of the former group mostly work in their own fields while the children of lower castes and tribes largely sell their labour to affluent farmers. About 83 per cent of the fathers of the child workers are illiterate and those few literate have not studied beyond primary school level. Indeed, only 2 per cent of them have studied up to standard V. That means the literate parents are, in fact, barely literate. Those belonging to peasant castes have relatively better representation in such level of literacy than the lower parents of child workers are conspicuously illiterate or bearely literate.

The occupational background of the families of child workers reveals that only about 22 per cent belong to those families whose primary occupation is cultivation while secondary occupation is wage labour. They primarily belong to the traditional peasant castes. In contrast, 40 per cent of child workers belong to wage labour families. And about 38 per cent belong to families with wage labour as primary and cultivation secondary (Table 2). We have already noted that through all castes have child employment (except the Brahmin), none of the child workers of Kulata, Belama, Dumal, Kalinji and Telenga belong to wage labour families. In fact, primary occupation happens to be cultivation for most of the Kulata and Belama households whose children are engaged in labour in their own-farms, the lower castes and tribes mostly belongs to agricultural labour and small peasant families. Hense, internal differentiation in the nature of child employment and its association with the caste hierarchy is very explicit.

Expectedly, most of the working children belong to families with no land of small uneconomic holdings. Forty per cent of the child workers hail from landless families and 45 per cent from households with less than one acre holding each, whereas only 4 per cent belong to households owning over 3 acre of land. Similarly, while none of the children of capatalist landlords and rich peasants are engaged in productive work, not even in their own farms. 55 per cent of child workers belong to farm worker and 41 per cent to small peasant families (Table 3).

Table 1 : Castes and Literacy of Parents of Child Workers

Case	No. and percentage of families with child labour	No. and percentage of literacy among the parents of child workers
Brahmin (N=28)	Nil	Not Application
Kulata (N=97)	17 (17.5)	6 (35.3)
Belama (N=58)	20 (34.5)	12 (60.0)
Dumal (N=74)	28 (37.8)	8 (28.6)
Kalinji (N=39)	24 (61.5)	6 (25.0)
Alia (N=30)	25 (83.3)	4 (16.0)
Odiva (N=14)	10 (71.4)	Nil
Teli (N=10)	9 (90.0)	2 (22.0)
Telenga (N=16)	6 (37.5)	Nil
Gauda (N=17)	14 (82.3)	1 (7.1)
Gudia (N=6)	2 (33.3)	Nil
Bhandari (N=4)	2 (50.0)	Nil
Keuta (N=77)	10 (58.8)	Nil
Khadala (N=31)	27 (87.1)	2 (7.4)
Scheduled Castes (N=46)	40 (87.0)	2 (5.0)
Scheduled Tribes (N=22)	18 (81.8)	Nil -
Total (N=509)	252 (49.5)	43 (17.1)

Table 2 : Caste-Wise Occupational Distribution of Parents of Child Workers

Caste/Occupation	Cultivation primary and wage labour secondary	Wage labour primary and cultivation secondary	Wage labour only
Brahmin (Nil)	-	-	-
Kulata (N=17)	14 (82.3)	3 (17.7)	-
Belama (N=20)	15 (75.0)	5 (25.0)	-
Dumal (N=28)	13 (46.4)	15 (53.6)	-
Kalinji (N=24)	3 (21.5)	21 (87.5)	-
Alia (N=25)	4 (16.0)	13 (52.0)	8 (32.0)
Odiva (N=10)	-	3 (30.0)	7 (70.0)
Teli (N=9)	2 (22.2)	4 (44.4)	3 (33.3)
Telenga (N=6)	3 (50.0)	3 (50.0)	-
Gauda (N=14)	-	5 (35.7)	9 (64.3)
Gudia (N=2)	-	2 (100.0)	-
Bhandari (N=2)	-	-	2 (100.0)
Keuta (N=10)	-	3 (30.0)	7 (70.0)
Khadala (N=27)	-	9 (33.3)	18 (66.7)
Scheduled Castes (N=40)	1 (2.5)	6 (15.0)	33 (82.5)
Scheduled Tribe (N=18)	-	3 (16.7)	15 (83.3)
Total (N=252)	55 (21.8)	95 (37.7)	102 (40.5)

$x^2 = 114.75$ Df=56 d<.01

Table 3 : Class & Land Position of the Families of Child Workers

Class	No land	Upto 1	1-2 acre	2 acret	Total
Capitalist landlord (N=11)	-	-	-	-	-
Rich peasant (N=41)	-	-	-	-	-
Middle peasant (N=92)	-	-	-	10	10 (4.0)
Poor peasant (N=142)	-	76	27	-	103 (40.9)
Farm workers (N=223)	102	37	-	-	139 (55.2)
Total (N=509)	102	113	27	10	252 (100.1)

$x^2 = 175.91$ df= 45 D<.01

If annual family income of Rs. 5.000 is considered minimum need for an average sized family to cross the poverty line, then only about 5 per cent of the families of child workers belong to that category (Table 4). In fact, more than one-third of the families have an annual income of less than Rs.3.000. While 30 per cent of the families owning land above 3 acre each have more than Rs.5.000 annual income, the said percentage is less than 3 among the landless and very small peasants. In any case, their belonging to low income, powerty stricken groups is obvious.

Table 4 : Annual Income of Families of Child Workers by Land Size

(in Rupees)

Landsize	Upto 2000	2000-3000	3000-4000	4000-5000	Above 5000	Total
No land	15	27	48	9	3	102
Upto 1 acre	7	36	50	17	3	113
1-2 acre	-	5	6	11	5	27
2 acret	-	-	1	6	3	10
Total	22 (8.7)	68 (27.0)	105 (41.7)	43 (17.1)	14 (5.6)	252 (100.0)

$x^2 = 140.28$ df= 30 D<.01

Not only they belong to landless or small peasant and poor families who cannot reproduce themselves without introducing their children into the labour process but also as many as one-fifth of these families have sold their tiny parcels of land during the decade 1975-85. Of course, less than 4 per cent of the families have also added small fragments to of dry land. A couple of families could indulge in this unusual practice of buying land because of remittances from the migrant workers of their families. Anyway, this is insignificant. Abour 22.2 per cent of the families hbave leased—in some land from the capitalist landlords and rich peasants as well as from some of the kin members who have migrated to distant places for employment. These sharecroppers mostly (77%) leased-in less than one acre of land. Those few leased-in more land belong largely to traditional peasant castes like Kulata and Belama. The higher castes and middle peasants normally employ their children in their own fields while the lower caste landless and small peasants tend to send their children for wage employment. The primary objective in the latter case is to supplement the family income. Tenancy does not provide a marked solution to the problem of wage employment of children.

With reference to the debt of the families of child workers, it is found that as many as 83.3 per cent are indebted. Moreover, 70.6 per cent of the indebted families have taken loans in both cash and kind from moneylenders, who are also the members of affluent agrarian classes-cum-speculative traders. The liberal institutional credit is insignificant in comparison to usurious monevlenders. It may be worth noting that 40 per cent of those who sold their lands during 1995-85 did so just to repay the earlier debt. The inter linkage of caste, land, credit and labour market ensures and reproduces a form of semi-feudal bondage. Here, the labour of children is often used as pawn to procure loans an even to lease-in land. In spite of the pomous declaration of the government to save the rural poor from the clutches of moneylenders, the small peasants and moneylenders to meet their immediate survival needs. Sometimes, to repay an earlier loan, a new in taken from some other moneylender. This debt trap reduces them to perpetual indebtendness. As a result, the bankrupt families are often forced to sell or mortoage their tiny land holdings or even family members.

Nonetheless, the amount of loan appears quite low that 58.7 per cent of the families have a loan of less than Rs.600. Only 4 per cent of the families, all belonging to Kulanda, have taken loans over Rs. 1.000 (Table 5). But the point is that given their low family income and negligible immovable assets, the amount of loan is consierable. Moreover, the compound rate of interest fattens the original loan amount very raipdly. For instance, during the rainy months, just a couple of moths before the harvest, the small peasants and tenants often take paddy loans under the contition that soon after the harvest they will return it in paddy calculated in terms of one and half times the original price. Not only 50 per cent interest is charged for three to four months but also the calculation being made in terms of cash at pre-harvest and past-harvest times, actually doubles the repayment. Similar is the case with regard to agricultural inputs.

Table 5 : Amount of Loan Taken by the Parents of Child Workers

Amount of loan (in Rs.)	Krlanda	Chhadiapalli	Total
Upto 200	10	11	21(08.3)
200-400	22	37	59 (23.4)
400-600	30	38	68 (27.0)
600-800	12	18	30 (11.9)
800-1000	14	8	22 (08.7)
1000+	10	-	10 (04.0)
Not applicable	26	16	42 (16.7)
Total	124 (49.2)	128 (50.8)	252 (100.0)

The household consumption requirement is the major cause (25.8%) of loans, followed by marriage (16.7%), agricultural expenses (13.5%) and purchase of land and cattle (8.7%) (Table 6). As many as 45 per cent of indebted household have not repaid even a part of the loan and others have paid only a portion of the debt. In other words, most parents of child a workers, being always in debt, find no other alternative than seeking supportive hand from their children to augment survival of the families.

Given the fact of their poverty, illiteracy, low social and economic position, perpetual indebtedness, continued dependence on the rich to eke out a living, it is not surprising that over 96 per cent of the parents do not have membership in any formal institutions of the village.

Table 6 : Purpose of Loan of the Parents of Child Workers

Purpose	Kulanda No.	Kulanda Percentage	Chhadiapalli No.	Chhadiapalli Percentage	Total No.	Total Percentage
Household consumption	24	19.3	41	16.3	65	25.8
Marriage	14	11.3	28	21.9	42	16.7
Health	6	4.6	4	3.1	10	4.0
Agriculture expenses	19	15.3	15	5.9	34	13.5
Purchase of land or cattle	13	10.5	9	7.0	22	8.7
Education	8	6.4	6	4.7	14	5.5
Others	14	11.3	9	7.0	23	9.1
Not applicable	26	21.0	16	12.5	42	16.7
Total	124	49.2	128	50.8	252	100.0

Interestingly, when inquired why the children are sent to work, the parents one-fourth of the workers convened that it was to meet an obligation to their employers. Another 28 per cent pledged their children to repay their debts. Only 22 per cent disclosed poverty as the cause of child employment, About 12 per cent of the parents, mostly belonging to small-sized households, opined the necessity of assistance of their children in the farming operations and some 11 per cent justified it in terms of their children's poor performance at school (Table 7). In short, poverty and debt constituted the chief reasons for employment of children.

Further, when asked what are the major benefits they accrued from the employment of their children, over 40 per cent conveyed that they could procure loans easily. This is followed by financial help (32%), exchange of labour (14%) and supplementary help at work (13%). And when asked how the problem of employment of tiny children can be reduced, more than half of the parents opined that if only their economic condition improve (50.4%) and gainful employment at the rural set-up increases (23.0%). A quater of the parents, however, told that rise of consciousness (13.5%), compulsory free and productive education (7.1%) and strict enforcement of the esisting labour legislation (6.0%) may alleviate the problem.

Table 7 : Reasons Given by Parents for Directing Children to Enter into Work Force

Purpose	Kulanda No.	Percentage	Chhadiapalli No.	Percentage	Total No.	Percentage
Obligation to employer	37	29.8	26	20.3	63	25.0
Repay the debts	34	27.4	37	28.9	71	28.2
Poverty	18	14.5	37	28.9	55	21.8
Need of assistance of children	28	18.5	7	5.5	30	11.9
Bad at school	8	6.4	19	14.8	27	10.7
Others	4	3.2	2	1.6	6	2.4
Total	124	100.0	128	100.0	252	100.0

However, without reiterating the obvious social and economic background of the child workers in the advanced agricultural setups let us analyze the nature of work and the terms and conditions of employment of children. Of course, the labour of children, both inside and outside the household. is always considered inferior to that of the adults. But the changes in production system and the socio-economic position of the child workers differentiate the degree and intensity of child labour. The nature and character of employment of children under subsistense economy, feudal system, and matured capitalist production system vary widely. Besides, the multi-structural formations provide a complex system of roles and statuses to different categories of child workers belonging to different strata of society.

Child Workers and their Work

The studied child workers belong to the age group between 8 and 15 years, but 72 per cent of them actually are within the range of 13 to 15 years, while 25 per cent are aged between 10 and 13 years, and 3 per cent come within the range of 8 to 10 years. Younger children sometimes attend school, besides helping in domestic chores and allied agricultural activities. Soon, however, they spend more time in productive and remunerative activities. It may not be out of place to recall the off repeated assertion that there is a negative correlation between child work and formal eduction, and extension of educational facilities constitutes one of the most effective remedies to the evil of child labour. This is simplistic and the correlation is superfluous. High drop-out and low attendance rates in the rural areas evidently suggest the importance of employment of children in the production process. Moreover, it is erroneous to presume that for the rural poor, education is an investment towards enhancing earning capacity. So long as education has a limited economic value, and contribution of children in the work process in considered essential, enhancement of educational facilities and forced enrollment will not be able to make any dent into the problem. Perhaps a reasonable suggestion could be restriction of hours of work for children, and restructurisation of school timings and curricula to impact essential ingredients of functional education in the shortest available time.

In all, 56 per cent of the child workers in the two village are illiterate. One-third have barely studied in the school. Only one-tenth of them have passed between standard III and V and none of them gone beyond the primary school level. The child workers of low caste families are mostly illiterate whereas those of the peasant castes are laroely literate. For instance, illiteracy among child workers of Gudia and

Bhandari households is cent-percent. Those of the scheduled tribes are 89 per cent and scheduled castes 85 per cent. Khandala 81 per cent, Keuta 70 per cent, and so on. And the children who are literate have never gone beyond standard III. In contrast, all the child workers of Kulata caste are literate. 79 per cent in case of Kalini. 75 per cent in case of Belama and 57 per cent of Dumal, are literate. Moreover, the child workers above standard III largely belong to these castes alone. The association between castes and educational status is significant. The fact that over 43 per cent of child workers are literature in an atmosphere of 70 per cent overall illiteracy may tempt some to presume that the child workers are relatively better placed in this regard. But this is incorrect. Free education and persuasion of the school teachers simply account for the marginal increase in literacy among the younger generation. The literate peasant caste child workers normally work in their own farms while illiterate of barely literate child workers belong to lower castes and tribes and mostly sell their labour power others.

Notwithstanding the development of capitalism in agriculture caste seems to continue to play a crucial role even with to resect to the child labourers. As many as two-thirds of child workers engage in both their own farms and works as casual laborrers of others peasants. They mainly belong to the peasant castes like Dumal. Kulata, etc. which are numerically as well as economically dominant in the village. They are now facing a pattern of immigration due to the techonological growth in agriculture. In other words, they are both economically and sociaily better-off then the other castes landless households. In contrast, most of the 30 per cent of child workers who rely on wage labour belong to the families of servicing castes, scheduled castes/tribes. They work largely as attached, semi-attached or contract labourer. Thus, there is a broad correlation between the caste status and degree of the child workers. This, however, does neither mean that the attached and semi-attached child workers are absent among the backward peasant castes nor does it convey that lower caste child workers do not seek the greatest insecure contract and casual labour. It only highlights differential concentration of unpaid free child labour in terms of caste. Moreover, the fact that attached and semi-attached child workers are often employed in domestic chores and that purity and pollution still dectates social relationship in the village set-up, no matter whatever is the level of agricultural growth, there is also preference of workers of the same or upper caste than the lower caste. In case, however, the child workers are only needed to look after the cattle and carry out agricultural operations, preference is given to the lower caste whose employment is more advantageous to the employer than when one's own caste or of higher caste worker is employed. Curiously, even the lower caste child worker prefer attachment to higher caste households than to the lower level, precisely because they cannot take water. Let alone cooked from the lower caste master. In other words, besides the economic position, caste position dircetates the child workers and their family members in the selection of the employer. If this relationship slightly weakened in the recent years. It is largely due to the growth of capital-intensive agriculture and changes in the need to employ any child worker for a longer time and mass immigration of outside labour. Also perhaps the land and labour legislations might have contributed to the apparent marginal alteration.

The child workers are internally differentiated in terms of their degree of attachment to the employers. This means not only the children and their involvement in the production is primarily decided by their parents in accordance with their socio-economic position but also their parents freedom to change the employers of their children is terribly restricted. Under such condition, of a scenario of multiple domination and dictation, the right of the children to choose their masters in terms of their own volition is immensely sabotaged. Table 8 indicates that 2 per cent of the child workers engage only in their own farms or tepented lands. They belong to two traditional peasant castes. Attached and semi-attached child workers constitute half of the total underage workers. The remaining are casual wage earners. Attached labourer is defined here as the one who is employed by the employers on an annual basis or for an agricultural season. Their wage is fixed while the assignments remain unstructured, although a couple of primary works constitute the basis for decision on the guantum of wage. Among two-thirds of these cases, the attachments are usually renewed every year for a prolonged period. Only in exceptional cases, with the permission of the employer, they are allowed to sell their labour to others, In all but five cases, they are paid a fixed amount of case and kind in several irregular instalments during the contract period. The amount depends on the age of the workers, status of the employers, major tasks assigned to him/her, and whether lunch is provided by the employer on the working days etc. Ironically the attached child workers and their parents, by and large, consider the attachment as a favour of the capitalist landlords and rich peasants. Besides, as nearly one-fourth of the attachments are related to current consumption loans and more than one-fifth to the conditions of whole debt, the notion of favour is reproduced. This may appear to convey that the relations of contract are based less on extra-economic coercions of the dominant class, than on mutual economic advantage to the employer and the employee. But the nature of the production system being such that the labour has little other means to secure livelihood than submitting to the demands of the ruling classes, who can go to any extent to preserve the unjust and obsolute order, cannot be ignored (Pathy, 1984).

Table 8 : Caste and Pattern of Child Labour

Caste	Attached labour	Semi-attached labour	Casual labour	Labour in family farm
Brahmin (Nill)	-	-	-	-
Kulata (N=17)	11.8	29.4	58.8	-
Belama (N=20)	-	10.0	75.0	15.0
Dumal (N=28)	14.3	25.0	53.0	7.1
Kalinji (N=24)	8.3	12.5	79.2	-
Alia (N=25)	24.0	20.0	56.0	-
Odiya (N=10)	60.0	20.0	20.0	-
Teli (N=9)	33.3	44.4	22.2	-
Telenga (N=16)	-	66.7	33.3	-
Gauda (N=14)	21.4	21.4	57.1	-
Gudia (N=2)	-	100.00	-	-
Bhandari (N=2)	-	-	100.0	-
Keuta (N=10)	30.0	40.0	30.0	-
Khandala (N=27)	25.9	22.2	51.8	-
Scheduled Castes (N=40)	47.5	25.0	27.5	-
Scheduled Tribes (N=18)	61.1	22.2	16.7	-
Total (N=252)	26.2	24.2	47.6	2.0

$x^2 = 110.17$ df = 25   d < .01

The semi-attached child workers are operationally defined as those whose farm enployment is based on monthly basis. In their case, the obligation to the master is relatively limited. Of course, a large number of them are not tied to their employers through credit nexus. Small peasants belonging to traditional peasant castes normally opt for casual wage labour along with their other family members, Evidently, attached and semi-attached child labourers mostly belong to the scheduled castes. Half of the child workers of kulanda and more one-third (37%) of Chhadiaballi are attached and semi-attached labourers. The wage rate for attached labourers is lower than the casual wage labourers, although the former perform more tasks and for longer periods of time. The rural credit system seen as the potent instrument to ensure the continued attachment, of the labourers. The loan demands not only exorbitant interests and multiple unpaid labour service but also the family measurement, manipulation of accounts an pricing system at different seasons, contribute to the perpetual indebtedness of the rural poor. In the village Kulanda, many of the tribal immigrant families do not possess house sites to their own. The landed interests of the village temporarily provide them sites for construction of house under condition that at least a member of their families be attached to them in return of food and festival gifts. This shows that capitalist landlords and rich peasants have found a cheap and profitable source of labour appropriation in the attached and semi-attached labour system.

Turning to the annual income of child workers (Table 9). Sahoo (1995), notice that as may as 30 per cent of them get less than Rs. 500. Indeed, 36 per cent of attached and semi-attached workers belong to that income group while only 22 per cent of casual wage labourers have such meager income. Nearly four-fifth of the child workers recive less than Rs. 700 each per annum. Only 5 per cent earn above Rs. 1.000 annually. Low wage is under-standable, but in this case average per day income being around Rs. 1.60 indicates the extent of poverty, unemployment and destitution. On the days of farm employment, the child labour receives between Rs. 2 and Rs. 3 on an average as against Rs. 8 to Rs. 10 for male adult workers performing the same type of work. The wages are fixed arbitrarily and unilaterally. Along with such a less than subsistence wage, the frequent ill-treatment, the deplorable working condition and hours of work have endangered the physical, and mental health of the child workers. In any case, parents take away the wages of their children, except some pocket expenditure, during festival and other times.

Table 9 : Nature of Child Employment and Annual Income

Nature of employment	Upto Rs. 500	500-700	700-900	900+	N.A.	Total
Attached labour	19	28	13	6	-	66
Semi-attached labour	27	25	9	-	-	61
Casual wage labour	27	70	15	8	-	120
Labour in own farm	-	-	-	-	5	5
Total	73 (30.0)	123 (48.8)	37 (14.7)	14 (5.6)	5 (2.0)	252 (100)

Immigration into the developed village of Kulada by the poverty-sticken tribal and Harijans from the drought-prone neighboring areas has increased not only the employment of children but ironically more as attached and semi-attached labourers (50%). The other village with marked commercial agriculture has witnessed out migration of a substantial proportion of male adult work force to far distant semiskilled occupations and thereby raised ther necessity of employment of more children but largely as free wage laboures (55%). The phenomenon of migration can no longer be explained simply in terms of 'push' or 'pull' factors (Todara, 1976: Connell et al. 1976: Barik, 1988). At this moment, it is probably difficult to say how the simultaneous migration and immigration shapes the division of labour between the children and adults and the forms of dominance in the village production system. Nonetheless, the point is that the advancement of agriculture instead of declining the employment of tiny workers has in fact made them more vulnerable to economic and social exploitation. The major source of surplus appropriation still continues to be the cheap an unoranized labour force, in which childen and women are most vulnerable. The labour seying modern mechanisms and inputs have not displayed the singificance of cheap labour to the controllers of the productive assets. Besides, the survival of the small parcels of land demonstrates the need to utilize the domestic labour would further diminish the meager value of the produce. This indicates that articulation of capitions of production. There is thus no imminent need for the powers that be to transform or eliminate such atrocious institutions and relations.

Regarding the labour days spent in agriculture, it is found that one-third of the child workers get employment for over 200 days per year. This appears on the higher side of average employment available to agricultural workers in Indian rural context, irrespective of the level of development. But 80 per cent of all those who get such higher employment, actually are attached labourers who perform not only agricultural work but also domestic chores. Hense, greater employment at lower wage cost. Another one-third of child labourers get employment for 150 to 200 days per year, followed by 23 per cent between 100 to 150 to days, and about 9 per cent between 50 and 100 days (Table 10). Those who work between 150 and 200 days mostly belong to the families of less than 2 acre of landholding, end engage about 100 days in their own farms and rest in other fields. The primary employers for over half of the child workers (54%) belong to the class of rich peasants and 33 per cent by capitalist landlords, while 13 per cent by middle peasants. This shows the inclination of use cheap labour power for surplus product.

Beside farm work, they also indulge in stone cutting, brick making, canel digging, road construction and other non-agricultural summer activities. In fact, one-third of them work up to 30 days in non-agricultural occupations and one-fourth between 30 and 60 days (Table 11).

Table 10 : Labour Days Spent in Agricultural Sector

Type of labour	Upto 100 days	100-150	150-200	200+	N.A.	Total
Attached	-	-	-	66	-	66
Semi-attached	5	32	24	-	-	61
Casual	17	26	60	17	-	120
Others (non available)	-	-	-	-	5	5
Total	22	58	84	83	5	252

These activities are contract works performed along with the family members and close kin groups. Here, they get a slightly better wage of about Rs. 4 per day but calculated in terms of piece rate. These works are also more strenuous than farm work. Besides the aforesaid works, child workers of small prasants and farm workers involve in carying livestock, collecting firewood, looking after the siblings, gathering fodder for cattle and so on. Although some of these activities are not strictly productive in the sense of generation income but are essential tasks for the reproduction of the households. Indirectly they are also production as by their engagement, they free other members of the households to engage in productive labour (White, 1975: Cain, 1977), Be that alone: the difference in the amount and type of work performed by children of land owning and landless families is, however, striking.

Table 11: Labour Days Spent in Non-Agricultural Wage Work

No. of days	Stone cutting	Brick making	Canal digging	Others	Not applicable	Total
Up to 30	5	22	19	35	-	81
30-60	8	22	16	25	-	71
60+	3	9	4	18	-	14
N.A.	-	-	-	-	66	66
Total	16	53	39	78	66	252

In the farm sector children engage in diversified activities. Considering the average child labour's involvement, it is found that he indulges in plaughing for 20 days, sowing eight days, harvesting 30 days and others like watching crops, weeding, measuring, leveling etc.. around 50 days. Nearly 8 per cent of child workers said that last year they could not earn more because of frequent ill health. Time duration of payment of wages varies depending upon the contract between the employers and labourers. Only one-third of child workers are paid daily while the rest received after a long duration, including quarterly or half yearly. The mode of payment also varied primarily according to the nature of employment. They are paid in cash (15.1%) or kind (9.1%) or both (48.8%) or even in terms of repayment of loan (22.2%) and exchange of labour (4.8%).

Incidentally, 70 per cent of attached child labourers and half of the semi-attached labourers have changed their employers: about 30 per cent once. 22 per cent twice, and 9 per cent thrice. This indicates that they are not employed recently and that their dependence on a given employer is impermanent. Indeed. half of them changed due to low wages or violation of the oral contract and a quarter on account of excessive work and unreasonable behaviour including physical assault, by the employers.

Weak economic background and credit nexus have forced them into the uniust labour market. Lack of consciousness and organizational activities and obviously the apathy of the state has aggravated the problem. Surprisingly, one-fifth of the child workers opined that they are not in a position to extrapolate their future and an equal number was not sure of finding any better alternative. They, of course, feel and desire for a resoite from such hard and unremunerative work. The parents and relatives who ask the children to work are equally helpless themselves, and thus tend to console in terms of having an extra supportive hand to family income. Without repeating, it may be sufficient to note that the dominant assumption of agricultural growth declining the employment of under-aged workers and precapitalist relations of production is found untrue. In this study. Instead what is noticed is the co-existence of commercial agriculture with large-scale employment of children in both agriculture and non-agricultural sectors, and that too often under procapitalist obligations and relations. The pitiable working and living environment of the child workers can be made more explicit through a few case studies.

Case Studies

It may be useful to categorize the cases to arrive at a better comprehension of the phenomenon. Of course, as well be seen, the diverse cases essentially convey the overall trend in advanced agricultural context, which reproduces the employment of underaged work force at a cheaper rate and with mulitple obligations. The first one comop ises fifteen cases belonging to farm worker or poor peasant classes. They work mostly as attached or semi-attached to the capitalist landlords and rich peasants, and recieve a relatively lower wage. Besides the tradition, the impoverishment of peasantry, artisan and servicing castes has facilitated their forced employment. The second category comprises two cases belonging to small and middle peasants households, who face constant threat of unemployment, and work both on their own farms and hire out to other employers. The last category includes three cases where the children are compelled to accept familiar responsibility due to some unexpected calamities at home and primarily engaged in self-cultivation.

Case-1

Ramest Dakua (15) is a attached labourer to a Brahmin rich peasant of Chhadiapalli village. He belongs to Bhandari caste. His father and elder brother are working in some power loom units at Surat. He lives along with his father and sister. Till recently his famaly had an acre of land and also leased in some land. The income from farming as well as rural wage being inadequate for the survival of the family, his parents incurred debts. Besides for the marriage of his brother the tiny farm was sold to a rich peasant. The two male adults migrated to Surat and Ramesh become attached to the Brahmin rich peasant. He says: "Because of the honesty and intergrity of my father the Sahukar (the creditor/master) has given me the job and rejected the offers of other parents." Presumably, he considers getting the assignment as a credit. Anyway, he is primarily assigned the duty of herding the cattle and cleaning the cattle shed, but more often then not given unspecified agricultural and households chores from 7 a.m. to 7 p.m. without any fixed hours of break. Mother rece ves the wage, paid monthly or at times in shorter intervals upon request. During the Dasahara festival in October, the master given him a pair of new clothes and a few extra coins. His mother often works as a casual worker in the farms of the rich peasant, though she receives a lower wage than the prevailing market rate. The immigration of his father and brother to Surat has not changed their condition of existence, and a major protion of the debt to the Brahmin rich peasant persist. He is told that the recurring illness of his father and frequent retrenchment of his brother forbade them to remit any appreciable amount of money to lessen their sufferings at home. Ramesh is unhappy due to the low wage and wishes to immigrate to some city but only if his father and brother permit.

Case-2

Subhash Das (13) is an illiterate attached labourer of Kalinji caste of Chhadiaplli. His father was a coal miner at Samastipur. At the age of eight. Subhash got his first employment as an attendant in the house of an office of the mine. His salary was Rs. 50 p.m.. besides food and other facilities. But as his father suffered from T. B. the family returned back to the native place. Meanwhile, an acre of land was purchased from the savings. Farming the land led the family to a debt trap and thus it is mortoaged. In order to pay the loan. Subhash is employed in the house of a capitalist landlord-cum-money lender. During the last two years several times he conveyed his unwillingness to work thre but his father being promise bound has persuaded him every time. But now his father is arranging for his migration to Surat to work in a textile processing unit at Surat. He is looking forward for the freedom and better wage in Surat.

Case-3

Sudhakar Patra (16) is a semi-attached labourer in the house of a rich peasant of Mangalpur village. His family consisting of seven members own 1.25 acre of land. His father works at Surat an frequently remits money for household expense. In fact, Sudhakar having faired poorly in the school went to Surat to work along with his father. But within a year due to harsh working environment, twelve hour shifts and filthy living conditions without civic amenities, made him ill and thus returned to the village. At the moment he appears content working in his own field as well as in the rich peasants frame. He says though the wages are low in the village, from the health point of view. It is far better than the city employment. Sudhakar's only concern in on the present and tomorrow is left to the consideration on the parents, particularly father.

Case-4

Ram Kunda (15) is an Semi-attached labourer to a capitalist landlord of Kulanda. Some two decades back his parents immigrated from Bolangir and worked as an agricultural labour in Baragarh region, followed by digging canel under a contractor. Since the age of none. Ram used to help his father, and subsequently he became an attendant in the common mess of the labour contractors. Working hours stretched from 6 a.m. to 8 p.m. with unspecified leisure time, depending on the availability of work. His monthly salary was Rs. 20 plus three times food. Lured by the rich peasant of Kulanda, his father shifted to the village. Initially they received Rs. 500 as advance to be repaid through labour. Presently, his whole family comprising of parents, two sisters, three brothers and himself work in the land of rich peasant, and on an average receive around Rs. 20 per day. Ram is paid only Rs. 45 per month without food while his younger brother (10 years) is only given a meal per day. Ram washes clothes, cleans vessels, mopes house floor and does many unspecified works. He feels suffocated and cannot escape. Once in two or three years, the family visits their kites and kin in their ancestral village. The whole family is illiterate and none knows any civil and political rights.

Case-5

Bipin Das (15) is a literate (standard II level) attached labourer to a rich peasant of Kulanda. His joint family consists of seventeen members. Their small holding at Rangali of Sambalpur area forced the members to opt for diverse occupations. Bipin started as a railway employee's house at Jharsuguda with a monthly wage of Rs. 15 and food. After an year he shilfted to a hotel of the same town with Rs. 50 salary and food. Ill-treatment and overwork forced him to join as a helper to a forest contractor-cum-capitalist landlord. His father was persuaded to be attached to his farm and accordingly five members of his family have shifted to Kulanda. All the them work for the capitalist landlord at a lower wage rate than the prevailing market rate. The household chores are unpaid except for occasional left over foods. Very often, the lady of the house scolds them. During the off season, they are allowed to work outside, and then Bipin earns an average of Rs. 6 to Rs. 7 on repairing canal and dam.

Case-6

Bipin Pradhan (17) is an illiterate tribal boy. His landless family having faced the constant atrocities of the forest contractor in the remote village of Sundargarh migrated to a construction sita near the Rourkela Steet Plant, working under a contractor. Bipin used to recive Rs. 4 per day. Iregular payment and frequent denial of work, made them to leave the place. Along with his parents, he arrived Kulanda some three years back. Since then the whole family has been working for a given capitalist landlord. Bipin does not know specified life is no better than before, except for the availability of secured employment.

Case-7

Achutya Nag (13) belong to a five membered artisan family. Though his father suffers from a chronic stomach ailment, he continues to catty out the caste occupation both within and outside Chhadiapalli. His mother also suffers from chest pains. Due to their illness, the family incurred a debt and subsequently sold half and mortaged the other half of the total one are holding. Elder brother also works in the family work occupation as well as does casual farm work. Achutya never entered school. He mostly goes for farm labour and receives between Rs. 3 and Rs. 4 a day, when hired to harvest sugar cane, he is paid Rs. 3 for every 100 bundles, each containing between 8 and 12 pieces of sugar cane. His wage then comes to about Rs. 6 besides for carrying the bundles to the roadside he gets an extra wage of Re. 1 or. Rs. 2. depending on the distance. The children are given this task only if they can carry at least 100 bundles a day. A chutya also helps mother in household work and wishes to practice his caste occupation.

Case-8

Dharani Sahoo (14) is an illiterate attached labourer to a capitalist landlord. The contract is renewed annually and the wage adjusted as repayment of an outstanding loan. Curiously, neither Dharani knows the amount of debt nor how much is repaid. He only gets two meals in return for his back-breaking farm and non-farm jobs like tending animals, sweeping house, drawing water from the well, watering the vegetable garden on alternate days etc. He is nurturing a hope to migrate to Surat and escape from the drudgery.

Case-9

Muneshwar Das (14). a milkman by caste, belongs to a family of landless. For long the family was surviving on tending the cattle of the village and selling the milk from the four cows and three buffaloes, besides of course farm labour. As better milch cattle are bought by the affluent through bank loans, their survival support declined. Moreover, to meet the funeral expenses of grandmother, two cows were sold and a buffalo died of some unknown disease. Due to the fall of grazing land, fodder became castly. Maneshwar is looking after the gattle from early childhood but now he works as a casual labourer and gets employment for about 150 days per annum. During summer months he tends the cattle often better off peasants and gets Rs. 30 per month. He thinks of having one hybrid cow which would give ten liters of milk. But how can he and his family afford?

Case-10

Kameswar Rao (14) has studied upto standard V. He belongs to a Telugu migrant family. His father has purchased one and half acre of irrigated land and also leased-in another half an acre. Kameswar remains busy throughout the year in multi crop farming of their field. Sometimes he also participates in reciprocal labour exchange with some Telugu speaking small peasants. Roughly he spends 40 days per annum in other fields on exchange basis and an equivalent number of days in Telugu rich peasant's farm to get a share in water and some modern inputs. Such non--waged labour relationship is. however, restricted only a few migrant families.

Case-11

Ravikanta (14) belongs to a small peasant family. His father worked also as a contract labourer in eastern Orissa and as a worker in Bihar coal mines. He used to remit money for family maintenance, and also managed to buy one and half acre of land. But, unfortunately, his father died in an accident in the mine. This forced Ravikanta, the eldest child to look after the family consisting of two brothers and two and two sisters. The farm is not adequate for the survival of the family and hense he also works as a labourer in others fields. And yet, he has already borrowed heavily from the village moneylender. The marriage of the elder sister forced him to sell one-fourth of land to a rich peasant. Anyway. Ravikanta is pulling on disinterestingly without knowing the future.

Case-12

Brahmar Jena (15) a self-employed agricultural worker belongs to a small peasant-cum-tenant family. His father had worked in Assam and Asansol, but ill health forced him to return back to village. And then he went to Surat along with Brahmar, who became a twister in a small power loom unit. Both of them earned about Rs. 1.500 pere month. Facing continues health problems. Once again, they returned to native village. Brhmar works in his family farm, leased in farms and occasionally in others fields. He says that the only thing they get from year long labour is just minimum food any clothing needs.

The case studies provide the implicit support to the quantitative information. Suffice here to note that rapid agricultural growth in the recent years has endangered the survival rights, of the children of exploited social class and status groups, and that their future, if any, is rendered bleak.

Conclusion

The observations will not only be as concise as possible, but also deliberately provocative, in the hope that it might encourage others to study these problems more closely. Nothing has been concluded of course. The discourse and dialogue do not end.

Despite the recent proliferation of child labour studies in India, there is a paucity of new ideas and insights into the process of the historical and social conditioning of the phenomenon. The conventional wisdom explains the existence and change of the phenomenon in terms of poverty, illiteracy, chronic unemployment, rapid demographic expansion, regional backwardness and apathy of the state. These factors, though crucial, are not sufficient for the comprehension of the nature and dynamics of employment of children. The treatment of the phenomenon in isolation from the larger historically evolved political economy provides little sociological insights into the issue. In other words, the conventional approach indicates only certain dimensions of phenomenal existence and conveys little about the structure of its reproduction. It is time to move beyond simple truisms to a more profound anlysis of the machanisms perpetuating the phenomenon of child labour. Not only the child labour studies refrain from holistic and historical analysis of the penomenon but are also confined to urban unorganized sector which employs barely one-tenth of the total child work force. Meanwhile, agriculture and allied sectors which employs over 90 per cent of the under-aged work force has received little academic of political concern. In fact, there is almost little substantive research on child labour in advanced agricultural regions. Surprisingly, it has been found impossible to arrive at any generalized propositions on the formation, nature and character of child labour force: their structural position in the total production context, their consciousness, struggle and future. This study starved to formulate and develop new dimensions and approaches in the child labour research. It also questioned the widely held fallacious notion that agricultural growth would contribute to the decline of employment of children in productive process. Instead, this study has demonstrated that the nature of agrarian capitatism being primitive is prone to employ and expropriate the cheap labour, including that of the children.

The criterion of age has been euphemistically used as the sole indicator of determining the child on employment. This juridico-administrative demarcation is hardly sociologically convincing, for it ignores the socio-economic conditions circumscribed by culture, ideology and above all the production relations. The need to work-out an alternative to the preyailing age criterion and the over popularized notion of universal significance is strongly indicated.

This study has argued that the nature of child labour varies in space and time depending on the character and strength of the given political economy. The two major propositions—that higher the development of agriculture (primitive accumulation of capital), the greater is the peasant pauperization and consequent increased employment of children: and that uneven development of agriculture tends to larger recruitment of children into the underpaid force from among the lower classes and castes—

are amply substantiated.

Nonetheless, there are quite a few important methodological problems in the study of class structure at micro level. This is precisely because of the openness of village agriculture in terms of labour and produce. Similarly, though noting the objective classes is indequate to understand a class society, and that a complete picture demands the exploration of the mediation structure between objective classes and their consciousness and actions, it was rather found insurmountable to extrapolate the potentiality and trend of the structure. The apparent permanence of the system at the given moment is only partially responsible to this limitation. Besides villages studies, however powerful may be, can hardly extend in full strength to the regional political economy.

The multi-structual regional system has certainly not been able to disintergrate all forms and relations of pre-capitalism, rather has tended to co-exist with many of them albeit in slightly modified forms. This did not give the labourers the much talked about freedom from obligations. Meanwhile, severe unemployment and underemployment, uneven capitalist growth, discovery of profitable usages of pre-capitalist relations of production, and unorganized labour market contributed to the growth of primitive accumulation of capital, without the necessary strength to transform the absolute relations in the production.

The assumption that with the modernization of agriculture, the children will be rerely employed in the production, is found untenable. The chldren of capitalist landlords, rich peasants and Brahmins do not engage in farm work. Nearly 85 per cent of the child workers belong to farm worker and small peasant families of lower castes and tribes. Those who belong to peasant castes normally work in their own farms, though occasionally also hire out themselves. Mostly their parents are illiterate and poverty-stricken. During the last decade, one-fifth of these families have sold their tiny parcels of land. Moreover, 83 per cent are indebted, mostly to moneylenders and no wonder 28 per cent are employed to repay the debts. In fact, 40 per cent of the families of child workers said that the major benefit from the employment is to procere loan. Obviously, poverty illiteracy, low social and economic position perpetual indebtedness, etc.. forced them to employ their children to eke out a living. This conveys volumes on the nature and impact of agraian capitalism.

Over one-fourth quarter of the children are of less than 13 years of age. None of the child workers have studied beyond primary school level while 56 per cent, largely belonging to lower castes and wage earning families, have never entered school. It is false to assume that extension of educational facilities would be one of the most effective deterrents to the evil of child employment. For the rural poor education is not an investment.

So long as education has a limited economic value and considered essential, educational expansion per cannot alter the situation.

There seems to be a broad correlation between the caste status and the degree of freedom of child workers. Of course, purity and pollution dictates employment of children for domestic labour but when they are needed for animal husbandry and farming, preference is given to lower castes. Surprisingly, half of the child workers are attached or semi attached whereas just 2 per cent work in their own farms. About half of the attachment is due to debt and consumption loan. Though their wages are low, curiously attachment to an employer is considered as a fovour. Immigrant families from drought prone areas have been compelled to attach their children to capitalist landlords or rich peasants. About 80 per cent of child workers earn less than Rs. 700 per annum. The average wage being Rs. 1.60 indicates the extent of destitution. A casual child labour normally gets between Rs. 2 and Rs. 3 a day as against Rs. to Rs. 10 for a male adult worker. Performing the same type of work. One-third of them work over 200 days a year. The primary employers of child workers are the rich peasants (54%), capitalist landlords (33%) and middle peasants (13%). Besides farm work and looking after cattle many of them go for stone cutting, brick making, canal digging, road construction. etc.. durng summer months. There, of course, they work under labour contractor and along with their parents.

In short, advancement of agriculture, instead of declining the employment of tiny workers, has in fact made them more vulnerable to economic and social exploitation. While articulation of capitalism profitably used the cheap child labour of explaited social classes and status groups, the continuance of small holdings too neecessitated the utilization of children in the farming. The future of these under-aged work force, it any, has been rendered bleak. Intervention of democratic instituations and processes may perhaps case the situation, but as yet there is nothing in sight. But is appears that neither the employers nor the state on their own can take any decisive step towards solution of the problem without united challengers from the working people at large, supported by other democratic and progressive forces. Subjective beneyolent intentions and endeavours can hardly resolve the issue.

References

Achrya, Poromesh 1982, "Child Labour". Seminar No. 275, July, pp.18-21.

Aghaianian. A. 1979, "Family Economy and Economics Contribution of Children in Iran: An Overview". Journal of South Asian & Middle Eastern Studies... Vol.3. No.1.

Alavi. Hamza 1980, "India: Transition from Feudalism to Colonial Capitalism." Journal of Contemporary Asia. 10(4).

Alexander, K.C. 1973, "Emerging Farmer-Labour Relation in Kuttanad." Economic and Political Weekly. Vol. VIII. No.34. August.

Amin, S. 1974. Accumulation on a World Scale. New York: Monthly Review Press.

Anon. P. 1983, "Child Labour Abolition: Sivakasi Match Units Threaten to Mechanize." Financial Express. October 17.

Appu. P. S. 1974, "Land Reforms for Agricultural Growth." Community Development and Panchayat Raj Digest. V(3).

Appu, P. S. 1975, "Tenancy Reform in India." Economic and Political Weekly. X(33-35).

Aries. P. 1979. Centuries of Childhood. Harmondshworth: Penguin Books.

Arnold. F. et. al. 1975. The Value of Children: A Cross National Study. Vol. 1. Honolulu: East-West Population Institute.

Arrighi, Giovanni and Saul. S. 1973, Essays on the Political Economy of Africa. New York: Monthly Review Press.

Baneriee, S. Child Labour in India: A General Review—With Case Studies of the Brick-making and Zari Embroidery Industries, London: Anit-Slavery Society.

Bardhan. P.K. 1979. "Wages and Unemployment in Poor Agrarian Economy: A Theoretical and Empirical Analysis," Journal of Political Economy. No.3.

Barik. B. C. 1988. Class Formation and Peasantry. Jaipur : Rawat Publications.

Barrah, P. 1977, Working Children in Urban Delhi : A Research Report. New Delhi, Indian Council for Child Welfare.

Becker, G. and Lewis. H. G. 1973. "On the Interaction Between the Quantity and Quality of Children." Journal of Political Economy. Vol. 81. April.

Beteille, A and Madan, T. N. 1975. Encounter and Experience: Personal Accounts of Field Work. Delhi: Vikas Publishing House.

Bhadur, A. 1973. "A Analysis of semi-Feudilism in East India." Frontier, Autumn.

Bhalla, G. S. 1983. "Peasant Movement and Agrarian Change in India." Social Scientist. 11(8).

Bhall, G. S. & Alagh, Y. K. 1977. Food Growth: A District wise Study. J. N. U. Planning Commission Project (Mimeographed).

Bhall, G. S. and Alagh, Y. K. 1979. Performance of Indian Agriculture, New Delhi : Sterling Publications.

Boissevain, J. and Friedi. J. (eds) 1975. Beyond the Community. The Huge: Ministry of Education and Science.

Boulding, E. 1979. Children's Rights and the Wheel of Life. New Brunswick : Transaction Books.

Braverman, Harry 1974. Labour and Monopoly Capital. New York : Monthly Review Press.

Breman, J. 1985. Of Peasants Migrants and Paupes: Rural Capitalist Production in Western India, New Delhi : Oxford University Press.

Breet, E. A. 1973. Colonialism and Underdevolpment in East Africa 1919-1939, London, Heinemann.

Byres, T. J. 1977. "Agrarian Transition and the Agrarian Question," Journal of Peasant Studies. Vol, 4 No. 3 pp. 258-74.

Cain, Read. M. T. 1977. "The Economic Activities of Children in a Village in Bangladesh," Population and Development Reveiw. Vol. 3, No. 3.

Cantwell, Nigal 1985, "Un Child Labour Seminar : An Intolerable Evil" International Children's Rights Monitor. 2 (4th Quarter).

Chakrabarti, Prafulla. 1970 "Quantificition and Social Research : A Trend Analysis." Economic and Political Weekly, Vol. V. No. 38, Septembar 19.

Chakravarty, Kumaresh 1972. "Education in the Fifth Five Year," Social Scientist, Vol. 1, No.3.

Challis J. & Eliman. D. 1979. Child Workers Todya, London, Questionnaire House Ltd.

Chandra R. 1982, "Child Labour in Tamil Nadu," Bulletin of Madras Development. Seminar Series. 12(12) : 672-86.

Chattopadhya, Paresh 1972, "On the Question of the Mode of Production in Indian Agriculture: A Preliminary Note" Economic and Political Weekly, Review of Agriculture, 25th March.

Chaudhari, K. 1976. "Bonded Labour", Economic and Political Weekly, No. 10.

Choudhury, Sadananda 1979, Economic History of Colonialism : A Study of British Salt Policy in Orissa. Delhi :*Inter-India Publication.

Clearke, M. 1975. "Survival in the field implications of Personal Experience in Field Work" in Theory and Society. No. 2.

Cliffe, Lionel. 1977. "Rural Class Formation in Africa." The Journal of Peasant Studies, IV (2).

Clopper. E. M. 1970. Child Labour in City Streets, New York : India," American Anthropologist, Vol. 67. December.

Coles, R. 1964. Children of Crisis : A study of Courage and Fear, London : Feber and faber.

Connell, J. and Lipton. M. 1976. Assessing Village Labour Situation in Developing Countries, Delhi : Oxford University Press.

Costa, D. M. and James, S. 1973. The Power of Woman and the subyersion of the Community, Bristol : The Falling Wall Press.

Da, Costa 1971. "A Portrait of Indian Poverty" in A. J. Fonseca (ed). Challange of Indian Poverty. Delhi : Vikas Publishing.

Dalton, G. 1971. Economic Development and Social Change, New York: Natural History Press.

Danniel Christopher 1976, "Child Worker has Come to Stay", Social-Welfare. XXII (8) : 6-9.

Dasgupta, B. 1977. Village Society and Labour Use, Delhi: Oxford University Press.

De Mause, J. (ed) 1974. The History of Childhood, New York : The Psycho-history Press.

Desai, A. R. 1966. Social Background of Indian Nationalism, Bombay : Popular.

Dev, S. M. 1986. "Growth of Labour Productivity in Indian Agriculture" Economic and Political Weekly, XXI (25-26) : A 65-75.

Duba, Leela 1981. "The Economic Roles of Children in India." Methodological Issues. In Rodoers and Guy Standing (eds) Child Work Poverty and Underdevelopment, Geneva : I.L.O.

Dutta, Aroti. 1981. "Helping the Family through the Children," Social Welfare, Vol. XXVIII, No. 1-2, April-May.

Elizabeth, B. Hunock 1972. Child Development, Londeon: Mcgrow Hill.

Engels, Fredrick 1969. The Condition on the Working Class in England. St Albans, Panther.

Engels, F. 1963. The Origin of the Family Private Property and the State. Moscow : Progress Publishers.

Enid. Schildkrout, 1980. "Peasantry as an Economy Category." The Journal of Peasants Study 4 (4).

Ennew, J. and Young. P. 1981. Child Labour in Jamaica : Its nature and incidence, Report No. 6. London. Anti-Slavery Society.

Erikson, E. 1963. Childhood and Society, London : Penguin Books.

Espenshade T. J. 1972. "The Value and Cost of Children." Population Bulletin, Population Reference Bureau, 32 (1).

Fabian, Johannes, 1971. "Language. History and Anthropology," Philosophy of the Social Science. 1 : 19-41.

Fanon, Frantz 1966. The Wretched of the Earth, New York: Grove Press.

Fee, T. 1976. "Domestic Labour : And Analysis of Housework and Its Relation to the Production Process. "Review of Radical Political Economy, VIII(2).

Fine, Ben and Harris, L. 1979. Reading Capital, London, Macmillan.

Firth, R. 1961. Elements of Social Organization Boston : Beason Press.

Frank, A. G. 1967. Capitalism and Underdevelopment in Latin America. New York: Monthly Review Press.

Frankel, F. 1971. India's Green Revolution: Economic Gains and Political Costs. Princeton: The University Press.

Gangrade, K. D. 1979. Child Labour in India, Delhi: Delhi School of Social Work.

Gangrada, K.D. and Joseph. Gathia A. 1983. Women and Child Workers in the Unorganized Sector. New Delhi: Concept Publishing Company.

Ganguly, Piyus. 1984. "Child Labour Rules Fouled with Impunity," The Telegraph (16.4.86). Culcutta.

George, K. N. 1975. "Child Labour in the City of Madras" Paper presented in the National Seminar on Employment of Children in India. New Delhi.

Ghatek, M. 1984. "Child Labour in India" in N. Dash (ed.) The Worker and the Working Class: A Labour Studies Anthropology, New Delhi: Public Enterprises Centre for Continuing Education.

Ghose, A.K. 1983. Agrarian Reforms in Contemporary Developing Countries, London: Croom Helm.

Ghoshal, H. R. 1966. Economic Transition in the Bengal Prsidency (1793-1833), Culcutta.

Goddard, V. 1981. "Child Labour: An Introduction to Some Relevant Issues" Paper presented at the Workshop on Child Labour, University of Sussex. Institute of Development Studies.

Godelier, Maurice 1977. Perspectives in Marxist Anthropology. Combridge University Press.

Gorowtiz, I. H. 1928. "Some Aspects of the Child Labour Problem". Social Service Review, Vol. II, pp. 598-617.

Gough, I. 1972. "Marx's Theory of Productive and Unproductive Labour" New Left Review, No. 76.

Ganga, Kathleen 1980. "Modes of Production in Southern India," Economic and Political Weekly. XV.

Government of India. 1949. Abstracts of Agricultural Statistics of India, Delhi: Director of Economics and Statistics.

Government of India, 1971. Census of India, New Delhi: Census Commissioner and Register General Series I.

Government of India, 1975. Statistical Abstract of India. Ministry of Planning: Central Statistical Organization Department.

Government of India, 1978. Rural Labour Enquiry. Summary Report, Labour Bureau.

Government of India, 1979. Report of the Committee of Child Labour, Ministry of Labour.

Government of India, 1980. Basic Statistics Relating to Indian Economy, Ministry of Finance: Economic Intelligence Service.

Government of India, 1981. Census of India, New Delhi, Census Commissioner and Registrar General, Series I. Part II 15 (I).

Government of India, 1985. Agricultural Situation in India. Ministry of Agirculture and Rural Development.

Government of Orissa, 1970-71. Agricultural Census of Orissa, Bhubaneswar, Board of Revenue.

Government of Orissa, 1971. Economy Survey of Orissa, Vol. I, Cuttack: Government Press.

Government of Orissa, 1974. Orissa Land Reforms Act, Cuttack: Publication Division.

Government of Orissa, 1982-83. Agricultural Statistics, Bhubaneswar: Directorate of Agriculture and Food Production.

Government of Orissa, 1983. Economic Review of Orissa, 1981, Vol. XXI, No. 4.

Grewel. S. S. and Sidhu, M. S. 1981. "Migrant Agricultural Labour in Punjab," The Indian Journal of Labour Economics. XXIV. No. 3.

Gupta, Sulekh Chand 1962. "Some Aspected of Indian Agriculture," Enquiry, Delhi.

—, 1979. "Child Labour Revisited," Haryana Labour Journal 12 (4), October-December.

Habib, Irfan. 1963. The Agrarian System of Mogul India: 1556-1707, London: Oxford University Press.

Habib, Irfan 1983. "The Peasant in Indian History," Social Scientist, Vol. II, Non. 3, March.

Halim, Fatimah. 1980. "Differentiation of the Peasantry," Journal of Contemporary Asia. 10 (4) 400-422.

Hasan, Amir 1978. "The Silk Wayer of Varansi," Social Welfare. XXIV, No. 17, pp. 13-15.

Henderson. A. 1950. "The Cost of Children, Parts II & III" Population Studies, 4(3): 207-299.

Heywood, Colin 1981. "The Market for Child Labour in Nineteenth Century France," History, Vol. 66, No. 216.

Hoben, Allan and Tmberg. T. A. 1980. "Micro and Macro Data in Village India," Economic and Political Weekly. XV (48) 2019-202.

Horowitz, David 1969. The Abolition of Poverty, New York: Prager.

Hovles, M. 1979. Changing Children. London, Writers and Readers Publishing Cooperatives.

I. A. M. R, 1977. Manpower Development in Rural India: A Case Study, New Delhi.

I. L.O. 1978. Children and Work: An ILO Policy Framework for the International Year of the Child, Geneya.

mimeographed.

—, 1979. Convcention Concerning Minimum Age for Admission to Employment, Geneya.

IYer, G. and Das. A. N. 1976. "Orissa: A Case Study of Poverty and Bondage," National Labour Institute Bulletin, No. 5.

Iver, K. V. 1968. "Role of Children in the Indian Economy," Social Welfare, Vol. XV, Nos. 2&3.

Jain, D. et. al... 1979. "Rural Children at work, Prelminiary Results of a Pilot Study," The Indian Journal of Social Work, Vol. XI, No. 3.

Jain, S. N. 1981. "Child Labour." Journal of Indian Law Institute, 23(v), pp. 336-48.

Jena, K. C. 1978. Land Revenue Administration in Orissa during the Nineteenth Century, New Delhi: SPS Publication.

Jena, K. C. 1978. Socio-Economic Conditions of Orissa during the 19th Century, Delhi, SPS Publication.

Johnson, C. 1983. "Ideologies in Theories of Imperialism and Dependency, "in Chiloote. R. H. and Johnson. D. L. (ed), Theories of Development: Mode of Production or Dependency? London: Sage Publication.

Joshi, P. C. 1979. "Field Work Experience: Relieved and Reconsidered" in M. N. Srinivas et. al. (eds.), The field worker and the field, Delhi: Oxford University Press.

Joshi, P. C. 1981. "Field Work Experience: Relieved and Reconsidered, The Agrarian Society of Uttar Pradesh," The Journal of Peasant Studies, Vol. 8, No. 4, July.

Joshi, P. C. 1982. "Poverty, Land Hunger and Emerging Class Conflicts in Rural India," in S. Jones et. al. (eds) Rural Poverty and Agrarian Reform, Delhi: Alliged Publishers.

Juval, B. N. et. al. 1985. Child Labour: The Twice Exploited, Varanasi: Gandhian Institute of Studies.

Kakar, Sudhir. 1979. Indian Children Cultural Ideals and Social Reality. Bombay: Oxford University Press.

Kabra, Vijendra. 1983. "Rehabilitating the Child Labour in India," Indian Worker 31(16).

Kaur, Jasbir 1982. A Study of Nature and Extent of Child Labour in Kalavat (Jind) & Kathura (Sonepat): Block of Haryana, Hissar: Haryana Agricultural University.

Kesser, W. 1975. Children in Chine, New Haren: Vale University Press.

Khandekar, Mandeine 1970. A Report on the Situation of Children and Youth in Greater Bombay, Bombay: Tata Institute of Social Sciences.

Khan, M. A. 1980. Sociological Aspects of Child Development, New Delhi: Concept Publishing Co.

Kishwar, M. and Horowtiz, B. 1984. "Family Life: the Unegual Deal" in Kishwar. M. and Vanita. R. (eds). In Search of Answer: Indian Women's Voices from Manushi. London: Zed Books Ltd.

Knight, N. 1980. The World's Exploited Children: Growing up Sadly, Manograph No. 4, Washington DC: Bureau of International Labour Affairs.

Kosambi, D.D. 1975. An Introduction to the Study of Indian History, Bombay: Population Prakashan.

Kishanji, N. 1984. "Family Size, Level of Living and Differential Mobility in Rural India: Some Paradoxes" Economic and Political Weekly, XIX (6).

Kulshreshtha, J. C. 1978. Child Labour in India, New Delhi: Ashish Publishing House.

Lecguman, Haq 1983. "Child Labour and the Law," Southern Economist, Vol. 22, No. 4, June 5.

Lenin, V. I. 1967. The Development of Capitalism in Russia. Moscow: Progress Publishers.

Levine. R. A. 1977. "Child reasing as Cultural Adaptation." in P. H. Leiderman. et. al. (eds). Culture asnd Infancy: Variation in the Human Experience, New York: Academic Press.

Luxembury, Rose. 1925 (1954). What is Economics? New York: Pioneer.

Maltby, T. J. and Lemen. G. D. 1918. The Ganjan District Manual, Madras Government Press.

Mamdani, M. 1972. The Myth of Population Control, London. Monthly Review Press.

Mangold, G. B. and Hill L. B. 1929. Migratory Child Workers, New York: National Child Labour Committee.

Margaret. Crompton, 1980. Respecting Children: Social Work with Young People. London: Edward Arnold.

Marla, Sarma 1977. "Bondage in Medak District (A.P.)" NLI Bulltin. 30(10), October; pp. 424-30.

Marx, Karl 1964. Pre-capitalist Economic Formation, London.

—1970. Capital, III New York: International Publishers.

Mark Karl, 1971. Capital. Vol. I, Moscow: Progress Publishers.

Mark. K. 1971. The Grundrise, New York: Harper and Row.

McGill, N. P. 1929. Children in Agriculture, United States Children's Bureau, Bulletin No. 18%.

Mead. Lain. et. al. "Labour Market Structure. Child Employment and Reproductive behaviour in Rural South Asia." I.L.O.W.E.P. 2-21/W.P. 89 (June).

Meced, T. Cain 1977. "The Economic Activities of Children in a Village in Bangladesh," Population and Development Review. September, pp. 201-227.

Mehta. Manahabhai, 1983. "How Children are Exploited in Socialist India," Organizer,. January (Republic Day) Number 34, (36).

Meillassoux, C. 1971. "From Reproduction to Production: A Marxist Approach to Anthropology" Economy and Society. Vol. I, No. 1, 90-110.

—, 1979. "Historical Modalities of Exploitation and Overexploitation of Labour," Critiques of Anthropology IV (13-14).

Mencher, J. P. 1974. "Problems in Analyzing Rural Class Structure," Economic and Political Weekly, Vol. IV, No. 35.

Mendelivitt. Elias 1979. "Child Labour," International Labour Review, Vol. 18, No. 5, September-October.

Menon, Usha 1982. "Women and Household Labour," Social Scientist, Vol. 10, No. %.

Minge-Kalman, W. 1978. "The Industrial Revolution and the European Family: The Institutionalization of 'Childhood' as a Market for Family Labour" Comparative Studies in Society & History, Vol. 20, No. 3.

Mishra, B. 1979. "The Pattern of Agricultural Development in Orissa," Orissa Review. XXXIV (4-5), p. 5.

Mishra, G. P. 1977. Some Aspects of Change in Agrarian Structure, New Delhi, Sterling Publisher.

Mishra, P. K. 1979. Political History of Orissa: 1902-1936, New Delhi.

Mishra, P. K. 1981. Cost and Benefit Analysis of Rural Electrification: A Case Study of Orissa, Unpublished Ph. D. Thesis, Bombay University.

Mishra, S. 1967. Economic Survey of Orissa, Cuttack.

Mitchell, D. J. and Clapp, J. 1980. "The Impact of Child Labour Laws on the Kinds of Jobs Held by Young School-Leayers," in Journal of Human Resources, Vol. XV, No. 3.

Mitra, Ashok. 1982. "Citizen of Tommorow: Children Neglected and Exploited." Statesman, May. 22.

Mitra, A. K. and Mukherjee, S. 1971. Population, Food and Land Inequality in India. Bombay: Allied Pub. Pvt. Ltd.

Mitra, N. 1980. "The Slave Children of Mandsaur" Sunday, No. 8, 19th December 10-17.

Mody, A. 1983. "Rural Resources Generation and Mobilization," Economic and Political Weekly, Annual Number.

Mohanty, M. 1984. "Social Roots of Backwardness in Orissa: A Study of Class Caste and Power," Social Science Probing I(2).

Mohanty, Nivedita, 1982. Oriya Nationalism, Delhi, Manohar Publication.

Mohsin, Nadeem, 1979. Problems of Slum Children in Patna. Patna: A. N. Sinha Institute of Social Studies, Patna.

Moshin, Nadeem, 1980. "Poverty: Breeding Ground for Child Labour." Mainstream June 7.

Mhshin, Nadeem 1982. "Exploitation of Child Labour" National Labour Institute Bulletin. Vol. VIII, No. 3 and 4.

Molyneux, M. 1979. "Beyond the Domestic Labour Debate," New Left Review, No. 116.

Moolgadar, Leela. 'Rural Child' Social Welfare, 27(3), 80. JI-3.

Morice, Alain. 1980. "The Exploitation of Children in the "Informal Sector:" Some Proposition for Research" Working Paper No. 87. Population and Labour Policies Programme, I.L.O., Geneva, (W.P.) 87, W. E.

Mazumdar, Madhumita, 1981. "Caution: Children at Work," Future Development and Perspectives on Children. Fourth Quarter, 4.

Mueller, E. 1976. "The Economic Value of Children in Peasant Agriculture" in R. G. Ridker (ed). Population and Development. The Search for Selective Interventions, Baltimore, Johns Hopkins.

Mukherjee, D. P. 1981. "Child Labour in India," Capital 187 (4678), pp. 27-28.

Mukherjee, p. 1957. "The Orissa Famine of 1866," Orissa Historical Research Journal, Vol. VI.

Mukhrjee, R. 1957. The Dynamics of a Rural Society, Berlin: Academic Verlag.

Mukherjee Ramkrishna, 1974. "The Sociological and the Social Reality," Sociological Bulletin 23(2): 169-172.

Mukherjee, R. K. 1967. The Economic History of India, Allahabad.

Muller, R. 1973. "The Multinational Corportation and the underdevelopment of the Third World" In C. K. Wiber (ed), The Political Economy of Development and Underdevelopment, New York: Random House.

Mundle, Sudipto. 1976. "The Bonded of Palama. Economic and Political Weekly, Vol. Xi, No. 18, pp. 653-56.

Murthy, N. L. et. al. 1985. "Child Labour in Agriculture," Mainstream, Vol. XXIII, No. 49, August.

Nag, M. 1972. "Economy Value of Children in Agricultural Societies: Evaluation of Existing Knowledge and an Anthropological Approach." In J. T. Fawcett (ed). The Satisfaction and Costs of Children: Theories, Concepts. Methods, Honolulu: East-West Center.

Nagi, M. H. 1972. "Child Labour in Rural Egypt," Rural Sociology, Vol. 37, No. 4.

Nadu, Accdikersareely, D. 1981. "Child Labour Participation in India: A Statewise analysis," Man Power 16(4) January-March, 95-112.

Nangia Parveen 1981. "Child Workforce in India." New Delhi, Centre fFor Studies in Regional Development, Thesis (M. Phil): Jawaharlal Nehru University.

Narvan, S. 1980. "Children of Bihar." Illustrated Weekly of India, 101(44), December.

Nash, M. 1961. "The Social Context of Economic Choice in a Small Society," Man No. 29.

N. P. P. C. 19975. Perspectives on the Child in India. Delhi University Press.

N. I. P. C. 1978. Working Children in Bombay, New Delhi.

Novak, George 1971. Empiricism and its Evolution, New York.

O. Laughlin, B. 1975. "Marxist Approach in Anthropology." Annual Review of Anthropology, pp. 341-71.

O. P. C. 1985. "High Incidence of Child Labour," Economic Times. November 10.

Ossowski, S. 1969. "Old Nations and New Problems: Interpretations of Social Structure in Modern Society," In Andre Beteille (ed) Social Inequality, London: Penguin Books.

Pandhe, N. K. (ed.), 1979. Child Labour in India. Calcutta: India Book Exchange.

Panda, N. K. 1983. "Agricultural Growth and Rural Poverty in Orissa," Vision II (4) 19-24.

Panda, P. C. 1984. British Administration in Orissa 1912-1936, New Delhi: Inter India.

Parr, J. 1980. Labouring Children: British Immigrant Apprentices to Canada 1869-1924, London: Croom Helm.

Pathy, J. N. 1975. "Social Stratification in an Orissan Village," Economy and Political Weekly. X(23).

Pathy, J. N. 1981. "Land Reform and the Problems of Agricultural Development is Orissa: A Discursive Review," Indian Journal of Regional Science, XIII (2): 148-149.

Pathy, J. N.. 1984, Tribal Peasantry: Dynamics of Development, New Delhi: Inter India Publications.

Pathy, J. N. 1985. "A Note on the Structure on Working Class in India." paper presented in a seminar on Industrial workers and Social Change, in Centre for Social Studies Surat.

Pathy, J. N. 1987. Ethnic Minorities in the Process of Development, Jaipur: Rawat Pulications.

Pati, Biswamgy 1983. "Peasants, Tribals and National Movement in Orissa (1921-36)," Social Scientist, Vol. XI. 7.

Patra, K. N. 1971. Orissa Under the East India Company, New Delhi: Hunshiram Manoharlal.

Patternson, Orland 1979. "Slavery in Human History," New Left Review, No. 117.

Pattnaik Utsa, 1987. Peasant Class Differentiation, A Study in Method with Reference to Haryana, New Delhi, Oxford University Press.

Pichholia, K. R. 1980. "Child Labour in a Metropolitan City: A Study of Ahmedabad," Indian Journal of Labour Economics, XXII. No. 4, pp. 99-106.

Polyani, K. 1975. Trade and Market in Early Empires, Glencoe: The Free Press.

Poulantzas, Nicos 1975. Classes in Contermporary Capitalism. London: New Left Books.

Poul, Clan, 1980. "The Forgotten Little People: A Study of Urban Child Labour in a Developing Economy." Asian Economics (Segul), No. 35, December, 67-79.

Prasad, P. H. 1982. "Regional Aspect of Agricultural dynamics in Indian, Journal of Social and Economic Studies, Vol. 3 No. 4.

Premi, M. 1973. "Student Workers in the Age Group 5-14: A Socio-Demograhic Analysis," Manpower Journal. Vol. XVIII, No. 4.

Prembhai, 1984. "Report to the Supreme Court Regarding Child Weayers of Mirzapur, Bhadohi & Varanasi, unpublished.

Punekar, S. D. 1975. "Child Labour in Unorganised Industries,." Paper presented at National Seminar on Employment of Children in India, New Delhi: November.

Puthenkalam, J. 1977. Child Labour in Unorganised Sector: A Field Study in a Fishing Village in Trivandrum District in India, New Delhi: National Institute of Public Co-operatives and Child Development.

R. B. I. Report of the All India Rural Credit Review Committee, Bombay (Mineo), p. 18.

Pande, C. G. 1986. "Growth of Productivity in Indian Agriculture." Economic and Political Weekly, XXI (25-26), A 75-80.

Rao. B. B. S. 1972. "Bonded Labour in Orissa." Man in India, I, pp. 67-69.

Rao, B. S. 1983. "Growth of Farming in Orissa." State and Society, Vol. 4, No. 2, January-March.

Rao, J. S. Narain 1980. "Agricultural Child Labour," The Indian Journal of Labour Economics, Vol. XXIV, January.

Ray, B. C. 1981. Orissa Under the Mughals, Calcutta: Panthi Pustak.

Rayappa, P. H. 1979. "Economic Cost and Benefits from Children," Paper Presented at the Seminar on Denongraphic and Socio-Economic Aspects of the Child in India, International Institute for Population Studies, February.

Raychaudhuri, Tapan 1985. "Historical Roots of Mass Poverty in South Asia: A Hypothesis." Economic and Political Weekly, XX(18).

Rele, J. R. and Tara. Kathar, 1979. "Demographic Profile of an Indian Child," in Sharad, Gokhle and Neera Sohoni. Child of India, Bombay: Somaiya Publication.

Rey, P. P. 1975. "The Lineage Mode of Production," Critique of Anthropology, Vol. 1.

Robbins, L. 1952. The Subject Matter of Economics, London: Macmillan Press.

Rodhers, G. And Standing G. (eds), 1981. Child Work, Poverty and Underdevelopment, Geneya, ILO.

Resenzweing, M. R. and Evenson, R. 1979. "Fertility, Schooling and the Economic Contribution of Children in Rural India: An Econometic Analysis," Vol. 45, July.

Roy, B. C. 1960. Foundations of British Orissa, Cuttack.

Roy, B. C. 1960. Orissa Under the Maraths, Allahabad, Kitab Mahal.

Rudra, A. et. al. 1969. "Big Farmers of Punjab: Some Preliminary Findings of a Sample Survey," Economic and Political Weekly (Review of Agriculture), September.

Rural Wing, 1977. "The Dark World Jeeta Gadus," National Labour Institute Bulletin, III, Decmber.

Russell, James, 1980-81. "Dialectics and Class Analysis." Science and Society, 44 (4).

Saberwal, Satish, 1969. Stress and Response in Field Work, New York: Holt Rinchart and Winston.

Sadhu, A. N. and Amarjit Singh, 1982. "Employment of Children in Different Occupations, Study of its Pros and Cons," Southern Economist, 2(2). 22-23 February.

Sahlins, M. 1961. "The Segmentary Lineage: An Organization for Predatory Expansion." American Anthropologist, Vol. 63.

Sahlins, M. 1974. Stone Age Economics, London: Tavistock Press.

Salisbury, Richard F. 1962. From Stone to Steel. Melbourne University of Australia Press.

Sahoo, V. C. 1995. Child Labour in Agrarian Societ,. Rawat Publication, Jaipur, p. 187.

Sahrma, A. N. 1979. "Child Labour in Indian Industries," The Indian Journal of Social Work. XI(3): 345-52.

Sahrma, M. T. R. 1978. Economic Value of Children in Rural India, New Havan: Conn, Yale University, Economic Growth Centre Mimeographed.

Satapathy, B. 1977. Land Reforms Administration in Orissa, Bodhgava: Institute of Behavioural Sciences.

Sau, Ranjit 1973. "On the Essence of Manifestation of Capitalism in Indian Agriculture," Economic and Political Weekly, 31 March.

Schildkrout, F. 1978. "Chanding Economic Roles of Children in Comparative Perspective," in Coppong (ed): Marriage, Fertility and Parenthood in West Africa, Ganbera: Australian National University.

Schildkrout, E. 1980. "Childwork Reconsidered" International Social Science Journal. Vol. XXXII.

Schultz, T. W. 1973. "The Value of Children: An Economic Perspective," Journal of Political Economy, Vol. 81. No. 2.

Scott, C. D. 1976. "Peasants. Proleterianization and the Articulation of Modes of Production," The Journal of Peasant Studies, III(3).

Seal, K. C. 1979. Child Labour in India. Paper presented at the Conference on Children in India, Indian Association for the Study of population, March.

Searight, S. 1980. Child Labour in Spain, London: Anti-Slavery Society.

Sebastian, A. 1979. "Child Migrants and Child Migrant Labour." in Srinivasan. K. et. al. (ed) Demographic and Social-Economic Aspects of the Child in India. Bombay: Himalaya Publishing House pp. 181-98.

Secombe, W. 1975. "Domestic Labour" Reploy to Critics." New Left Review. No. 94.

Sen, B. 1962. Evaluation of Agrarian Relation in India. New Delhi: Peoples Publishing House.

Senapati, Nilamani, 1971. Orissa District Gazatteers. Cuttack. Government Press.

Sengupta, P. 1975. "Children Work to Live." Social Welfare Vol. XXII. No. 1.

Shanin, Tegdor 1977. "Measuring Peasant Capitalism: Russia's 1920a And India's 1979s." Economic and Political Weekly. XII.

Sharma, A. N. 1977. "Child Labour in Indian Industries." Indian Journal of Social Work. 40(3). 333-43.

Singh, B. et. al. 1982. "Impact of Technological Change in Farm Employment." Indian Journal of Labour Economics, Vol. XXV, No. 3.

Singh, Musafir. et. al. 1980. Working Children in Bombay: A Study New Delhi: NIPCCD.

Sinha, D. 1981. Socialization of the Indian Child. New Delhi: Concept Publication.

Spargo, J. 1906. The Bitter Cry of the Children, New York, Macmillan.

Srinivasan, K. et. al. (eds.) 1979. Demographic and Socio-Economic Aspects of the Child in India. Bombay: Himalaya Publishing House.

Stabenhagen, Rodolfo 1975. Social Classes in Agrarian Societies, New York: Anchor Press.

Stern, D. et. al. 1975. "How Children Used to work." Law and Contemporary Problems, Vol. 39. No. 3.

Stolzman, James and Gamberg. Herberg. 1973-74. "Marxist Class Analysis vs. Stratification Analysis as General Approaches to Social inequality." Berkeley Journal of Sociology 18:!05-26.

Sud, S.K. 1985. "Illiterate Child Labourers of Chandigarh" Patriot, January 12.

Sumanta, Banerjee, 1979. "Child Labour in India : A General Review: With Case Studies of the Brick-Making and Zari Embroidery in Industries," Anit-Slavery Society, London.

Swamy, D. S. and Gulati. Ashok 1986. "From Prosperity to Retrogression: Indian Cultivatiors during the 1970s." Economic and Political Weekly. XXI (25-26) : 56-63.

Terray, E. 1972. Marxism and 'Primitive' Societies, London: Monthly Review Pron.

Terray, E. 1975. "Class and Class Consciousness in an Abron Kingdom of Gyamaa." in M.Bloch (ed). Marxist Analysis and Social Anthropology, London.

Thompson, E. P. 1977. The Making of the English Working Class. London: Penguin Book.

Thorner, Daniel. 1969. "Context for a Cooperatives in Rurai India," in A. R. Desai (ed.). Rural Sociology in India Bombay: Asia Publishing House.

Thorner Denial, 1974. Land and Labour in India. Bombay, Asia Publshing House.

Thorner, Alice, 1982. "Semi-feudalism of Capitalism/contemporary debate on Classes and Modes of Production in India. Economic and Political Weekly, 17(5) 14-18.

Todaro, M. P. 1976. Internal Migration in Developing Countries, Generva: I. L. O.

Tripathy, P. K. 1985. "Political Economy of a Village in Orissa," Social Science Probings, II, No. 4.

UNICEF, 1969. Child Malnutrition in the Developing Countries. *New York.*

Vaidvanathan, A. 1986. "Labour Use in Rural India," Economic and Political Weekly, XXI (52): A. 130-146.

Valcaranghi, M. 1981. Child Labour in Italy, Landon Anti-Slavery Society.

Verma, R. B. S. 1980. Child Labour in Agriculture, Department of Social Work, University of Lucknow.

Vlassof, M. 1979. "Labour Demand and Economic Utility of Children: A Case Study in Rural India," Population Studies, Vol. 33, No. 3.

Vyas, J. 1978. "Is it Easy to do Away with Child Labour," Eastern Economist, Vol. LXXI, No. 17.

Wallerstein, Immanuel. 1983. Labour in the World Social Structure. London: Sage Publication.

White, B. 1975. "The Economic Importance of Children is a Javanese Village" in M. Nag (ed.) Population and Social Organization, The Hague, Mouton.

World Bank, 1979. World Atlas of the Child. Washington DC, International Bank for Reconstruction and Development.

Zachariah, K. C. and Sebastian. A. 1966. "Juvenile Working Migrants in Greater Bombay," Indian Journal of Social Work, Vol. XXVIT, No. 3.

10

THE CHILD POTTERS OF KHURJA

William Wood. 9 years old, was 7 years 10 months old when be began to work. He ran mould (carried ready-moulded articles into drying-room, afterwards bringing back the empty mould) from the very beginning. He came to work every day in the week at 6 a. m., and left off at about 9 p.m. I work till 9 o'clock at night six days in the week. I have done so far the last seven or eight weeks. Fifteen hours of labour for a child of 7 J. Murray, 12 years of age, says: I turn jigger and run mould. I come at 6, sometimes I come at 4, I worked all night last night, till 6 o'clock this morning. I have not been in bed since the night before last. There were eight or nine other boys working last night. All but one have come this morning. I get 3 shillings and six pence. I do not get any more for working at night. I worked two nights last week. Fernybough, a boy of 10: I have not always an hour (for dinner). I have only half an hour sometimes: on Thursday, Friday, and Saturday.

(Karl Marx quoting from the Children's Employment Commission, First Report of 1863 describing the conditions of children working in the pottery industry of England).

The Pottery Industry of Khurja

Children in the pottery industry of Khurja today do exactly the same work as children did in nineteenth-century England. Their work is described locally as *uthai rakhai* (pick up and put down). They carry empty mould to the worker who works on the jigger jolly and carry the filled moulds out in the sun to dry. The boys who do this work are called *phantiwalas* (the boys who carry the phanti which is a piece of wood on which five or six moulds are kept). About 95 per cent of all working children in Khurja are phantiwalas. The only difference in the conditions of children in the pottery industry today and in nineteenth-century England is that they work not more than nine or ten hours a day and rarely do night-work.

The pottery industry of Khurja is over 600 hundred years old and is considered to be the traditional occupation of the people of Khurja in Bulandshar district of Uttar Pradesh. It may be clarified here than when people speak of pottery being a traditional industry of Khurja, they are really referring to the few families of Multani Kumbhars (potters) who came with the Mughal armies. The local village potter, part and percel of Indian rural society, is not included in this description, (Burra 1987c).

There are almost 20,000 workers engaged either directly or indirectly in the pottery industry. Of the total workers, approximately 5000 or 25 per cent are children below the age of fourteen years.

However, these are only estimates and no-one is sure of the actual figures. But factory owners say that the total work-force within the factories is 6000 adults and a few hundred women and children. They arrive at these figures by calculating at the rate of nine workers in each factory and there are officially about 500 pottery units. But a study of about 25 per cent of the units revealed that except for a handful of units where there were less than ten workers, 90 per cent of them had more than twenty-five workers each with about 25 per cent of the work-force being made up of children below the age of fourteen years. Some units had almost eight to ninety workers employed.

The pottery industry of Khurja makes a variety of ceramic goods such as flower vases, object diart, crockery, industrial ceramics like chemical procelain, ball mill linings and balls, electrical and electronic ceramics like low tension (L.I.) and high tension (H.T.) insulators, spark plugs, sanitary ware, stoneware jars, etc. Crockery and insulators account for the major share of what is produced.

The annual turn-over of the Khurja pottery industry is Rs. 8 crores (Bhattacharya, 1982). If these are the official figures. I was told in Khurja is that actual production is three times what is declared and the estimate is deliberately kept low in order to evade excise. Individual units purposely show turn-over figures of less than Rs. 7.5 lakhs to claim exemption from excise and retain their classification in the small-scale sector.

Other important pottery centres in Uttar Pradesh are located At Chinhat, Chuna, Basti and Ghaziabad.

I visited more than forty-nine units where pottery was being made in factories, ten units where work was being done exclusively with help of family labour, ten units where, in addition of family labour, some hired help was also used and eight familes or rural potterns who did not made the famous Khurja pottery but were exclusively involved with supplying pots for the local market. I spent nineteen days in Khurja. I was able to interview people from different segments of the pottery industry: hundred workers-me, women and children-twenty factory owners, eight *thekedars* (contractors), five master craftsman, five traders, two doctors and a few government officials.

The Khurja Pottery Industry : Genesis and Development

Khurja is a small located in the Bulandshar district of western Uttar Pradesh. It is hemmed in on both sides by the rivers Ganga and Yamuna, which flow at a distance of forty-five kilometer. It is approximately eighty-three kilometers by road from Delhi. Khurja junction is well connected by rail, situated as it is on the main Delhi-Howrah railway line. Thus it is very conveniently connected with some of the major towns and cities of India both by road and by rail.

The Khurja pottery industry has a long history. It is believed that Timur Lang, who sacked Delhi in 1398, had a band of soldiers amongst whom were also skilled potters. These potters stayed back and settled down in Multan (non in Pakistan) and near Delhi. They were adept at making blue pottery with Persian designs and colours. About 600 years ago, in reign of Mohammad Bin Tughlak, some of the potters, families moved from Delhi to Khurja (Bhattacharya, 1982:8:Sharma, 1978:208). They started with red Clay pottery and then went on to introduce blue glazes on redclay articles with an englobe or coating of white clay, painting floral designs with cupric oxide and applying a soft glaze containing glass, red lead, quartz and borax. The basic raw material was the locally available red clay.

At first the traditional potters made *hookahs* (pipes), *surahis* (water-containers) and vessels as well as decorated wares. They attracted the attentiton of the outside world when two of the master potters from Khurja were invited to the Coronation Exhibition in London in 1911 to demonstrate their skill on the potter's wheel. The grandson of one of the master potters. Rasheed Ahmed, is one of the leading master potters of Khurja and has recently won the master craftsman's award.

Until the 1930s, the pottery industry of Khurja was the preserve of two families of Multani Kumbhars. In 1934, in order to develop the pottery industry the Government of Uttar Pradesh took the initiative and sent Professor H. N. Ray of the Banaras Hindu University to investigate the feasibility of making white ware goods using modern technology and newer raw white-ware goods using modern technology and newer raw materials such as China clay, feldspars and quartz. The local potters were quite receptive to the new methods. But their activities did not make much headway till World War II.

The Second World was largely instrumental in giving a boost to the cermic industry because there was a ban on use of various metal for making household utensils. During the war, import of ceramic goods was drastically curtailed and to meet the demand of ceramic wares for the was hospitals, the Uttar Pradesh government set up a factory in Khurja in 1942 for making such articles under the supervision of H. N. Ray. When the war was over, the factory had to be lossed down in 1946 due to lack of demand for the products. It was decided then to convert the factory which had three small kilns, two chimneys and three ball mills into the Pottery Development Centre. The workers of the now defunct factory were provided with alternative employment. They were given the processed body and other raw meterials from the Centre and were also allowed the facility of firing their green wares or unbaked goods in government kilns on payment of a nominal rent. This Centre is the first Common Facility Centre in the country and the main cause for the development of the Khurja pottery industry.

The Centre started in 1946 with only eight potters. Initially, it was purely a cottage industry producing cheap quality products, which had a limited market. In 1953. Dr, T. N. Sharma, a ceramic expert, sent to Japan for training. On his return in 1955, he demonstrated the use of better technology using local raw materials, he also improved the jigger jolly mechines and the shape of saggars (fire resistant containers in which unbaked pots are baked) and was primarily responsible for a number of schemes for the development of the pottery industry under the Second Five-Year Plan.

The Khurja pottery industry today has three types of entrepreneurs. The oldest are master craftman, also known as traditional potters, who have adapted to the new technology and now make art-ware largely with the help of the new technology using the terra cotta moulds rather than the potter's wheel. But they have not given up their old methods of decoration, painting and glazes.

The Second type of entrepreneur is the one who learnt the skills offered by the Pottery Development Centre and set up his own unit. And the third type of entrepreneur is the person who had the finance to set up his units but has not actually learnt the job himself. Interestingly, the traditional village potter has not entered the industry. He continues his traditional work for a totally different market and is not included in the list of Khurja potters. By definition, the Khurja pottern makes his wares for an outside market, while the local village potter produces to meet local needs.

The pottery industry in Khurja was set up because it was felt that there was a tradition of pottery in the area and a market for the goods. The people who ware pioneers in this industry, like Dr. Sharma, had envisaged that by setting up an industry and providing facilities many people would get employment here. In face, in the early years, the training was very rigorous and those who wanted to set up independent units had to prove their knowledge and ability, for the facilities provided by the government were crucial for their economic upliftment. But in later years the pottery industry developed indepently: many people seeing the potential of the industry set up units without actually knowing the work just because it was a good business proposition. Today, therefore, there is not much similarity amongst the different types of entrepreneurs.

A common complaint of traders or financiers-turned entrepreneurs is that the skilled worker-turned-entrepreneur has ruined the market because of his lack of knowlege, illiteracy and absence of financial staying power. Many of the smaller entrepreneurs are heavily indebted to local dealers who are making all the profits. The worker-turned-entrepreneur knows so little about the business side of pottery that he has knows so little value of his goods at a low price. Since the goods produced in all the factories are, guality-wise, almost on par with each other, the financier-turned-entrepreneur is not able to make as large a profit as he would like to cartel of them has started marketing their own goods in order to bypass the local dealers. So great is the resentment against the skilled worker-turned-entrepreneur that these educated entrepreneurs, some years ago, tried to force the government to pass a resolution that coal quotas would only be given to those units which had a certain area of factory, size of klin and quantum of capital. The idea was to displace the small entrepreneur but it did not succeed.

The Pottery Industry Today Structure and Market

The are four types of pottery units in Khurja not including the local potter who produces red clay goods for the local market. Most of the other pottery units produce for the outside market. Out of a total of almost 500 units, less than 50 per cent actually function. The reason is the large-scale black-marketing of coal, which is the primary raw material need in this industry. Workers told this resercher that small unit owner could easily earn Rs. 10,000 a month by just a black-marketing coal and was also saved the problems of actually running a unit. Out of the 500 units that are registered with the Government Pottery Centre, approximately 300 are run by traders, twenty-five by traditional potters and seventy-five units belong to skilled workers who have save money and set up on their onw. About hundred units belong to people who have received training in the manufacture of pottery but who no longer use their own hands.

Looked at from another point of view, the units in the industry could be classified differently. The first and largest category is made up to independent pottery units, which are equipped with their own machinery and manufacture their own processed clay called body and glazes and have their own forming and firing facilities. Some of them also do decoration work on their products. There are 398 such units.

The second category consists of dependent units which have no processing and firing facilities of their own. They obtain the processed body, glazes and other raw meterial from outside, make the green wares at their units and after applying the glazes, get the wares fired at the kilns provided by the Uttar Pradesh Small Industries Corporation Potteries Ltd, and pay a nominal rent. There are 126 registered dependent potters in Khurja.

There are twenty units which only manufacture the processed body and glazes and sell them to the dependent units which do not have these facilities. While the Government Centre is supposed to do this, dependent potters require credit which the Centre cannot provide and there private manufactures area able to do good business. There are also units which only undertake the decoration of pottery articles on a piece-rate or job work basis. There are twenty such registered units.

Another category of pottern who makes clay goods in Khurja is formed by the local potters who do not make goods for outside market, but only for the local market. There are colonies of the local Kumbhar in the city and in the surrounding villages who make large containers for water and gain, Kulhads (clay cups) which are sold to halwais (sweetmeat sellers) and sakuras (small plates) bought for feasts and weddings. These traditional potters also make plates which are no longer in demand because of plastic and paper goods.

In a recent report on the development of the ceramic industry in India, it was estimated that there would be a crockery demand of 33 million sets during the Seventh Five-year plan period. It is estimated that the demand for clay-based crockery from the urban sector would be 1,28,500 tonnes. According to the 1985 figures. 10, 700 tonnes were produced in the organized sector and 71,000 in the small-scale sector. Ofr these all-India figures, the contribution of the Khurja units was 15, 000 tonner or more than 20 per cent of all the crockery produced in the small-scale sector in India. The small-scale sector, under which the Khurja pottery industry falls, supplies mostly stoneware items to people with little purchasing power. The middle-class purchaser is fed by both the small-scale and the organized sector manufacturer of quality stoneware, earthenware, etc., and the higher economic strata buy superior bone china products. Khurja makes about 50 per cent of low tension insulators in the coutry and about 10 per cent of kit-kats. The only sanitary goods made in Khurja are foot-rests for Indian-style toilets.

While the demend for pottery is very high and gowing, the goods produced by the local village have less demand than before. The village potter in Khurja is facing competition from plastic, paper and dried leaf plated and bowls. As one potter said:

There is at least a 25 per cent fall in the demand for our goods even in the local villages because of the paper and plastic plates and saucers. Even though our goods are cheaper, there is more prestige in using plastic goods and these have become status symbols.

The local potter who used the red clay locally available has not made any advance in technology from the government. The Khadiand village Industries Commission, which was set up to help village artisans, introduced white-ware pottery in the villages instead of promoting local methods. This venture failed miserably for a host of reasons: there was no market in the villages for these goods, the villages potter did not have resources for raw material or fuel and, in any case, could not find avenues for selling the goods produced.

Process in Pottery Industry

In most of the big ceramic units, the raw material is processed on the premises with the help of machines called jaw crushers, edge runners, clay blunger, etc. The processes in the pottery industry of Khurja are many depending upon the goods made. One commontly used method is by throwing clay on the potter's wheel. This is the traditional method of making red clay potteries throughout India.

In Khurja, the traditional potters even now use the kick-wheels for making decorated potteries. The potters use his hand pressure to shape the body. This process is wholly manual.

Another method is known as the beating or patting method. This consists of formation of clay-ware by beating a roughly thrown piece of leather-hard clay with a wooden beater to the required shape and thickness. This process reduces the porosity of the clay body and makes it homogeneous and strong. In Khurja, this process is used only for making the saggars or containers in which the unbaked clay goods are put before firing the kilns. The sagger body is put on the outside of a wooden frame and beaten into the required shape and thickness by a woden beater.

Most of the crockery, plates, cups and suacers, etc., are shaped on the jiggar and jolly machines. The jiggar and jolly process is used to produce hollow single shapes on a mass scale. A jiggar consists of a vertical shaft having a cup-shaped wheel-head which receives the mould made by plaster of paris. It is mostly power-driven and is provided with a foot-brake. Some units produce jiggered items without using power, by pedalling. A jolly consists of an inclined arm mounted on a pivot with a balancing counterpoise on one arm. The opposite are carries a profile which is an iron tool to give shape to the article. Depending upon the goods being made, a quantity of clay is put into the mould fitted to the head and pressed to shape by the profile by lowering the arm of the jolly. For every article, a separate mould is fixed to the jiggar head.

All the ceramic units a Khurja making crockery use this process. This technique, however, cannot make the complete product. Handles for teapots, jogs, etc. are made by the slip casting and then joined to these articles.

For slip casting, a plaster of paris mould is made and the slip which consists of semi-viscous slurry of the ceramic body is pured into it. The excess liquid is poured out after some time. The inside of the mould becomes covered with a thin layer of the body after the water is soaked by the plaster mould. After sometime, the layer becomes hard and is removed from the mould. It is then finished by scraping off the extra clay, smoothened with fine sandpaper and, finally, with a soft wet sponge. This method is also used for making complicated shapes such as soup spoons. In Khurja, this method is widely used for making both chemical porcelain as well as crockery and tableware.

The slip is made from finely ground plastic body by adding small amounts of sodium sillicate or sodium carbonate to act as deflocculent. For both the slip method and the jigger jolly method, units make their own mould of plaster of paris. But not more than three of four castings can be done from one mould efficiently. Making articles of complicated shapes or large sizes requires the use of several mould for making the component parts which are subsequently joined.

Pressing in steel dies using hydraulic presses in used of making tiles and high-tenssion electro-porcelain. One tile manufacturing unit and a few high-tension insulator units (up to 11 KVA) At Khurja are using this technique. The technique is also being used by other units for making electrical kit-kats, technical ceramics and other products of simple shapes. Small articles are being made by hand presses.

In the organized sector, the green-wares are dried in rooms using a hot blast of air. But by and large, drying is done in the shade by keeping the green-wares on the floor outside or by stacking them in shelves for a few days. Once the goods are dried they are scraped for any rough edges and smoothened with water. If they are hand-pained or decorated otherwise, they are given over to the painter and decorators. The dried goods not pained are sent for direct glazing.

The earliest of Khurja used indigenous red clay for their goods. But today all the raw material comes from outside. The China clay comes from Rajmahal in Bihar, Ahmedabad in Gujarat, Chandia in Madhya Pradesh and Bikaner in Rajasthan. The ball clay is available only in Rajasthen, Andhra Pradesh, Gujarat and Kerala. The feldspars comes from Rajasthan and quartz comes from Rajasthan, Andhra Pradesh, Gujarat and Madhya Pradesh. The main source of fuel, coal, come from the collieries of the eastern coal fields situated in Bihar and West Bengal. The independent units get their coal against allotment directly from the mines. The dependent units are allotted the requisite quantity of coal from the coal dump of the pottery Development Centre for firing in the rented Kilns.

Glazes are homogenerous mixtures of silicate minerals and chemicals which melt to form glass and are used to provide a lustrous coating to the porous fired products to render them impervious. They fit the body intimately as the materials are mostly the same in both the bodies and the glasses. A ball mill us used to powder the glaze to the desired fineness.

The basic raw material for the unglazed pot are quartz, feldspars, plastic clay and china clay, marble or calcite, zinc oxide, barium carbonate, etc. In Khurja, mostly raw and opaque glasses are used which mature at medium temperatures. Different colouring oxides are used by Khurja potters for colouring glazes. Cobalt or copper oxide is used for all shades of blue and black. Copper and chrome oxide is used for the green colour. Iron oxide is used for giving the brown colour and manganese oxide is used for pick or violet colour. The traditional Khurja potters who have about twenty units now use commercially available glazes but some of them still prepare their own blue glazez and jealously guard the secret of their blue pottery.

The Khurja ceramic industry follows an intermediate level of technology. The wares are all single fired. Raw glazes insoluble in water are generally used. Barium glazes containing zirconia and /or titania as the opacifying agents are commonly used by the potters. The glazes is generally applied by dipping the dried green wares in the glaze slip. In some decorative wares, glazing is done by spraying. For various artistic designs, the colours are generally applied by hand painting by artist.

Once the goods are pained the glazed, they are baked in coal-fired, down-draught kilns. The kilns are of various sizes ranging from 2.4 metres (8 feet) to 7.3 metres (24 feet) in diameter. The wares are packed in saggars prevent direct contact of the wares with the flames and fumes of the fuel which would otherwise spoil the colour and glaze of the products. They also help to keep the glazed articles in position without sticking to each other. The temperature of the kiln in highest at the top, around 1250-1280 C for insulators and 1200-1500 C for crockery.

Participation of Children in the Pottery Industry

The first job for the young child is to carry lumps of clay to the *kataiwala* (the worker who makes pots on the jiggar jolly machine). Each *kataiwala* has one or two helper, the *phantiwalas*, who are always children. Since this work is always done through a *thekedar* because the employer faster production. The work is done at a fantastic speed with both adults and children working at break-neck speed. An average *kataiwala* cuts 4000 pieces in an eight-hour shift and the *phantiwala* has to carry 4000 moulds outside in the open to dry to dry and carry back 4000 empty moulds to the *kataiwale*. In one factory. I noticed young children of nine and ten carrying six moulds on a phanti. The mould contained three-inch mugs, each of which contained 100 grams of clay. The could itself weighed 300 grams. The combined weight of the moulds, the clay and the wood was about eight kilograms which the child carried on every trip. In an eight-hour day, he ran five kilometers a day at the very minimum with this load.

At another factory I saw children carry weight up to eleven kilograms on the *phanti*. I was told that on an average, the children made a thousand return trips in an eight-hour working day and covered a distance of six or seven kilometers. This was the work that children were mainly engaged in and their work was described as that of helpers.

This was not the only work that children did. Once the pots were partially dry, these children took out the half-dry pots and carried them to the workers who were engaged in finishing the work. In several factories, I noticed children stacking ninety mugs on a wooden platform and then carrying them on their heads to the adult workers. The weight of this burden. I was told by adult workers and factory owners, was more than ten kilograms. The children doing this work were so young that their hands and legs would tremble after they had put down the weight.

In one factory, I saw children unloading saggers, six at a time. Each saggar weighed half a kilogram. In one factory, a child of thirteen was carrying three saggars, each weighing eight kilograms. His body was bent double with the strain.

Another job that children are engaged in is removing handles from the moulds and carrying them to adults who finish them, some children were engaged in just cutting handless to the required size. On the average, they had to cut at least 3000-4000 pieces in an eight-hour shift. The children were engaged in the scraping of the rough edges from the mugs and other crockery pieces. Others helped with the final water finishing.

The children who have had a little experience work on the jiggar jolly machines, clean out the blunger machines and remove the pebbles from the processed clay. I saw children of ten, knee-deep in cold liquid clay, removing the large pebbles from the processed clay while the employer was standing out-side the pit and giving instructings, children are also sent into slip pits to get liquid clay for the mould because adults do not like the work. It is taken for granted that children will clean the premises and do all the other menial tasks for which adults would be reluctant—such as running errands.

From village Bavanpur, approximately theiry-five workers come daily to work in potteries and these include or ten boys of the ages of ten to twelve years. Most of these children come from families of khet mazdoors (agricultural labourers). Some of them own two or three bighas (a unit for measuring land). The fathers of three boys also work in the pottery industry. Most of the children from this village belong to the caste of dhimar or thakur.

Sondha village is about fourteen kilometers from Khurja town and about hundred worders including thirty to forty boys and adolescents leave home daily at 7 a. m. to work in the potteries. Most of the parents working children have less than five bighas of land. Most of the families own one or two milch animals which the parents tend, while the children labour in the potteries. The parents of ten to fifteen boys also work in the potteries of Khurja. Interestingly, when I asked why children were being sent to work when there was so much adult unemployment, the answer that twenty-six-year old Manohar Ram gave was: many adults don't know how to cycle and even if they know, they don't own one. Children don't have that problem. They sit behind us and hitch a ride.

Some of the children working in the potteries whom I had the opportunity to interview in depth seemed to be sole earning members of their families. Kalu Ram is twelve years old and comes daily from village Dharaon. He has no father and his mother keeps poor health. He has been working for the past five or six years and supports three younger brothers and two sisters. Vijay Pal and Hira Singh are thirteen years old. They are orphans and also come from Dharaon. Vijay Pal lives with his grand-mather. He has no brothers and sisters. He started working in the potteries recently, and grazed the landlord's cattle before this. He said: In the villages, there is no work for children. We are expected to work without wages only for a little grain. My grandmother thought that it was about time I started bringing in a regular wage.

Hira Singh has a brother who is the local quack. They have fifteen bighas of land. He studied up to the fifth standard and then his brother told him stard working.

Laxman Das is twelve years old and is a local Khurja boy. He and his younger brother, aged nien years, are the only earning members of their family. Laxman Das was embarrassed at being asked what his father did and said: 'He has retired'. He and his brother support a seven-member family. The contractor, who was standing nearby when I was interviewing Laxman Das. said: 'The man's a drunkard. The mother is lazy. The do not work because they have children to support them'.

Ompal is fourteen years old. He started working a year back when he failed his sixth standard exam. It was also the time when his sister was getting married. He said:

My parent needed money for my sister's marriage so my brother and I started working in the potteries, I thought that after a while would go back to school but once you leave school, there is no going back. We still have sisters to settle. My parents have very little land.

I asked several children how they heard that work was available in the potteries. Fazal said :

Thekedars come to the villages and say they want children so we know that there is work. Often the *thekedars* don't want to give the work to adults. We are young, we can work fast and we don't get tired so easily.

Adults working in the pottery industry who took their children to work said : 'Out wages are so low that often we have no choice but to take our children to work to supplement the family income.'

Sometimes, as Karimbhai pointed out, a child has no aptitude for studying :

My boy is working in the factory with me. He is thirteen years old. When he failed his exams. I decided to put him to work. My other children are at school. If the boy is not studying, he might as well earn and pay for his own expenses.

But not all parents have this attitude. Savita, who has been working in the potteries for the last ten years, said :

My husband and I feel that we should not put our children to work at a young age. This is the age to play and run about, not to work in factories inhaling clay dust the whole day. We have decided that as long as we can manage, we won't send our children to work.

There are roughly speaking, three categories of children working in the pottery industry. The children of master craftsmen all have to learn the work of moulding clay on the tradition at potter's wheel. But they do this work for a couple of hours in a day after school only because the parents feel that the child should know the technique even if he is later going to be managing the business and not doing the actual work. These children probably help out occasionally when the pressure of work is high but they are not regular workers. The number of children in this category in negligible since there are only two families of traditional potters who are master craftsmen today.

In the second category are children of skilled workers, mainly biharis, who have set up their own units and run these exclusively using family labour. Here are children do not go to school but work full-time with their parents. This category of entrepreneur rarely employs hired labour and works solely with the help of his family. Such working children as described above probably account for about 5 per cent of the total child labour force.

In the third category are children who work full-time in factories doing the jobs described earlier. Occasionally. Whole family is employed because there are small children who can help out with the work. But usually, children work alone. This type of working children accounts for more than 90 per cent of all children in the industry. Children working the potteries of Khurja were by and large illiterate. Many of them had studied up to the fourth standard but could barely read and write. While some children had left school because their parents wanted them to work, many children had failed their examination and the parents had felt that the child did not have an aptitude for studying and had withdrawn him from school.

One noticeable factor was that units producing quality goods did not employ child labour. Or only one or two children were present out of a total labour force of forty of fifty workers. Most of these units had tall racks next to the jigger jolly machines and the same adult worker would stack the phanti with the moulds on it. There was no need for a worker to run with the phanti. These units also came under the Factories Act and the owners said it was not worth their while to employ children when child labour was illegal in factories. Nor were children employed in units making inculators which require certain kind of skills. By and large, children are employed in units making crockery for bulk production.

While adult workers belong to almost all castes and communities, the children were either from Koli. Dhimar of Jatay families-Scheduled Castes or Muslims. I did not come across any children from high-caste families.

Most of the work that children do in the pottery industry can be done by adults as well. In fact in many factories, where children were not being employed, the same work was done by either adolescent boys or adults. But adult workers said :

We don't like this work because it is tiring. The body of the child is supple and can run fast, bend down and get up quickly without any problem. When you are older. It is difficult to do this work.

Factory owners and *thekedars* also said the same thing : 'If an adult is asked to do this work of fetching and carrying. He would take too long. Adults can't move with the speed that children can. It is not work meant for adults.

Wage Structure and the Organization of Work

The wage structure is very flexible in the pottery industry. According to the Status Report on the ceramic industry at 'Khurja :

In the beginning very cheap labour was available at 50-75 paise per day for the skilled workers and 25-50 paise per day for unskilled one. The present wage of a skilled worker ranges from Rs. 300-600 per month while an unskilled worker gets only Rs. 150-300 per month. Jobs are generally done on piece rate basis but the pattern of income remains more or less the same. Cheap child labour is also abundantly available and utilized. Because of the low wages, ceramic industry has found a favourable labour pulled location at Khurja (Bhattacharya, 1982 : 9).

As has been mentioned earlier, there are three types of pottery units. The traditional potters who largely make art ware goods, supply them to boutiques in the major cities of India and to the five-star hotels. Their goods are quality goods and all the skilled work is done by members of their families but not that business has expanded, they do employ other workers mainly painters-who get paid on a job basis and earn upto Rs. 1500 a month. Many the them are art students who have got a BA degree as well. Their other workers earn about Rs. 500 to Rs. 600 a month and children earn on the average Rs. 150-200 a month. Most of the work in these units is not done on contract because here it is important to maintain quality rather than increase quantity.

In the second category are those run mainly by Biharis using family labour and few hired workers. Here the wages normally do not exceed Rs 300-500 a month for adults and less than Rs. 200 for children.

The bulk of labour force is employed in independent units where they work on piece-rate wages. In every factory, there are a few workers who are employed on *amani* (monthly wages). But the majority of the workers are engaged by *thekedars* on piece-rate wages. Even those workers who are working on *amani* for many years are not considered permanent workers and such not entitled to any leave. On days the worker does not come, his wages are cut. In some factories where the workers have able to fight for better conditions of work, the factory owner gives two paid holidays in a month. But in most factories this is not the practice and workers work seven days week without a break.

Since most of the worker are employed by the *thekedars*, the factory owner does not consider himself responsible for the workers. Many workers said that *thekedars* sometimes did not pay wages on time because they said the factory owner had not paid them or for some other reason. The *thekedars* some-factories cut the wages of the workers as commission. In most factories, a skilled worker earned not more than Rs. 400 a month and unskilled workers less than Rs. 200 a month.

Many workers interviewed said that wages in the pottery industry were low because of the large influx of Bihari migrant labour. One worker said:

Most of these people belong to Gaya or Nayada districts of Bihar. For them, it is impossible to earn even Rs. 200 a month at home. When they are happy with their wages, then who is going to raise our wages?

Another Adult Worker, Mahabir Ram, Said:

The factory owners know how to exploit these Biharis. They offer them space in the factories to stay and coal to cook their food on. The Biharis are quite happy even though they get paid almost a hundred rupees less then the local adult workers for the same job.

Shafeeq, Age Forty, Said :

These people work overtime without wages as a sign or gratitude to their employers. That is why they are employed.

Different categories of workers were paid different wages. Some firemen said they were paid Rs. 600: others said they were earning Rs. 1100. Those earning monthly salaries earned more than those workers who were engaged by *thekedars*. Hardly any of the children interviewed earned more than Rs. 150 a month for an eight-hour day.

Kalu Ram, allow twelve, commuted daily from Dharaon, a village near Khurja. He started working five or six years ago at a daily wage of Rs. 5 a day. Today, he earns Rs. 8 a day as a *phantiwala*. He is the sole supporter of his family of five brothers and sisters and an ailing mother. If he works theiry days in a months, he earns Rs. 150 month.

Vijay Pal and Hira Singh, mentioned earlier, earn Rs. 180 a month if they work thirty days in a month and don't take any time off. They also work as *phantiwalas*. Laxmi Das and his eight-year old brother earn Rs. 150 a month and between the two of them support a seven-member family.

In one unit I visited, one women with three children between the ages of eight and ten was able to earn Rs. 12 in an eight-hour day after finishing 1000 mugs.

By and large, the wages were as follows: the *amani* workers doing Katai (wire on the jigger jolly machine) got Rs 500 a month, *phantiwales*, if children, earned approximately Rs. 150 a month but if they were older, they earned up to Rs. 300 a month: those who fixed handles earned up to Rs. 500: those who did finishing got Rs. 300 a month. The workers who did finishing got Rs. 300 a month. The workers who did glazing received Rs. 400 a month. The workers on *theka* (contract) could earn as much in a month, they had to work twice as hard. Even the monthly wage workers had to complete a certain amout or work every day: othewise, their salaries were cut but their work-load was not as heavy as that of contract labour.

In one factory, the workers told me me that for scraping and water finishing the mugs, they got paid Rs. 11 for 1000 pieces. Two people together could finish 2000 pieces on a day. Usually an adult would team up with a child and together they would do the work. It seemed that even individual workers tried to exploit children by making them work hard and then keeping a part of their wages for themselves as commission. This way, the adult worker could take it a little easy because the child would work harder. On contract labour, those who cut the handles earned approximately Rs. 200 a month and those who jointed the handless earned Rs. 400 a month. To earn this much, the man had to work at break-neck speed and cut and fix 4000 pieces in eight hours.

Factory owners justifies the use of contract labour thus:

Workers on salaries become very lazy. An *amani* worker will cut only 2000 pieces on the jigger whereas the contract worker will cut 4000 pieces in eight hours. If you want production and increased profits, you cannot have salaried employees.

Ramesh, a Work Supervisor, Said :

These *Maaliks* (owners) are clever people. They want profit without responsibilty for the workers. They is why 90 per cent of the work is done through *thekedars*. The factory owner then does not feel anyu responsibility for the labour. He fixes a rate with the *thekedars* and it is the responsibility of the *thekedars* to pay the labour.

The bulk of the work is done through sub-contracting though the work is all done in the factory premises. The general pattern is the factory owner has a few adult workers on what is called amani or a monthly gone. They supervise the work of the *thekedar* and maintain quality. In some of the thekedar also helped out and thus saved on one adult's wage, the *thekedar* also helped out and thus saved on one adult's wage. It was the dream of every adult worker to because a *thekedar*. All the workers working under the *thekedar* were paid piece-rate wages. Since they were daily wages workers, no labour laws applied do them.

An interesting fact I observed was that worker who had started very young and worked for fifteen or twenty years earned exactly the same amout as the new adult entrants. The reason for this state of affairs. I was told was:

If you start working young mentality changes and you lose all purpose in life except to carry on with whatever you get. There is no fight left in you so you don't ask for your just dues. That's why employers prefer children. Also, you have to be really desperate in the first place to start work so young and the spirit is beaten out of you by the time you are an adult. Those who start working as adults earn more than those who started off as children.

Health Hazards

In England in the nineteenth-century, writes Karl Marx, the pottery industries were amongst the hazardous for the health of the workers. The Children's Employment Commission Report of 1863 drew attention to the kinds of health hazards faced by workers in the potteries of Stoke-of-Trent and Wolstanton. Marx, using the reports of the public health committees, has this to say:

Dr. Greenhow states that the average life-expectancy in the pottery districts of Stoke-on-Trent and Wolstanton is extraordinarily law. Although only 36.6 per cent in the potteries in the district of Stoke, and 30.4 per cent in Wolstanton, more than half the death among men of that age in the result of pulmonary diseases among the potters. Dr. Boothroyed, a medical practitioner at Hanley, say: Each successive generation of potters is more dwarfed and less robust than the proceeding one. 'Similarly another doctor. Mr McBean states: 'Since I began to practice among the potters 25 years ago. I have observed a marked degeneration, especially shown in diminutions of stature and breadth'. These statements are taken from Dr. Greenhow's Report of 1860 (Marx [1867] 1982).

Futher he writes:

Dr. J. T. Arledge, senior physician of the North Staffordshire Infirmary, says: 'The potters as a class, both men and women, represent a degenerated population, both physically and morally. They are, as a rule, stunted in growth, ill-shaped, and frequently ill-formed in the chest: they become prematurely old, and are certaily short-lived: they are phlegmatic and bloodless, and exhibit their debility of constitution by obstinate attacks of dyspepsia, and disorders of the liver and kidney, and by rhenumatism, to pneumonia, phthisis, bronchitis and asthma. One form would appear peculiar to them, and is known as potter's asthma, or potter's consumption.

While it may seem as if the work of *uthai rakhai* is not apparently hazardous because it is merely carrying pots from one place to another it is the total environment which makes the industry hazardous. According to Dr. N. C. Saxena, the Hospital Superintendent at the local Khurja hospital, most potters who come to the hospital at the local Khurja hospital, most potters who come to the hospital had asthmatic bronchitis, which then became tuberculosis. Out of 300 tuberculosis patients registered ast the hospital for regular care, 70 per cent were ptters. In his own experience of two years, there have been four of five patients with silicosis. Accoding to Dr Saxena: four or five patients with silicosis. According to Dr. Saxena:

If we have got 300 patients in our hospital, there would be another 700 patients being greated outside by private practitioners and quackes. But most of the patients must be going undiagnosed. There are at least two or three patients with asthmatic bronchitis in every pottery. The children working in potteries suffer from extra pulmonary tuberculosis and out of every ten, one has pulmonary tuberculosis.

Dr. Saxena has been trained to indentify silocosis but most of the local doctors treat as tuberculosis. Silicosis is a pulmonary fibrosis coused by the inhalation of dust containing free silica. It is the most common and severe of all pneumoconoisis. It is basically a nodular fibrosis of the lungs. The lungs' vital capaicity is reduced and the patient dies. There is no cure for silicosis which has now been identified as an occupational disease.

Dr. Masood Ahmed runs a clinic in the centre of the town. Most of his patients are potters. He gets on the average twenty-five or thirty adult potters a day and an equal number of children. The most common complaint of his patients is asthmatic bronchitis and pulmonary tuberculosis. Out of 200 patients he had recently examined, 75 per cent were potters and 87.5 per cent of them had pulmonary tuberculosis, bronchitis and asthma. According to him:

By the time the potter is thirty to thirty-five years old, the upper respiratory infection has gone into the third stage. By the age of forty of forty-five, the man dies. Most of the workers are too poor to take treatment. Many for them do not get paid regularly. We advice rest but that is impossible for them.

According to the International Labour Organization Encyclopedia on Occupational Health and Safety (Parmeggiani) 1983, the silicosis hazard is encountered in a wide variety of occupations including the manufacture of pottery, porcelain, refractory materials, etc. 'Cough with sputum, is an indication of bronchitis, and chronic bronchitis is frequntly associated with advanced silicosis. The three main complications of silicosis are also the most frequent causes of death and those are pulmonary tuberculosis, respiratory insuficiency and acute pulmonary infection. According to the above-mentioned encyclopedia:

Pulmonary tuberculosis is, even today, still the cause of death in a quarter of cases, and is the most request complication. It has recently been proved that tubercle bacilli grow and mulitply for more actively in macroplages that have phagocytised silica particles than in those that have not done so, perhaps because the former have suffered a lose of vitality and are no longer capable of destroying the tubercle bacilli.

There are specific hazards in the pottery industry. According to same encyclopedia; 'Ball clay contains up to 50% free silica and so presnets a potential hazard to sliphouse workers handling raw clay'.

Further, it is stated:

The major heath hazard is pneumoconiosis, which results from the prolonged inhalation of siliceous dust within the respirable size range, that is, particles up to about 7 microm in diameter. The risk arises from the combination of materials and methods and is proportional to the percentage of free silica in the inhaled dust: in gerneral, it is confined to the pre-firing processes.

These are not the only health hazards faced by workers but these are the most common ones. Workers who as firemen at the kiln, lose their eyesight. I was told, by the age of about forty-five or so. Their main job is to stoke the fire and to periodically remove samples of pottery to check whether they have been properly baked, as workers said: '*Ankhon ko aach lag jati hai*' (the eyes get affected by the heat). Those who work on the ball machines become deaf after some time. Children complained of frequent caughs and colds. The main reason, as one child told me, was: '*Selkhari se nazla ho jata hai*' (soap dust causes cold.) Most of the workers who were affected by silicosis were those working on disintegrators. These were machines used to powder the broken saggar for re-use. In fact, most factories had this process not in their main area but outside because of the dust that flew out. But operators of the machines were affected.

When workers interviwed in the factories, they said that the work was not hazardous. Part of the reason for this is that colds and coughs are not considered illnesses and no one wants to admit that they have tuberculosis. In fact, local doctors said they had no idea what happened to many of their patients as the minute a person heard that he had T.B.. he would rerely come back to them. Most doctors, therefore, in order to keep their custom did not tell the patient that he suffered from T. B. but gave him whatever reflief they could give.

Workers in Sondha village said that it was not uncommon to hear about accidental deaths in potteries. The main explanation offered was bad house-keeping on the part of the factory owners. A young adolescent, Birpal, recently died in a factory because the belts which rotate the grinding machines and he was trapped. Birpal's family was of course not compensated. Some workers said: '*Bachaon ko slip ke tank me bhej deta hein. Kai bacche thandi se behosh ho jate hein*' (They put children into the slip tanks and some children become unconscious because of the extreme cold.)

This was varified by Dr. Ahmed as well who told me that one of his patients had even gone into a coma because of this experience. Others workers in the village said that often working for some years in the potteries: '*Dum ghut jaata hai*' (One starts suffocating).

While there is substantial documentary evidence that pottery is hazardous work because of the large-scale use of silica which is one of the essential raw materials used, most workers interviewed at the factories did not complain of any health problems. Cold and caugh and slight breathing difficulties were common but were not taken serioulsy by the workers themselves. It seems that not all worker in the pottery industry are exposed to health hazards because many are working with wet clay so there is a minimum of dust in the air. However, those workers directly grinding the raw material would be the most affected. This is also a relatively new industry and the impact of the working conditions on the health of workers may only manifest itself at a later stage.

Labour Laws and Their Implementation

Under the Factories Act of 1948, which also applies to Uttar Pradesh, a factory means any premises where ten or more workers are working, or were working on any day of the preceding twelve months, and where in any part of which a manufacturing process is being carried out with the aid of power. If any manufacturing unit has more then ten workers, they are supposed to provide certain facilites to their employees such as rest-room, drinking water facilities, toilet, etc. Workers are not supposed to be employed beyond a certain number of hours a week without being paid overtime. There is a strict ban on the employment of children in factories under the age of fourteen years.

In order to evade the Factories Act, 90 per cent of the units show that they have less than nine workers. In some factories I visited, I noticed around fifty workers. But when I asked the employer, he said there were only eight people working there! In every singly factory I visited, there were over twenty workers employed and the factory owners made no bones about the fact that they were breaking the law. As one factory owner said:

If there are more than nine worker, then we come under the purview of the Factory Act. This a nuisance because we have to give bonus and provide employees medical insurance. ets. That is why we show fewer workers. But this was an isolated response. Every single factory owner in Khurja I interviewed me the same thing. Workers felt bitterily about it and said: 'Factory insepectors come. Labour inspectors come. They take money and go away. Who cares about labour?

Every where talked to workers, the story was the same. Some worker said that one of the reasons why the industry was listed as cottage and small-scale industry was because this sector was exampt form duty. One worker said:

The factory owners make twice as much as they show in books. All of them have two books. This way they have double benefit. They claim that there are only nine worker so that they do not come under the purview of the Factories Act. But you must have seen that this is a lie. There is no job security here and that is why there is so much child labour. Everyone in Khurja-workers, employers, contractors and traders-were aware that under the Factores Act, child labour is expressly forbidden. When I first visisted Khurja and talked to people, everyone denied that child labour existed. But when I showed them photographs of working children, they said that the reason for their denial was because there was a ban on the employment of children under the Factories Act.

Many factory owners expressed the view that the main reason that there was no progress in the country was that there were labour laws. One factory onwer said: 'You can either have production or you can look after the welfare of workers. Isn't it enough that we people are giving the poor employment? Why do we need laws to protect them as well?

Soon after this study was published in a local newspaper, there were questions in Parliament. The reply of the then Minister for labour was that it was the State Government's responsibility to enforce the Factories Act and the Child Labour (Prohibition and Regulation) Act, 1986. He admitted in Parliament that although the Labour Ministry had received an unofficial report (mine) about child labour in the pottery industry of Khurja, the State Government maintained there was not a single case of child labour to be found in this industry! (Times of India, 26 March 1988). When the author took up the matter in the press, the Minister admitted that the Central Government was surprised at the report they had received from the State Government that although forty-one inspections had been carried out and twenty-four people prosecuted, there was not by single of child labour in the pottery industry (Times of India, 12 April, 1988).

What seems clear from this brief study is that child labour is a fairly new phenomenon in the pottery industry of Khurja largely because of the need to mass-produce goods of low cost. The traditional Khurja potter did not have a very large market and therefore did not need children. Children only worked as part of apprenticeship training and long with getting regular education.

But with changing technology and the use of moulds, it became possible for such people to enter the pottery industry as had no background of pottery. It was also possible then to hire unskilled labour to do jobs which hitherto required specialized skills- e.g. the technique of moulding clay on the potter's wheel. Once the new technology came in, the demand for the goods grew along with an easy availability of cheap labour and this made Khurja a well-known pottery centre. The changes in the pottery industry also come at a time when in the rural areas mechanization of agriculture, the introduction of electricity and better technology created a class of rural enemployed youth who could not find sustenance in the villages. They flocked to the town for work and the only employment available was in the potteries. The local towns people found that the wages were so low that most of them tried to seek work outside. It was only when they found it impossible to get other work that they continued in the potteries.

Thus amongst the adults, the local people try to find work outside Khurja, prefereable in big citiecs while Bihari and eastern Uttar Pradesh migrants leave their homes in large numbers in search of work and a livelihood and some end up here. It is because of a combination of factors that wages and conditions or work in the pottery industry are so bad. Low wages has meant in turn that families have to send their children-out ot work in order to sustain the family.

Obviously, the children who need help are economically and socially from the lowest strata of society. They are the most vulnerable to exploitation and are in fact working like machines for the profit of others. None of the work they do is of the type that leads to the acquiring of skills which may lead to better prospects and can thus be justifies. If anything, the wages paid to adults who had started working as children are a little less than those who do the same work but entered the work-force at a later stage.

The conditions of most factories in Khurja are not so different from those described by Marx obtaining in the potteries of nineteenth-century England. In faft, Marx has been frequently catied in this study in order to draw attention to what is likely to happen to potters in another or one or two generations. The pottery industry of Khurja that employs child labour is relatively new and some of its ill-effects may not be noticed expect in a later generation. But the reports from England in the nineteenth-century need to be taken seriously in order to prevent the same kind of consequences!

The pottery industry does not need child labour except as a source of cheap labour. Compulsory education strict child labour laws will go a long way to remove child labour from the pottery industry in India as has been the case in England and Japan. There is nothing a child can do that cannot be done by an adult. But the children who come to work do so because of object poverty. The only solution is to provide them with free, stipendiary primary education and find alternative employment opportunities for their unemployed or under-employed parents. There are laws against employing children in factories which need to be strictly implemented and employers employing children strictly penalized. The industry will not collapse if children are withdrawn from the work-force. It will only provide more work opportunities for adults.

11

TRADITIONAL CRAFTS AND CHILD LABOUR

There is an old and popular belief that certain craft-oriented industries would die out and the skills be lost permnently if child labour was to be banned. The picture painted is one where traditional occupations pass on from father to son, generation to generation. That picture does not fit the facts any longer. While it is true that there are still artisans in a few crafts who earn their living with the help of family labour and cater to the needs of local markets, they are not representative. In many traditional industires, the artisan has been displaced either wholly or in large measure by the entrepreneur and the trader/financier. The artisan who would buy his raw materials, process them and then sell them-functioning more or less as an autonomous producer with some interest in small-scale agriculture-has been adversely affected by industrialization, the injection of capital and the growth of the new markets. Skills previoulsy the preserve of a few families are now widely available in the labour market because of state sponsored training programmes which cover many industries. Morever, new artisan has been transformed into a factory worker by the large-scale nature of production.

Consider, for example, the case of the carpet industry of Mirzapur-Bhadohi-Varanasi in Uttar Pradesh. Eighty per cent of the carpet production in India takes place in that belt and is primarily export-oriented. The industry employs 200,000 workers, of whom 150,000 are children, not counting those working as part of family labour (Juyal, 1987:27). Juyal observes that traditionally most of the weavers came from low peasant groups like the Binds. These groups were small or merginal owner-cultivators and combined weaving with agriculture, more so because the looms remained idle for long intervals and did not provide regular employment... Weaving with agriculture, more so because the looms remained idle for long intervals and did not provide regular employment... Weaving is, by and large, still a supplementary occupation for the small cultivation class.

The growth and potential of the industry led to major structural changes. Juyal points out that:
...some new leaders (like the Mishras, Dubes, Rajputs, etc have sprung up. They are all from the dominant castes in the agraian structure of the region, with the dominant castes in the agrarian structure of the ragion, with no background of trade, commerce, industry or artisan ship.

As a result, Juyal goes on to observe:

Thus, far from being an industry of self-employed weavers, there has been increasing concentration of ownership of looms in the no-artisan class. The looms may be placed together in factory-like sheds or in domestic premises, or even in the cottages of the weavers on a dispersed basis. But the fact remains that the emergence of this non-artisan owner class is, in fact, a major contributory factor to the migrant-capative type drafted from outside the village of locality (ibid: 11).

As regards the imparting or skills, the rapid expansion of the industry was largely a result of the 600 carpet-weaving training centres that were set up by the Government of India, and which annually trained about 30,000 child weavers. The Government of Uttar Pradesh contended that carpets woven by the 'nimble fingers' of children were of superior quality to other (GOUP 1986b:2). V. R. Sharma, a carpet manufacturer, admitted in an unusually frank interview:

It is a myth that child labour is essential and the children are capable of weaving better carpets than adults. The carpet manufacturers would have no objection whatsoever if children are being employed to heap their families (*Indian Express*, 16 June 1987).

According to this prominent employer's perspective, the skills related to carpet-weaving could be passed on to others in training programmes.

I have already noted earlier how the traditional potters of Khurja run only twenty-five establishments today as against 300 run by rank ousider: in the pottery industry as well, government organized training programmes have helped the growth of the industry. Where it expanded because of an increased demand, new recruits were helped by government training programmes, as in the case of the carpet and gem-polishing industries. In the lock industry where the village artisan is still visible, factories account for the major share of production and the social back-ground of factory owners-largely Punjabi Hindus—is quite different from that of the traditional Muslim craftsmen.

Sivakasi, in the State of Tamil Nadu, is the home of the match industry and employs 45,000 children. A study conducted for the Government of India by the Madras Institute of Development Studies (MIDS) has this to say about the reasons for child labour:

Although the 'nimble fingers' argument is widely accepted even by those who otherwise are opposed to child labour, the study indicates that there is not truth to it. Examination of the seventeen processes in match manufacture shows that children are employed in all twelve of the piece rated or contracted operations.... The major operations of frame-filling, box-filling and labeling and band-rolling are, of course, the principal employment generators. These are all simple tasks requiring a speed of movement and co-ordination of action but no special aptitude, which children might possibly have, and adults lose. In fact, not only were adults employed in all these sixteen operations, but they outnumbered children in the surveyed units and most crucially, their model rate or physical production was more than that of children. There is no reason, therefore, to accept the 'nimble fingers' 'argument either on the grounds of adults' inability to work or due their allegedly lower pace of work (MIDS, 1985: 54).

It is a common myth in Ferozabad that glass bangle-making and glass-blowing are hereditary occupations and therefore children should work so that this ancient craft is not lost. But skilled workers denied this. According to them the glass industry was only sixty to seventy years old. They pointed out that earlier most of the craftmen were Muslims and now a large percentage belonged to the Hindu community. The workers said that the myth of a hereditary occupation was important in justifying child labour on the grounds that if children were not to work, the art would be lost. Even the work of a *taarkash* (the man who threads hot glass onto a rolling pin) can be learnt by paying him a fee. This is, however, not to say that a *taarkash* will not teach his child if he wants to learn. But there is nothing inherited about these skills, and are not confined to perticular families.

The argument regarding hereditary occupations does not pass muster in the brass ware industry either. I have already referred to the findings of a study (IDS, 1983: 29) to the effect that whereas 66 per cent of workers were self-employed in 1959-60, that proportion fell to less than 1 per cent by 1974. Here again the migration of traditional Muslim craftsmen to Pakistan at the time of the Partition of India and the reverse flow of Punjabi entrepreneurs with their capital, the changes in international demand and the new technology it called for toghther led to the transformation of a household or cottage industry to one where the factory and the workshop became dominant and wage about became the norm. In order to seek protection of law, an image is still projected of the industry as retaining its household or cottage character.

Child Labour and Adult Unemployment

A recently study done by the Inter-disciplinary group of the Aligarh Muslim University (AMU) revealed that while there is a demand for child labour, there is also high adult unemployment and under-employment. This study was concentrated in thirty *mohallas* (residential localities) of the Upper Kote areas where 46 per cent of the Muslim population was engaged in lock manufacture. The sample used was rather large. They did a preliminary house-listing of 4166 household with a total Muslim population of 24,657. Later, an in-depth study was done on 562 households, i.e. 5 per cent of the total number of households listed in the area by the Aligarh Municipal Board. In the course of this study, it was observed that:...There are many children who are earning and many adults who are not able to find remunerative work (AMU n.d. : 20).

It is stated emphatically in the draft report of this study on Muslim entrepreneous that adult workers are not fully employed. The average number of days in the year that employment was possible was 264 days. Those artisans:.... Who are able to get work for eight to nine months a year regard themselves as fully engaged. A lock assembly worker feels himself fortunate if he gets work for the fourth day in a week (ibid : 52).

This study defined permanent workers as those who were working for more than 180 days in a year. Temporary workers were those who were busy for at least 160 days and casual workers were those who had worked for less than ninety days in the previous year. It was found that:

Even the so-called permanently employed artisans unemployed for more than three months, whereas others are unemployed for periods longer than 105 days, ranging from six to nine months. Thus the state of underemployment of labour is true for all the artisans, more for some and less for the others (ibid).

It was also found that:... The number of hours worked are highest 11.94 for the lowest income stratum earning less than Rs. 500 p. m.

I have already noted in the case study on the glass industry of Ferozabad how the black marketing of coal yields large profits and thereby permits factory owners to shut down their operations for several months in the year, a situation then is deliberately engineered in which workers are laid off for long periods of time leading to sever uemployment. Even when the factories of time leading to servere unemployment and workers are frequently and arbitrarily thrown out. In view of large-scale unemployment there are always fresh recruits to take the place of those whose services are terminated. The large-scale unemployment there are always fresh recruits to take the place of those whose services are terminated. The large-scale employment of children can be attributed to the savings on account of wage cost, increased productivity and the greater docility and vulnerability of children at the hands of employers.

In the carpet industry, Juyal says there is evidence that child labour is enhancing unemployment and underemployment of the adults. Within the industry, they not only seem to displace adult workers but also depress the incomes of adults doing similar work (Juyal, 1987 : 33).

Vishwarpriya Iyengar, on a visit to Sivakasi interviewed both parents and children, writes about Chinnadorai and his young ten year old brother Devraj, who work at match factory in Kalgumali, Says Iyengar:

Kadaval, their father, told me about Devraj. Like the others he too works ten to fourteen hours a days for Rs. 4 to 5... Returning from the factory he falls asleep without being able to eat any dinner. His legs ache and he has to drug himself to walk. His eves smart without enough sleep and his chest is congest all the time.... Every morning at 2.30 a. m. he is killing me. It is too difficult for me. Please let me stay at home. The mother shakes the child awake. Your father has no work. We have to work. There is no-other life for us. 'Kadaval feels helpless watching this day after day... (Iyengar, 1986a).

In the carpet industry or Kashmir, writes Suraj Gupta, 100,000 children of school-going age are working, Gupta reports:

One Bashir Ahmed Batt whose two sons, ages twelve and ten, have taken to carpet (weaving) has this to say: 'Can you beat it that the owners and the management refused to give me a job? They openly say that they young children suit them better, Why? Low wages are the chief reason', replies. To cap that, children are not the ones who would grumble against the bad working conditions or organize a protest rally' (Gupta, 1985).

In industries like the pottery industry of Khurja and the brass ware industry of Moradabad, there is tremendous demand for labour to the extent that factory owners have started hiring Bihari migrant labour but there is also adult unemployment amongst local people. The preference was for Bihari migrant workers because they would stay away from work during peak agricultural seasons and city labour was thought to be arrogant. But in all units except for the very big factories using modern techology, child labour was the preferred form of labour even when adults were unemployed.

Some might argue that if child workers were not employed the production would discontinue, but given the low wages of adults, that argument has little appeal. It seems a clear case of the substitution of children for adults, on grounds of cost and ease of control.

The Vested Interest in Child Labour

Definding Child Labour: The Industry's Viewpoint

As described earlier, there is virtually no control over hours of work, the conditions of work are appalling and the wages paid are meager and well below a living wage in most of the case studies dscribed in detail earlier. The prevelanece of a high rate of adult unemployment goes hand in hand with an impressive demand for child labour. The obvious explanation for this phenomenon is that children are a source of cheap labour and can be exploited in ways that adults may not accept. Yet, child labour is sought to be justified by the unit owners on the grounds that if the children of the poor did not work, they would starve.

Recently, the premises of some lock-manufactureers who employ children were raided: this resulted in a furore and factory, owners were up in arms. The Lock Times, a journal published by the All India Lock Manufacturers Association (AILMA). Aligarh published an editorial titled 'Aparadhi Kaun?' or 'Who are the guilty?' In his editorial, Ramesh Arora, the General Secretary of AILMA, said that the blame for the existence of child rest upon the Government which has not been able to implement Article 45 of the Constitution of India which states that all children below the age of fourteen years shall be given free, compulsory, primary education within ten years of the commencement of Constitution.

Arora's self-serving argument portrays factory owners as saints who come to the rescue of desperate parents mired in poverty. In his version of reality, compassion for the children on the verge of death and disaster compels factory owners to employ them even if it is against the law. Government officials emerge as heartless enforcers of labour Legislation who penalize factory owners for their humane works (Arora, 1986).

By the large, factory owners and smaller *karkhana* owners were aware that child labour is illegal. They justify the employment of children with much the same arguments as the editorial cited above. At best, the justification is partial: if poverty is one side of the coin, then the profits of manufaturers is the other.

V. R. Sharma, the carpet manufacturer, contradicted himself first by saying that child labour was essential because otherwise the wage cost would go up by 50 per cent and later by saying that:

The employment of children in the carpet.. industry is necessitated not because of the requirements of the industry but because of the needs of the concerned children and their families (Sharma, 1985+).

Simply put, employers prefer child labor because it is cheaper than adult labour and because children, unlike adults, cannot question the treatment meted out to them. Evidence indicates that the child's wage in any industry is a third to a half that of an adult for the same output, with the child working half that of an adult for the same output, with the child working for as many, if not more, hours than the adult. Socialized into work at an early age, the child works without pause: an adult would balk at the monotony of the tasks performed. We saw would balk at the monotony of the tasks performed. We saw earlier, how children in some industries are bonded, offering virtually 'free, labour and how in others with an apprenticeship scheme, they are not paid for months or even years.

The greater amenability of children to exploitation is succintly described in a conclusion from a study of the match industry.

Docility may create long-term economic advantages in that children are more likely to undertake unpaid work slipped in between piece-rated jobs, thefts of meterial and wastage which are elemental forms of protest may be smaller, and deductions from wages of fines and 'donations' by more feasible. However, the non-enonomic advantages are probably greater. Docile workers will not protest if they are used like instruments of production, moved from operation to operation as the demands of the manufacturing process dictate. They will work as long as the management requires, particularly when they are on piece-rated occupations. Most important of all, they will not have the capability and experience to organize mass protests against wages and working conditions, even though their knowledge of their situation may be acute (MIDS, 1985).

Smitu Kothari was told by a foreman at the Standard Fireworks Factory in Tayyalpatti village that 'we prefer child workers. They work fast, work longer hours and are dependable (Kothari, 1983c).

There are definite economic advantages in employing children in the match industry although there is server adult unemployment in that area. Indicative of that, when the Tamil Nadu government threatened to implement the ban on child labour, the owners of match and fireworks factories protested vociferously. The Secretary of the All India Chamber of Match prohibited, the factory owners would go in for mechanization or deversification of business (Financial Express. 17 October 1983). He added that the opponents of child labour were being financed by a multinational firm, the chief competitor of the Sivakasi match units, which together hold 30-35 per cent of the market. He contended that there was to alternative to child labour as there was an acute shortage of labour in and around Sivakasi. He also argued that if the children were sent away from the factories they would beg in the streets.

There are other factors which need to be kept in mind when discussing the need for child labour by employers in the match industry. According to the Madras Institute of Development Studies report, factory owners employ 'pannaiyal' or bonded labour, where whole families are working for the employers in a condition of slavery. As the report concluded. 'The open admission of this practice provides evidence for the pre-industrial nature of employer-employee relations in the area and has its effect on industrial relations in the match industry (MIDS, 1985). The second machanism for controlling the labour force is the provision of housing for workers.

The report point out that those households which had a large number of women and children were preferred in the allocation of housing and also that if production targets were not, the families faced eviction. The conclusion drawn is that the aim of such measures was less to provide welfare than to ensure control.

It must be noted here that children are harded into factory buses at 2 a. m. and return from work after dusk (Area Development Programme Report n. d.). The age of the youngest child found working by *Kothari* was three and a half years! (Kothari, 1983c).

Thus, as the MIDS Report Points Out :

> The curx of the problem of the child labour is... the conditions of the households providing child labour. Not only are they poor, their sources of income are unstable and the income itself fluctuates. They are dependent on agricultural wage work in an area of low agricultural potential. Most important of all, they find themselves unorganized in a situation where the manufacturers are organized, they are in a social millieu where the employer has almost unlimited right, now found only in the most backward parts of the country. And finally, residents of their own village are liable to report on any action they may take to change the conditions in which they and their children are forced to work (MIDS 1985).

The match industry is controlled by the powerful Nadar lobby. Kothari points to the fact that the eleven families of Sivakhasi and Kovilpatti are responsible for over 70 per cent of the production in the non-mechanized sector and together, their output is more than of the mechanized sector (Kothari, 1983).

Similarly, although there are 200 fireworks factories in the Sivakasi area the distribution of production again favour the Nadars: five of whom (with more than Rs. 50 million). A few others have a turnover of over Rs. 5 million.

The carpet industry is another major industry where there is vested interest in keeping child labour. When the Government of India introduced the idea of leaving a cess on employers of child labour, the carpet industry was alarmed. The Carpet Council News, which is a monthly published by the Carpets Export Promotion Council, frackly admitted in its September 1986 issue that the intended comprehensive legislation on child labour would decrease production and increase costs and that the aim was to prevent such legislation form going through (Chadha, 1986).

V. R. Sharma. a large-scale manufacture, wrote in 1985 that the major cost in the production of carpets was the labour cost. He argued that if the government were to try to bring this industry under protective labour laws and impose a cess on employers of child labour, it would be disastrous for the industry. He noted that a major part of the work in the said that such legislation would bring an end to the flexibilty that existed. That wages would rise by at least 50 per cent and that consequently the industry would close. He also felt that such legislation, besides being impossible to implement would increase corruption amongst the labour laws enforcement staff. He concluded that irreversible demage would be done and the result would be to have killed the hen that lays the golden eggs (Sharma, 1985). Needless to say, the much discusses cess that the government was intending to impose was not included in the new Child Labour Act.

The glass, lock, carpet and match industries are not the only industries that have a vested interest in child labour, Venkatramani reports from Coimbatore, where more than half the cotton hosiery in the country is produced, that Tirupper's 200-odd hosiery units have an annual turnover of Rs. 900 million and an export turnover of Rs. 280 million. Tiruppur shares the hosiery market with Calcutta. However, Tiruppur's hosiery in 2 or 3 per cent cheaper than Calcutta's and the main reason for this, as explained by T. V. Ratnam, Director of the South India Textile Reserch Association, Coimbatore, is that: 'labour is only 10 per cent of the total production cost in the hosiery industry. But the employment of child labour gives Tiruppur an edge over Calcutta in terms of costs (Venkatramani, 1983). Factory owners do not deny using children.

Child labour may be illegal, but what can we do? asked Mohan P. Kandaswamy, President of the South India Hosiery Manufacturers' Association.... From the drought-hit villages surrounding Tiruppur, children continuously flock to the town, literally beggin for work. And we are also in dire need of labour.

B. N. Juyal, writing about the silk textile industry of Varanasi, cites the admission of some employers that the entire industry would be in serious trouble but for the continued availability of child labour (Juyal et al 1985).

It will thus be seen that in a wide range of industries, employers are willing to admit the economic value of children to their industries. While one can understand and even sympathize with the need of poor parents to place an economic value upon their children, it is utterly reprehensible that in the eyes of their employers, the value of children lies primarily in the cheapness of their labour.

12

CHILD LABOUR IN CHIKAN INDUSTRY

Chiken Industry is a totally Rome-based indusry. It has been seen that the Chiken embroidery is basically done at home by the female member of the household. Because of the strict *purdah* system observed in the families which are predominatly Muslims, none of the female chiken workers gets out of his/her house and consequently know little about the outside world. As a result of this, the employers exploit these workers extensively and pay them very low wages. This accrues a very large profit for the employers, and also middlemen are able to make a neat sum of money.

Summarily it can be said that the unoganised nature of the Chiken Industry leaves a lot of room for exploitation of the workers by the employers and the middlemen. Thus, there is a need to organise these women and children workers, supported by legislations regarding minimum wages and honourable working conditions.

The home-based workers should be brought under the purview of various Labour Laws. The legislators, administrators ane social workers should bear in mind that amelioration of the socio-economic condition of these home based workers should be accorded top most priority while enacting or emplementing any legislation for regulating the working and living conditions of Chiken Workers.

The National Commission on labour has not been able to define 'this unoganised sector' but describes it as an assignment of conditions which have not helped organisation in present economic objective because of certain constraints such as the following:

(a) Casual nature employment.
(b) Igronance and Illiteracy,
(c) Small size of establishment with low capital investment per person employed,
(d) Scattered nature of establishments.
(e) Superior strength of the employers operating singularly or in combination.

The Commission has also given the types of child worker who have been engaged in the unorganised sector. These types are the following:

1. Contract Labour including constitution workers.
2. Casual Labour.
3. Labour employed in small scale industry.
4. Handloom/Powerloom Industry.
5. Bidi and Cigar workers.
6. Employees in shops and commercial establishments.

7. Sweepers and scavengers.
8. Workers in tanneries.
9. Tribal labour.
10. Other improtected labour.

The illustration noted above points out that the Chikan Industry has all the characteristics of an unorganised industry. Most of the workers that are employed there-whether they are adults or children, man or women—are found completely illiterate and ignorant and also there is low capital per investment per work. The workers are always exploited. Thus we can safely assume that the Chikan Industry should be placed under the unorganised Sector or industries employing child workers.

It has been seen that "Chikan" embroidery is just like a shining feather in the artistic cap of Lucknow.

The art of Chikan Embroidery was mostly confined within the walls of old localities of Lucknow but later on, it stretched within a radium of about 100 km from North to South. West to East of Lucknow. About 50.000 to 60.000 people are engaged in this art and it has become a profession of the members of the Muslim families and it is passing from generation to generation.

Saleha Khatoon

(Recipient of National Award) Development Training Centre, Government of India, 482/24, Nai Basti, Iradat Nagar, Deliganj, Lucknow.

Even Saleha Khatoon belongs to the traditional family where Chilkan Embroidery is in the blood. One of her table covers was chosen for National Award in 1982. After that she got aid form the Government and opened a Training Centre for children in her house only in 1983 but due to insufficient aid from Government she had to closs down the centre in 1987. Now all the workers are engaged in their respective homes and get the orders from—

UPICA HANDICRAFTS,
89, Crowngate Chock.
Lucknow.

From the area of kaliganj, 50 children were selected from amongst who were working in their homes.

Sex Composition

The following Table shows the sex-wise distribution of respondents in the sample selected for study.

Table 1 : Showing sex composition of the respodents

Sex	No. of respondents	Percentage
Males	2	4
Females	48	96
Total	50	100

The Table shows that 96 per cent of the respondents are females. It proves that embroidery is basically done by females who do a better job then males and it does not usually attract males as the Zardoji industry does because of low wages.

Generally girls only do this because they are not allowed to go out of the house after they cross certain age and they have to observe purdah because of their Muslim background their parents feel that if the girls are going to star at home, they must do some job contribute to the family income.

Age Composition

While selecting the children for survey, the only consideration was that the child selected for the survey should be below the age of fourteen years as per the difinition of the child given by the Child Labour (Prohibition and Regulation) Act, 1986.

The following Table shows the age of 50 children surveyed in Daliganj.

Table 2 : Showing Age, Composition of the Respondents

Age (Years)	No. of Respondents	Percentage
6-8	2	4
8-10	10	20
10-12	21	42
12-14	17	34
Total	50	100

The above table reveals that the majority of the children belongs to the age groups of 10-12 years, followed by 12-14, 8-10 and 6-8 in that order.

The average age of starting work has been 8.57 years. 'Gangrade' has also maintained that "the usual age of entry into employment seems to be 8-10 year..."

Religion of the Respondents

The Table 3 shows religion of the child workers because it plays a perminent role in shaping the outlook of life in later yeras.

Table : 3 Showing Religion of Respondents Family

Religion	No. of Children	Percentage
Hindus	--	--
Muslim	50	100

Above the Table shows that all the respondents were Muslim's and it only proves that Muslims still preserve the art of Chikan Work.

Reasons Behind Taking up Chikan Work

It has been found that generally Chikan Work was the traditional occupation of the family, 50 children came into this field because of the encouragement provided by their parents or other close relatives.

The families which were selected in the sample were affiliated with UPICA Handicrafts. The head of the family had enrolled his/her name at the office at 'Crowngate' and got the pieces to be embroidered at their residence. Conveniently Tuesday has been a fixed day when they had to take the complete work deposit it there and get the new orders.

Table 4 : Persons who Encouraged the Respondents in Chikan Work

Persons who brought them in Chikan work	No. of Respondents	Percentage
Parents	45	90
Other relatives	5	10
Total	50	100

The Table 4 unreavels that 90% of the respondents were encouraged by their parents to come into the Chikan Work.

Reasons for Taking up Chikan Work

The following table shows the reasons due to which the respondents worked.

Table 5 : Showing Reasons for Respondents Taking up the Chikan Work

Reasons for doing Work	No. of Children	Percentage
Family tradition	40	80
For earning	9	18
Hobby	1	2
Total	50	100

The above Table shows that it has been due to family tradition that 80% respondents have been working. The number of children coming in the Chikan Work for earning themselves and as part of their hobby been quite low.

Table 6 : Showing the Training Aspects of the Respondents

Whether trained	No. of respondents	Percentage
Yes	5	10
No	45	90
Total	50	100

Training

The Table 6 shows the percentage of trained and untrained and workers.

The Table 6 makes it clear that the majority (90%) of the respondents are untrained. Only 10 per cent of them were trained in Chikan Work.

Table 7 : Showing Training in Relation to Age

Whether untruined	One Groups				No. of respondents
	6-8	8-10	10-12	12-14	
Yes	--	--	2	3	5
No	2	10	19	14	45
Total	2	10	21	17	50

The above Table unreavels that children who were trained generally belonged to a higher age group (i.e. 12-14). Among the untrained children the highest percentage come from 10-12 age group, followed by 12-14, 8-8.

Duration of Work

The following table given the time span for which these children have been engaged in the work.

The Table 8 shows that 76 per cent of them have been working for more than 1 year, 20% of them have been doing this work for six months and 4% of them had recently joined this trade.

Table 8 : Showing Duration of Engagement in the Work

Time upon engaged in this work	Number of respondents	Percentage
For more than 1 year	38	76
Between 6 months and 1 year	10	20
For less than 6 month	2	4
Total	50	100

1. The majority of children in this trade has been the females.
2. The highest number of children doing the Chikan Work has been found to be in 12-14 age groups.
3. All the respondents have been from Muslim families.
4. Overwhelming majority of the cases have been encouraged by their parents to join the Chikan Work.
5. Keeping up the family tradition has been the general reason behind the respondent's coming for Chikan Work.
6. Only a lesser number of children are trained for the Chikan Work.
7. The majority of respondents have been in the Chikan Work for more than one year.

Family Profile of Child Workers

Family is the main institution in shaping the child's personality. Therefore, the form and character of the family is of utmost importance for developing the child's personality.

It has been seen that the form of the family is greatly affected by the social and economic changes that have taken place in recent years but the basic biological and social needs which guide the essential functions of the family have not yet changed. Though some of the original functions of the family such as the educational, recreational and relioious have been taken over by other social agencies get its basic function which centres around the bio-psycho and social needs of man have not been affected.

The importance of the family has been rightly summed up by Mciver and Page in these words :

"..of all the organisatsons, large or small which society unfolds none transcend the family in the intensity of its sociological society."

The Psychological and environmental influence of the family on the child is so deep and takes place so rapidly that Psychologists say that the child acquires all the traits of his personality and character of his adulthood before he attains the age of 5 and in some cases even earlier. Since the family forms such an integral part of the child's life, it is essential to study the family background of the child.

It was found during the survey that the average size of the family was large. The main reason was that they had the viewpoint that family planning was prohibited by Islam and they also believed that they needed extra hands to earn and contribute in the family income. Unfortunately they could not understand the underlying fact that large size of families means that there are extra mouths to feed and bodies to cloths. Consequently a large number of children are found in the families which were selected for the study.

Table 9 : Showing Sex Composition of Respondents Families

composition	Total number of family members N=500 (100%)	Percentage
Male	220	44%
Female	280	56%
Total	500	100%

From the total 50 families surveyed the average size of the family is 10-0 where as the desired size of family members is 3.8 by 2000 AD. The breakup being 220 male members or 280 females.

Table 10 : Showing Siblings of the Family

Number of siblings	Number of families	Percentage
1 child	--	--
2-3 children	8	16
4-5 children	10	20
6-7 children	20	40
7 and above	12	24
Total	50	100

The present survey has revealed that as many as 280 number of siblings have been found in the sampled families. The following Table has given the breakup of the families according to the number of siblings there in.

The Table 10 shows that the highest number of families were having the 6-7 number of siblings, followed by the families having 7 or above number of siblings, 4-5 number of siblings and 2-3 number of siblings in the order. The average number of siblings per family was 5-6.

It is stated that one of the major causes of child labour is said be to illiteracy and ignorance of parents. This leads to a lack of appreciation of education on the parts of the parents and also limits the outlook towards life. Such parental handicapes are at once reflected in the child as it is primarily in the family the early socialization of the child takes place.

Table 11 : Showing Literacy/Illiteracy of Father

Education of father	Number of children N=47 (100%)	Percentage
Yes	12	25%
No	35	74%
Total	47	99%

Table 12 : Showing Literacy/Illiteracy of Mother

Education of mother	Number of children	Percentage
Yes	5	10
No	45	90
Total	50	100

The Tables 11 and 12 show the educational status of the parents (father and mother separately) of children studies in this research, employed in the Chikan Industry.

It is seen from the Table 11 that 24% of the children's fathers was educated and 70% of the children's father was not eductated. Six percent of the children has lost their father.

The Table 12 shows that out of 50 children 10% of their mothers was educated, and 90% of their mothers was uneducated. In comparison, educational status of fathers was better than mothers. Yet the overall educational status of both the parents was far from satisfactory. In the families where both the parents are illiterate, children are bound to be called upon to take up some job or occupation to contribute to the income of the family.

Numberous studies, have brought to light the crucial role the mother plays in the development of the child. And if the mother follows the Purdah system and if she is uneducated, she becomes economically and psychologically dependent and socially backward. She is hardly capable of bringing up her children as healthy boys and girls and well adjusted adults. It is important to determine the occupation of the head of the family as it has an impact upon the children's job, work or economic activity.

Table 13 : Showing the Occupation of the Head of the Family

	Occupation of the Head of family	Number of families N=47 (100%)	Percentage
1.	Government servant	3	6.38
2.	Hawker	8	17.02
3.	Vegetable vendors	6	12.76
4.	Cycle repair shopworker	8	17.02
5.	Rickshaw puller	8	17.02
6.	Factory worker	8	17.02
7.	Causual labourer	6	12.76
	Total	47	99.98

The Table 13 contains the information regarding the parent's occupation. It reveals that though the occupation of the head of the household varied yet the most common occuption was that of hawker (16%). Richshaw puller (16%) and factory worker (16%). Only in 3% of the cases the children's father was a Government employee and 12% was vegetable vendors and 12% was casual labourers.

Most of the heads of households are employed in occupation requiring little or no skill. Most of them work in the unorganized sector. Unorganized sector has been defined as that sector which has not been able to organise itself in pursuit of common objectives. Casual nature of employment, ignorance and illiteracy on the part of the workers, small size and scattered nature of establishments and superior strength of employers, are some of the charocterstics, of unorganized occupations. There is also little security of employment or assurance of a stable income in these occupations. Under such circumstances parents have little choice but to send their children to work.

It is immense importance to determine the family income. Since one of the major couses of child labour is the low income of the family and the general poor economic condition. The family income comprises of the income of the head of the household, and income of the earning dependents, that is of wife and children or of any other person in the family.

The unwillingness on the part of family members to disclose the actual income has left a wide margin of error. We relied on observation about the standard of living and also on the secondary services to give us an estimate about the family income. The following Table shows family income (monthly).

Table 14 : Showing Family Income of the Respondents Family

Family income monthly (in Rs.)	Number of families	Percentage
0-200	4	8
200-400	10	20
400-600	11	22
600-800	6	12
800-1000	19	38
1000 and above	--	--
Total	50	100

It is revealed from the above Table that out of total number of families, 8% had family income less than Rs. 200/- per month, 20% had family income between 200-400. 22% from 400-600. 12% from 600-800 and 38% above per month.

It s evident from the above Table that the standard of living was poor. In these families the income could be supplemented by the effrots of extra earning members—the wife and children who were engaged in home based industry, like Chikan, Mukesh and Zardorzi industries. Low income compelled the parents to send their children to work in the above said industries.

After seeing the children involved in the Chikan work one is likely to assume that the Chikan craft is handed over from generation to generation and in this case it becomes the family occupation. Thus an information with regard to the number of family members engaging in this work (Chikan) was gathered in this study. The following Table shows the number of family members engaged in Chikan craft besides the children interviwed in the study.

Table 15 : Showing the Number of Persons of the Family Engaged in Chikan Work

Number of person of the family engaged in Chikan Work	Number of families	Percentage
1-2	19	38
3-4	17	34
5-6	12	24
7 and above	2	4
Total	50	100

From the above Table it is evident that most of the families have two or more members engaged in the Chikan craft while the highest percent of families were engaging between one and two family members in this work number of families engaging between 3 and 6 members was substantially high.

38 per cent of the families had 2 members while 17 families or 34% had 3-4 members engaged in Chikan craft. Another 12 families or 24% had 5-6 member in the Chikan craft and only 2 or 4% had more than 7 members in Chikan work.

Summary

1. The average size of the respondent's family members is 10.00 (per family).
2. The average number of siblings of the respondents families has been 5.6 (per family).
3. The per cent of respondent's father being illiterate was predominatly high.
4. Ninety per cent of the respondent's mother was also illiterate.
5. Most of heads of the households wer casually employed persons.
6. None of the families surveyed had the income above Rs. one thousand per month.
7. The number of family members engaging in the Chikan work, beside the children interviewed, was quite high.

Educational Determinant of Child Workers

Education had been defined as the "Art of developing and cultivating physical, intellectual, aesthetic and moral faculties of the individual with a view to enabling him to respond positively to demands and responsiblities of his social being.

In all developing countries including India, there is no lack awarness of the importance of education, primary, secondary, intermidiate and higher nor any shortage of commitment to achieving the educated society. But there are many constraints which come in the way of achieving the coveted goal. These are poverty, low status of women and conseqquent neglact of girls education, child marriage, chornic shortage of building and equipment, and defective supervision and administration in the field of education. These factors people's participation and development.

The directive Principles of State Policy of the Indian Constitution (Article 45) include the following: "The State shall endeavour to privide within ten years of the commencent of the Constitution free and compulsory education, for all children upto the age of 14 years."

Although the Indian Constitution has been in existence for more than 4 decades, the literacy percentage in the country as not gone up beyond 35 per cent. The literacy among the women and the scheduled castes, tribe population is more depressing. Thus, time stipulate in the Constitution has been extended several times to wipe out illiteracy and ignorance from the Indian scene. The educational system in India was devised not for universal learning, but to produce small numer of clerk and junior officials needed to run the status-guo administration during the British rule.

The United Nations Declaration of Rights of the child has emphasized the importance of education in the life of a child in these words:

"Education is an essential need of the child especifically the kind of education that will help him to develop the knowledge judgement and social and moral values to play his proper role in society when he becomes an adult".

Thus in fufilment of this constitution no child should be allowed to work on the street or in other palces of employment. The child should indeally be attending school to grow into a responsible adult. But this is not to be : the following table attempts to show how many of the children in Daliganj area have been to school ? How many of them have dropped out and how many have never been to school?

Table 16 : Showing Distribution of Children According to Status of Their Schooling

Status of Schooling	Number of Children	Percentage
Currently attending school	5	10
Had attended school	19	38
Never attended school	26	52
Total	50	100

Looking at the Table it can be found that there was only 10% of 50 children who wer currently attending school. Thirty eight percent of the children had dropped out of school while a large percentage *i.e.* 52% of the children had never been to school.

Table 17 : Showing the Present Level of Standard of Education

Classes	Number of Children	Percentage
I	1	20
II	1	20
III	1	20
IV	--	--
V	2	40
Total	5	100

By speaking to the mothers of children employed on the Chikan craft. We discovered that although they were aware of the imporatance of education their girls. They could not send their girls to schools because of various constraints and pressures of poverty. The table 16 gives information with regard tot he present state of children's (interviewed) schooling,

The Table 17 revealed that there were only five children who were attending the schools preently. Out of the children attending the schools two were in the class Vth whereas the other three children were in equally divided in classes Ist, IInd and IIIrd.

The following Table provides information with regard to the type of school (whether private or public) being attended by children presently:

Table 18 : Showing Type of School Being Attended by the Children

Typology	Number of Students	Percentage
Private (Semi)	1	20
Public	4	80
Total	5	100

Table 19 : Showing Who Supports Their Education

Person supporting	Number of Stadents	Percentage
Father	2	40
Mother	1	20
Other relatives (elder brother)	1	20
By himself	1	20

The Table 18 revealed that the higher percentage of children attending the school presently were in public schools, only one out of five children was found to be in a private School.

The Table 19 contains information regarding the question who supported their schooling :

The Table 19 revealed that the majority of the cases the children's schooling was supported be either of the parents, father in two cases and the mother in one case, out of the total number of five children attending schools presently, However, in one case child was supporting his schooling by himself.

Discussion

The Table 16 has revealed that as many as 52 per cent of the children interviewed had never been to Schools.

On speaking to the mothers of children employed in the Chikan craft, it was discovered that although they were aware of the importance of educating their girls, they could not send their girls to schools, because of various reasons. Roverty was the main couse for not sending the children to the schools. They could not affort educaction their children.

Regarding school drop-outs, the most important reason was stated to be that all girls belonged to the Muslim community where there was a very strict pudah system. The girls on attaining the age of puberty were made to observe purdah strictly. And thus the parents kept their girls at home rather than send them to schools. These parents preferred earning on the part of these girls rather than allowing them to sit idile at home.

Summary

The picture obtaining with regard to the educational standard of the children interviewed was very depressing with the state of affairs regarding the educational background of the children. One must look at the government policies already existing with regard to the education of children. One easily discovers that there is an emphasis an the education of girls, vocationalization of secondary education and free and compulsory education for all children under 14 years.

Thus, it is abundantly clear that although the Government is giving due importance to education by including it in the Five Year Plans, a lot still needs to be done in this field.

Health Department of Child Workers

It is fairly established that health of any nation depands upon the health status of its population especially that of the younger generation. But it is amazing that in India even after forty years of andependence, the overall health and nutritional situations continue to be bad. Although India has made tremendous progress in all other spheres of life like industry, science and techonology, space and son on, the sphere of health seems totally neglected. It will be clear by the folling figures:

(1) The infant mortality rate is 125 to 1000 whereas in developed countries it is 10-14 to 1000.
(2) Life expectancy at birth is 54-5 years as compared to 75 years in developed countries.
(3) 36% of school children are malnourished.

But now the efforts are being made to improve the standard of health of the population through a nationwide programme of immunization under Integrated Child Development Scheme (I.C.D.S). In evaluating the health condition of the children, one of the major constraints was that there was no possibility of any clinical examination and no records were available to substanitiate the information collected with regard to the death of the children. The limited response and the ability of the respondents to communicate gave us some picture about the prevailing health situation of the children employed in the Chikan Industry.

The factors affecting the health of the children are of two kinds. First, there are the health problems to which the children are exposed because of the fact they they are required to work for long hours without rest. Secondly, the children are also exposed to certain environmental, social, biological factors together with the poor economic conditions prevailing in these families.

Looking at the occupational health hazards because the child which doing Chikan work sits in a small poorly lit and ventilated homes in crowded mohollas, which provides him both the workplace and living space.

Sitting in the pasture of cross legged or with leges out-stretched with their bodies bent slightly forward on floors and working for such long periods results in backaches and due to poorly lit rooms, it damages the eye or the child.

The following Table shows the diseases from which the children are suffering.

Table 20 : Showing Various Ailments of Working Children

Ailments	Number of Children N=50	Percentage
1. Eves water often	37	74
2. Headache	36	72
3. Backaches	42	84
4. Pain in the arms	31	62
5. Giddiness	17	34
6. Pain the joints	10	20

The Table 20 shows that 84% respondents complained about their backache, 74% complained about their evesight problems, followed by 72% complaining about headache, 62% about pain in arms, 34% giddiness and 20% pain in joints.

It most be noted that a child often complained of more than one ailment. Thus a child had headache, backche, or pain in the arms.

The next inevitable questions are whether or not any treatment is undertaken for the above mentioned ailments and if any treatment is undertaken then where has it been taken, in government hospitals, private practitioners or any other place?

The following Tables 21 and 23 provide information on the above two questions:

Table 21 : Showing Whether or Not Treatment was Obtained

Nature of response	Number of response	Percentage
Yes	6	12
No	44	88
Total	50	100

It is found from the above Table that the majority of the children (88 per cent) did not take any treatment, while the rest i.e., 12 per cent consulted some physician for their ailment. The findings of this table further proves that the families where Chikan work is taken as a source of employment often suffer from poor economic condition which does not allow them to incur any expenditure on health problems.

146 / Child Labour in Various Industries

The Following Table deals with question which, place was consulted by the resondents for treatment of ailments.

Table 22 : Showing the Type of Treatment Undertaken by Respondents

Type of treatment	Number of respondents N=6=100%	Percentage
Government Hospital	2	33
Private practitioner	1	16
Quacks treatment	3	50
Total	6	99

The above Table shows that the highest percentage of respondents consulted the quacks for their treatment followed practitioners in the sequential order.

The next question which was asked pertaining to the health of the child was whether or not the child has been vaccinated in his/her childhood. Since the child was unable to answer the question the mother was asked this question.

Table 23 : Showing the Status of Vaccination and Immunization

Nuture of response	Number of response	Percentage
Yes	5	10
No	45	90
Total	50	100

It is found from the above table that only 10% had been inoculated whereas the rest 90% had not received any incoulation.

It should be noted of the 10 per cent who were vaccinated none of their mothers could specify the exact names of the vaccinations given to their children. During the discussion it was found that some of the vaccinations like D.T.P. and Polio which required administration of three doses specified period of time, could not be given in their full doses.

Summary

To sum up, it can be said that general public is quite indifferent and apathtic towards immunization. The main cause of this apathy is the lack of awareness and information regarding the benefits of immunization on people's part.

It has also been found that if the child develops minor reactions such as burning fever etc. after getting inoculated, the parents develop aversion towards inoculation. They refuse to get their children inoculated in future.

Another cause for general apathy towards inoculation is that male members of the family never find time to take the child to hospitals for inoculation or to acquire awarenes and knowledge about the benefits of immunization. The need, therefore, is to spread the general awareness on the part of general public regarding varies inoculations and immunizations.

Nutritional and Dietary Derterminant of Child Workers

Nutrition is an important factor in building up of the health a nation and malunutrition is a very serious problem of developing countries. The most severaly and chronically malnourised are the poor, specially the infancts, children and mothers. Nutritional status affects health, labour productivity, learning capacity and their income. Mainutrition leads to deficiency and acts as a major cause of impairment in the proper growth of the children and women specially in the rural areas. In fact malnutrition makes a particular class of people a vulnerable class.

We shall attempt to study the nutritional level of the children employed in the Chikan Industry. Since the children doing Chikan Work are girls, their naturitional standard is very poor. The main criteria for judging the nutritional level was height, weight, protein and calories intake. However, due to absence of specified knowledge in this field only an estimate could be made of the nutritional level of the children through observation.

Table 24 : Showing the State of Nutrition Among the Child Workers

Sate of nutrition	Number of child workers	Percentage
Malnourished	30	60
Healthy	20	40
Total	50	100

Table 25 : Showing State of Diet Among the Child Workers

Opinion	Number of respondents	Percentage
Getting enough to eat with good quality	2	4
Not getting enough/the quality food to eat	23	46
Unable to Answer	25	50

The Table 24 shows that only 40% of the respondent seemed to be nourished. The Table 25 shows that majority of the respondents were suffering from nutritional deficiency. Only 40 per cent of the respondents was stated to be healthy whereas the rest 60 per cent were nutritionally deficient children.

The information with regard to the respondents diet was collected. It is being presented in Table 26.

The Table 25 shows that the 46 per cent respondents were dissatisfied with the diet and its quality and only 4 per cent were satisfied with the diet and its quality.

It is noticeable that exactly half of the respondents (50 per cent) could not provide and definite answer with regard to the diet and its quality.

The next question was regarding the type of food being taken through the day by the respondents.

Table 26 : Showing the Type of Food Taken at Different Points of Time in the Day by the Respondents

Type of food	Break fast %	Lunch %	Dinner %
Whether fresh cooked	20.40	10.20	15.30
Whether left overs	21.42	38.76	34.68
Whether brought from market	9.18	2.4	1.2
Total	50.100	50.100	50.100

It is found that in the break fast only 40 per cent of the workeres ate fresh cooked food while 42 per cent had often left overs to eat and 18 per cent bought biscuits or *somasa*, etc. from the market. The Table 2% also points out that for lunch only 20 per cent of the child workers ate fresh cooked food while 76 per cent had leftovers to eat and 21 per cent of the chlid workers bought puri, etc. from the market.

The general finding from the Table 26 only substantiates that the quality of the food had been far from satisfactory. It had how nutritional value. Most of the child workers either ate the left-overs or bought food from the market to satisfy power being poor they could not have bought enough and quality food from the market.

Summary

(1) The health of the majority of the child workers had been very poor.
(2) Among the child workers who provided answer regarding the question as to their diet and its quality, it was found that that the majority were deprived of their full diet and also the quality of food was poor.
(3) The vast majority of child workers either depended on the left-over food or the food bought from the market.

Working Conditions of Child Workers

It has been faily established that complete abolition of child labour in any underdeveloped society is not practicable. Child labour has come to stay in our societies as a necessary evil. In fact, child labour continues as long as there is poverty in any society. Though we have made so many laws banning it, yet it won't be of much use as people much satisfy their basic wants and when their income is so meagre they will ask their children to work and supplement the family income. Thus a ban chilld labour will neither be feasible nor practical.

The working condition of children employed in India are absolutely inhuman. The ILO categorically states—

"The child's creativeness and ability to transcend reality are blurted and his whole mental world in improved."

Despite the fact that the Constitution has been in existence for the last forty years the working conditions of children in various occupations continue to be inhuman. It was felt that since a complete ban on child labour was not practical nor feasible, the working conditions under which children worked could be regulated.

The child labour (Prohibition & Regulation) Act, 1986 was promulgated with a view to regulate the working conditions of child labour. Although this Act is a step in the right direction, it is very difficult to enforce it in a country which is poor and over populated. The appaling working conditions under which children are forced to work makes a mockery of Article 24 of the Directive Principles of Sate Policy which states—

"No child below the age of 14 years shall be employed in any factory of mine or enganged in any other hazardous employment."

Although girls constitute a large percentage of child labour, they are mainly engaged in home-based work. The Act makes no mention of the home-based category of child labour. Because of this short coming it is very difficult to regulate working conditions of children working at home.

Hours of Work

The following Table 27 contains the information regarding the working hours of child workers engaged in Chikan Industry.

Table 27 : Showing Relationship Between Child Workers and the Hours of Work

Working hours (daily)	Number of child worker	Percentage
Upto 2 hours	5	10
2-4 hours	13	26 64%
4-6 hours	14	28
6-8 hours	17	34
8 to 10 hours	1	2

The above Table shows that 64% of the child workers were working for less than 6 hours a day (in accordance with provisions of the Act). These children usually take a break in between the working hours to do some other work in the house. A few of the girls also go to school that is why they work for about six hours. It has been generally observed that the female child workers work for lesser hours

150 / Child Labour in Various Industries

because they have to do household course like cooking and sewing clothes and also as the baby sister. It is also noteworthy that about 34% of the child workers were working for more than six hours a day.

Duration of Employment

The information regarding the duration of Chikan work by the child workers was also collected and the same is being presented in the Table 28.

Table 28 : Showing The Distribution of Child Workers According Their Duration of Chikan Work

Duration of the Chikan Work	Number of child worker	Percentage
Less than 3 months	1	2
6 months-1 years	1	2
1-2 years	10	20
2-3 years	10	20
3-5 years	11	22
5-6 years	14	28
6 years and above	3	9
Total	50	100

The Table 28 shows the duration of employment of the children. A large percentage of the children started work at a very young age and hence had been working for more than 5 years or so. The highest percent of child workers had been found to be working for between 5 and 6 years, followed by 22 per cent for 3-4 years, 20 per cent for 2-3 years.

Table 28 : Showing the Distribution of Child Workers According to Length of Chikan Workers and Number of Working Hours

	2	2-4	No. of working hours Upto 4-6	6-8	8-10
Less than 3 months	1	--	--	--	--
6 months -1 year	1	--	--	--	--
1-2 years	2	5	2	1	--
2-3 years	1	5	4	--	--
3-5 years	--	2	5	4	--
5-6 years	--	1	2	11	--
6 years and above	--	--	--	2	1
Total	5	13	13	18	1

It has been observed that the working hours increased as the duration of employment increases. Thus, the Table 29 attempts to show a relationship between length of time employed and number of working hours per day of the working children.

It has been also observed that if a girl was employed for more than 5 years, her working hours decreased. This is because of the fact that as they grow older they have to help more in the household course and also look after younger siblings of the house.

Distribution of Children According to Place or Work

We attempted to study the distribution of child workers according to their place of work. Although the children are found to be mostly working at home, some of them are found to be working at different places other than that of their homes.

The following Table shows the distribution of children according to their place of work.

Table 30 : Showing the Distribution of Child Workers According to Their Place of Work

Place or work	Number of children	Percentage
At home	34	68
At neighbours	16	32
Total	50	100

Thus, it is clear from the Table 30 that 32% of child workers worked at neighbour's house. These neighbours get pieces of work which require different stitches. Since not every girl child worker knew stitching work of chikan, different girls work at the same piece. However, the mothers of the child workers were found to be working at their homes only, it has been observed that the working conditions prevalent are found to be lacking in several basic amenities. Thus the following table contains the information whether the working place had the basic necessary conditions of work.

Table 31

Items	Satisfactory	Percentage	Poor	Percentage
Cleanliness	18	36	32	64
Ventilation	23	46	27	54
Lighting	23	46	27	54

It is apparent from the above Table that very few households had fulfilled the requirements for a healthy and clean working atmosphere. Usually the area resided by the child workers were characterised by open drains, garbage dumps and poor sanitation and environment facilities. Ventilation was also not satisfactory. 54% of the households had poor ventilation. Similarly, the majority of house of the working children did not have satisfactory lighting. As many as 54 per cent of the workers informed about the poor lighting. Only 46% of the child workers informed that their place had the satisfactory lighting conditions.

These living and working conditions often make home based workers particularly vulnerable to various diseases and had health. In the end it may be worth mentioning that though the Chikan work is available throughout the season, the burden on the workers increases in Summerdays when it becomes quite hot.

Summary

It is evident from the survey that the working conditions were far from satisfactory. The long working hours often left no time for the child workers for any other household activities. These long hours have several detrimental effects on the child worekers. These working conditions cause tremendous damage to the physical health of the child workers and hence they grew into a weak adult in the future.

When a child workers is made to perform dull, laborious and repetitive tasks day in and day out, his mind becomes tired out. At this young age, they should be free from responsibilities but circumstances forced them to become wage earners. Consequently they lose the inclination for formal education.

It is very difficult to regulate the working hours and conditions of work without the proper implementation of legislation. Since it was not possible to ban the children to work and that too in the unorganised sector, a new legislation should be enacted to regulate conditions of the child workers working in their houses. Besides passing such a legislation the authorities should take other steps to improve the environmental conditions of the localities which are predominantly inhabited by the child workers of Chikan Industry.

ECONOMIC DETERMINANT OF CHILD WORKERS

Wages

Once of the hardest and unfortunate aspect of poverty is that children are required to work as wage earners and India is a country where more than 60% of the population still lives below the poverty line and the parents, who are cought in the web of poverty, put the child to work and marginally increase the family income by their labour. However, the family remains as poor as ever.

During the survey we found that very household had 2 to 3 child workers along with the adult females doing the Chikan work. It has also been found that although with the increasing numbers of years of employment, their works become better and better and yet their wages remain the same as before.

Most of the children now have permanently adopted doing 'Chikan Work.' Most of these workers are not paid daily wages but get payment according to piece rate. This payment depends upon the volume of embroidery done on the piece. Sometimes more than one person works on the piece because not every girl knows all the stitches like Phanda, tepchi, murri and so on.

Table 32 : Showing the Piece-work Rates

Rate given per piece of work

Items	Workdone	Rate (in Rs.)
Kurta-1 plain	Murri	20
Kurta-1 Daraidar	Murr	12
Kurta-3	Murri Phanda	8.25
Kurta-4	Bakhia	7
Kurta- tericott/4	Bakhia	5
Saree fine Wayal	Phanda	6
,, ,, ,,	Bakhia	75
Salwar Suit Tericott	Phanda Murri	60
,, ,, ,,	Bakhia	25
Paijama Suit Tericott	Phanda Murri	25
,, ,, ,,	Bakhia	25
Salwar Suit Cotton	Phanda Murri	25
,, ,, ,,	Bakhia	25
Paijama Suit Cotton	Phanda Murri	25
,, ,, ,,	Bakhia	25
Saree Argandi 5-2	Phanda Murri	115
Saree Argandi 5-3	Phanda	75
,, ,,	Bakhia	60
Saree Wayal 5-9	Phanda	45
,, ,,	Bakhia	25
Blouce piece	Phanda	7
,, ,,	Bakhia	5
Dupatta Border Pallu	Border	20
,, Jaldar	Jaal	30

The Table 32 only suggests that the child worker are not paid according to their hours of work but on piece rate basis. No effort till now has been made to get the authorities to enforce minimum wages. The child is not paid according to the number of hours that she puts in doing the Chikan embroidery work. The child workers informed that if they were paid more, they would definitely make an effort to improve the quality of their work. Since they were paid the same wage irrespective of the quality of work done, they did not bother about the quality of work.

Summary

The child workers are not paid any fixed wages. They are paid on piece-rate basis. The pathetic situation about the payment system in the Chikan work is that quality of work is not given due importance in payment of wages to the workers. Consequently the payment of wages is also not related to the number of years put in by the child workers. Often group of 2-3 child workers work on a piece and hence the payment on that piece is shared by the workers doing on the said piece and hence the economic condition of the workers does not improve.

LIVING ENVIRONMENT DETERMINANT OF CHILD WORKERS
Housing

Various reports have confirmed that India's urban population is constantly rising over the years. The constant rising in the population has further aggravated the urban housing problem. In most of the large Indian cities we find narrow and congested lanes with improper drainage, lack of drinking water and inadequate housing facilities. The study of housing conditions of the households in which children are found working in the Chikan Industry, is of permanent importance as environment plays a major role in determining the development of the personnality of the working child. The impact of these conditions, which are sub-human to a large extent, on the child, is so immence that it leaves a permanent scar on physicals as well as moral development of the child's personality. Lack of proper accommodation is harmful for mental, physical and moral development of the working child as well as the entire family. These houses lack privacy, and this has certain psychological repercussion on the growing members. The small and *kutchcha* houses offers little or no protection from rain, cold or sweltering heat conditions.

The following table throws light on the types of the houses in relation to their ownership.

Table 33 : Showing Distribution of Child Workers According to the Type of Dwelling and Ownership

Type of house	Number of child	%	Own	%	Rented	%
Pucca	41	82	30	77	11	100
Semi-Katchcha	9	18	9	23	--	--
Total	50	100	39	100	11	100

The above Table shows that majority of the houses were *pucca* as well as owned by the families of the child workers. Only 18 per cent of houses were *semi-katchcha* and 22 per cent on rent. It is also worth mentioning that the amount of rent varied from Rs. 100-300 depending upon the accommodation and the standard of house and the locality.

The following table contains information regarding the extent of accommodation available in the houses occupaied by the workers.

Table 34 : Showing the Distribution of the Child Workers by the Number of Rooms Available in the Worker's House

Number of Rooms	Number of child workers	Percentage
One room only	22	42
1-2 rooms	15	30
More than 2 rooms	13	26
Total	50	100

From the above Table we find that out of the total households surveyed 42 per cent were having one room and 30 per cent houses had 1-2 rooms while only 26 per cent of the houses had more than two rooms. The Table had shown that 18% families were living in *semi-kutchcha* houses. These houses were made of mostly small bricks and thatches whereas in *pucca* houses the walls were brick-laid cemented.

The essential aspect of the urban housing is whether the houses contained the following facilities :
1. Water facilities,
2. Ventilation,
3. Lighting,
4, Latrine,
5. Kitchen, and
6. Water supply.

It was found that most of the families had municipal water connections. These of the had hand-pumps installed in their houses. Seven household were using water from public water taps in the near vicinity. Pollet facilities were available only in some houses. Only 10 houses holds had proper flush fitted toilets. The rest had *katchcha* toilets.

It was interesting to know that most of the *pucca* houses had electric connections and some of the *kutcha* houses had also electricity connections.

All the *pucca* houses had some clean corners which were used as kitchens, even the *kutchcha* houses too managed the same corner to use as kitchen.

Summary

To conclude, we can say that the over flowing drains, big heaps of refuse, congested and crowded living quarters, absence of toilets etc. are harmful for the child workers and their family members. The Lucknow Mahapalika sould take effective measures to ensure that centain basic civic amenties are available specially in the area which are pre-dominantly occupied by Chikan Workers.

Recreational Determinant of Child Workers

The word 'recreation' means the proper and constructive use of leisure time by the individual. This gives dimension and release of tensions from monotonous long working hours. Therefore, recreation is an essential factor for the proper physical, mental and spiritual growth of an individual, specially the working child.

Leisure time is one of the gifts of a mature civilization. The way leisure time is spent determines to a long extent the culture of the individual and collectively of the country as a whole. It has been rightly said that leisure is work's greatest achievement.

During the course of survey, it was found that the children who were found doing Chikan embroidery were all girls. They mostly came from the Muslim families where *purdah* system is very strictly observed. As soon as girls cross the age of puberty they are not allowed to go out of the house alone.

It is also striking to not that as the wages of the Chikan Workers are fixed on piece-rate basis the work for pretty long hours with little break of time in between the work. Even holidays and Sundays are not spared in working.

By discussing with the child labourers it was found that the girls sometimes wathced televisions, visited movies along with their family members for their recreation.

One of the most obvious aitivities or children is 'play' a spontaneous, free, joyful and pleasurable activity for them. By observing it could be inferred that the child workers could not devote their free time to this natural arge because there was hardly any place playing games in their homes and neighbourhood.

An important indication that children are imaginative can be seen from the imaginary work they indulge in that is the drawing of the motives.

We have already noted that girls have less free time boys. They are less free than boys to come and go to at will. They must help the household work, which is less required of the boys. The following Table present rank orders of the recreational activities preferred by the child workers.

Table 35 : Showing the Rank Order of Recreational Activities Prefered by Child Workers

Recreational activities	Rank Order	Frequency N=50
Singing and dancing	1	23
Radio listening	2	21
Television viewing	3	20
Indoor games	4	19
Movie visiting	5	17
Dramatic display	6	16
Outdoor games	7	8
Hobby activities	8	7

This Table transpires that the child workers being the females prefer singing and dancing with top most priority, followed by Radio listening. Indoor games, movie-visiting, dramatic displays, outdoor games and hobby activities, which include collection of photographs, coins, painting, sewing and embroidery etc. in that order.

The recreational needs of a person become greater when we see the nature of the work done by him which requires long working hours and concentration in performance of the activities. Therefore, steps should be taken by the government to develop some parks and playgrounds in the vicinity of houses occupied by child workers to provide recreational facilities therefor the children. These parks should be built in the very area from which the children come. Recreation is very important for the proper physical and mental growth of the child workers.

Summary

The above discussion makes it clear that female child workers have less time than male child workers. In between the working hours they also have to assist in household activities. Nonetheless, the female child workers have some preferences for the recreational activities. Singing and Dancing, Radio listening, Television viewing, Indoor games are some of the preferences of the child workers for their recreational activities.

Recommendations and Suggestions

Child Labour in any industry and Chikan Industry in particular, is a grim reality, a reality that has to be accepted for many years to come in the future too. This is because it is not realistically possible nor practical to totally abolish Child Labour in India. Several reasons contribute towards this thinking. The foremost reasons being that most of the children come from families with very low income, though their wages are very nominal yet they supplement the family income. Secondly, these child workers do not have any education or training that could be of use to them while looking for alternate jobs. They earn very little which is in most cases the income of Rs. 10/- to Rs. 100/- per month. Sitting in their homes and being mostly females and observing purdah has made the totally onaware of sharoes going on out of four walls of their homes. New educational facilities on the lines of the condensed course have to be provided more and more to meet the needs of these children. If these children are forced to attend conventional schools. then they will join the teeming millions of education unemployed youth which will increase their frustration and aggravate their pitiable conditions.

When the parents were informally asked why Mahajans preferred employment of children in Chikan Industry, several reasons were advanced. Some of them were as follows:

If the child started work at an early age, the quality of work is bound to improve and on maturity they attain the height of good work in Chikan. In turn these children supplement the meagre family income.

The real reason for employing children is stated to be the economic one. The payment of low wages leads to Mahajan's higher profit. The mahajans convince the working children by saying that they were doing a favour to the children's families.

The reasons given above cannot be used as justification for the perpetuation of child labour in the Chikan Industry. As was pointed out earlier, early employment to the child retards his physical and mental development and leads toreduction in his or her earning capacity in the future years.

The recommendations for improving the conditions of children employed in the Chikan Industry can be summarized as under:
1. Inclusion of children doing chikan work in Child Labour (Protection and Regulation) Act 1986.
2. All the schemes under Child Welfare Services being run by Government be so directed so as to reach the children employed in Chikan Industry, their families and communities. Proper monitoring should be undertaken by Government officials to ensure that they are being run properly.
3. Meeting the vasic needs of the children employed in the Chikan Industry viz, health, nutrition and recreation.
4. Undertaking measures to meet the basic needs of the families to which these children belong.
5. Undertake long term measures in order to regulate the working conditions of children in Chikan Industry.
6. In August 1987, the National Child Labour Policy was adopted comprising three thrust areas,

namely, is legal action plan: (ii) Focasing of General Welfare and development programme on child labour and the families. (iii) A project based 'Plan of Action'. The policy will works out strategy for strict and effective inforcement of the Child Labour Act. 1980 and utilize the on going development programme for the benefit of working children and their families.
7. Jawahar Rojgar Yoina (JRY) launch by the Govt. in 1989 aims at providing relief to the weaker section of society. If the benefit of JRY do percolate down to the real target beneficiaries, the picture of child labour that would emerged is the 1991 census would probably be quiet different, and there might actually be a downward tread.

The suggestions listed above need further clarification. These are as under:

1. Inclusion of Children Doing Chikan Work in the Child Labour (Protection and Prohibition) Act 1986

The child labour (protection and prohibition) Act 1986 was passed in 1986 with the main objective :
"To ban the employment of children in certain specified occupations" and to "regulate conditions of work of children in employment where they are not prohibited from working."

The schedule which lists the occupation in which children are prohibited from working does not include chikan work. The provision relating to working consistions also can not be applied since chikan is a home-based industry.

The first step should be to include Chikan embroidery and other home-based work in the unorganised sector under the purview of the Child Labour (Protection and Prohibition) Act 1986 with the help of a suitable amendment. This law was passed mainly to regulate working conditions and in some cases prohibits employment of children mainly in the unorganised sector has ignored a large number of occupations in which children are employed. The earlier discussion in the main body of the report pointed out that working conditions are far from satisfactory and because of the unorganised nature of the Chikan Industry, nothing has been achieved through the Child Labour (Prohibition and Regulation) Act 1986. Thus, the first and foremost need is to regulate working conditions of child workers engaged in the Chikan Industry through the following steps :

(1) These children should be so organised that they sit in a room which might be in their home or in their neighbourhood with proper facilites like lighting, ventilation, safety of building and so on. The supervisor, in charge of these workshops should be a local muslim women whom the parents can trust and who will ensure that no exploiting incidence takes place.
(2) Steps should also be taken to ensure that a child does not work for more than a certain period of time as laid down by the Law. The child should be entitled to a rest interval of atleast one hour.
(3) The entire work period including the rest interval shall not exceed six hours.
(4) Inspectors from the local labour Office should came for regular inspection of these workshops to ascertain facts such as :
   (a) Address of workshop to which communications regarding the workshop should be sent.
   (b) Name and location of the workshop.
   (c) The nature of the occupation carried on in the workshop.
(5) All these workshop so established shall be asked to maintain a register of children employed or permitted to work in any establishment. The register shall contain.

(a) The names and data of birth of every child employed or permitted to work.
   (b) The work and duration of work of every child and also the rest he is entitled to.
   (c) The nature of work whether he is doing embroidery stitching or any other work in Chikan work.
(6) Regular inspection should be made of these work centres with a view to checking the following :
   (a) Cleanliness of the place of work.
   (b) Proper Ventilation.
   (c) Adequate lighting.
   (d) Provision of drinking water.
   (e) Provision of toilets.
   (f) Maintenance and safety.
(7) For above mantioned purpose, the Government should appoint inspectors.
(8) The Supervisors and their employer shall be punished in accordance with the Law, if necessary.
(9) The Government should take steps to see that the training centres being run by those who have won awards offered by the U. P. Government and the Central Government for excellence in handicrafts are being properly organised. These people are given Government grants to run training centres for girls who do not know any Chikan work. But in practice these people take the girls who already know Chikan work. They get orders from the shops, and make these girls do their work and pay them very low wages and keep the profit for themselves. This looses the basic objective of the programme. Even the stipend that these girls are supposed to be given is pocketed by the person in charge.

Proper selection should be done to ensure that these girls selected for the work actually do not know any Chikan work and that they belong to the family of chikan workers. The course whould be for period of one year. After the completion of the course, a final examination should be held and accordingly grade certificate should be given. These certificates should be used by the girls when they apply for jobs such as Quality Inspector in some Government agency.

II. Implementation of Child Welfare Scheme being Run by the Government

Although there are various Child Welfare Schemes being run by the Government, they have not reached the children in the Chikan Industry. So steps should be taken to ensure that these programmes reach the children in Chikan Industry.

Some of the Programmes that the Government is running are :
1. Integrated Child Development Scheme (ICDS).
2. Supplementary Nutrition Programme (SNP).
3. Maternity and Child Health Centres (MCH).
4. Provision of free education at the primary level.
5. Mid-day meals.
6. Scholarship for higher education.
7. Creches and day care centres.
8. Grants to voluntary organisations for providing recreational facilities.

III. Meeting the Basic Needs of the Children in the Chikan

Each basic of the child, *i.e.*, health, food nutrition, education and recreation, has to be recognized in its own right and while planning programmes all of them have to be integrated as they are all inter dependent in nature.

The basic needs of the children employed in the Chikan Industry are common to all children but there are some additional needs arising out of the problems that are unique to this Industry.

The basic needs determinates of the children are :

(A) Health

The overall health situation of the children is quite depressing. The following recommendations can be made, keeping the health needs of children into consideration :

 (i) Regular health check-up by a Pedratrician and provision of treatment, if necessary.
 (ii) Immunization programmes.
 (iii) Regular testing of eyes with provision of corrective measures when necessary.
 (iv) Imparting health education to children with special emphasis on aspects concerning the Chikan work including teaching the correct postures for sitting while at work.
 (v) Provision of mobile clinics by voluntary organisations.
 (vi) Proper and regular disposal of garbage in the areas occupied by the child worker should be done by the Lucknow Nagar Mahapalika as garbage dumps increase the risk of epidemics if not done regularly.
 (vii) The drains which had not been cleaned may becomes a breeding ground for all kinds of germs. Drains in these areas should be cleaned regularly by the Lucknow Nagar Mahapalika.
 (viii) Congested and bad housing increases the susceptibility to various kinds of diseases and is harmful from the health, hygiens and safety point of views. Tuberculosis is rampart in these areas primarily because of poor housing conditions, *Kutchcha* houses provide little protection from rains, bitter cold or scorching heat. Therefore, steps should be taken to improve the living conditions of these areas inhabited by child workers engaged in the Chikan Industry.
 (ix) Since most of the people surveyed were reluctant to go to the Government Hospitals for treatment because of reasons such as heavy rush and long queues, expensive medicines; so Government doctors should make regular visits to these areas and check-up the children and their families regularly.

(B) Nutrition

The most important need of the child is adequate food. There is little purpose in planning to safeguard measures and protect him from disease and accidents if he is likely to succumb to malnutrition.

The nutrition status, as previously stated is far from satisfactory. The recommendation with regard to the food and nutritional requirements of the children engaged in Chikan are:

 (i) Providing supplementary nutrition with special emphasis on the need for a balance diet.
 (ii) Imparting nutritional education to mothers and children.

(C) Education

Education is of particular relevance in under-developed countries where it is an indispensable instrument for economic and social development :

At any given time, around half or more children of the primary school going age may be out of school. This keeps the goal of universal primary education rather distant. The majority of the non-school going children including girls are burdened with household courses or earning a living for adding to the income of the family.

The following recommendations specify how the current educational programme can be modified and adopted to suit the needs of the children doing Chikan work.

(i) Since these girls work for an average of six to seven hours and also do household work, it is not possible for them to attend formal school. Classes should be held either in the mornings or after they complete their work. The duration of the classes should not exceed two hours a day.

(ii) Due to the heavy work load, classes should be held on alternate days.

(iii) Education should enable them to do the basic mathematics. reading and writing.

(iv) Apart from 'conventional' type of education the other methods of imparting education and practicals, use of mass-media, institutional visits, should be used.

To reach the first goal of the universal education it is necessary to convince the planners and administrators that education embraces much more than 'academic' skills and has to have a curriculum both explicit and implicit which can build skills useful for household, for occupational purpose, for problem solving and for continuous self-learning in the field of work.

Thus sechmes should be started for providing functional education with adult education. The course should be the one set by the NCERT. New Delhi. There year courses should be started. During the courses they should be given education and also they should be made to make samples so that the quality of their work improves.

(v) These girls should be taught how to organize themselves by social workers and voluntary organizations, already working in this filed.

The girls should awareness classes about their rights and status by Labour Inspectors and other social workers.

The girls can then organize themselves into cooperatives with a minimum membership of twenty. The girls themselves should look after the marketing of the finishied products.

The U. P. Government should give loans of Rs. 25,000/- for self-employment which these girls can utilize. These cooperatives should be used for the upliftment of the families living there and also the entire community.

It is only when they are educated and made economically independent, will the mahajans stop exploiting them. It is because they are uneducated and unorganized that they are being exploited by the mahajans. These cooperatives can later on be merged into a trade union which will fight for their rights.

(vi) Steps should be taken to improve the standard of education for these child workers. Since these children come from Muslim families, importance should be given for teaching Urdu, which should be included in the school curriculum.

(vii) Schools should be opened exclusively for girls in Daliganj as also for child workers living in other localities. The Company on Child Labour states :

"The education curriculum for each area should be drawn up keeping in view the basic requirements of the invironment. The present craze for uniformity in the educational policy needs to be noted down. At present there are not satisfactory provisions for providing educational facilities for child workers under Labour Laws."

(D) Recreation

Recreation is important for the physical, mental and spiritual growth of the child. The following recreational activities are recommended for the children doing Chikan Work :
   (i) Since children sit for such long stretches which affect their physical growth, steps should be taken to promote physical exercise.
   (ii) Since mental and creative abilities of the child are limited, appropriate forms of recreation for improving the child's creative and mental abilities are greatly needed.
   (iii) Since they have little scope for developing their general awreness, so their interests, hobbies, etc. should be organized at their place itself to give them greater exposure.

The Report of the Committee on Child Labour states :

"If facilities for recreation or cultural activities are provided either at the place of work or residence, children will be able to regenerate themselves after a day of monotongus toil. Otherwise it will increase juvenile delinguency.

IV. Meeting the Needs of the Child Worker's Family and Community

An important aspect of child workers includes the family in any programme of services being organized for them. The family is an integral part of the child's life. The services which benefit the family shall also benefit the child.

The recommendations pertaining to the family and the community are as follows :
1. Adult education classes should be organised for the parents with a focus for bringing an awrensess in them regarding the legal provisions available in the Chikan work.
2. Education on health, nutrition and child rearing should be given to the mothers of these children.
3. Education the women will broaden their horizons thereby bringing about a change in their attitude which is important to the child also.

(E) Long Term Measures

The complete eradication of child labour should be a cherished dream in any developing country, though it is difficult to be accomplished. Thus, certain long term measures with a view to arresting the child labour phenomenon should be taken. The following are some long term measures that can be taken while dealing with the problem of Child Labour.
1. Steps should be taken to eradicate poverty as poverty is the root cause of all social evils, especially the child labour. Statistics show that even after four decades of planning, the percentage of population living below the poverty line has infact increased. The programmes being run by the government should reach the beneficiaries, specially families of Chikan

workers, thereby increasing their income and reducing the necessity to send their child for work to supplement the family income.
2. Today a growing majority of the child population falls in contex of deprivation, which is born not necessarily so much from economic poverty-but to appropriate technoligies to infrastuctrure and managerial ability. This sort of poverty can not be sucessfully overcome by improved GNP and per income measures or by enhanced resources but requires deliberate measures to expand the availibility, efficiency as well as the utilization of services and to make them more responsive to children and their developing needs.
3. The profit margin of the shopkeepers and the mahajans is quite large in the Chikan Industry and hence the worker is exploited.
A system of minimum wages for workers as well as those doing embroidery work should be imposed and implemented effectively. Although prices of product increase, the wages remain the same. Therefore steps should be taken to reduce exipoitation.
4. Girls from the cooperatives should be assisted by the U.P. Handicrafts Board to market their goods. The profits should go to the girls themselves.
5. Family planning should be given wide publicity. The large size of families in the lower income group compels them to send their child out to work to supplement the family income. So the norm of small family size should be popularised.
6. Public conciousness and awarness of the ill effects of child labour should be publicized through the mass-media. The public is yet to be awakened to the shocking implications of child labour for the development of the nation.

A wind of change must blow through society and through the minds men, for it is only if men adopt a redical new outlook that the ullimate aim, the elimination of child labour can be achieved.

Suggestions

The evil of child labour exists in this country mainly because of wide-spread poverty and ignorance: and till these twin problems continue to exits, it will not possible to affectively tackle the problem of child labour. Since with the present state of development in the country it is imposible to eradicate poverty and ignorance in foreseeable future, it is hardly of any use to talk about abolition of child labour which is not only unrealistic but is also likely to do more harm than good to the million of poverty stricken people in the country who are forced by their awfully poor economic condition to seek the help of their children to come out and work for their existence. Chikan work in some of localities of this city is still the most predominant occupation enganing an overwhelming majority of the families residing there. People depending upon chikan work as their economic pursuit live below the poverty line and hense any step in the form of an attempt to ban child labour in Chikan work will, instead of mitigating and alleviating, will aggravate their sufferings and miseries. What seems to be realistice at the present stage of development is to develop such conditions in which children, instead of being forced to take up employment, may be able to go to school and picture their studies effectively, and those children, who have unfortunately been driven to work, may also be able to start getting their aducation and to work in a healthy and congenial atmosphere in such a manner that their involvement in work should not effect development suggestions are being extended which may be taken note of while considering the problem of Child Labour by all those who are interested in it :

1. All out efforts should be made to attack the problem of poverty from all sides by sincerly implementing all developmental programmes directly as well as indirectly concerned with promoting the interests of weaker sections in general and child labour in particular.

2. Since many parents/guardians involve their children in work because they do not understand and realise the significance of education, it is necessary to develop education consciousness among them by making use of all possible means, especially by organizing adult education programme. The present situation in which educaged youngman fail to get suitable employment consonant with their educational attainments and also find it difficult to take up traditional family occupations creates feeling of uselessness of education in the minds of parents/guardians which in turn gives rise to a feeling of apathy, and in many cases even aversion, towards education. Such a situation can be retrieved by suitably reorienting the education to meet the demands of reality and by giving it required vocational and technical bias.

3. The constitutional obligation of providing free and compulsory education to all children upto the age of fourteen years should be fulfilled without any further delay. It will be necessary to take the following steps for the fulfilment of this obligation :

    (i) Education should be made legally compulsory.

    (ii) A chain of educational institutions, within easy reach of children should be established so that any child desirous of getting education may not have to go more than one kilometer.

    (iii) Education to children upto 14 years of age should be given free. The present restrtction in U.P. of providing free education to boys up to VI class only should be removed. The facility of free education, without fixing any class limit should be extended to all boys and girls at least up to 14 years.

    (iv) The entire expenditure on educartion of children should be borne by the government.

    (v) The school security programme of aid to families with dependent children to suitably compensate parents/guardians for the loss they suffer because of withdrawal of their children from work should be started.

    (vi) Community creaches should be established in areas having concentration of child workers in order to enable the child looking after the youngones in their families to attend the school.

    (viii) For the time being, keeping in view the necessity of children's work in Chikan work, school timings should be suitably adjusted to meet the requirements of Chikan work so that child workers may be able to learn while they earn; and if necessary, formal/non-formal education centres should be started in night with the help of existing voluntary organizations. In case of child workers who have never been or left going to school, the Government should make it obligatory for their employers to provide educational facilities to them.

4. Since some of the child workers has been destitutes Union Department of Social Welfare has been running a scheme of assistance to voluntary organisations through State Government/ Union Territory Administrations for extending both institutional and non-institutional services

to children upto 12 years of age, in need of care and protection. There is need for giving preference to volutary organisations coming forward to take up this scheme in rural areas.
5. Since for the time being child labour is a necessary evil, special employment bureau should be set up, to help the needy children in getting such work which neither comes in the way of their schooling nor exerts any serious kind of adverse effect on their personality development. Provisions regarding payment of munimum wages, maintenance of registers and records, etc. made under the minimum wages Act should be strictly enforced by strengthening and suitably orienting the implementation machinery and assisting it by developing a cadre of voluntary workers. Provisions rerarding penalty for payment of less than prescrebed minimum rates of wages or less than the amount due to an employee under the act should be amended on the lines suggested earlier in the context of adult workers; and the general provision of fine of upto Rs. 500 in case of contravention of any provision of the Act or of any rule or any order made thereunder, should be amended by converting it into an imprisonment upto one year of fine upto Rs. 1000.
6. In order to provide opportunity to warking girls for supplementing the income of their families by contributing their share to the family fund, it is desirable to develop cooperative societies of these young working girls having responsibility for organising traning, making raw material available and selling the produced goods.
7. In order to prepare children for future, it becomes necessary to equip them with certain skills suited to their aptitude. It will, therefore, be desirable to develop suitable aptitude tests keeping in view the Indian conditions and to administer them on both the types of working children viz. those who combine their work with studies and those who are completely involved in work. After ascertaining their aptitude, suitable training should be imparted by the Training Institues/Centres for the child workers in general and in vocations for those working children who combine their work with studies.
B. The Government should immediately enact a comprehensive legislation for Chikan Industry to provide for working hours, rest intervals, overlime, leave and holidays, health, safety and other related welfare.
9. The Government of Uttar Pradesh should effectively enforce the Children Act.
10. As a matter of long-term strategy, a National Children's Code incorporating provisions of the Children Act with model rules and uniform standards and norms regulating employment of children in different occupations should be made. The Code should lay down the minimum age of more than 14 years for entry of children into any employment. The code should be flexible enough to provide an opportunity to concerned administrative authorities for evolving necessary regulatory means and measures and should prescribe working hours, conditions of work etc.
11. The Government should intiate a dialogue with trade unions at its earliest in order to prepare institutional framework necessary for collective bargaining with regard to improyment in working conditions and conditions of work and to control the magnitude of child labour, specially engaged in the Chikan work.
12. Minimum need programme with all its components should be effectively implemented.
13. Young persons, clubs, libraries and reading rooms fully equipped with necessary meterial suited

to the taste of the local children should be established by voluntary social welfare agencies which should be given grant-in-aid by the Central Social Welfare Board.
14. The National Children's Board/State Children's Board should more closely associate themselves with problems of Child Labour and should take necessary steps immediately to improve the lot of child workers by checking their exploitation and imporving their working conditions and conditions of work.
15. Studies on Child Labour in Chikan Work on bigger scale in different parts of Lucknow city should be sponsored in order to throw light on regional variations in different aspects of Child Labour. This may be helpful in evolving a comprehensive pieces of legislation having uniformity in standards and norms regulating the problem of Child Labour but at the same time making necessary provision for ensuring flexbility to suit regional variations.
16. Seminar, Symposia, Discussions. etc. on various aspects of Child Labour should be organised from time to time, and the problem of Child Labour should be widely publicised through different types of mass-media in order to create awareness of this social evil among people and to motivate them to come forward to gradually eliminate it.

13

CHILD LABOUR IN LOCK INDUSTRY

The patients were all workers in the lock industry employed in paint workshops, polishing or electroplating units. They complained of continuous coughs, blood in their sputum and a feeling that their heads were about to burst. The compounder was making up packets of multi-vitamin tablests.

The doctor was very matter of fact when I asked him why be was prescribing only multi-vitamins when the complaints seemed so serious. His reply was : 'Most of these people are already to for gone'. You can't do anything to save them. At least this medicine gives them a feeling that they are being treated. The multi-vitamin capsule looks like a strong medicine. It makes them feel good, when they reach the last stages, I give them cortisone. But death is only a matter of time.

'How can you be so callous?' I asked.

He replied, 'It's not can tell a lock-maker to stop working if he wants to live? That is his whole life. There are no other opportunities in Aligarh. The entire population is dependent on lock making'.

Aligarh City : The Background

Aligarh city is divided into two clear-cut halves by a railway line, which divides the city north/south. In the northern part.

There are between 80,000-90,000 workers involved either directly or indirectly in the lock industry. Of the total workers, approximately 7000-10,000 are children below the age of fourteen years. However, these are factory owners and government officials, there are only 5000 children working out of 55,000 workers, comprising 9 per cent of the total labour force. The actual numbers are, however, much larger (Burra, 1987 a).

Field-work

During field-work I visited about fifty polishing units, fifty electroplating units, twenty painting units as well as thirty homes where either filing or assembling or packing was being done. I was able to visit ten factories in the industrial area and meet scores of workers who were working at home in the city and in the outlying villages. The villages I went to were Bhambola, Jaffarabad and Barola in Aligarh tehsil : however, these visits were not very useful as childen were not engaged in hazardous work there. I also visited the inner city a couple of times between 8 p. m. and 11.30 to see whether children were working at night. I spent twenty-one days in the field on three separate occasions out of the project period of three months.

The Research Assistant, who was employed for a month, had two helpers, to assist him. He was assigned the job of listing the number of units and assesting the number of child, adolescent and adult workers in each unit in thirty mohallas (localities) of the Upper Kote area, which boasts the highest concentration of the most hazardous processes in the lock industry. He went only to those units that were visible from the street but did not attempt to interview the employers of employees both for lack of time and because he did not want to arouse suspicion. In these thirty mohallas, he saw 683 units where the processes of electro-plating, spray painting and polishing were being carried out. Apart from these processes, he also observed that the jobs of operation hand-presses, assembling and making keys were being performed in many of these units.

According to the information collected by the Research Assistant, out of 6936 workers in the 683 units visited, there were 2475 children below the age of fourteen years, accounting for 35.68 per cent of the total work force in the sample. Children accounted for more than 50 per cent of all workers only in two areas, Qazi Para and Tan Tan Para, out of the thirty mohallas studied. The data collected indicated the size of the problem even though formal sampling techniques were not employed of the city is the Civil Lines and in the southern portion, the old city. These two portions of the city display a striking contrast where the over spill from the old city, population growth and urban development have resulted in the formation of two distinct cultures and patterns or settlement.

The old city is the ecological centre of Aligarh. This has the tightly knit core or the centre business district and fans out towards the eastern-southern suburbs. Most of the Muslim majority mohallas (residential localities), which house both business and homes, are located in the centre and are surrounded by Hindu localities. This area is communally sensitive because the residential areas are populated by Muslims but trading and commercial activities are in the hands of the Hindus. It is in centre of Upper Kota, that several small and medium-scale lock-making household industries are located. There is almost on contact between the two areas of the city, the civil lines and the old city.

According to a stury on communal violence and its impact on development and national intergration conducted by the Centre for Research in Rural and Industrial Development (CRRID), in Aligarh district of about 1575 registered manufacturing units, it was found that only 7 per cent of the manufacturers were Muslims. And of these 7 per cent, about a fourth of them were involved in the lock-making industry (CRRII n.d. : 28). Thus, a very large proportion of industries and manufacturing units in Aligarh are owned by Hindus.

This study also made the significant point that Muslim majority mohallas have fever educatonal facilities and the drop-out rate and non-attendance rate of Muslim children were much higher than those of children belonging to other religious, communities. Around 80 per cent of the Muslim school children either drop-out or fall in the category of non-attendance.

Most of the traditional lock-makers-both Hindu and Muslim are engaged in this work for part of the year as agriculture alone cannot support them. Since most producers are dependent upon others for supply of components, there is a great deal of inter-dependence amongst the castes/communities as certain processes are the exclusive or near-exclusive preserve of certain casts/communities. Thus, the Kohlis (a Scheduled Caste community) are mainly involved in casting activities. Muslims are more of less exclusively doing polishing work and in the final products is done by Muslim Safis, Mathur Brahmins and Jatavs. The suppliers are mainly Hindu Banias (Varshneys). The relationship between the traders and the direct producer of locks is that of super ordination and subordination (CRRID : 47). With the coming in of marchant capital, the position of the direct producer has been worsened. His working day has been lengthened and his earning power reduced substantially (ibid.). With the influx of outside capital into the lock industry, there have been structural changes in the industry which have brough about a shift from the household to the factory system, especially in the mode of producing locks.

The big lock industry, owned by Hindus, is locked in the outskirts of the city, while the smaller units, owned by Muslims, are in the interior. While most of the manufacturing units are owned by Hindus, the labourers are either Muslims or Scheduled Castes leading to tension between them for scarece jobs.

The Lock Industry : A Histrorical Background

The lock industry of Aligarh was started in 1860 by the Postal Department. In the early years, the making of locks was a village industry and locks or components of locks were made by the artisan in this home, with the help of his family labour. Many families, who found it difficult to support themselves only by agriculture, started making locks. There were also many castes like the mainthile Brahmins and others, whose lands were usurped by the Thakurs and big landlords of the area, who then also joined the lock industry. Most of the padlocks were made in the surrounding villages. As the demand for locks increased, the lock-maker found it difficult to commute and many families sold their lands and shifted to the city. But these were essentially small village craftsman.

After the Partition of India in 1947, there was sudden shift in the social composition of lock-makers. Many of the traditional lock-makers in Aligarh city were Muslims who when away to Pakistan leaving a void. They were the real craftsmen and for a while thee was slump in the lock industry. While Muslim artisans or master-craftsmen who were the backbone of the lock-industry went to Pakistan, there was a migration of Punjabi Hindus to Aligarh. These families were not engaged in lock making traditionally. But realizing that the lock industry was a profitable veture, they set up small units by hiring labour and this led to the mass production of locks.

Thus, whereas the villages craftsman or lock-maker was able to provide for the needs of fewer people, once the industrialist stepped in, locks began to be manufactured on the factory scale by people whose main contribution was their capital. The demand for locks has increased tremendously and the lock industry is seen as one with a very good future.

Thus, whereas the village craftsman or lock-maker was able to provide for the needs of fewer people, once the industrialist stepped in, locks began to be manufactured on the factory scale by people whose main contribution was their capital. The demand for focks has increased tremendously and the lock industry is seen as one with a very good future.

But inspite of mass-production of locks in factories, the villages craftsman has not been wholly displaced. Locks are still being made in the adjoining villages of Palakhana, Atrauli and Barola. The village artisan brings a model to the financier of well-known lock trader, gets his order, buys the raw material and components, finishes the product and gives it to the trader who then puts a brand name on it such as Parker, Plaze and so on. But the bulk production of locks is locks is done by financiers and lock manufactureers in the big factories.

The Lock Industry Today

According to A. L. Anand. in 1982 there were about 3000 units both in the organized and the unorganized sector, manufacturing, assembling locks and their components. There were only five or six units in the large sector : the rest were in the small scale sector. Out of the total units in the small-scale sector, about 150 units were registered and the remaining units were run by artisans as household and cottage industry (Anand, 1982 locks or parts of locks are made in almost every home in the old city. The practice of using children as part of family labour is very common. It is estimated that about 80 per cent of the country's locks are made in Aligarh district.

Processes in the Lock Industry

There are two methods of making padlocks. One is the traditional method where the lock-maker designs a lock and gets an order from the trader. The trader is usually also a financier who may give a loan to the lock-maker to buy raw material and other components. Once an order is placed, the lock-maker gives the raw material, namely brass or iron, to the dhalai (moulder, who usually belongs to a Scheduled Caste community) along with a model. The *dhalai* casts all the pieces according to specifications and returns them to the lock-maker who then files them. Those components like the handle, springs, keys, etc., which have not been cast by the *dhalai* are bought from the market, the lock assembled and then returned to the trader. The trader gets a final polish given to the locks and his brand name engraved on.

Most of the heavy brass and iron locks are made this way. The smaller and less expensive locks with names such as Link, Horseman and Mohaj as well as well as mortice and cycle locks are mass producted in factories. In this process, the lock manufacturers have their own production units where they cut scrap iron sheets called MSA sheets—which they get from the automobile industry- on power presses. Thus the outer cover of locks, the lid, flat keys and other parts are all cut from MSA sheets. Some parts of the lock like the handle are also cut and bent and grooves made in the big factories. Once this is done on power-presses, the work shifts to the hand-presses where the components are smoothened and holes pierced in keys or key-holes pierced in lock-cases. Hand presses and power-pressess are used for a variety of jobs. A die is fitted into the machine which will do a particular job. For every process, there is a separate die.

These rested components of locks are either sent for *dhol* (drum)—this is a term used for drum polishing—or polishing on buffing machines. Those parts of lock which are visiable from outside such as the handle, cover or keys, which need to be electroplated, are first polished on buffing machines. Those parts which are not visiable are sent for *dhol*. If visible parts are not electroplated, they they are spray painted.

Children do no work with *dhalais*, or in *dhol* polishing, dhol plating or on power-presses. But children are used in all other processes like working on hand-presses, polishing on buffing machines, in electroplating and spray painting units, for filing machines, in electroplating and spray painting units, for filing components, making springs and assembing and packing of locks.

It is important to note here that some of these processes like working on hand-presses, electroplating, buff polishing and spray painting are also done for the hardware industry in Aligarh. Children working in these units are therefore not exclusively working for the lock industry.

There is not even one factory where all the processes (of which there are approximately forty-five are carried out in the same premises. Most of the factory get some parts made outside. The work is given on a contract basis and it is the responsibility of the contractor to get the work done. All workers are paid on a piece-rate basis and work anything upto forty-eight hours at a stretch when the work-load is heavy.

In the big factories, components are cut and then farmed out to artisans to do the filing, finishing, etc. There are different contractors for different jobs and varying systems for getting the work down. Some people are paid by the gross, others are given a weekly wage and still others are remunerated according to lots. Ninety-five per cent of the workers have no protection as they are piece-rate workers.

In some units, popularly known as *karkhanas* (literally means factory and legally) they would come under the Factories Act, 1984 the premises and machines may belong to a man directly hires labour and gets work done on a lot basis. In yet others, the man who owns the machines may rent them out to different sub-contractors who arrange for the labour. Sometimes a sub-contractor may himself work on the machines, but this is rare. By and large, those who own these machines do not work on them.

In the lock industry the putting-out system prevails for a variety of reasons. Small firms are able to survive because they act as sub-contractors to the larger firms and supply special components and help out at certain stages or production during periods of peak demand. Secondly, legislation such a as the Factories Act and various Labour Acts help perpetuate the 'putting out system, which is the best way of maintaining profits without any obligations to the workers. A third major reason which allows the 'putting-out' system to flourish is that there exists a large number of small peasants in the countryside around Aligarh city, whose lands do not provide a full livelihood; through the 'putting-out' system, they are able to save and then invest the capital in the financing of cottage industry rather than in the factory system.

The small entrepreneur is himself fairly poor and he survives primarily by exploiting those who are ever poorer. The small entrepreneur is almost as uncertain about getting work as the labourer and therefore there is a high mortality rate with smaller units having to class down because of economic insecurity.

Wage Structure

There is no uniform wage structure in the lock industry. The method of payment is, by and large, the piece-rate system. In one assembling unit, the owner said he paid children Rs 25 a month for a ten-hour day Workers in a polishing unit said that children, if they work twelve to fifteen hours, can earn up to Rs 15 a day and an adult Rs. 25. In electroplating units, child workers can earn Rs. 5 to Rs. 10 a day depending upon the number of hours of work. Many children interviewed said they worked for more than twenty hours at a stretch. They would take a short nap or drink tea if they were very sleepy and continue to work. I met two children who had worked thirty-six hours at a stretch and who were paid 60 paise an hour as over-time. Many children, I was told, worked for several months without wages, particularly in the polishing units. After that, they earned Rs. 50 a month. Only after working ten to fifteen years was a man able to earn Rs. 600 a month and that also for a fourteen-hour day.

The payment of low wages to workers have other ramifications as well. Poor parents are not able to afford the expenses of school-going children if the education is not subsidized. But more importantly, as pointed out earlier: 'The generally prevailing low wages/remuneration for work of the parents forces them to involve child labour in the traditional business of the family' (ibid, : 26-7).

There is no fixed wage rate and different jobs/processes are paid according to different rates. For example, for cutting a keyhole with a pointed chisel in the lock-case called *dibbi* (a term used to describe a flat and small box) and also fitting a key, a child earns Rs. 3 per thousand and he can complete 1000-1500 holes in a whole working day. Sometimes, a child is paid 30-35 paise per gross. Likewise, in a electroplating unit, in an eight to ten hour working day a child could tie 1000-1500 locks/handles on copper wires. For this work, he is paid Rs. 2 or Rs. 3 per thousand The rate was also fixed at 30 paise per gross.

While there is no uniform wage structure in the lock industry, my interviews revealed that on the average, a child earned nothing for the initial period of apprenticeship, after which he began to earn Rs. 50 per month. This unpaid period for learning the skills varied from process to process but rerely exceeded one year. For the first couple of years, the child earned a monthly wage of Rs. 50 a month but his working day normally lasted twelve to fourteen hours. He was paid no over-time. On the days that the units was closed, he got no wages. All units are closed on Wednesday and units owned by Muslims are also closed on Friday.

After a few years, the child earned between Rs. 125-150 per month for a nine-hour working day. He was also paid over-time depending on the urgency of the order and the mood of the contractor. These workers were considered permanent by *thekedars* (contractors) because they were regular employees but they were not entitled to any other benefits such as medical assistance. Provident Fund and so on. The salaries of these children were also cut for days they were absent due to ill-health or on Wednesday, when units were closed.

Thus, a child earned Rs. 50 a month or about Rs. 1.60 paise per day for an average of a twelve-hour day. Any day he did 125 a month for a nine-hour day got approximately Rs. 4 per day and was not paid for the days he was absent or the factory was closed.

Many explanations were advanced for preferring the piece rate system to a fixed-rate system. According to factory owners, the labourers employed in polishing, electroplating and painting units were prone to alcoholism: if workers were paid fixed wages, they would disappear for day at a time and not come to work. Another unit owner said that this system of payment was best for both labour and factory owners because the factory owner has assured output and the labourer, if he is hard-working and sincere, can earn a lot money.

But the main reason, as another factory owner frankly pointed out, is that polishing, electroplating and spray painting are the three most hazardous processes in the lock industry and felt that contract labour was not convert by any labour laws. The unit owner has no responsibility to the worker if he falls ill or gets seriously hurt when working and he does not have to provide medical assistance or compensation if the worker dies. This is the primary reason for getting work done on a put-out system, where the wages are paid according to out-put and there is no job secrurity.

Workers were interviewed randomly from the neighbouring areas. Most of the workers and unit owners were engaged in electroplating, polishing on buffing machines and spray painting. Most of the workers engaged in polishing work live near Mehtab Ka Nakla near Shahja Marg. In this locality, almost 500 children go every day to work in the polishing units in the Upper Kota region. I interviewed six children and seven adults who had been working on buffing machines. They were covered in black emery powder. Although they had bathed after returning from work, the colour of their skin was black. I was told that children, when they start larning this work, do not get any money except for the occasional rupee or two to go to the cinema.

They worked twelve to fourteen hours and were paid monthly wages. The children were between the ages of seven and eleven years. One boy had come home at 2 a.m. when the work was over. He was eleven and has been working for three years. In the first year, he got paid nothing because he was learning the job. In the second year, he received Rs. 50 a month. Now, he earns Rs. 150 a month. His father is a rickshow-puller and he has three unmarried sisters. He was never sent to school. He then went to work with another polisher. In the unit where he works now, there are almost twenty workers of whom fifteen are children of his age.

An old man pointed to two small children who were his grandchildren. They were both working as polishers. When I told him that *thekedars* said they paid children Rs. 500 a month, the crowd of about fifteen adults and eight children laughed and said that the children were not even paid Rs. 50. And if a person got ill, as was inevitable, he not only his day's wages, but also had to borrow money for treatment. On the weekly day off when the power supply was shut off, the worker loses the day's wages.

After working for six months, they start earning Rs. 50-60 a month. A child starts working at the age of six or seven years. He usually ages to work along with his neighbours. An average working day is between twelve to fourteen hours. Since there is a shortage of power and most small units cannot afford generators, work continues through the night. The thekedar or unit owner decides what constitutes a working day. If units are not operating because of electricity breakdown, then the working day (that is the number of hours that constitutes a working day) stretches out way into the night.

After the third year, the child starts earning Rs. 150-250 a month if he is about twenty-five to twenty-six years of age that he may be able to earn as much as Rs. 500-600. But as the workers pointed out, after working under such conditions, very few are able to manage a twelve-hour shift. Within a matter or six to seven years, that is by the time a child is thirteen or fourteen years old, he is afflicted by tuberculosis, bronchitis, asthma and other diseases.

Processes in the Lock Industry and Participation of Children

Children are employed to work on hand-presses which cut different components of locks. Of all the processes in which children are employed, the activities of polishing, electroplating, spray painting and working on hand-presses are the most hazardous for the health of workers, particularly child workers. The hand-presses become particularly dangerous because children are made to work very long hours-anything from twelve to fourteen hours a day. Carelessness caused by exhaustion is the main cause of accidents and often, children loss the tips of their fingers, which get cought in the machines.

Polishing on Buffing Machines

The work of polishing is perhaps the most hazardous job undertaken Rusted pieces of metal are polished on buffing machines. The bobs on these machines against the bob and the rusted portion is polished off. The face of the worker is withing ten inches of rotatin machines which run on power.

The worker is bent over and directly inhales the emery powder and metal dust. Polishers can easily be identified because they look like coal-miners. They are covered from head to toe in this black powder. If a piece slips from the hand of the worker, it can severely injure another worker.

I visited about fifty such polishing units where more than 60 per cent of the workers were less than fourteen years of age. Children of eight and nine years could be seen working very late at night. I saw some children sleeping on the premises an some eating there as well. There were no exhaust fans in any of the units. Children who were too young to work on the machines could be seen gumming discs and then covering them with the black masala (as this mix is called. It is a term used to describe a mix of ingredients). This process generates a lot of dust and therefore factory owners keep buffing machines in a separate place.

Most factories in the industrial area had a separate place where buffing machines were kept. But factory owners felt that they were not responsible for the working conditions as the machines and the space were given on rent to the contractor, who hired the labour.

While large factories have their own buffing machines, most of the polishing work is done in the Upper Kota mohallas. This is where there is a maximum concentration of such unregulated units. Most of them are unregistered and there is on control over working a conidition, hours of work or wages. In the lanes and by-lanes of Upper Kota, child labour is very visiable. In many buffing units I visited, more than 70 per cent of the workers were children. Buffing units are also found in the Khirni Gate area and in the other parts of the city, but the highest concentration is in the Upper Kote area.

Electroplating

Electroplating is another extremely hazardous process in which more thanm 70 per cent of workers are children below the age of fourteen years. These children are engaged in tying polished metal pieces on copper wires, which are then strung on rods and submerged in acid and alkaline baths. In many of the units I visited (approximately fifty), it was not possible to enter the premises because of the noxious fumes which also one's eyes water. Electroplating is hazardous for a variety of reasons. For one thing, the chemicals used such as potassium cyanide, trisodium phosphate, sodium silicate, hydrochloric acid, sulphuric acid, sodium hydroxide, chromic acid and barium hydroxide are extremely dangerous. The hands of children were in these solutions for the better part of a twelve-hour day, if not longer. Secondly, an electric current passes through these chemical tanks and children often get shocks. The floors of these units were wet and accidents were frequent.

Although most units had a convertor, which transformed AC current into DC current and though the current passed did not exceed ten volts, illegal electricity connections taken from street-lights made this extremely dangerous. There were cases of electrocution.

Electroplating units can be found in all parts of the city though they are concentrated in the Upper Kota area. In none of the units did workers wear gloves of aprons and there were no exhaust fans installed anywhere. Many of the smaller units were run by people who had worked in a supervisory capacity in larger factories, saved money or taken loans and then set up their own units. Every single unit owner interviewed said that he would not allow his on own children to even go near the unit. There children were all in local schools. But these very owners used child labour because they admitted that it was cheaper than employing adults. Many units were working at night as well.

Spray Painting

At least 50 per cent of the total labour force in the spray painting units observed was made up of children below the age of fourteen years. They were engaged in placing pieces of metal on trays which they then carried to the painting table. They were also employed to pass on pieces to the man who held the spray gun. In this process, they inhaled substantial quantities of paint and paint thinners. Many children were found working beyond midnight.

HAZARDS TO HEALTH

Polishing

Fazal Ahmed is thirty-five years, and has been working on a buffing machine for ten years. Now his two sons have also started working. Ahmed said that almost all polishers suffer from chest disorders, particularly tuberculosis, polishers inhale vest quantities of metal dust and emery powder in the course of their work and consequently find if very difficult to swallow. Another worker said that after a few years, polishers also find it difficult to breather. I met two boys, eight and twelve respectively, both of whom were working as polishers and who already had TB.

Electroplating

One electroplating unit owner, Nabi Ahmed, had himself worked for twenty years in an electroplating plant. Although most workers were adjectly poor, some were able to set up small units but could not afford to hire labour. I now about forty-five to fifty years old. Nabi Ahmed had a servere asthmatic condition and could hardly breathe. He has stopped working and employs others. On being asked whether his children were working, his answer was; So long as I am alive, I will never let my children work. Look at my condition. I cannot even breathe easily. I do not let may children even enter the premises. Both my boys aged seven and nine years are studying.

However, Nabi Ahmed has to employ other children if he wants to make enough money to avoid having his own children work. But that is described as *duniya dari* (ways of the world).

Nabi Ahmed said that electroplating work is very dangerous. He recalled the case of a child who, by accident, put some potassium cyanide in his mouth thinking it was salt and died instantaneously. Ever so often a child tastes some of the liquid in the chemical tanks out of curiosity, as small children tend to do, and gets seriously ill or dies. But there is no one who can say exactly how many deaths, eccidental or otherwise, take place.

Gyan Prakash, aged thirty-five (though he looked older), worked for several years in the Tigar Lock Factory near Marris Road. They had a big electroplating plant in which he was a supervisor and was responsible for mixing chemicals in solution with potassium cyanide and dissolyed it with his hands, eating; the minute he took a break and washed his hands before eating; the minute he put the food in his mouth, he started vomiting blood. He vomited four of five times and was rushed to the Employees State Insurance Corporation (ESIC) Hospital. He was ill for a long time and never went back to work. He think that perhaps the glove was lightly torn and some chemicals had stuck to his nails and and these did not come off with washing.

Gyan Prakahs has worked in several *Karkhanas* but he finds it hard to work in electroplating units. The smell of acids gives him a headache and he is unable to eat. Now he works only in a supervisory capacity in this unit. He has three children who go to school. He does not want his children to work so long as he can work, and particularly so for children. As he said, 'Although every child who comes to work is warned not to put his fingers in his mouth, children are, after all, children. How can I keep such vigil? But we know that potesh (potassium cyanide) is used and we have to be careful.

This is not the end of the story. Liquids in these tanks are heated, and strong fumes are inhaled by adults and children alike. Many workers, both adults and children, work continuously for days on end, night and day. As another worker said: '*Maalik ko to kaam se matlab hain, Admi mare ya jiye, usko kya frak padta hein*'? (the owner is only interested in the profit margin. What difference does not make to him if the worker lives or dies?)

In the electroplaiting plants, hazards to health arise not only from the acids and alkalies used but also from electricity. In Tan Tan Para, a mohalla in Upper Kote, an eleven-year old worker was recently electrocuted when his foot touched a naked wire. The poor wiring system, the presence of water and illegal connections from street-lights are the main reasons for people being electrocuted or reciving servere shocks. One adolescent youth complained of severe problems of breathlessness ever since he recived an electric shock. Another electroplating unit worker said that in his work-place, a worker had been saved in the nick of time. Two wires got joined together and the nickal bath got electrified. The young worker of about fifteen or sixteen was arranging wires on the rods. He was unconscious for a long time.

Workers, whether polishers, painters or electroplanters, say that a lot depends on what can afford to eat. If he is able to get decent food, milk, butter and so on, he can word off illness more easily. Otherwise, it is a downhill path. Needless to say, those who work in these units cannot afford to eat well.

Spray Painting

A painter working for last fifteen years in a spray painting unit, strated his work at the age of ten. After five or six years of working twenty hours at a stretch, he found that his body would get very hot and he felt like hitting someone. He said that this went on for five or six years. He was always close to losing his temper and many times he felt that he was close to murdering some one, according to him, this was a physiological condition and not just a psychological state. He could actually feel the blood rushing to his head. Finally, he left the job because he felt that he might not be able to control himself. He thinks that this was due to the combined impact of paint thinners, the bright lights, the heat of the ovens and the long hours of work. he was alright soon after he changed the job. Now he has set his own spray painting unit where he employed both children and adults. He plans to remove his own son to do some other work.

An Over View

Doctors, workers and unit awners say that except for those cases where a child gets electrocuted or dies by consuming acid or alkaline solution, there is no immediate health hazard to children! Or in other works, since no systematic medical survey has ever been done, the exact nature of the health problems children are affected by is not known. The common ailments reported are cough, cold, temperature and breathlessness. But these are not taken seriously. Signs of pneumo-conionsis, tuberculosis and bronchitis are visible after a child has worked for five or six years. By that time, he is already an adolescent. When the child gets very ill and cannot continue working, only then does he go to the doctor.

Local doctors and hospitals do not even have a clue to the number of children afflicted. Figures of pneumoconiosis, which is an industrial occupational hazard, vary from 5 per cent to 40 per cent. Many doctors who say that a person suffers from pneumoconiosis do not even know what its exact symptoms are. All they can say is that it is an occupation-related lung disorder. Some doctors say that the capacity of the lungs of those working in polishing units get greatly reduced causing breathlessness but they cannot say to what extent this happens and what the mortality rate. Everywhere I went in the Upper Kote area, people talked of death and disease stalking their *gali mohallas* (by-lanes in a residential locality) and this, they said, was directly related to the work people were doing. However, no one could give any exact numbers or percentages. But they said that the number of people, specially children, who got ill, was very high. Doctors say that almost all the workers—adults and children—who work in these units get tuberculosis.

While pneumoconiosis exists among workers in buff polishing units and electroplating units, no doctor knows what happens to these patients! According to a textbook on Preventive and Social Medicine (Parke 1974), pneumoconiosis is caused by dust particles within the size range of 0.5 to 0.3 microns. After a period of exposure to these dust particles, fibrosis is caused in the lungs which may cripple a man and reduce his working capacity.

Pneumoconiosis is definitely an occupational disease caused by working conditions. There is also no cure for it. The only thing that can be done is to prevent secondary infection and to remove the person from the place of work. But doctors point out that workers are not in a position to take long-term treatment and leave their jobs. Children, since they are not legally workers, cannot avail of the facility of the Employees State Insurance Corporation (ESIC) hospital. As a worker's condition worsens, he goes from doctor to doctor looking for an instant cure. He is also deceived by local medical quacks who call themselves Registered Medical Practitioners (RMP). There people are not qualified doctors. Many of them have worked for a while as compounders and dispensers and promise the patient quick results. They pump the patient with cortisone tablets and powders which give the man some instant relief. What ultimately happens to patients, both adults and children, is difficult to tell. Not one doctor I interviewed in Aligarh could give any authentic information!

Other occupational diseases prevelent amongst lock-makers, particularly those working in electroplating and painting units, are occupational dermatities, eczema and perhaps even cancer. Workers in electroplating plants are also exposed to lung cancer.

Not many studies have been done on the health status of lock workers. One important study is that of Mohammad Anees in 1978 (Anees, 1978). Although he concentrated only on chest disorders amongst adult workers, nevertheless his findings are relevant for an understanding of the health conditions of working children in this industry.

Anees's study, which also reviews the work done by other doctors on occupational health, says that exposure to vapours of lead, copper, zinc, brass and iron, may produce metal fume fever, an acture febrile illness that clinically may resemble bacterial infection of the lungs (ibid. : 7). His study shows that the inhalation of nickel in the form of carbonyl or dust, which is necessary when working in electroplating units, gives rise to broncho-pneumonia or cancer of the lungs and nasal sinuses. Likewise, Anees says that :

That air contaminated with chromic acid mist or with the dusts of chromates and bichromates is the principal source of exposure to this metal in this industry. Chronic bronchitis and cancer of the lungs are occupational risks in the chromate producing industry (ibid. : 8).

Anee's study points out that in the lock industry, the worker is exposed to mineral dusts, specially that of iron and brass, while in polishing he may get an additional exposure to chrome mist, nickel and other inorganic and organic dusts. Since the majority of workers are employed in ill-ventilated and over-crowded premises, the likelihood of chest diseases is very high.

It was noticed that the proportion of workers from small factories had a higher percentage of chest diseases (40 per cent) against 23.6 per cent from the bigger factories. Anees's research showed that pulmonary tuberculosis, chronic bronchitis and short respiratory illnesses were the common chest diseases suffered by lock workers.

According to the inter-disciplinary study undertaken by the Aligarh Muslim University and cited earlier, while the number of children below the age of fifteen years numbered 1560, the number of persons above sixty years of age were only sixty-two. It was observed that:

> One serious feature noted... is the considerably small number of persons who have attained 60 years of age. In fact, in the age group of 41-60 years... the number of individuals [goes] on reducing as the age advances. The poor living and working conditions cause so much damage to the health that living beyond 50 years becomes difficult (IDS n.d.: 20).

Labour Laws and Their Implementation

Though the lock industry per se is not a forbidden occupation under the Child Labour (Prohibition and Regulation) Act, 1986, children are not allowed to work in processes which involve the use of certain chemicals. But since most lay persons do not know what these chemical compounds actually contain, it would be surprising if the staff of the Labour Department was able to identify these chemicals. Children are not allowed to work in hazardous employment, but the lock industry is certainly hazardous.

Though the lock industry is not a forbidden occupation either under the Employment of Children Act, 1938 (now repealed) or under the Child Labour (Prohibition and Regulation) Act, 1986, children may not work in factories or in hazardous employment according to the mandate of Article 24 of the Constitution. From what has gone before, it will be evident that the Constitutional directive is not being implemented.

When we examine the provisions of the Factories Act of 1948, it becomes apparent that they are being blatantly violated in the lock industry of Aligarh. The Act unambiguously lays down (Section 67) that children below the age of fourteen years are prohibited from working in a factory. The evidence collected in this study points to the fact that this provision is implemented largely in the breach.

Some factory owners evade the law by circumventing it. For example, any premise in which the manufacturing process is being carried on is considered a factory if there are ten or more workers and if power is used; if power is not used, there must be twenty or more workers involved (Section 2 (m)). By this definition, most electroplating, polishing and spray painting units would fall within the purview of the Act. Yet, factory owners seek a loop-hole by partitioning their premises and isolating the areas where work is being done with power. Workers then need not be paid according to law nor do they receive the benefits of paid leave, medical assistance, Provident Fund, etc. By this device, they also evade excise duty as their units are then considered to fall under the categories of small-scale or cottage sectors.

The Act also provides (Section 14 (1)) that effective measures shall be taken to prevent the inhalation and accumulation of dust or fumes or other impurities which are likely to be injurious or offensive to the workers. My observation as well as medical evidence clearly reveal that the activities of electroplating, polishing or spray painting are manifestly injurious to the health of both child and adult worker. Not a single exhaust fan was found in any of the factories visited excepted for the spray painting units, where work could not have been done without it.

The Factories Act lists twenty-two notifiable diseases that are caused by direct contact with chemicals and paints and these are considered occupational diseases. The Act also casts a duty upon medical practitioners (Section 89 (2)) to report such cases without delay. This is not being done.

Another provision (Section 16 (1)) states that no room in any factory should be overcrowded to an extent injurious to the health of workers. Most of the smaller units in the Upper Kote region were overcrowded and the pavement outside used as an extended work-place. It was physically impossible for all the workers to fit into the cramped premises. I was told that in polishing units the most common type of injury that occurred was when a piece of metal slipped from the hands of a worker and hit another. It was also noticeable that buffing machines were far too closely arranged for safety.

The regulations under the Factories Act to protect the interests children above the age of fourteen years are also not followed. All children above fourteen years are supposed to be registered (Section 73(1)) but no one maintains any registers. Also, children are not supposed to work for more than 4½ hours and not at all during the night (Section 71 (1)). In fact, they commonly do.

In almost all cases observed, children worked for far more than 4½ hours and usually for even more than eight hours. Children and adults working late at night were a common sight as well. One justification for night work was said to be the regular power-cuts (usually between 1 p.m. and 5 p.m.) during the day. Contractors were keen to finish the job at hand as even they were not assured of regular work; workers could not afford to refuse night work because employment was not available throughout the week or month and they needed the money.

The nine-hour day shift would normally continue well into the night, for the contractor counted only the hours the work was actually done, and not the hours the worker was present. As mentioned earlier, children came early and left very late; it was not practicable for those lived to go home and return and also, power could theroretically come on at any time.

State government are given powers under the Factories Act to declare some processes or operation as dangerous and can also declare a unit to be a factory even if it has less than ten workers and does not use power. But Section 85 (1) exampts units where owners manufacture products only with the aid of their families. The State Government of Uttar Pradesh does not appear to have exercised the powers it has in this regard. The escape clause that unit owners may employ their own children has come in very handy for them. My interviews revealed that almost nobody engages his own children in hazardous processes: there was only one such case of a man who worked along with his sons on two rented buffing machines. Even he was aware of the dangers involved and though one son developed a severe chest problem, the father was too to keep his children at home. On being asked, unit owners would invariably say that the children working with them were their own: they knew this was permissible under the law. If one was to believe this story, a convincing explanation would be needed for the extraordinarily large size of the families of the lock-makers of Aligarh!

In conclusion, there is unmistakable evidence that the jobs of polishing on buffing machines electroplating and spray painting are injurious to the health of workers, whether adults or children. Polishers inhale emery powder and metal dust and they work is such crammed spaces that workers frequently get injured because pieces of metal hit them. Working in electroplating units for children means that they have to keep their hands in solutions of dangerous chemicals like potassium cyanide for long periods and, die when the universal curiosity of children to taste anything new, in this case these foul liquids seizes them. Moreover, electric current taken illicitly also causes disability and death. Children in spray painting units inhale unacceptably large doses of paint and paint thinners leading to servere chest disorders. Breathlessness, fever, tuberculosis, bronchitis, asthma and pneumoconisosis are some of the symptoms and diseases that effect the children of the lock industry. Malnutrition and poverty combine to exacerbate the ill-effects of their working conditions and considerably shorten their lives. The most telling evidence of the hazards involved in polishing, electroplating and spray painting is found in the fact that no unit employer employs his own children in any of these processes. The other processes of the lock industry do not seem to be hazardous in themselves for the health of children. But children working on hand-presses do lose the tips of their fingers when fatigue blunts their senses.

The only course of action in the circumstances is to impose a ban on children working in this industry and enforce it strictly. Even if some of the processes in the industry are not hazardous in themselves, once a child enters the units, it is impracticable — to say the least — to try to confine his/her work in only non-hazardous processes. If it was feasible to physically isolate the hazardous processes by clear geopgraphical demarcation, and possible to count on the co-operation of the owner, the question of children being permitted to work in non-hazardous processes could been considered. Since all the operations are inextricably intertwined in the present arrangement of the lock industry, a ban appears to be the only solution.

14

CHILDREN WORKING IN AGARBATTI INDUSTRY

Child labour is very much prevalent in our country. They are engaged in a number of occupations which varies from state to state and within the state from district to district. The type of job in which the children are engaged broadly can be grouped into two i.e. the urban areas and the rural areas. In the rural areas mostly children are engaged in agricultural sector and also in the construction of road and buildings in the villages and the nearby areas of villages where they reside. So far as the prevalence of child labour in urban areas are concerned these are starting from hotel, restaurant, Larri, Garage, household chores and a number of other home based activities. This particular study is aimed to make a survey of children working in Agarbatti Industry in Ahmedabad city. The Ministry of Labour, Government of India asked us to conduct a survey of the children engaged in agarbatti industry in Ahmedabad city. The amount sanctioned for the project was only Rs. 20,000 hence the area of study was restricted only two areas of Ahmedabad city though we have identified six such areas where children engaged in Agarbati industry were doing their job. The aim of this study was to identify the number of the children in this particular profession in these two areas on the basis of which the Government can think of opening non-formal education centres to impart education to these deprived children. For the purpose of identification of the number of child labour engaged in Agarbatti industry a questionnaire entitled "A survey of child labour employed in Agarbatti Industry in Ahmedabad City" was prepared. It consisted of 19 questions/statements. It was thought proper by the researchers to gather some additional information in addition to simply identifying the number of the children so employed. The objectives of gathering additional information was to give data regarding the demographic characteristics of the children, the duration of their job in this industry, the number of days they get the opportunity to do the manufacturing Agarbatti, working hours per day, the main profession of their family, monthly income they get from this profession, the total income of their members, the number of their family members working in Agarbatti profession and the average number of Agarbatti manufactured by the child per day.

Data Collection

First of all the investigators went to these two areas of the city vis, Saraspur and Bapunasgar. The investigators contacted the significant persons in those two areas and could know the names of the various industries engaged in this activity and they could also get the information regarding the chawls, houses and societies where the children either along with their family members or at the houses of others were engaged in manufacturing Agarbatti. The another source of information available to the investigators were to different shops where the agarbatti was being sold and those shopkeepers could help considerably to the investigators to indentify the names of the industries and the other different places where this type of work was going on. Investigators could also take an opportunity to meet and discuss with the office bearers of the association of Agarbatti manufacturing industries and could discuss with them the objective of the project and sought their cooperation in this endeavour and most of the office bearers could come forward to extend their cooperation and help in the collection of data. The investigators want to the places where a group of people including children and grown up poeple were engaged in manufacturing Agarbatti in Groups and they requested the owner of that particular industry to part information by allowing the child labours to answer questions printed in the questionnaire. At the initial stage the owner were very much apprehensive and showed the stubbornness to part with any information. But after explaining the purpose of the project and through pursuation they did allow the child labours working at their place to give the answer of the questions which the investigators asked them. But when the investigators went to the individual houses where either the whole family was engaged in manufacturing Agarbatti or they could hire children of others and were manufacturing Agarbatti at their own houses, the gathering of information from them was not very difficult.

Results of the Survey

The total number of the children employed in Agarbatti Industry in Ahmedabad city in the areas of Saraspur and Bapunagar is 2788 out of which 785 are males and 2003 are female child labours which has been shown in Table number 1. Table 2 gives the distribution of child labour on the basis of age group. 41 children are of 5 years, 627 children are within the age group of 6-9 years and 2120 children are within the age range of 10-14 years.

1025 children are Hindus and 1763 children are Muslim which is presented in Table 3. So far as the educational level of these child labours are concerned we find that 312 children are illiterate, 651 have got their education within the range of 1-3 standard, 1023 childen have received the education within the range of 4-6th standard and 802 children have got the education within the range of 7-9th standard. 1969 children are continuing their education, 819 children have stopped their study. These data are shown in Table 4. If we look at the working period in terms of years since when they are doing this Agarbatti manufacturing activity it is clear from Table 5 that 42 children have started their work of manufacturing activity of Agarbatti from 1-15 days, 5 children have started their activity from 16 to 30 days, 18 children have started their work from 1-2 months, 89 children have started their work from 3 to 5 months, 116 children have started their work from 6 to 9 months, 1365 children have started their work from 1-2 years, 629 children have started their work from 3-4 years, 266 children have started their work from 5-6 years, 925 children have started work from 7-8 years, 77 children have started their work from 9-10 years.

The average number of days in a month the child labours get work in manufacturing Agarbatti is presented in Table 6. We find that a chidren do their work within the range of 1-9 days, 48 child labour get their work for 10-15 days, 321 children get their work for 16-20 days, 1416 children get their work for 21 to 25 days and 999 child labour get their work for 26 to 30 days.

The average hours a child labour work in a day is presented in Table 7. 235 children work for 2-3 hours, 2125 children work for 4-5 hours, 333 labour work for 6-7 hours, 76 children work for 8-9 hours and 19 children work for 10 and more hours.

Tabe No. 8 furnishes the information regarding child labours families main profession. 246 children's families main profession is Agarbatti. 131 child labour's families main profession is rickshaw driving. 256 children's families' main profession is using larries, 1563 child labourers family member work either in the factory or in mills, and 623 children's families main profession in pan-gulla (pan-shop and others). So far as the child labourers monthly income from Agarbatti is concerned it is found that 699 children earn Rs. 2 to 50 per month, 984 children get income of Rs. 51 to 100 per month, 818 children get monthly income of Rs. 101 to 200, 235 children get monthly income of Rs. 201 to 300, 52 children get monthly income of Rs. 301 to Rs. 400. This data is presented in Table No. 9.

Table 10 gives information regarding child labour families whole income. It is found that 617 chidren's families whole income is within the range of Rs. 400 to Rs. 500, 889 children's families whole income is Rs. 501 to Rs. 600, 443 children's families whole income is within the range of Rs. 601 to 801. 410 children's families whole income is within the range of Rs. 801 to 1000 and 423 children's families whole income is within the range of Rs. 1001 and more.

Table 11 depicts total number of family of the children engaged in Agarbatti industry. 52 children have 1 to 3 family members, 1288 children have 4-6 family members, 1195 children have 7-9 family members 216 chidlren have 10-12 family members and 37 children have 13-15 family members.

Table 12 gives the information regarding number of family members working in Agarbatti industry of the children engaged in Agarbatti manufacturing. 1219 children's 1-2 family members are working in Agarbatti. 1328 children's 3-4 family members are working in Agarbatti. 187 children's 5-6 family members are working in Agarbatti. 54 children's 7-9 family members are working in Agarbatti.

The perusal of Table 13 makes it clear that 1089 children manufacture 500 to 1000 Agarbatti in a day. 826 children manufacture 1001 to 2000 Agarbatti in a day. 430 children manufacture 2001 to 3000 Agarbatti in a day. 205 children manufacture 3001 to 4000 Agarbatti in a day, and 238 children manufacture 40001 to 6000 Agarbatti in a day.

Table 14 gives the name of the places where the children are working in Agarbatti manufacturing in Bapunagar are and number of the children working there. There are 35 places where children are engaged in manufacaturing Agarbatti.

Table 15 gives the name of different manufacturing Agarbatti industries in Bapunagar area. In total there are 36 manufacturing Agarbatti industries where child labourers are engaged in manufacturing Agarbatti.

Table 16 gives information regarding different places in Saraspur area where the children are engaged in manufacturing Agarbatti in industry. There are total 38 places where Agarbatti manufacturing work is going on.

Table 17 furnishers the information regarding the name of the manufacturing Agarbatti industries in Saraspur area. These are the following.

(a) Smt. Taraban Vimalbhai Shah Industry.
(b) R. C. Industries.
(c) Maganbhai Centre.

Conclusion

The result of the survey shows that is total there are 2,788 child labourer working in Agarbatti Industry in Ahmedabad city in the area of Saraspur and Bapunagar out of this number 785 are males and 2300 are femal child labourers.

2. 1, 025 child labourers are Hindus and 1,763 are Muslims, 48.9 per cent of the child labours have started their work from one to two years and 33.1 per cent of the child labourers have started their work from 7 to 8 years.
3. 50.8 per cent of the child labour get their work for 21 to 25 days in a month. 35.8 per cent of the child labours get their work for 26 to 30 days in a month.
4. 76.2 per cent of the child labour work for four to five hours a day.
5. 25.1 per cent of the child labours get income of Rs. 51 to Rs. 100 per month from manufacturing Agarbatti. 29.3 per cent of child labours get monthly income of Rs. 101 to 200.
6. 46.2 per cent of the child labours working in Agarbatti industry have family size of 4 to 6 members and 42.9 per cent child labours family size is of 7 to 9 members.
7. 39.1 per cent child labour manufacture 500 to 1000 Agarbatti in a day, 29.6 per cent child labour manufacture 1001 to 2000 Agarbatti in a day. 15.4 per cent child labourers manufacture 2001 to 3000 Agarbatti in a day. 7.4 per cent child labours manufacture 3001 to 4000 Agarbatti in a day and 8.5 per cent child labour manufacture 4001 to 6000 Agarbatti in a day.

Table-1 : Distribution of Child Labour Working in Agarbatti Industry in Ahmedabad City on the Basis of Sex

Area	Male	Female	Total
Saraspur Area	306	828	1134
Bapunagar Area	479	1175	1654
Total of Both Areas	785	2003	2788

Table-2 : Distribution of Child Labour Working in Agarbatti Industry in Ahmedabad City on the Basis of Age Group

Area	5 yrs.	6-9 yrs.	10-14 yrs.	Total
Saraspur	13	193	928	1134
Bapunagar	28	434	1192	1654
Total of both areas	41	627	2120	2788

Table-3 : Distribution of Child Labour Working in Agarbatti Industry in Ahmedabad City on the Basis of Caste

Area	Hindu	Muslim	Total
Saraspur Area	38	1096	1134
Bapunagar Areas	987	667	1654
Total of both areas	1025	1763	2788

Total-4 : Distribution of Child Labour Working in Agarbatti Industry in Ahmedabad City on the Basis of Education Level

Area	Illiterate	1-3rd	4-6th	7-9th	Total
Saraspur Area	142	212	340	440	1134
Bapunagar Area	170	439	683	362	1654
Total of both Areas	312	651	1023	802	2788

Study is Continuing?

Area	Yes	No	Total
Saraspur Area	732	402	1134
Bapunagar Area	1237	417	1654
Total of both areas	1969	819	2788

Table-5 : Distribution of Child Labours Working in Agarbatti Industry in Ahmedabad City on the Basis of Working Period

Area	1-15 days	16-30 days	1-2 mth.	3-5 mth.	6-9 mth.	1-2 yrs.	3-4 yrs.	5-6 yrs.	7-8 yrs.	9-10 yrs.	Ttl.
Saraspur	13	2	65	36	32	524	197	135	65	65	113
Bapunagar	29	3	99	53	84	781	432	131	30	12	165
Total of both	42	5	164	89	116	1365	629	266	95	77	278

Table-6 : Distribution of Child Labour Working in Agarbatti Industry in Ahmedabad City on the Basis of Average No. of Days of Working in a Month

Area	1-9 days	10-15 days	16-20 days	21-25 days	26-30 days	Total
Saraspur	4	29	171	433	497	1134
Bapunagar	0	19	150	983	502	1654
Total of both areas	4	48	321	1416	999	2788

Table-7 : Distribution of Child Labour Working in Agarbatti Industry in Ahmedabad City on the Basis of Averge Hours of Working in a Day

Area	2-3 hrs	4-5 hrs	6-7 hrs	8-9 hrs	10 & more hrs	Total
Saraspur	93	701	265	56	19	1134
Bapunagar	143	1424	68	20	-	1654
Total of both	235	2125	333	76	19	2788

Table-8 : Distribution of Child Labour Working in Agarbatti Industry in Ahmedabad City on the Basis of Family's Main Profession

Area	Agarbati	Rickshaw	Lari	Factory/Mills	Pan Galla & Others	Total
Saraspur	133	39	33	483	446	1134
Bapunagar	113	92	192	1080	177	1654
Total of both	246	131	225	1563	623	2788

Table-9 : Distribution of Child Labour Working in Agarbatti Industry in Ahmedabad City on the Basis of Monthly Income from Agarbatti

Area	Rs. 20-25	Rs. 51-100	Rs. 101-200	Rs. 201-300	Rs. 301-400	Total
Saraspur	51	351	493	189	50	1134
Bapunagar	648	633	325	46	2	1654
Total of both	699	984	818	235	52	2788

Table-10 : Distribution of Child Labour Working in Agarbatti Industry in Ahmedabad City on the Basis of Family's Whole Income

Area	Rs. 200-400	Rs. 401-600	Rs. 601-800	Rs. 801-1000	1001 & above	Total
Saraspur	294	421	93	173	154	1134
Bapunagar	323	468	350	244	269	1654
Total of both	617	889	443	416	423	2788

Table-11 : Distribution of Child Labour Working in Agarbatti Industry in Ahmedabad City on the Basis of Total Number of the Family

Area	1-3	4-6	7-9	10-12	13-15	Total
Saraspur	21	523	463	100	27	1134
Bapunagar	31	765	732	116	10	1654
Total of both	52	1288	1195	216	37	2788

Table-12 : Distribution of Child Labour Working in Agarbatti Industry in Ahmedabad City on the Basis of No. of Family Members Working in Agarbatti

Area	1-2	3-4	5-6	7-9	10-12	13-15	Total
Saraspur	629	438	67	-	-	-	1134
Bapunagar	590	890	120	49	5	-	1654
Total of both	1219	1328	187	49	5	-	2788

Table-13 : Distribution of Child Labour Working in Agarbatti Industry in Ahmedabad City on the Basis of Average Number of Agarbatti Manufactured by a Child in a Day

Area	500-1000	1001-2000	2001-3000	3001-4000	4001-6000	Total
Saraspur	373	303	205	98	155	1134
Bapunagar	716	523	225	107	83	1654
Total of both areas	1089	826	430	205	238	2788

Table-14 : Name of Place Where the Children are Working in Agarbatti Manufacturing in Bapunagar Area and the No. of Children Working there

S. No.	Name of Place	No. of Children
1	2	3
1.	Jhopadpatti in front of Dispensary No. 20	50
2.	Bapunagar Char Rasta	22
3.	Jhopadie in front of Charodia Police Chowki	47
4.	Juni Rangwali Chal	46
5.	Jhopadapatti Nicol Road, Bapunagar Char Rasta	4
6.	Gujarat Housing Board	335
7.	Malik Saban Dargah	75
8.	Ram Rajya Nagar, Ulainagar Chal	4
9.	Karnataka Chali, In Front of Nagarveli	16
10.	Mohan Nagar Vibhag, 1 and 2	74
11.	Leela Nagar	70
12.	Indira Garib Nagar	323
13.	In front of Rajan School	1
14.	Sanjay Nagar	3
15.	Bharat Bobbin Factory Chal	14
16.	Bhavna Society	3
17.	Lakhandwali Chal	64
18.	Ghadawali Chal	30
19.	Naseeb Nagar	47
20.	Aman Chawk	53
21.	Mahadeva Nagar	3
22.	Shastri Nagar	2
23.	In front of Anand Nagar, Jalaram Society	13
24.	Abad Nagar	45
25.	Vaishalee Nagar	2
26.	Shree Ram Krupa Nagar	2
27.	Juni Chal	13
28.	Urban Nagar	64
29.	Hari Das Nagar Challi	19
30.	Vishnu Chal	24
31.	Subhlarmi Flat	36
32.	Navlakha Hangla	12
33.	India Colony	59
34.	Sonaria Block	63
35.	Fakeer Das Chal	16

Table-15 : Name of Place of Agarbatti Manufacturing in Nagar Area of Ahmedabad City

S. No.	Name of Places	No. of children
1.	Amina Agarbatti Works	10
2.	Sellar Agarbatti Factory	95
3.	Gope Agarbatti Works	66
4.	Chetan Agarbatti Works	28
5.	Bharat Industries	16
6.	Anand Agarbatti Works	2
7.	Sukhadia Perfume Works	5
8.	Devendra Agarbatti Works	3
9.	R.C. Industries	52
10.	Sanjay Agarbatti Works	15
11.	Akas Agarbatti Works	60
12.	Gujarat Dhup Sugandh Factory	89
13.	Patodia Agarbatti Works	4
14.	Gautam Agarbatti Works	3
15.	Shamim Agarbatti Works	13
16.	Punam Agarbatti Works	13
17.	Neelam Agarbatti Works	4
18.	M.M. Agarbatti Works	17
19.	Vijaya Agarbatti Works	29
20.	Ramdev Agarbatti Works	25
21.	Mayank Agarbatti Works	11
22.	Ambika Agarbatti Works	2
23.	Chamunda Agarbatti Works	20
24.	Pankaj Agarbatti Works	64
25.	Mahila Vanat Kendra	31
26.	Jyoti Agarbatti Works	32
27.	Devikrupa Agarbatti Works	5
28.	Aradhana Agarbatti Works	17
29.	Ravajee Bhai Factory	13
30.	Jaysattandhar Agarbatti Works	2
31.	Vinod Agarbatti Works	16
32.	Rajendra Agarbatti Works	3
33.	Asheerbad Agarbatti Works	12
34.	Deepak Agarbatti Works	9
35.	Ram Kishor Agarbatti Works	5
36.	Mamta Industries	7

190 / Child Labour in Various Industries

Table-16 : Place Where the Children are Working in Agarbatti In Saraspur Area and the No. of Children Working there

S. No.	Name of Places	No. of Children
1.	Bai Rukhi's Chawl	143
2.	Arvind Mill Society Chawl	20
3.	Mohanlal Sindhi's Chawl	4
4.	Kotwali Chawl	55
5.	Tulsidas Chawl	26
6.	Mela Duka's Chawl	16
7.	Jaya Keshav's Chawl	3
8.	Atmaram Ambalal's Chawl	1
9.	Manilsal Kadiya's Chawl	24
10.	Fruitwali Chawl	8
11.	Phoolchand Old Chawl	51
12.	Bapala Kadiya's Chawl	36
13.	Shantilal's Chawl	2
14.	Manchhani Masjid Slum Qurters	37
15.	Chunilal Jethlal's Chawl	2
16.	Balubhai Kambhar's Chawl	20
17.	Pathan's Chawl	66
18.	Mangal Prabhat's Chawl	21
19.	Patrawali's Chawl	127
20.	Naranbhai Kumbhar's Chawl	6
21.	Somnath Nagardas's Chawl	44
22.	Parmanand's Chawl	5
23.	Phoolchand's New Chawl	3
24.	Shah Kantilal Gokaldas Chawl	11
25.	Chahwali Chawl	6
26.	Radheshyam's Chawl	9
27.	Popatlal Mohanlal Chawl	25
28.	Jalampuri	62
29.	Vakil's Chawl	7
30.	Balabhai Chaganlal's Chawl	89

31.	Bhavsar's Chawl	48
32.	Sawantilal's Chawl	38
33.	Ammu Mills Chawl	10
34.	Bai Jeevi's Chawl	8
35.	Vikram Mills Chawl	94
36.	Chandulal's Old Chawl	4
37.	Kantilal Kasturchand's Chawl	4
38.	Dahya Malino Bagicho	11

Table-17 : Name of the Manufacturing Agarbatti Industries in Saraspur

1. Smt. Taraben Vimalbhai Shah Centre
2. R.C. Industries
3. Maganbhai Centre

15

CHILDREN WORK IN THE BRASS WARE INDUSTRY

The job of the moulder is a very delicate operation and it there is a slight mistake or accident the boy can get very badly injured and can even lose his limbs. He wears no protective gear and stands barefoot on top of the furnace to either put in the crucible or to remove it. The temperature in the furnace is about 1100 C. As one exporter/manufacturer, explaining the processes in his factory, said: 'See how dexterous this young child is. He has to be. Because even if a drop of molten brass fall on his foot there will be a hole in it.

The Brass Ware Industry of Morababad Uttar Pradesh

Moradabad is one of the most important centres of production of art metal wares in the country. It is the district headguarters of the district of the same name in the State of Uttar Pradesh and is situated about a hundred miles from Delhi on the right bank of the river Ramganga. Flower vases, planters, plates, dinner services, tea sets and various decorative object d' art the all made here.

The history of the brass industry of Moradabad is lost in antiquitey. According to the Moradabad Gazetter, the original method of moulding was the para method by which earthen moulds were used to give shape to molten metal. After 1920, the *daria* (box moulding) system was adopted but only for small articles like handless and spouts. Cutlery began to be manufactured around 1925 and power began to be used towards the end of 1930. Imported brass sheets were used as raw material in the manufacture of utensils but as the they were in short supply around 1940, the prodution of sheets from scrap, virgin copper and zinc was taken up locally.

In 1947, there were only three big exporters in Moradabad: *Lala Bhukan Saran, Mousin Yaar Khan and Haji Kallan*. After 1947, when there was large-scale migration from Punjab to Moradabad and other cities, the Punjabi Hindus saw the industry as a good investment and began sending samples abroad for orders.

As the industry developed, many outsiders came to settle down in Moradabad. They would get things made by the multiprocess unit manufacturers who were known as *Karkhanedars* (owner of a Karkhana or factory). Many of the local Muslim elite also realized the potential of this business and began exporting goods. Haji Mohammad Jan Mohammad Dawood, who now have almost eight firms, and Haji Mohammad Jikaria Mohammad Yahiya, who also have several firms of exporters, are amongst the earliest ones.

After 1970, a new process of sheet work was introduced and this was done on lathes. Goods like planters began to be manufactured in this fashion which did not require a high level of skill. These goods were made in factories and a large number of the unemployed rural poor came to the city to work there.

The term 'art metal ware', though not very precisely defined, is generally used to denote metal articles which have a higher input of 'artistic skill' as compared to functional household metal wares. More than 90 per cent of the goods produced in Maradabad are exported.

There are almost 150,000 workers engaged directly in the metal ware industry. This figure would include manufacturers, suppliers, exporters, and administrative staff. Of the total workers, approximately 40,000-45,000 are children below the age of fourteen years. The basis of the figures of the numbers of workers, both adults and children, has been discussed in detail later.

While the figure of 150,000 workers is an estimate for the metal ware industry. The study was primarily of the brassware industry. It is however very difficult to differentiate between the two as many of the goods made in a particular unit may be for both metal ware and art-metal ware, for the sake of consistency, the industry will hense forth be referred to as the brass ware industry.

Common items produced are flower vases, planter, wallplates, candle-stands, dinner services, cutlery and so on. The estimated turn-over of the Moradabad brass ware industry for 1986-7 has been Rs. 90 crores (Rs. 1 crores is equivalent to Rs. 10,000,000) and was likely to cross Rs. 100 crores (U.P. State Brass Ware Corporation : Personal Communication). Other important art metal ware centres in Uttar Pradesh are located in Varanasi, Jalesar and Almora.

There are several categories of manufacturing units in Moradabad. Some of the largest units-both in terms of size and in the number of workers employed-will be referred to as factories. At the next level are smaller manufacturing units, where more than one process is carried out—and these are known as *karkhanas* the literal translation of which is factory. The owner of *karkhana* is known as a *karkhanedar*. The term *karkhanedar* is also used to describe a contractor because many owners of mulit-process or double-process units also act as middlemen for procuring items not made by them, from others. At the bottom level are single-process units also act as middlemen for procuring items not made by them, from others. At the bottom level are the single-process workshops referred to as artisan units. While there are a large number of factories, most of the business is in the hands of the middle-level entrepreneur who both employs artisans directly in his multiprocess unit. gets work done by them and supplies the goods to exporters (IDS, 1983 : 11). In some cases, factories do not get all the processses done in their own premises but place orders directly with multi-process unit owners, the *karkhanedars*. For the sake of simplicity, the term factory of factory owner will be used for those units or owners of units which are very large both in size and in numbers or workers employed on the same premises. The term multi-process unit will be used to refer to *karkhanas* and the term workshop for single-process units.

It is difficult to give authentic information about the number of establishments working in Moradabad. If a particular unit wishes to avail itself of concessions and facilities given by the government, it has to be registered with the District Industries Centre (DIC). According to the DIC, there were 3000 units registered with them as small-scale units with a capital of less than Rs. 35,00,000. But many people this researcher spoke to said there were at least another 3000 units which were unregistered. According to the Factories Act, any unit employed more than twenty workers and not using power or more than nine workers using power is considered a factory. Once the unit is registered as a factory, its workers become entitled to certain rights under the Act. These rights include Employees State Insurance. Provident Fund, leave with pay and so on. Only 381 unit were registered as factories and everybody agreed that this was a gross underestimation because employers were chary of becoming legally liable to provide statutory benefits to workers. It will be seen, therefore, that the statistics regarding the number of establishments and factories are quite misleading.

More than 90 per cent of the goods produced in Moradabad are meant for export and this explains the dominant role of the exporter in the industry. Exporters are of two types : manufacturing exporters are few in number and are those who have very large businesses.

Exporters who have entered the field of manufacturing have done so in order to maintain quality control and to preserve the secrecy of their designs. The directly employ few workers themselves and these are either supervisory staff or artisans with a high degree of skills. Their modus operandi is to have a number of captive mulit-process units, who use their building space and machinery on the payment of rent. By this means, the manufacturer exporter is sure that his work will be done according to schedule but he has no direct responsibility for or reletionship with the workers in these captive units. These workers are the employees for the multi-process unit owner, who usually works on the machines himself as well. Though the building and machinery belong to the manufacturing exporter, it is for the multi-process unit owner to organize his supplies of raw materials like black powder, chemicals and coal and with the help of hired-labour, complete the job contracted out to him. In this type of arrangement, it was also found that many of the units in the premises of the manufacturer exporter were single-process units specializing in particular activities like moulding, scraping, welding, polishing and electroplating.

The non-manufacturing exporter is the more representative figure and accounts for a larger share of the business. His way of working is to ask a multi-process unit owner to give a sample and then place an order after tendering that sample to a number of possible competitors. Scraping, welding, and grinding (fine scraping) are activities commonly carried out in these mulit-process units. It is rare for the processes of moulding, polishing and electroplating to be carried out in these multi-process units for these jobs reauire separate space as they generate a great deal of heat and pollution. The multi-process unit owner is charged with the responsibility not only of completing the processes which he himself carries out in his unit but usually also of getting the goods finished in other respects through different single-process units or workshops.

It will be seen from the above description that, the multi process unit owners, who are given orders by the non-manufacturing exporters differ significantly from the multi-process unit owners who are tied to the manufacturing exporters. The former have their own buildings and machinery and not necessarily linked to a particular exporter. Besides, they operate on a wide canvas and normally get the wares readied in all respects for the exporter. While the multi-process unit owner is an artisan-turned-entrepreneur, the single-process unit owner attached to the manufacturing exporter is more commonly a worker, with a high degree of initiative but who does not perform full-blown entrepreneurial fuctions.

It was found that of the exporters, 75 per cent were Hindus and 25 per cent were Muslims. The Hindus were either Punjabi's who went to Moradabad after Partition on Banias, local trading castes. Punjabi Mussalmans. Ansaris and members of the Khan clan made up the Muslim exporters. As regards the multi-process unit manufacturers, about 65 per cent of them are Muslims (Ansaris, Mansooris, Ghosis, etc.) and 35 per cent are Hindus (mainly Punjabis). Most Hindus labourers belong to lower castes like Bagvans, Balmikis, Lodhas and Ahirs. Amonst the Muslims, the poorer Ansari and Quarishi families work as labourers, while the bulk of the Muslim work force is to be found in small workshops, the majority of Hindu workers are engaged in the large factories.

Methodology and Fieldwork

Data for this study were collected over a period of nineteen days on two separate field trips to Moradabad and its surrouding villages. During these visits, opportunity was taken to hold frank and participatory discussions (where possible) with workers, entrepreneurs, exporters, contractors, and others connected with the trade. An addition, there were interviews with government officials, doctors, social activists and others. During the period of field-work, I spoke to about 300 people belonging to different categories for varying lengths of time.

I visited fifteen large factories. They were large in terms of size of premises and by number of workers employed, who ranged between more than twenty and up to about seventy-five. Visits to the first few factories helped me understand processes of manufacture, and, later I began discusssing issues with the factory owner or his representative. Access was made possible since a helpful government official accompanied me. But it was evident that the absence of a questionnaire creates suspicion amongst some factory owners; in particular, those who were exporters or their employees were most reluctant to part with information.

However, several factory owners—who were not exporters but supplied them with goods-spoke freely to me for they felt that government gave undue concessions to exporters and did not treat simple manufacturers with the same solicitude. Though the number of large factories visited was relatively small, they took up a disproportionate share of my time as they were dispersed in different parts of the town and had a large number of processes in operation.

I was able to visit some thirty medium-size multi-process units in which the number of processes were limited and less sophisticated as compared to those in the larger factories refer to above. Here I received cordial treatment almost uniformly. These units fell under the jurisdiction of the official accompanying me which was of great advantage for my work. Except for the old child, children were not found working either in the larger factories or in the medium-sized ones. In many of the units I went to, I could disarmingly that a lower number of worker is reported in order to evade the provisions under the Factories Act that call for certain facilities to be given to worker if the unit is deemed to be a factory.

I saw about a thousand single-process workshops in the by-lenes of Moradabad, away from the main road. This statement needs clarification. These workshops are involved with the precesses of moulding, polishing, scraping, welding, engraving and colouring. Of all these small workshops I saw, more than half were moulding units. Most of the workshops I saw had three or four workers, adults and children. Usually, these small workshops were closed off on three sides and faced the streets for the natural light and ventilation they offered. Commonly, these spaces were part or extensions of the residential complex but clearly demarcated. However, there were also some larger sheds where several adults and children were working in separate units with their own equipment but sharing common space.

Out of nineteen days of fieldwork, twelve days were spent walking through these populated Muslim localities, observing what was going, on spending a few minutes and sometimes engaging there in long conversations with the local people. The purpose of this exercise was to gain a representative understanding of what could be considered the most common form of industrial activity in Moradabad in which the largest number of people are employed, particularly children. One question that I invariable asked was whether the children working in these workshops were part of the families of the adults working there. And this I did by asking the children present what their fathers did and the adults about where their children were and what they did. I shall return later to this theme of children working as hired labour—for it is my contention that official policy rests importantly upon the belief that children in the brass ware industry work along with their families and learn traditional skills.

Since I was there for many days and visited the same localities again and again, sometimes people would offer to take me to their workshops which were in their own homes. I then got the opportunity to see what kinds of units people were running at home. These visits also gave me the chance to talk to people at langth-particularly women and girls—who were otherwise invisible. I learnt about the history and development of the industry and the situation of the labour force from older people and others who were not currently employd and involved directly in the industry. Very rerely did the children speak in the presence of adults and it was not possible to get to know what they felt about their work. The children would either listen to what the adults were saying or, if they were asked a direct question, would answer in monosyllables and them lapse into silence. Invariable when a question was asked of a child, an adult would answer. In units where the largest number of children were working—the moulding units—it was risky to ask children questions because of the hazardous nature of the work. Concentrations interrupted might have led to accidents!

One day, leaving early in the morning, I visited six villages within the radius of ten kilometers from Moradabad town. In spite of the fact that it was so early in the morning, both adults and children were getting ready to leave to leave for the day's work. I had an opprtunity to discuss with many mothers and their neighbours the social and economic conditions they lived in and was able to get information about the castes and communities they belonged to.

Processes in the Manufacture of Brass Ware

There are several processes involved in the manufacture of brass ware. The basic raw material used are copper and Zinc. The making of ingots and sheets is the first stage of the production process. Ingots can be of two types: *silli* (oblong) and *qulli* (round). Oblong or round ingots or brass sheets are used depending upon type of article to be produced.

There are very few factories where ingots are made and these factories supply the other manufacturing units. Copper, zinc and scrap material are put into large graphite crucibles and heated to high temperatures. The resultant molten *metal* (brass) is then poured into smaller earthenware mould to make the ingots. The shape of the mould is either oblong or round depending on whether oblong or round ingots are being made. Only adults are involved in the manufacture of ingots.

The oblong ingots are sold directly to the *darja bhattis* (box mould furnaces) in which the which the worker moulds the various parts of the final product—for example, handles, spouts and lids—as well as small bowls, plates and so on. He breaks off as much of the oblong ingot as necessary, melts it and fashions his goods.

In the box mould furnaces, the following operation are undertaken continuously. The mould or die is put into the box and packed with a black powder made up of sand, clay oil, molasses and borax and sprinkled with a mixture of ammonium chloride. A piece of the oblong ingot is put into the graphite crucible and when heated, the molten metal is poured through a spout into the box. The metal solidifies almost immediately into the required shape and the box is then opened to remove the article with a pair of tongs. The mixture of black powder falls out and is then beaten up by hand in perparation for further use. This process is then repeated. Children are used here to rotate the cycle wheel and fans the furnace, to put the ingot into the crucible and heat it, to remove the crucible containing molten brass and hand it to the adult worker and to grind the blank powder for re-use.

Round ingots are not sold in that fom. In the factories where they are made, they are put onto rolling machines and pressed into sheets of the required specifications. Both round ingots and the sheets that they are fashioned into are manufactured according to the requirements of the indenter. Bowls and plates are examples of the type of goods which have a circular or spherical shape that are made from round ingots.

Apart from oblong and round ingots, the third possible starting point in the production chain in brass sheets. Here, children are not employed. There sheets are maily manufactured by the Uttar Pradesh State Brass Ware Corporation and then supplied to the manufacturers of brass ware. The goods that are to be made from these sheets are not moulded. The most important item made from these sheets is the planter. The sheets are pressed in factories and given shape and design on electrically operated machines which have dies in them. Them planters or pots are moved several times between the press and the furnace before they are given a final shape. They are then scraped by adults on power-operated lathes. In this semifinished form the goods are normally sent to other multi-process manufacturing units, which specialize in the processes of polishing, soldering, electroplating and so on. Goods like planters, which are one of the most important export items, sometimes need ancillary parts like handless and chains. which are manufactured in box mould furnaces and later joined.

When the article in question reaches the stage of being given a shape-whether—whether the starting point be oblong or round ingot or brass sheet—the processes to follow are by and large common, for example, all semi-finished goods are scraped, welded, polished and electroplated or silver-plated. Some wares are engraved and coloured as well.

Semi-finished articles are to be scraped in order to make them smooth and iron out the rough edges. Scraping can be done either by hand or by machine. When it is manual, this involves the used of chisel and hammer. Mechanical scraping, which involves the fixing of the articles on moving rods, is done only by adults in the case or larger wares but young boys can also be found doing this work for smaller pieces.

Welding can be done in three ways : using small furneces stoves or gas cylinder. Children are engaged in large numbers in welding workshops and their main job is to hold the pieces together which are to be welded. Young women and girls the metal wires around the parts to be welded in their homes an send them to the workshops for welding.

Once the semi-processes goods are scraped and welded, they are then to be washed and polished to give them the reguisite gloss. Washing is done in a mixture which has hydrochloric acid and this work is unusually done children. The article is first cleaned, polishing by machine involves mounting the piece on a spindle or lathe with polishing paint the revolving article as a result of which it gets the required finish : if they are plain, they are polished on machines rotating faster and using discs covered with emery powder. Polishing machines are also called buffing machines.

Engraving is the cutting of design into the surface of a metal. The engraver cuts the required design on the ware with the help of engraving tools and light weight hammer. In the case of ordinary work, the design can be carved by the engraver from memory. If the design are intricate, the design are the first drawn on paper and outlined on the ware. After engraving the resultant depressions are filled with shellac by heating the aricles and appliying shellac sticks. The articles are then glazed by rubbing with wood ash. Children and women are also engraved in this work. The main raw materials used are shellac, lacquer, colours, thinners, soft coke and zinc oxide. Frequently, goods are polished both before and after engraving.

Though not all wares electroplated or silver-plated, when they are, it is the last stage in the production process. The purpose the this activity is to prevent or postpone the tarnshing of wares. It involves tying the goods on metal wires and then immersing them in baths of a solution containing potassium cyanide and silver nitrate while and electric current is passed. The next step is to cover them in ammonium chloride powder, which absorbs moisture and hastens drying. Children are to be found both in the activities of tying these articles to the wires and covering them with ammonium chloride powder.

It has been reported that till the late 1950s or early 60s, 89 per cent of all establishments in Moradabad worked without power with only 11 per cent using power. The establishments using power were engaged mainly in scraping, electroplating and polishing. Today, many item, particularly those made from brass sheets, are made by using mechanized methods. The large units have facilities for mechanical rolling cutting and fabricating pressed sheets articles. There is still no mechanization in sheet beating, casting, engraving and emameling, but more and more units are introducing a low level of mechanization in the processes of sheet work, soldering and scraping.

Changes in Demand : Impact upon Technology, Labour and Structure

There was time about twenty-five or thirty years ago when the brass ware industry was entirely a cottage industry in which the artisan worked with the help on his family labour an virtually no hired help. I was told that the goods produced at that time were vases, decanter, wine glasses, decorative plates and the like. Though there was a small export market in the Middle East, most of the goods made were sold in India. The designs that were carved, the colours that were used and the wares that were thus made—all bore the unmistakeble stamp of Moradabad and made that town famous for its particular type of brass ware. The skilled craftsman was in control of the industry to the extent that he purchased the raw materials himself, fashioned the goods and then sold them. Since there was specialization in different types of skills, processes that could not be done at home were got done by other artisans.

The self-employed artisan of your, who was the representative figure in the production system until a few years ago, is now conspicuous by his substantially reduced presence. In 1959-60, it was estimated that 66 per cent of workers were self-employed. By 1974, the proportion of self-employed workers was estimated at less than 1 per cent (IDS, 1983 : 29). This was not an isolated development.

The kinds of changes that have taken place in the organization of production of the brass ware industry of Moradabad have been well analyzed in a study on the subject undertaken by the Industrial Development Service (IDS), it will be useful to quote here at length from the report.

There has been an organizational change in terms of (i) and increase in the averge number of workers per establishment... (ii) and increase in the number of multi-process establishments (*karkhanas*) (iii) decline in the category of workers described as 'self-employed' (iv) an increase in the number of manufacturers, suppliers and exporters who co-ordinate the completion of a number of operation through different sets of artisans. This is reflected in the shift in the ownership of working capital. In 1979-80 exporters accounted for 67 per cent of the working capital employed, while the other 33 per cent was accounted for by suppliers and manufacturers. Even allowing for a margin of error of a definitional discrepancy, it supoorts the decline in the self decline in the self-employed category and an increase in the proportion of wage earners among the craftsmen (ibid. : 5-6).

What accounts for these changes? Earlier, even though artware always earmarked for export, there was in important domestic market for brass utensils. Rises in the prices of raw meterial, the difficulty of keeping brass utensils from tarnishing and the growing popularity of stainless steel gradually eroded the domestic market. At the same time, there were significant changes in the nature and scale of demand from international market in the USA and Europe.

Planter, dinner plates, tea services and other items of table-ware were sought for in international markets. These were not the traditional brass ware item made in Moradabad like flower vases, decanters, wine glasses, decorative table tops and so on. The traditional methods of manufacturer of the traditional items of brass ware which I have described earlier in Chapterl consisted of a series of operations being performed by a particular manufacturer such as, moulding is box moulds, welding, scraping, polishing, engraving and colouring. The technology thus employed was not suitable for mass production and mass production was called for by the new, enormous scale of international demand. Morever, the kinds of goods that found a market abroad were such that they lent themselves to the technology of mass production.

Planters, dinner services, bowls and so on could be manufactured by machines on which there were dies containing designs which were impressed upon large numbers of pieces simultaneously, Factories manufacturing sheets of different specifications sprang up in response to the new climate of demand and such sheets could now be ordered by other entrepreneurs according to their needs. The introduction of mechanization in the production of brass sheets made the procurement of this raw material much easier for the entrepreneur. It can thus be seen how the change in the quality and scale of demand was importantly responsible for the changes in technology that followed.

I have earlier drawn attention to the fact that the traditional methods of manufacture required artisans who had skills in particular areas such as mouding, engraving, scraping an polishing. With the advent of mechanization, certain skills became redundant. Scraping and polishing which were traditional femele preserves were now done by machine.. As a result, female workers were displaced in large number. In a later section, the situation of the female worker will be accused in greater detail. Moulders still have an important role to play because they mould all the new technology. Engravers, on the other hand, have suffered a substantial set-back for they have role in the new technological processes and there is little demand for traditional carvings.

The growth of the industry created a demand for a large work-force and this demand was met by workers from the rural areas of Moradabad and from Bihar and eastern Uttar Pradesh. The level of mechanization is not particularly advanced : unskilled and semi-skilled workers are quite capable of handling the machines currently used. This is an additional reason for the changed profile of the brass ware worker as be becomes transformed from being a skilled artisan to wage labourer.

The children of artisans, it would be safe to say, were always involved with work of their fathers and mothers whether on a part-time or full-time basis. But such a situation obtained when the industry had a primarily cottage character. A combination of factors resulted in significant change. The prices of raw materials rose, there was a change in the nature and scale of demand, mechanization was introduced and women were displaced.

Together, these events resulted in a substantial increase in the share of children in the work force though this did not occur in a uniform way. For example, in the larger factories of Moradabad, it was observed that there were virtually no children at all. When I asked factory-onwers why this was so, they offered two reasons. The first and more important one, which seemed convincing to me when, I saw the machines involved, was that the new technology was not suitable for the height and strength of children. The size of the machine and the nature of the process involved such as, removing the round ingots from the furnace, pressing them into shape, re-heating and pressing the unfinished wares several-times, seemed to be beyond the physical capacity of children. The other reason proffered by factory owners was that child labour was banned under the factories Act and they would not want to risk prosecution or harassment on that account. Of cource, it was easier for labour inspectors to inspect the comparatively fewer factories there are than the innumerable workshops. Yet, I felt that what the factory owner was doing was rational from his point of view in that it was not worth his while to employ children when the new technology was conducive to the use of adults rather than chidren, and the use of children would not yield ecconomic advantage. Furthermore, factory owners would subcontract the job of molding, polishing and electroplating to workshops in which child labour was freely used and abused without attracting any legal liability for doing so.

Even if it is true that children are hardly employed in factories, nevertheless they are employed in most multi-processes such as moulding, welding, polishing, scraping and electroplating. The main explanation for the use of children in these processes lies in the fact that, apart from it being feasible to do so, children are paid less than adults and hence production costs are kept relatively low.

I shall now look at how the changed demand for brass ware has affected the structure of the industry. The relatively self-contained skilled artisan of yester year is no longer an important factor in the production process. The IDS studh, referred to earlier in this section, points out how between 1959-60 and 1974 the proportion of self-employed persons dropped from 66 per cent to less than 1 per cent. The export market has increased the importance of entrepreneurial functions. There has been thus a shift in the pattern of ownership and control from the self-employed artisan to the entrepreneur or multi-process unit owner and middleman. In the late 1950s the general pattern was that either the artisan worked in his house, or in a room attached to his house but clearly for work purposes, or several artisans jointly rented a common shed. But today, there has been a shift in the pattern of ownership in the sense that those working in common sheds are more likely to wage earners under one establishment or *karkhana* rather than several individuals sharing the common space (ibid. : 21).

It is clear, therefore that the category of self-employed artisans, who work for themselves with an investment in fixed and working capital, has virtually disappeared. Most artisans have reduced to wage labourers even though outwardly the industry may retain the nature and structure of cottage industry.

It will be evident from the above that the most important factors in the changes that have taken place with respect to technology, the labour force and structure of the industry has been the qualitative and quantitative change in the international demand for the products of Moradabad.

Employment, Wages and Contitions of Work

I have referred earlier to the importance of the brass ware industry form the pointing of view of employment in Moradabad. Both governmental and non-governmental sources estimated that at least three-fourths of the population of the city was dependent for their livelihood on industry. At least 150,000 people could be said to be engaged in the metal ware industry and many more are employed indirectly, though most workers were employed on a full-time basis, about 20 per cent of them are from the rural areas. The latter work during the slack periods of agricultural activity and are usually not available during the sowing and harvesting seasons.

In 1980, there were communal riots in Moradabad that claimed several lives and much property. The aftermath of the riots was a climate of distrust and uncertainty and long-lasting tension. Export order could not be met in the time and there was a slump in the industry leading to high levels of unemployment. Other countries stepped in when India failed to supply its goods. And the impact of the riots could still be felt till as late as 1985. The long period of economic insecurity has conditioned the way in which worker look upon the industry : today they are grateful for the work that they have and concentrate their energies upon earning a living. The absence of other employment opportunities makes the workers wholly dependent upon the metal ware industry. Militancy and a trade union movement are both conspicuous by their absence.

When we look at the religious composition of the workers, it is apparent that those who work in big factories and large multi-process units are mainly Hindus and those who are employed in the smaller units are almost entirely Muslim. This is partly to do with the fact that the smaller units are located in the city centre which are Muslim dominated areas and where Hindus men are not encouraged because of the tradition of purdah (the seclusion of women). Moradabad is one of the few cities in India where Muslims outnumber Hindus.

Today, when business is thriving, there is hardly any unemployment for male worker in Moradabad. I was told that most people-excluding women-were assured of at least 200-250 days of work in a year. Most workers interviewed said that they could earn about Rs. 400 to Rs. 500 a month and nobody even referred to the minimum wages fixed for the industry as these were fixed many years ago and were much less than the prevailing wage rates.

In the last twenty years or so with the increasing demand for labour, there has been a large and growing component of migratory labour from the adjoining villages. Every morning, workers come from villages like Macheria, Hartala, Menather, Uchangaon, Langada, Betiyan, Majola, Khadakpur, Mulak, Kalyanpur, Dhakka, Jayantipur, etc. Those who own cycles, cycle to work. Early in the morning, the streets of Moradabad are packed with workers going to factories. Double Phatak is the area where workers can be sent at 7. 45 in the morning either walking or cycling to work. The Amroha passenger train mainly carries workers from the more distant villages to work in the brass ware industry of Moradabad. These are, by and large, landless labourers or people with a little land and belonging to the Scheduled Caste communities of they are Muslims. There is also now a very large component of Bihari labour.

Labour workers complain that their situation has worsened as a result of the entry of labourers from the rural areas and, in particular, because of those who have migrated from Bihar. For the Bihari workers and those coming from parts of eastern Uttar Pradesh, the brass ware industry has been a boon. The wages paid to them, even though lower than those paid to local people, are more than what they would have got in their own areas. Both these categories of workers, they felt, depressed the wages in the market as they were prepared to work for less. It was interesting to find in Moradabad that the wages paid to workers depended at least in part on whether they were city people, rural labour or migrant Biharis, the latter two categories being willing to settle for less. Conversations with factory in demand because they were the cheapest and always available. People coming from the adjoining villages were considered unreliable because they would stay away from work during peak agricultural seasons and city labourers were thought to be arrogant.

Three modes of payment are to be found in the industry : daily wages and piece-rate. The number of salaried employees is negligible both in absolute terms and as proportion of the work-force. Wherever, it is possible to quantify the work to be done, wages are paid according to the piece rate system. And where it is not feasible, people are on daily wage. For example, the moulder in a box mould furnace workshop was paid according to the amount of brass moulded. Polishers and electroplating workers were paid daily wages. Engravers and those who coloured the designs were paid piece-rate wages. Other workers who did miscellaneous jobs like fetching and carrying and are helpers were all on daily wages.

Most workers I spoke to had to work at least ten to eleven hours a day. When large export orders had to be met by dead-lines, people would work through the night as well. Over-time would be paid for the extra hours of work put in and workers had no complaint about their long hours of work or about working at nights; they did not consider themselves to be exploited. The power supply in Moradabad being erratic and uncertain, workers would often spend hours just waiting for it and then work into the night as well in order to earn a minimum amount of money. In this respect, workers in the bigger factories were better off since there would be generators installed them. Workers were not paid on days they did not report for duty or the factory was closed. All power-operated industries are supposed to be shut once a week as a measure of power conservation and so, whether they like it or not, workers get unpaid holiday every week.

As mentioned earlier, according to the Factories Act, any unit which uses power and employs more than nine workers or has twenty or more workers nut does not use power is deemed to be a factory and consequetly, workers in such units are entitled to various rights like Employees State Insurance. Provident Fund, leave with pay and so on. In the case of a leading exporter, there were more than 500 worker in his four-storied building but the Manager told me that there were only thirty-five workers who were regular employed be contractors. The factory owner did not incur any legal liability on their account although they were producing goods for him with raw materials purchased by him, using his machinery and doing the work in his promises. This situation may be said to be typical of other manufacturer exporters as well.

Two encounters I had are worth recounting for what they tell. In one factory, a worker told me in the presence of the owner that he was deeply indebted to the latter for the factory owner had spent Rs 2000 on private medical treatment for the worker's wife when she had an accident. He told me in all sincerity that had it not been for the owner's assistance, his wife would have lost an arm. When the worker left, the owner said to me:

I spent this money which I needn't have but I've got the loyalty of this man for life. He is a skilled worker and can supervise new recruits. He will never leave me to work for another man even at a higher wage. He keeps a check on other workers and reduces my burden of work. The money I spent is nothing compared to the returens I get.

One Works Manager said

If the employer is good, the workers will work well. We pay our workers monthly wages plus commission for production as well as provident fund, bonus, leave, employees state insurance, etc. People don't realize that if you treat workers well, they will never let you down. Our work is highly skilled. If we did not have permanent workers, we would lose a lot by training new recruits. This way we save money. And since we pay extra for exceeding production targets, the workers work well.

The instances cited above were exceptions and certainly do not exemplify a general trent. But where workers are treated well, there is a clear understanding on the part of the management that such treatment is justifies by the returns it gives.

People engaged in the job of polishing probably had the most harrowing experience in the brass industry. Some polishers said that if they worked continuously for thirty days in the month, they would be dead in two years because the work is so hazardous. For every fifteen days of work, they have to take a break for fifteen days. Employers, however, this as irresponsibility on the part of workers was that they were so unreliable. Electroplates told me that because the job was hazardous, they could not affort to work for more than twenty days in the month. I shall return to this question later.

Another story though not representative needs to be told. In one factory I visited, workers employed in moulding, polishing and scraping were locked up in cages. When the employed took me to visit this part of his factory, the supervisor first unlocked the main grill door. As we entered, there were large rooms with grills on the windows and grilled doors. Each process was being done in a different room and the grilled doors were locked from outside. Since part of the structure was open for light, it was also grilled. There was a small tea-stall inside the premises and whenever workers wanted drinking water or tea. it was passed through the grills. After we left. I noticed the supervisor locking the doors behind us! The exporter exlained that these measures were necessary because workers were by and large dishonest and would try an steal the raw material which was almost as expensive as gold!

Participation of Children in the Work-Force

There are no precise figures available for the number of workers in the brass ware industry, whether adults or children. Estimates made by different agencies vary and sometimes quite widely. The District Industries Centre, a government source, estimated that in 1987 out of a total of 16.000

workers, 9100 were men, 900 were women and 5000 were children. In sharp contrast, a study by Kulshrestha and Sharma in 1980 puts the total labour force at 1,00,00 of which 24 per cent or 24,000 were children (Kulshreshtha and Sharma 1980). Again, a study conducted in 1979-80 by IDS in Moradabad argues that of about 70,000 workers, 80-85 per cent are males, 10-15 per cent are children and rest females (IDS-1983 : 4-5). In other words, there are between 56,00-59,000 men, 7000-10, 500 children and rest are women.

An unpulished report of 1988 of the Labour Department of the Government of Uttar Pradesh refers to the findings of a survey begun in 1981 by the National Industrial Development Corporation (NIDC) and quotes them. These figures do not include registered factories but concentrate on small-scale units. According to the NIDC report (cited in Table III below), of 29,100 workers, 20,370 are men, 7566 are children and 1164 are women. Thus, nearly 70 per cent of all workers are men and more than 25 per cent are children.

The same report refers to the conclusions of samples survey carried out in August, 1986, by the Labour Department itself. This survey concluded that while 75 per cent of children work as part of family labour, only 25 per cent of them are wage earners. It went on to estimate that number of such children was between 1800 and 2000 from the point of view of rehabilitation under the National Child Labour Programme (Labour Commissioner, U.P. 1988 : 3). This researcher was told informally that in the absence of adequate staff, less than a hundred families were interviewed.

Table-1 : Break-up of Units (Process-Wise) of Brass Ware Industry at Moradabad

Nature of job	Total No. of units	Men	Women	Children	Total
Shapping	425	1860	23	296	2179
Polishing	1190	4068	284	1387	5651
Casting	2510	6072	276	1872	8220
Welding	431	746	-	18	764
Enamelling	85	712	63	96	871
Scraping	890	4346	386	2193	6925
Electroplating	256	1853	212	1613	3678
Engraving	1560	721	-	91	812
Total	7650	20,370	1164	7566	29100

Source: Labour Commissioner, U.P.: Project Report of Rehabilitation of Child Labour in Brass Ware Industry of Maradabad prepared by Labour Commissioner, U.P. January 9, 1988, pp. 1-2 (unpublished).

The number of children working in the brass ware industry has been thus estimated as 1800-2000 (by the Labour Department), as 5000 (by the District Industries Centre), as 7000-10,00 (by the Industrial Development Services report) as 7566 (by the National Industrial Development Corporation report) and as 24,000 (by Kulshreshta and Sharma). Even allowing for natural increase in number since the studies relate to different years, such wide variations need to be explained.

When I spoke to different categories of people in Moradabad like entrepreneurs, exporters, workers and others not connected with the government, almost everybody said that about 90 per cent of people in Moradabad worked in the brass ware industry. According to the 1981 Census, the population or Moradabad town was 3,45,350. But when I asked about actual number, I was given a renge of between 2,00,000 and 3,00,000 people as working the industry. I was also given to understand that more than 25 per cent of the work-force is made up of children, even though the proportion of children varies from process to process. Even if one takes a lower figure of 1,50 000 as the number of workers, it would mean that there are about 40,000-45,000 children working in the industry.

Government reports and government officials tend to severely underestimate the size of the problem. For one thing, no systematic survey has been carried out by them. For another, if the belief is that only 25 per cent of the working children are hired labourers in need of rehilitation, the size of the problem becomes automatically smaller. But twelve days of seeing and visiting several hundred small units in the by-lanes of Moradabad convinced me that in virtually no case were children working as part of family labour. To the last child, they were all hired by others. It is in the light of my observation of different processes and assessment of the propertions of children in each of them coupled with the discussions I had with a wide cross-section of people in Moradabad that I would estimate the number of workers to be at least, 1,50,000 and the number of workers in different process and the share of children in them have been calculated on a similar basis. Yet, I cannot claim that the figures offered in this report are free of error but am confident they are closer to the facts than official documents allow.

Seventy-five to 80 per cent of the children are Muslims from the town of Moradabad and 20 to 25 per cent Hindus, usually Scheduled Castes, from adjoining villages in a redius of five to six kilometers from the town. The latter can be seen at the railway station in the morning sitting on top of the carriage of the Amroha and Chaumasia passenger trains. The age-range of the child workers is between eight and twelve years. The Bhagvans, Jatavs, Lodhes and Khagis are the castes to which the children normally belong.

I was told by village officials that while adults go on their own in search of work, children are recruited by dalals (middlemen), who usually belong to the village and who paid a commission for bringing child workers. *Thekedars* (contractors) and workshop owners prefer children because they are easy to control. The middlemen look out for children. Their parents are offered an advance of Rs. 100 or the equivalent of a month's wages. If a parent takes an advance, the child has to work whether he likes it or not. If he plays hookey, the wages of other children from the same village are cut and this way the town itself, their parents are induced into sending them to work by the lure of an advance of say Rs. 500. This lump sum payment is a big incentive for parents and it is adjusted against a child's wages over a few months. Unlike as in the case of children in the rural areas, there are no middlemen involved to recruit urban cnildren into the work-force.

Moulding

Of the 30,000 odd workers involved in moulding in the box mould fournace workshops, about 50 per cent or 15,000 are children below the age of fourteen years. Their main job, as explained earlier. is to rotate the wheel which fans the under-ground furnace. These boys are known as *pandhawalas* (the person who fan the flames) and this is the first job given to a new child recruit. The ghadivawale (the person who melts the raw material in the graphite crucible) is the boy who heats the oblong ingot on top of the furnace, breaks it into small pieces with a hammer and melts the required amount of brass. When the molten brass is ready, he lifts the graphite crucible containing the raw material with long tongs and passes it to the adult worker, who then pours it into the moulds, some times. When the adult is holding the mould, he pours the brass into it and then replaces the crucible into the furnace. Often, the job of the boy who rotates the wheel also includes that of removing the crucible from the furnace and vice-versa. Both the boy who rotates the wheel and the boy who removes crucible help grind the hot black mixture into a fine powder with their bare hands and help remove the hot moulded metal from the moulds. These are all continuous processes and if the child is not rotating the wheel, he either removing the crucible or grinding the black powder or removing the hot moulded metal. There is not even a minute's rest in a ten-hour day for a child working at a box mould furnace workshop.

The jobs described above in these workshops are done only by children. Employers justified the use of child labour for these tasks by saying that children began this work at an early age, they would never be able to become moulders in their adulthood; a high degree of skill was said to be involved. Yet, I interviewed several adult moulders who had not done such work as children. In fact, in the 600 add box mould furnace workshops I visited, I found that the moulders were almost always under 30 years of age. People told me that children who work in box furnace workshops from a young age either do not survive as adults or become too ill to work. Tuberculosis (TB) is the most common consequence. In one unit I visited, as I was talking photographs, the child poured the molten metal into the mould and suddenly the room filled with fumes and everybody began to cough. It took me full fifteen minutes to recover from such a brief exposure and these children work in these conditions for ten hours a day, day in and day out! The moulder who employs children knows that his working life in limited and therefore tries to maximize his profits in the short time available to him by hiring children. The other costs of production like coal, sand, molasses, oil, etc., are beyond his control.

Polishing

The other process in which a large number of children are working is polishing the semi-finished goods. Polishing employs about 25,00 workers of whom about 12,000 are children. Unlike the lock industry where children can be seen working on the buffing machines in large numbers, in the brass ware industry children spend their time applying chemicals on the wares to be polished, dipping wares in acid baths before they are polished, putting masala (a term used for describing a mix of ingredients)– on the buffs so that they could be used again. Many children working in polishing units are from the adjoining villages. I was told that while children working the box mould furnace workshops invariably belonged to the city, children engaged in polishing work often came from outside. It was expained that polishing was a relatively unskilled activity into which untrained recruits could enter, while moulding required some training; living and growing up in the urban environment was supposed to help.

I visited six villages around Maradabad city from which people came to work in the brass ware industry. Dhakka village is five kilometers from Maradabad city. The total population of the village is 2000, of which 250 people go daily to work in the multi-purpose workshop units and about fifty are children below the age of fourteen years and about 150 are adolescents below eighteen years. The work of polishing and moulding is also done in the village and many people work here. All the workers working the village and in the city are Muslims. Kundanpur village has a total population of about 3000. This village is about four kilometers from the city. Most of the workers go to the polishing units in the city. Approximately 250-300 workers commute daily on cycles or walk to work. These are no multi process units in the village so they all work in the city. There are at least 160 children below the age of fourteen years. Most of the children had already left for work when I visited the village at seven in the morning and could come back home only as late as nine at night but sometimes only at eleven. Since they were afraid of walking home alone, they would wait for their friends and then come together. A common sight in the morning is young children holding on to their small tiffin-carriers as they set out to work. None of the children interviewed earned more than Rs. 100 a month. The children said they continued to work as long as they were asked to by the unit owner.

Dhimri village is six to seven kilometers from Moradabad with a total population of 5000 people. From this village, only children below the age of fifteen years go to work. Approximately 200 children commute daily. They are either Muslims or Satar by caste and belong to families of landless labourers or people with small amounts of land.

Menather, another village, is five kilometers from the city with a population of 5000 people. About 100 workers commute to work of whom fifty are children. Most of the workers are Muslim. Jayantipur village, which is six kilometers from the city, has a population of 3000. Out of 250 workers who go to work, 150 are children. Many children and adults work in the polishing units set up in the village. While the adults are mainly Bagvan by caste, the children are mainly Muslims. In Bhadora village, about three kilometer from the city, 150 workers go to Marodabad and they are either Bagvans or Muslims. Pandit Nagla is another village about three kilometers from Moradabad. While parents are engaged in Agricultural work, Children, about 150, go to work. They are either Muslim or belong to the lower castes of Jatav, Lodhe and Khaagi.

Most multi-process unit owners prefer children from the rural areas because they are cheaper than children of the city. Most children working in polishing workshops were in the age-range of twelce to thirteen years. earner about Rs. 100 a month and were kept on a monthly salary. The younger children, between the ages of eight and nine, earned Rs. 60 a month and their wages were cut and day they did not come to work. The adults were paid on a piece-rate basis. The children who worked with moulders earned Rs. 100-150 a month once they had gaind experience and reached the age of twelve or thirteen years. Nine or ten years olds earned Rs. 3 a day and still younger seven to nine-years-old earned Rs. 60 a month. No child below the age of fourteen years earned more than Rs. 200 a month irrespective of the kind of work he did or the number of hours he worked.

Electroplating

Out of 20,000 workers engaged in electroplating, about 5000 are children. The main job that children . The main Job that children are involved in is in the tying of articles with wires which are then submerged by adults in chemical tanks containing potassium cyanide. Once the goods are plated, the wires are removed also by children and the wares are taken out into the sun by children where they cover each article with ammonium chloride power so that all the moisture is obsorbed. In the evening, the children carry the dried goods inside the workshop.

Welding

There are porbably 10,000 workers engaged in welding, of whom about 7000 are children. It was common in the lanes of Moradabad to see children working as helpers to adults, who were welding. The adults usually wore protective glasses to prevent injury to his eyes but the child, who passed him the goods and watched him carefully, did not use anything at all. The workshops where welding was carried out were very small and there was not enough space for the children to sit. The adult would sit outside the workshop and the children sat inside, often on top of the cylinder because there was not enough space on the workshop floor. If the cylinder exploded, as has sometimes happened, it was the child who would be injured. One other feature of welding workshops was that the number of children was very large per adult. One frequently saw one adult and three or four children in one workshop, though there were also units where there were no one children at all. Children working in welding workshops wer very young. Most of the children were in the age-range of six to nine years.

Engraving

A few thousand children work in the processes of engraving designs and colouring. Children involved in these tasks more often than not help their fathers and contribute their mite to the labour of the family. The explanation for this phenomenon is that both engraving and colouring are highly skilled activities which require long periods of training. Parents who want a quick return by way of the child's wage cannot afford to wait the necessary time if their children were to take up these occupations. Because of changes in market demand, engraving and colouring are not at a premium any more and the wages for this category of artisans have in fact fallen. There is no certainty of employment for those who enter these lines. The rest of the workers were employed in factories, etc.

Wage Labour not Family Labour

Except in the process of engraving and colouring, child labour in the brass ware industry of Moradabad is not a part of family labour as it is usually made out to be. The Child Labour (Prohibition and Regulation) Act of 1986 does not apply to those children who work as part of family labour. In any case, in Moradabad, almost all the children work as wage labour and going by visual impression children do not seem to be remotely related to the adults they work with.

At one box mould furnace workshop in Dhakka village, a man and a boy were working together. I presumed that since this was a village and the work was being done in the courtyard of the house, the man and boy would be related. Since the man was not old enough to be the father or the child, I thought he was the brother and said, I suppose he is your brother' pointing to the boy. To which he answered in the affirmative. A little later, while we were waiting for the moulds to be prepared, someone said :

This boy has been working for at least six years. (This boy was about twelve or thirteen years). Even his younger brother works and he is only seven years old. Rasheed is the sole earning member of his family. His father is dead and mother unemployed with lots of little brothers and sisters to support. He now ears Rs. 5 a day.

-Then I asked, 'You mean you two are not related? This boy is not a brother? He said, He is not a real brother, but in the vocabulary of the village, everybody is a brother.'

During the course of the study in Moradabad. I visited nearly a 1000 units of different types and found that parents and children worked together in less than ten or fifteen of them. Such detailed investigation in not normally done by inspecting authorities even if they possessed the will and manopower to do so. Hence, the myth that most children who work in Moradabad work as part of family labour persists. Exactly the opposite is the case.

Attitudes of Parents

I interviewed several parents about their attitudes towards the fact that their children worked. Many time I got the distinct impression that parents believed that children wer born to serve and support them and saw nothing wrong in their not being in school or not being able to play. It is, of course, true that few parents could afford to send children to school or let them have the luxury of play. The attitudes of many parents reflected the expectations that society has of children with respect to their roles and, in particular, their filial duties.

When I asked Sunil's mother whether Sunil protested about being made to work, she said: 'If he doesn't work, he will die. We don't have a government job that we can feel him ourselves without lifting a finger. Whatever the is spent on him.'

At Bara Shah Shafa, Khajoor ki Sarai. Feel Khana and Lal Masjid, there are many polishing workshops. At one that I went to, two boys of twelve and fourteen years were working. The younger one told me that he lives on the premises and cooked his food on an electric stove. The room he lived in was small and most the space was occupied by a wooden bed on which the two boys slept. A section of the room was partitioned and two buffing machines installed. These boys got up at 6 a.m. and by 7 a.m. when I visited, they wer busy at work. Alam said that he earned Rs. 250 a month and went home once in eight days. He was the sole supporter on his family of six brothers and sisters and a mother. His father, a rickshaw-puller died two years ago, and since then the boy has started working. I was told that most the children who lived on the premises were those who had come from the rural areas. About 10 per cent of all working children lived in the workshops.

Health Hazards

The two most hazardous processes in the brass ware industry are moulding and polishing and it is in these two process that child labour is all-pervasive. I saw 600 box mould furnace workshops and this was the recurring pattern. For every adult, there were two children. The work in the box furnace work-shops is extremely dangerous. The child is employed to do two types of jobs. He rotates the wheel which is called a *pankha* (literally means a fan. In this context it is the rotation of the wheel which is called a *pankha* to keep the furnace fire burning). In some box mould furnace workshops there were only two workers, an adult and a child. In these workshops, the child would rotate the wheel. After the temperature had reached a certain level, the child tested it by opening the top of the underground furnace and throwing a little powder into it. If the material-molten brass was ready, blue and green flames would shoot up from the mouth of the furnace. The child then took a large pair of tongs and lifted the crucible of molten brass from the furnace and handed it over to the adult who poured the molten brass into the already prepared moulds. The boy then returned the crucible into the furnace with raw material and helped the adult to open the hot moulds and remove the pieces. As soon as this was done, he and the adult would grind the hot sand till it was very fine. Then, while the moulds were prepared by the adult, the child went back to sit at the wheel to fan the flames.

The job of the moulder is a very delicate operation and if there is a slight mistake or accident the boy can get very badly injured and can even lose his limbs. He wears no protective gear and stands barefoot on top of the furnace to either put in the crucible or to remove it. The temperature in the furnace is about 1100 degre C. As one exporter/manufacturer, explaining the processes in his factory, said: 'See how dexterous this young child is. He has to be. Because even if a drop of molten brass falls on his foot there will be a hole in it.

The child is not only in danger of getting badly burnt but both he and the adult worker inhale the fumes and gases which are let off from the furnace and again when the molten brass is poured into the moulds developed tuberculosis. A local doctor, Anwar Hussain of Peerzade, said that almost every brass-worker suffered from TB or other upper respiratory tract infections after a few years. This could be avoided only if the worker looked after himself and ate well. But since they cannot afford good food, the combination of poor nutrition and bad working conditions reduces the life span of workers by half. No one worked for more than ten or fifteen years and none lived beyond the age of fourty years. In fact, in the 600 or so moulding units I visited, the workers were remarkably young!

In Bhurra Mohalla, commonly referred to as *Jatavon Ka Mohalla*, near Prince Road, about 100 families live there and almost 500 people are engaged in polishing work. Some of them polish steel utensils and others polish brass. There are hundreds of polishing mechines installed in the locality: most of them are owned by workers who save and after a few years get a machine and then use hired help, mainly child labour. I talked to at least thirty people, many of whom had lost members of their families. Draupadi was a middle-aged woman whose child had started working at the age of eight and died the previous year at the age of twenty-five years. He was a polisher. Mangal Sein is sixty, and works as cobbler. His four adult sons are dead. The youngest died the week before my visit, after vomiting blood. Just across the lane from Draupadi's house, a young adolescent boy had died the night before and the family was taking the body for its last rites. People in *Jatavon Ka Mohalla* said that 60 per cent of them die soon after. A young adolescent boy, Prakash said: used to work on the machines, but since I started vomiting blood. I hire other workers. mainly children, being asked why people sent their children to work when they knew that the child would die in any case. If he doesn't work, he will die of starvation in a few days. If he works, then death is at least postponed for a few years.

Everyone told me that death, and a very painful one at that was inevitable for polishers at a very young age but there was no alternative. Chandrasen said: 'What can I say but that every family has lost one or two adolescent boys or adult sons? Now we have started taking this for granted.'

Local doctors admitted that brass-workers were prone to TB but they felt this was largely due to poverty, malnutrition and congestion in their living quarters. They were not willing to admit easily that these problems were particularly acute for brass-workers, especially those working in box mould furnace workshops and in polishing work. Some reluctantly agreed that there was correlation between work and as even in the city, it was mainly brass-workers who were affected. In the villages where people lived in relatively open spaces. The incidence of TB was negligible but those who were diagnosed as having the disease were brass-Workers. In fact, Moradabad is one of the two cities with the highest rate of TB in the state. The local doctors were certainly not in a position to make a distinction between TB and pneumoconiosis or silicosis, the latter being clearly an industrial disease.

Doctors in Moradabad felt that workers who came with chest problems did not get themselves treated. There was such fear in the minds of workers about TB that if their problem was so diagnosed, patients rerely came back even though the disease was curable. This was so partly because the first advice the doctor gave his patient to change his occupation and to improve his diet. Workers cannot afford to act upon these recommendations.

While local doctors said that the most common medical complaint of workers was chest diseases, workers themselves said that accidents at work were not unusual. Said Rafiabhai: 'Accident are very common. Sometimes, the arucible slips and your hands and feet get badly burnt.'

The most lazardous process was considered to be that of moulding in a box mould furnace workshop. One young man, painting to six children working in his workshop, said: 'None of these children will survive beyond the age of thirty. They will die of TB.' Harizbhai Namumewale said. Most parents who send their children to work are not even aware of what will happen to the child. They only realize it when a child gets injured and hurt. But by that time, it is too late to repent. And of course, poverty forces parents to turn a blind eye. If a ghadiya wala drops the ghadiva (crucible), he injures himself will take the hot *chimta* (tongs) with which the child holds the *ghadiya* and brand and complain to his parents. The mother will put some ointment on the would but will send him right back to work the next day! Ansari Sahib said:

Children who work on polishing machines are at considerable risk. Not only do they inhale all the metal dust and masala, but if a piece. It can severely injure the child. One of the main jobs the children do in polishig units is acid washing of goods before they are polished on buffing machines. You can't enter the room where this is done—all by children. You can actually see the green and blue vapors rising from the acid tubs. We people, who are workers, find it impossible to enter such a room. You won't be able to stand even outside the door. The stench is tremendous and the eyes burn. With polishing the person gets chest diseases. He suffocates to death.

I asked Hafizbhai whether the problem of child labour was better than before or worse. He said:

It's better. At least 5 per cent of parents are beginning to realize the harmful effect of work on the child. Look, you can see what happens to the child working as ghadivawala. His health deteriorates so fast. He is breathing in fumes from the furnace ten to twelve hours a day. Have you been near a *darja bhatti*? You won't be able to stand there for a few minutes. And this child spends his life in front of it. Within a short time he gets weak. His legs become obsolutely skinny. Parents can see this. Every other day the child has fever. It is only desporate parents who sent their child to work at a *bhatti* (furnace).

Most people interviewed said that accidents were very common amongst children but 10 did not see any injured children myself. I was told:

Only when the child is well can he come to work. These days major accidents are relatively few. In the earlier days, when the bhattis used to get scrap as raw meterial-most of it from the ordinance factories—sometimes whole mohallas used to explode killing adults and children. Now this kind of thing is rare because the raw material is centrally processed at factories which make sillis and gullis and this danger is relatively less.

But in Rasheedbhai's locality just recently, a child was killed and several adults injured in an explosion. In a box mould furnace, a child was breaking up scrap brass from an ordinance factory with a hammer. One of the pieces was a live grenade which exploded on his face. He died instantaneously. But this is rare.

People, paticularly local doctors, are reluctant to talk about health hazards to strangers for fear that they will get into trouble for not reporting obvious medico-legal cases. Parents to not talk about them for other reasons. Khalid Begum said: If the poor think of ill-health and illness, how can they work? Accidents are very common. My son lost four fingers. He was under treatment for a long time. Now he's alright.

Ruksana Begum had also toined the conversation she said :

Only a few months back. Mumtaz's fifteen-year old son dies. He had just started working as a welder with a stove welding workshop. God knows what happend, but there was too much gas in the strove and it burst. The boy caught fire and he died before he could be given any medical attention.

Suraiya narrated the story of her neighbours son in Feel Khana who lost his arm in the belt which rotates the buffing machine in a polishing unit:

Poor thing, he was only twelve years old. The story is that this clothes got caught in the machine. He tried to disentangle them and his hand got cought. Now he's OK. He can even work with one are.

Khalida said Smilingly

Accidents can happen any time on any job but you can't stop working. The disc of the grinder sometimes breaks and eyes get damaged. The crucible slips and hands and feel get burnt. But if a mother was to think of all these factors, how will she send her child to work?

I asked why most of the children were working in the three or four most hazardous jobs like moulding, polishing, electroplating and welding. Ruksana's answer was:

These jobs have quick returns. A boy who goes to work at a *bhatti* will get at least Rs. 5 at the end of ten hours. This is not the case with skilled jobs like engraving, colouring, etc. For these jobs, you'll notice only those children who are working with their own fathers. The training period is long and there are immediate monetary returns.

It takes a long while before the child can earn enough. As it is, the rate paid to adult engravers is so little that children will get nothing for this. This work is the least harmful. Your clothes don't get spoilt. You don't inhale fumes and dust. The children who used to do a lot of engraving earlier have now virtually disappeared. Many men want these jobs because they are relatively easy, so where is the questions of young boys getting them? It is only the very unskilled jobs that children get and unfortunately these are also the most hazardous.

It is clear that the majority of child workers in brass ware industry are engaged in intrinsically hazardous occupations. With the current technology, one does not see any way in which their health can be protected or the health hazards significantly lessened.

Education

None of the working children I met were educted. They worked a minimum of ten hours a day and their parents said they were not in a position to pay for their education. I talked to Sayeedbhai a painter. His older son was busy colouring a brass plate. He has not been educted. But the younger boy goes to school. He does not want to send his child to work. He said:

You can't sacrifice your family for work. It is bad enough that one son has not been educated and therefore he has to work that this job. But this little one will study. He can always learn the craft. After all, he belongs to a family of artisans. In any case, education will only improve his ability to work.

Others gathered around and said the same thing: 'Education is very important if one day you want to become an entrepreneur. To manage the business. The child will have to be given education.

I asked why some parents send their children to work and others do not. And the unanimous responses where: 'If you can't feed your children, where is the question of paying for their education? But when I said that primary school education was free for children, they said:

Are there enough schools in Moradabad? Our children don't get admission into government schools and we can't afford to pay Montessori school fees. If there were more schools, half our problems would be solved.

I asked whether parents come up with a scheme to provide education to all children and sets up schools, all these children working in *darja bhattis* (box mould furnace) would leave work and go to school. No one sends their children to work because they think that education is irrelevant. But if there are no schools, then children are sent to work.

The attitudes of parents sometimes differed. Zakiabi's husband has deserted her. She lives with her four sons in her sister's house. Although she did not work herself, she sent all her children to work, though they were under twelve years. She said, 'Their father has deserted us and gone away so they'll have to work. If he comes back, he can educated them".

She was so upset about having been desrted that she felt that it was the duty of her children to work and support her. Her young seven-year old son was working in a box mould furnace workshop. He had never been to school. When I asked him how many years he had worked, he said that he did not know how to count but he had been working for several years. The others workers said that he had worked for three years.

In Kathghar, Jamalbhai was working at a box mould furnace workshop with two boys aged eight and ten years. The three together earned Rs. 40 a day. The boys were not his sons. He said, 'I have only four daughters so that questions does not arise. But if I had a son I would send him to school. This is no work for a child. 'But in Peeruave, Kathghar. Lal Masjid and Idgah, none of the working children had been to school. Some parents felt that, 'If they study, they will dies of starvation'. They could not afford the opportunity cost of sending a child to school because every penny earned was crucial for bare survival of the family.

Hafizbhai Namunewale was adamant and said that the problem of child labour was closely linked to the problem of illiteracy. He said, 'I'll give it to you in writing that educated parents do not send their children to work. It is only illiterate parents who put their children to work at an early age. 'He went on to add:

It is a vicious circle. If you are uneducated, You don't even understand the implications of what you are doing. You only think of today. It is almost impossible to explain to uneducated people the valued of family planning, for instance. This only makes the problems more difficult to handle. For them, if a child is bringing in one or two rupees at the end of the day. it is good enough.

His son. Mushahid, interjected: 'Education is the most important thing. If you are uneducated, you don't even know the meaning of the work bhavishya (future)'. Hafizbhai said:

We have had a law to ban child labour for so long. Has it ever been implemented? Do you know the laws in Japan? You cannot employ a child there. What prevents the government from enforcing the Child Labour Act and forcing parents to educated their children.

I replied that government officials often say that banning child labour is impossible because the economic conditions of the families of working children will become worse. Hafizbhai had this to say:

It is true that many families rely entirely on their children. But not always because of economic necessity. In our neighbourhood, there are families where the father spends the whole day playing cards. The mother does housework. The only income of that family is from the children, do you think that this should continue? Parents can also be callous. I met a women this morning who was very upset because her twelve-years old son collapsed in a factory due to heat stroke and she had to spend Rs. 30 on doctor's fees and medicines. If parents do not know what is good for thier children, then surely the state has to intervene. The consequences of all this are very serious. These are the very children who as adolescent boys become irresponsible citizens. They have so much enger within them. They are the easiest targets for anti-social activity.

Some Muslim Social Activists Confirmed This

The child who is denied education and made to work is really frustrated. It comes out in little things like his inbility so read the film posters. He feels ashamed that he has to ask another child which film is showing. An this alone can build up into a tremendous anger. There is so much violence in our mohallas, in our families-because of this.

Rahim Khan, Designer, has Educated all his Children, He said:

The evidence of what education can do for you is all around us. Look at the exporters, they have become mulit-millionairers look at us artisans-uneducated—how easily we are being exploited. If you are educated, you know what the laws are, the govenment policy is. Even if government has a programme for helping the artisans, they don't know about these things. Exporters have got so many concessions and income tax exemptions that overnight they have become multi-millionaries. One of our biggest exporters has recently imported a twelve-seat Toyata from Japan. A car which will cost only Rs. 60 on diesel from Moradabad to Delhi. They have four gunmen and guard dogs. Their imported German dog costs them Rs 3000 a month on food and sleeps in an air-conditioned room with one attendant. It is more that what they will spend on ten workers. How have they become so weallthy but by exploiting the uneducated workers?

The people gathered around were very resentful of those who had made if big. Many of them felt that the main road to upward mobility was education. It was the very first step. Without it, the question did not arise. One or two people were of the view that:

The only way to implement a ban on child labour is to use police force. You have to make education compulsory. You provide school books, clothes, etc. Parents will protest. Employers will protest. But sooner or later they will realize that this is all for the good of the child.

Abidbhai Said

It is very important to educate women. If you educate a boy, it is like educating one person. But if you educate a girl she in turn wil educate her children. The condition of a family depends a lot on the women. Parents need to be educated on the harmful effect of work on the health of their children.

Hafizbhai added. 'Give education to children and their eyes will open up automatically'. Mukhtiarbhai spoke bitterly of the problems of education in Moradabad. He said. 'There is nothing callled a school teacher here. In front of my house there is a government school. There are supposed to be four teachers but not one comes. According to him, most of the schools are grant-in-aid schools getting funds from the government and run by registered societies. At the time of school admission and just before examination, they demand money in the form of donations on the slightest pretext. The private schools are not recognized by the government and their certificates and diplomas are of no use for college admissions. Muktiarbhai had a valied point regarding the medium of instruction which in Hindu :

The medium of instruction in Moradabad is Hindu because that is supposed to be our national language. Yet university education in places like Delhi is all in English. Our children are handicapped. And if truly the intention is to use Hindu, then why is all the literature on the subject or imports and exports in English? All the information we need about government policies and programmes regarding trade are in English. How are we supposes to understand that? Those who are educated in English are obviously at an advantage. Now any body who makes it as an entrepreneur sends his child to Nainital or Dehra Dun for education. Even the better-off artisans ar trying to send their children there. But very few can afford it.

Surinder Singh, an activist in Moradabad, but not working with brass workers, had ideas about the kind of education working children need:

I was a child worker myself so I know what it means to be a working child. My father died when I was seven years old and my mother forced me to work. My clothes were always torn and dirty and I was very ashamed of myself. It was only after I had worked for some years, saved some money and bought some clothes that I went to a teacher I knew in the village to let me come to school. Even then, the first day, I was scared. I didn't have the nerve to enter the school, so I stood outside the gate the whole day. It was only when the teacher I knew came that I went with her. Working children have very low self-esteem. They will not even go and talk to a child who is better dressed-because that signifies superior status. The teacher in our society is glorified as the guru close to god—a position that we can never hope to attain. The image must change if children are going to enjoy school. The teacher must come down from her pedestal. Any scheme to provide education to working children must take this into account. Children must be given unforms so that some semblance of equality can be maintained. If education is to be provided after work, it has to be qualitatively different from that given to non-working children. It must be fun. There must be a component of entertainment in it for it to be successful.

The most horrifying consequences of working in the brass ware industry for children is that their lives are shortened by the hazards they are exposed to. Those who survive are often ill. Their life-chances are bleak because of their illitercy and the question of bettering their lot simply does not arise: they are thus destined to remain poorly paid and unskilled workers for whatever is left of their lives. Given the nature and kind of for whatever is left of their lives. Given the nature and kind of work, part-time education is not a practicable proposition and it will be impossible to monitor such a scheme. The only solution is to lessen the awesome human cost and pay those parents who cannot affort the money to send their children to school.

Technology and Employment : Some Observations

One of the objectives of this study was to see whether any changes in technology could be recommended from the point of view of discouraging the use of child labour and promoting the employment of adults. On a visit to Bangkok in Thailand in 1988. I was able to visit four factorers manufacturing brass ware. At each factory there were only eight to ten workers employed but the premises of these factories were almost as large as some of the biggest factories in Moradabad. When I looked at the processes in these factories, it become apparent that the technology used in Bangkok was virtually the same as that used in Moradabad. However, there were no children working in the brass ware factories in Bangkok.

It is relevant to mention here the differences in the technology employed between Bangkok and Moradabad. For one thing, the moulds and crucibles used were of much larger size and could not therefore be handled by children. In one factory for example, where large statues of the Buddha were being made, I saw a crucible being lifted by two men with the aid of wooden supports. Clearly, such heavy weights could not be lifted by children. When I enquired with the factory supervisors as to why children were not employed, they gave three types of reasons. They pointed out that children were not fit by virtue of their physical attributes to work for the industry, that the work was hazardous and therefore not suitable for children and finally, that child labour could be obtained in Bangkok only on a monthly waoe as most children came from outside Bangkok to work and not on piece-rate wages. In one of the factories I visited where smaller decorative brass pieces were virtually identical to those in Moradabad. Even then, no children were to be seen.

It is not as if there is no child labour in Thailand in general or Bangkok in particular. In fact, Bangkok attracts working children from the poorer Northern and North-Eastern provinces of Thailand. Several studies point out that there are over two million working children in Thailand, a significant proportion of whom are to be found in Bangkok (Bond 1982 : 2 : Udomakdi 1986 : 36). But perhaps there are better options available for children than working in the brass ware industry and therefore no child works in this industry. It is therefore necessary to look at the relationship between technology and the employment of children in a larger socio-economic setting.

When I spoke to manufacturers and exporters in Moradabad, they informed me that the technology employed in Taiwan and Korea in the brass ware industry was far more sophisticated than that used in Moradabad. The level of mechanization was much higher. In these countries, brass ware is manufactured by the die-casting method where an initial model or die is made and fixed on machines and thousands of pieces are then churned put. Clearly, in more developed capitalist economics, technologies of mass production are more in vogue. Since I have not studied the growth and development of the brass ware industry elsewhere, it is not possible to make further generalizations regarding the situation in those countries.

If one was to posit that increased mechanization in the brass ware industry of Moradabad is a desirable goal from the point of view of discouraging the use of child labour, the first question that needs to be answer is whether there is any incentive for an entrepreneur to take such an investment decision. It was pointed out to me in Moradabad that there have been periods as long as four or five years—such as, for example, after the 1980 riots—when trade saw a sharp decline because there was virtually no production. The regain one's position in the last couple of years that the industry is on the upswing. Apart from other factors like the inherently unstable international market, the uncertain communal situation of Moradabad is a risk to be constantly borne in mind. Such reasons inhibit technological investment and change. Moreover, we have to ask whether it is not cheaper for the entrepreneur to continue at the present technological level when labour in general is cheap and child labour particulary so. The answer, it would appear, in the context of the uncertainties of production and the market, to stick to cheap child labour unless pressure is brought upon industry through importers.

Let us look at a small technological change that is possible. In the moulding units, there are usually one adult and two or three children. One child is exclusively engaged in rotating the wheel which fans the furnaces. In very few units I noticed that a low horsepower motor was installed which routed the wheel and climinated the need for one child. When I asked other entrepreneurs why this simple device was not more widely used, I was told about—and in fact experienced—the extremely erratic power supply available in the town, since power shortage is a way of life, most people preferred to keep a child worker fanning the furnace for, otherwise the entire production process would grind to a halt whenever why even such small technological changes are not introduced.

In the polishing units, which along with the mouding units are the largest employers of children, the buffs on the polishing machines wear away in course of time. These buffs, can be replaced by purchasing them in the market but until it becomes absorlutely necessary to replace them, recycled buffs are used for as long as possible. In every polishing unit, one or two children spend most of their time extending the life of these buffs by putting gum, emery powder and some mixture on them. We may infer that the entrepreneur has calculated that it is cheaper for him to employ these children to recycle these buffs rather than buy them from the market. This story illustrates the relatively weak financial position of the entrepreneur who owns a small polishing unit. One cannot expect substantial investment in new technology from persons of such standing, unless those who get this work done also share their profits more equitably. Pressure can again be brought upon these small entrepreneurs only through the industry and that also when there is pressure upon the industry from the buyers of such goods.

I have in the section on the female worker referred to the fact that when there were technological changes in the process of scraping and polishing, women who usually did this work at home were substantially displaced from the labour force. Men took over this job on machines in factories and workshops. As a result, incomes of families in which women did this work saw a decline, To make ends meet in such families, young boys who might otherwise have been in school were sent out to work.

Even if it were feasible to introduce mechanization in the brass ware industry in the background of the hardles described above, it is necessary to ask whether increased mechanization is a desirable goal considering the prevalence of unemployment and under-employment. Technological changes on a large scale would almost certainly diminish opportunities of employment and under-employment. Technological changes on a large scale would almost certainly diminish opportunities of employment for adults even if such changes made children unsuitable as workers in the brass industry. Perhaps a better alternative would be to bring pressure upon the industry as a whole from the buyers of these goods and entrepreneurs, both big and small are forced to improve working conditions for labour welfare as well as to ensure that no child labour is employed. When there is a continued demand for the goods and non-availability of child labour, it is likely that the prospects of adults workers will improve.

The Implications of Government Policy for the Brass Ware Industry

What holds good for the lock, gem, glass and pottery industries is also the case for the brass ware indstry of Moradabad everywhere, child labour is being passed off as family labour, despite facts to the contrary. And this is precisely because of the provision in the Child Labour (Prohibition and Regulation) Act. The fact that work is carries out in residential premises lends credence to the belief that the industry is cottage oriented and that father pass on their skills to sons. The labour Department of the Government of Uttar Pradesh organized a sample survey in 1986 and found that only 25 per cent of the children were wage workers and that, thereforee, protection was required only for 2000 children. My estimates were that there were between 40,000-45,000 children working in the industry. The vast majority of whom are wage workers, the sight of adults males working with children reinforces the view that children work as part of family labour. Patient investigation in needed into these appearances and governmental survey staff are notably untrained for this type of work. When government teams visit, they are blandly told on non-existent family connections for people are afraid of violating the law for fear of being penalized. In the short time violating the law for fear of being penalized. In the short time available, data collectors take what they are offered at face value. It bears repetition that while the work of engraving and colouring is done in family units, at least 75 per cent of the child labour force is engaged on work like moulding, electroplating, welding and polishing. These are all extremely hazardous occupations and, if properly investigated, would fall squarely within the purview of the Child Labour Act :

On plank of National Child Labour Programme (NCLP) is to effectively implement the various laws enacted for the benefit of working children. But the labour office in Morahad is grossly understaffed with only one labour inspector for the whole city. No organization, however sincere, could even get the facts straight—much less implement the law when it is so thinly people. It is necessary both to sensitize the labour enforcement machinery to the problems of workers both adults and children as so as to be able to cover the large area of the industry.

The Government of India has laid down the framework of the NCLP and left it for the local authorities to implement. A bureaucratic tendency to accept what has come form above has led to a plan divorces from reality. The identification of hazardous and non-hazardous activities has been left for the Deputy Director of Factories (Medical) of Uttar Pradesh to decide at a later date. In the meanwhile, it is planned to give vocational training to children in the age-groups often to twelve years and twelve to fourteen years in the trades of engraving polishing, foundry, gas welding, soldering and electroplating. To suggest that children between the ages of ten to twelve years should start with polishing and foundry work would be an express violation of Article 24 of the Indian Constitution. However, given the way in which the Child Labour Act is formulated, if these processes are taught in government-aided schools and institutions, these children would not come under the purview of the law. Thus what may be against the spirits of the Constitution may be perfectly legal!

But it would seem that the proposal under consideration to train twelve to fourteen year old children in solding electro-plating, gas welding, etc., in factories would also violate Section 67 of the Factories Act. The section unequivocally states that children below the age of fourteen years should not be allowed to work in any factory. The scheme for such training, if a approved by the Government of India, was to start in 1988-9 giving stipends and food to the children to be trained in local workshops.

Even if it were not the intention, a scheme to train children in the listed trades will result in providing skilled labour to the brass ware industry at no cost to the industry itself. Had free primary education been offered instead, these children would have had better life chances that their current prospects of remaining workers forever.

Under the NCIP, there is a plan to improve the working conditions in the workshop where children above the age of fourteen years are working. In the areas of child labour concentration, the removal of slum, improvement of sanitation and construction of approach roads are components of the plan in general. For anyone who has visited Moradabad, this scheme appears to be unrealistic for the improvement of working conditions would be close to being impossible unless the entire city is demolished and rebuilt. Obviously, this is not a practicable proposition.

When this case study was written in 1988, a scheme, the Peetal Vasti or colony for brass-workers was being set up outside the city centre by the U. P. States Brass Ware Corporation. This would enable the artisans to move out of this congested living and working quarters to a allocatged outside the city centre. Here, perhaps plots could be allotted only to those families who undertook not to send their children to work but to keep them compulsorily in schools in Peetal Vasti. If the problems that poor children face in schools are schools are taken care of and if an enforcement system devised, then such a scheme might well be viable.

Ultimately, the only solution to the problem of child labour, in the brass ware industry is a complete and unequivocal ban on its use. This step would be in keeping with the stated with the stated policy of the Government of India, which says that it will not allow children to work to hazardous occupations. The National Institute of Occupational Health could do an epidemiological study to verify the extent of the problem of health hazards to child workers. The ban would have to be enforced only when the government is ready to provide free, compulsory primary education with the added incentives of free meals, uniforms and books. Exporters, to whom various concessions are given by the government, could be prevailed upon to pay a cess to help fund such a programme.

16

MORADABAD CHILD LABOUR PROJECT

A Project to benefit child worker's engaged in the Brass
Industry Moradabad, Uttar Pradesh

1. Introduction

The Goverment of India has been greatly concerned about the plight of child labour in various sectors of employment in the country. In spite of the fact that employment of children is banned under various Acts, socio-economic compulsions force children to work. The result is that their education, health, physical and mental development are neglected and they have hardly any future except drugery and exploitation. What is worse, is that their working conditions are most unsatisfactory, the working hours are too long, wages paid are low often they do not get a weekly day off.

It is clear in such a situation, where children are forced to work due to proverty, mere enforcement of the legal provisions banning child labour will be counter-productive and only add to the misery of the poor families from which the child workers come. Child labour has been the focus of several government committee and numerous studies carried out under the auspices of the Minister of Labour. The Government of India established in 1981 a Central Advisory Board on Child Labour, headed by the Union Labour Minister, to review the implementation of existing legislation and welfare measures for working children, review the progress of such measures and identify industries and areas where there must be a progressive elimination of child labour. In December 1986, the government passed the Child Labour (Prohibition and Regulation) Act to prohibit the employment of children in certain hazardous occupations and processes and to regulate the employment of children in non-prohibited employments. The Act also provides for setting up of a Technical Advisory Committee to advise the Government on the additional industries and sectors which are hazardous to children and in which the employment of children below 14 years should be banned so that a gradual reduction and elimination of child labour can be achieved. The Act was followed by a National Policy on Child Labour which of child labour and outlines the action to be taken to benefit and improve the lot of the child workers.

The conclusions that emerge from the various studies on child labour and a review of the experience of government so far are that, notwithstanding the large number of legislations enacted to provide legal protection to children working in factories, mines, plantions, shops and commercial establishments, etc, and to regulate their these legislations has not been effective and that the provisions, for health and educational development are grossly inadequate. The possibilities for the application of the full force of legislation in unorganised sectors where pronounced are also severely limited. Even if it were possible it may not necessarily be in the best interest of economic situation of the families concerned. Child labour, however, objectionable it may be, will continue to persist so long as low incomes, high ratios and limited resources are required to contribute, even if modestly to meagre family income.

The problem of child has two distinct but related dimensions : a quantitative aspect, i.e., the quantum and incidence of child labour, and a qualitative aspect, namely the conditions of work and terms of employment. These two aspects must, however, be viewed jointly. A high and growing incidence of child labour other things equal; leads to greater adult unemployment and under-employment, lower child wage rates and greater child exploitation, such as excessive and uninterrupted hours of work, physical and psychological abuse, towards all of which children are far more vulnerable than other groups of workers of. Conversely, a reduction in the incidence of child labour can lead to increased adult earnings and improvements in overall employment and working condition and thus support efforts at improving, promoting and protecting the welfare of children. Therefore, public policy in the field of child labour must encampass these dimensions and aim at :

* first, the prohibition of child labour in work which is hazardour to their health and well being.
* second, the improvement of the conditions under which children work (where such work is non-hazardous and not banned by law) protection of such children from exploitation, and access to emproved nutrition and minimum levels of educations, health protection and skill development.
* third, the gradual abolition of child labour by adopting measures that bear on the factors that generate and sustain it.

With this in mind, this pilot project has been formulated. That project is intended to cover children employed in the brassware industry in Moradabad and Uttar Pradesh. Although these constitute the primary target population, the beneficiaries would also include : (a) the parents of these children, and (b) low income and disadvantaged groups who will have benefited directly or and income-generating schemes and social services.

II. Objectives

Long-term Objectives : The ultimate objectives of this project are :
   (a) the elimination of child labour, and
   (b) the physical and mental development of children and their protection against exploitation.

Immediate Objectives : The Immediate objectives are :
   (a) Improvement in health, nutritional status, working conditions, literacy and skill level of the child workers included in this project, and
   (b) reduction in the incidence of child labour in the project area.

III. Background and Context

The brassware industry of Moradabad is a traditional industry of Uttar Pradesh. There are factories and more than 7,000 workshops in which various processes are carried on. The important places where the brassware industry is localised at Moradabad are : Barylan, Lalbagh, Lal Masjid,

Faizgnj, Niyaria Mohalla, Peorjady, Duluya Bagh, Kochcha Bagh, Divan Bagh, etc.

The National Industry Development Corporation, New Delhi carried out a study of metal handicrafts during 1981. The survey identified various processes in the brassware industry at Moradabad. Table 1 indicates the number of units and the total employment in these units as ascertained during the survey. The units are all small scale. The registered factories where the more sophisticated work and diminishing work is undertaken have not many of these children were below 14 years of age.

The Uttar Pradesh Labour Department also carried out a sample survey during August 1986 and found out that children below the age 14 years were employed in foundries, wagraving and polishing units. All these jobs are taken up at workshops mostly situated at the dwelling places of the craftsman. Usually children belonging to the families of the craftsman assist their parents in these workshops, but roughly 25% of the children engaged in these jobs are employees drawn from other houses. Roughly 3600 children are deployed in 1800 foundries, 1400 children are engaged in 700 units of engraving and 2400 children are employed in 1200 polishing units, 25% of this strength of 7400 comes to 1850. Thus the children who are required to be rehabilitated, have been estimated to be normally in the range of 1800 to 2000.

Table 1 : Break-up of Units of Brassware Industry at Moradabad

Nature of Job	Total No. of units	Men	Women	Children	Total
1	2	3	4	5	6
Shaping	425	1860	23	296	2179
Polishing	1190	4060	284	1387	5739
Welding	431	746	--	18	764
Casting	2150	6072	276	1872	8220
Enamelling	85	712	63	96	871
Scrapping	890	4346	386	2193	6925
Electoplating	256	1853	212	1613	3678
Engraving	1560	721	--	91	812
Total	6987	20378	1244	7566	29188

IV. Project Content and Objectives

Specifically this project proposes to do the following :
(i) Reduce and ultimately eleminate through strict enforcement of the Factories Act, 1948, the U. P. State Shops and Establishments Act, 1962 and the Child Labour (Prohibition and Regulation) Act, 1986, the employment of children below 14 years in the industry.
(ii) Raise the income levels of the families of the child workers by covering them under existing income generating schemes such as IRDP, NREP, RLEGP, etc. and other income-generating schemes of the State Government or the Central Government in the area.

(iii) Provide non-formal education to the child workers and to their parents.
(iv) Provide better health care to the child workers.
(v) Improve the conditions of work and the terms of employment in the industry.
(vi) Improve the nutritional levels of the child workers.
(vii) Raise the general awareness and social consciousness of poeple of the area.

(i) Enforcement of Child Labour Laws

Employment of children below 14 years is prohibited in factories under the factories Act, 1948 and employment of children below 12 years is prohibited in smaller workshops under the U. P. State Shops and Commercial Establishments Act. Unfortunately, the employment of children in the brassware industry in both factory and non-factory establishment has been continuing for years in spite of these provisions. To ensure that no child below 14/12 years is employed in the industry, it is necessary to have both the Factories Act, 1948 and the U. P. State Shops and Establishments Act, 1962, strictly implemented. It will also be necessary to enfoce the Minimum Wages Act and other Acts to ensure that children between 12 years and 14 years employed in shops and establishments are protected.

With the commencement of this project, the Inspectorate under the Labour Depasrtment, U.P. posted in the Moradabad Region will give due priority to the enforcement of the labour laws relating to child workers. Every Labour Inspector will be required to carry out at least 10 inspections every month. The total yearly target of inspections per Inspector will be 12-15 units. The target of prosecutions will be 100% of the major breaches detected but not removedafter inspection. Similarly in case where children between 12 years and 14 years employed in establishments and workshops engaged in the brassware industry are paid les than the prescribed minimum rates of wages, claim cases will have to be filed in all cases of breaches which have not been removed after inspection.

The inspections requires to be carried out as also prosecutions and claim cases requird to be filed will be rigorously monitored by the Regional Labour Commissioner, Moradabad, so that an impact is created in the minds of the employers that employment of children shall not be allowed to continue, where prohibited. The target of inspections, prosecutions and claim cases will have to be achieved for every year of the project.

(ii) Income and Employment Generation

The importance of employment and income-generating scheme in any child labour project need hardly be stressed. Indeed, they are fundamental to the achievement of the second objective of the project, namely the reduction in the incidence of child labour through an overall improvement in the soci-economic status of the families or the child workers impoves, there will be less need for the child to go out to earn.

A number of employment and income generation programmes of the Government are in operation at present throughout the country. These are : the Integrated Rural Development Programme (IRDP), the National Rural Employment Programme (NREP), the Rural Landless Employment Guarantee Programme (RLEGP), the Development of Women and Children in Rural Areas (DWAGRA), the Self-Employment Programme for the Urban Poor (SEPUP), etc. The project management will make efforts to get as many child labour families as possible covered under the ongoing poverty amelioration schemes.

As the project management will themselves not be administering these programmes, their role will be more that of catalyst. However, each of these programme has its own parameters and constraints. It is, therefore, possible that despite efforts all child labour families may not be coverd under the existing poverty amelioration programmes of the State and Central Governments. Additional funds are therefore, proposed to be provided under this project to cover child labour families under povety amelioration schemes similar to those of the IRDP. As in the case of IRDP, the assistance will be partly in the shape of a bank loan at low interest rates and partly in the shape of subsidy. The same kind of economic assets provided under the IRDP scheme will be provided under this.

Efforts will also the made to start industries, which are labour-intensive but do not require much capital. In these industries, employment will be given predominantly to family members of child workers.

Since the principal objective of the project is to remove child labour, it will be necessary for the project management to ensure that every family which is given a benefit under this project, removes its child/children from the industry and puts him/her in school. This has to be strictly enforced.

(iii) Non-Farmal Education

Most of the children working in the industry are either dropouts from schools or have never been to school at all. Under the project, non-formal education will be made available to these children.

An essential purpose of non-formal education would be to impact literacy skills of primary education level in order that these children may be able to benefit from other sources of knowledge and information in their later life.

Under the New Education Policy, the Department of Education, Government of India has certain programmes for non-formal education. Non formal education programmes for working children in areas with a concentration of child labour are also specifically mentioned. Under the scheme of the Department of Education, the Central Government will give financial assistance to the extent of 50% for starting non-formal education centres. Where the centres are for girls, 90% assistance will be given by the Central Government. These programmes will be utilised in the project area as for as possible to give non-formal education to the children engaged in the brassware industry.

Various lacalities which have a high concerntration of child labour have been indentified, 18 basic primary schools, whose names are given in Annexure-I have been selected in these areas for providing non-formal education. One hundred children will be taught in each school in two fours—the first batch from 1.00 p.m. to 3.00 p.m. and the second from 3.00 p.m. to 5,00 p.m. every day. The Project Director will, in consultation with the Director of Education, draw up the proposals for these non-formal education centres and submit them to the Department of Education, Ministry of Human Resource Development, Government of India, for releace of funds.

Monthly evaluation of the progress of the child will be made by a Committee consisting of selected heads of schools and class teachers with the Project Director acting as the Chairman and Convener of the meetings. The record of evaluation and the suggestions given for improvement will be kept by the Project Director. These non-formal education centres may by named Bal Shramik Vidyapeeths.

Non-formal education is also proposed to be given through special schools under the project. In these schools emphasis will be laid not only on non-formal education but on vocational training, health care, nutrition, recreation, as well as on any other needs of the children that might emerge. These schools will be run by voluntary organisations will be indentified by the Project Officer and the proposals will be forwarded through him to the Minister of Labour. A hundred per cent financial assistance for these special schools will be given by the Central Government (Ministery of Labour) under this project. Like the other nonformal eudcation centres, (assisted by the Deptt. of Education), these special schools will also have to function during working hours. A provision has been made in the project budget to give stipends to the children who attend the special schools. This has been done so as to compensate the children for their loss in earnings as a result of giving up employment.

(iv) Vocational Training

Vocational training would be available to the children between the age group of 12 to 14 years. In the first year 90 children may be trained in 30 different units. For this 3 supervisors will be required to oversee the training and to ensure that the children are not otherwise exploited by the employers. The object of the vocational training is to teach the children traditional skills of brassware manufacture at Moradabad. To encourage children to take up vocational training, they will be provided with a stipend of Rs. 100 to Rs. 150 per month.

The training shall be given in selected trades such as engraving, polishing, foundry, gas welding, packing, soldering, electroplating, machining, turning, etc. Children selected for training will be in the groups of 12 to 14 years. It will be ensured that all these children get education as well.

(v) Health

It is usually found that the health state of child workers is inferior to that of non-working, school-going chidren. Therefore, providing for health care is sen an essential component of this project. Efforts will be made to get the School Health Progamme which covers school children in the formal school system to cover the children in the non-formal education centres also.

In addition the special school to be set up will have a specific health care component consisiting of medical chick-ups, treatment, maintenance of health hastory sheets, etc. The formal in which history sheets are to be maintained will be prescribed by the project management to ensure uniformity in report.

(vi) Conditions of Work and Terms of Employment

While the enforcement of the law is necessary to ensure that children below 14 years do not work in the industry, at the same time conditions in the industry will have to be created so that it is no longer profitable for the employer to engaged child labour. In addition to this, since many of the parents of child workers are also employed in the industry, improvement of conditions and terms of employment in the industry will have a direct impact on the child workers. The most important step that needs to be taken in this direction relates to wages. Wages should be fixed at a sufficiently high rate to ensure a reasonable income to the workers. Presently, under the Minimum Wages Act, 1948 children between the age groups of 14 to 16 years are paid wages at the rate of two-thirds of the wages admissible to adults. Efforts will be made by Labour Department, Uttar Pradesh to revise minimum wages at par with adults. If it is not possible, wages to children above 14 years should not be less than three-fourths of wages payable to adults. Economically and technologically feasibly improvements in the working environment and improvemtns in the manner in which work is designed and organised will be identified. The Directorate General of Factory Advise, Service and Labour Institute, Bombay (under the Ministry of Labour) will examine defects in lighting, ventilation, etc, in the work place and suggest corrective measures.

(vii) Raising General Consciousness

Efforts will be made by the Project Management through their own staff as well as through voluntary organisations to raise public awareness regarding the problems of child labour, Camps/Workers can be held and the Radio and TV network utilised. The Central Board for Worker's Education should also be used for conscopismess raising. In the adult education classes run by the Government as well as by non-Governmental organisations, efforts will be made to drive home the Government's message regarding child labour.

V. Survey

In order to assess the impact of the project, it will be necessary to take up a proper base-line survey to arrive at the actual number of child workers and collect certain information about them. According to preliminary estimates the number of children engaged in the brassware industry is approximately 7,500. The majority of the children are boys.

VI. Evaluation

At the middle and end of the project period, evaluatory studies will be taken up to assess the progress made towards achieving the objectives indicated. A financial provision has been made in the project budget for this purpose.

VII. Duration

The project has at present drawn up for two years. i.e., upto the end of the 7th Plan period.

VIII. Institutional Framework

At the national level, the programme will be carried out under the auspices of the Ministry of Labour.

At the project level, the following staff will be created :

A Project Director to be in overall charge of the Project, for effective implementation and coordiantion with the District and other authouities.

Two Field Officers to assist the Project Director. They will make frequent visits to the project area programme are properly implemented. These field officers will also be disignated as Labour Inspectors so that they can also enforce the provision of the various laws relating to child lavour.

One Typist-cum-Clerk-cum-Accontant to keep the records and accounts of the Project in the Project Director's Director's Office.

A stenographer to assist the Project Director.

A peon in the office of the Project Director.

A Driver for the vehicle to be provided to the Project Director.

A project level society will be constituted to supervise the programmes with the District Magistrate as its President, the representatives of one or more voluntary agencies with a demonstrated capacity and interest in non-formal education and training and elected representatives of the area. The Project Director will be the Secretary of the Society.

At the national level there would again be a National Monitoring and Evaluation Committee to be instituted by the Ministry of Labour, Government of India, for overall supervision and evaluation of various child labour projects started under the National Child Labour Policy.

IX. Funding

It is proposed to fund the activities fully by the Central Government of India, Ministry of Labour have been reflected in the project budget.

Moradabad Child Labour Project
Approved Budget for the Year 1988-89

1.	Project Staff Salaries		
	— Project Director (1) @ Rs. 3500 p.m.	42,000	
	— Field Officers (2) @ Rs. 2500 p.m. each	60,000	
	— Typist-cum-Clerk-cum-Accountant @ Rs. 1500 p.m.	18,000	
	— Peon (1)	10,000	
	— Driver (1) @ Rs. 1000 p.m.	12,000	
	— Steno (1) (@ Rs. 1500 p.m.	18,000	1,60,000
2.	Office and Support Expenditure		
	— Non-recurring	1,10,000	
	— Vehicle	25,000	
	— Recurring	1,50,000	2,,85,000
3.	Special Schools		
	10. schools for 50 children each @ Rs. 1,60,000 per school per annum	16,00,000	
4.	Income-Generating Schemes	3,00,000	
5.	Resomg Public Awareness	20,000	
6.	Survey	30,000	
	Total	23,95,000	

17

CHILD LABOUR IN NEPAL

The labour of young girls and boys is critical to the household economy my all over the developing world. Children "earn their keep" and contribute economically by assuming domestic responsibilities and "releasing" adults for productive, remunerative work. They may also do so by participating directly in the family occupation, be it agriculture or a trade, or else by working beyond the household for a wage which goes to supplement the family income.

In fact, children's involvement in the work of the family gives them the opportunity to learn traditional skills and the ways of their household and community; to that extent work constitutes an important part of their socialization. Sadly, however, in poor countries such as Nepal the labour of young children, especially girls, is exploited knowingly or unknowingly, both in the home and in the wider labour market.

When is Child Labour Exploitative?

In the context of the extersive poverty in Nepal, it may be unrealistic, even irrelevant to say uncompromising "no" to children's work without first distinguishing labour that is exploitative from other forms of work. Work that amounts to the exploitation of children could be categorized as follows :

* that which is inappropriate to the child's age and strength;
* that which is hazardous and injurious to the child's physical, mental and social well being;
* that which denies the child opportunities for schooling and play and inhibits thereby all around development;
* that which separates the child from home and family;
* that which employs children rather than adults (when large numbers of unemployed adults are available) because youngster can be paid less, threatened into submission, and because they do not have the "voice" or power to organize and bargain collectively (e.g. all forms of employment in the informal sector); and,
* that which uses the labour of some children, rather than others, on account of their membership in a group (such as their gener group), and thereby denies the group opportunities that other children might normally get (e.g. girl's involvement in domestic work because it is considered appropriate to their gender role and so that their brothers may go to school and their parents may work outside the home.)

The above categories are neither exhaustive nor mutually exclusive. They do however, cover most forms of work (ranging from cooking in smoke-filled kitchens to weaving carpets in surroundings that are protected and conditions that are not controlled) that are injurious to health or close down children's "developmental options."

Young Girl's Work

At Home

By the time they are 5 or 6 years old, girls begin to participate in demestic work. They cook and clean, catch water, fuel and fodder, tend animals, wash clothes, and manage and care for their younger siblings. Desipite all this work, girls are not valued as much as their brothers who are seen as potential wage earners. In fact, girls's work is regarded as familial duty than productive endeavour (Chatterjee, 1990). For this reason and because household tasks defy quantification and monetary valuation, girls' work is "invisible" In agricultural families girls in the fields and depending on the season, they may participate in back breaking agicultural activities, such as weeding, harvesting, winnowing, threshing and food processing. [It has been observed that where women are potential wage earners, female children receive a larger share of household resources, than where women are economically unproductive. "The economic productivity of women in adulthood is perhaps a more important determinant of female child survival than many other socio-economic factors. This is also supported by the hypothesis that high demand for female labour in agriculture (such as in rice gowing areas where women are crucial to transplating and other operations) supports less discrimination against female children" (Chatterjee, 1990,p.57)].

Girl's domestic work is considered to be "familial duty"

Children's Economic Participation Rates

Information gathered in micro-level investigations clearly demonstrates that on the whole girls do more work than boys of the same age. This however, is not reflectied in census data.

According to the 1981 census the economic participation rate of girls (10-14 years age group) was 52 per cent which is lower than that of boys in the same age group (61 per cent). The data clearly underestimate girl's labour as household activities are not considered to be "work". (See Table 17.1)

Household activities are not considered to be work in census data

Table 17.1 : Economic Participation Rate of Children (10-14)

Year	Total	Female	Male
1952/53	27.78	25.64	29.48
1971	50.45	40.06	59.24
1981	56.98	51.96	61.28

Source : (Population Censuses)

There appear to be rigional differences in girls economic participation. The highest rates are observed in the mountains and the lowest in the Terai. This possibly reflects the difficult living conditions (high density of population on land, small size of land holdings and ecological deterioration) in the mountains and the relative restrictions on girls' mobility (that increase with age) amoung the orthodox Hindus of the Terai.

There are regional differences in girl's economic participation

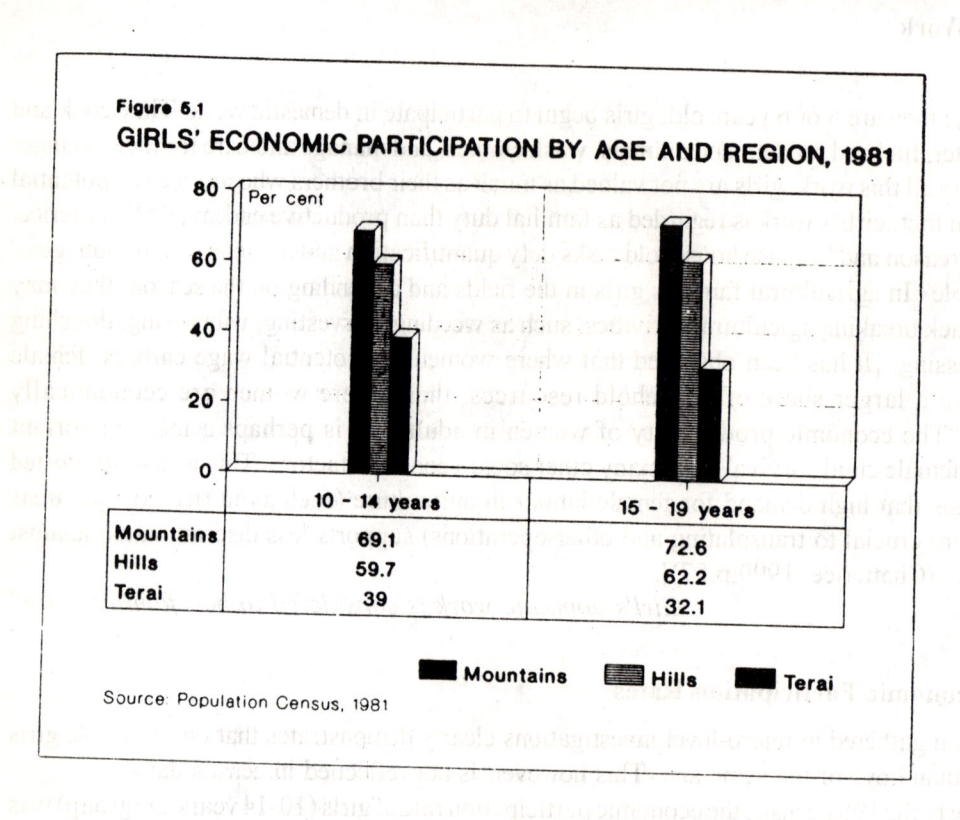

Figure 5.1
GIRLS' ECONOMIC PARTICIPATION BY AGE AND REGION, 1981

	10 - 14 years	15 - 19 years
Mountains	69.1	72.6
Hills	59.7	62.2
Terai	39	32.1

Source: Population Census, 1981

Girl's Workload

A more accurate picture of girl's workload is provided by research that examines the amount of time they devote to labour activities. The Nepal Rastra Bank/Multi-Purpose Household Budget Survey (NRB/MPHBS) data (see Table 17.2) clearly illustrate that :

Time use pattern data provide more accurate information about girl's workload

* girls work more than boys (sometimes more than twice) in all groups;
* their work burden increases with age
* their work burden is highest in the mountains and lowest in the Terai and in between in the hills.
* there does not appear to be a distinct relationship between grade of poverty and the number of working hours for boys and girls.

Time use pattern information based on NRB/MPHBS data reveal that domestic work, including child-care, constitutes 70 per cent of the total work burden of children of both sexes in the 6-9 age group, and over 50 per cent in the 10-14 year age group at all poverty levels and in all regions.

For the 6-9 year age group, child care accounts for about half of the domestic work burden.

Table 17.2 : Children's Work Burden by Age, Sex, Region and Poverty Level
(Times spent in hours)

Poverty Level[1]	Rural Mountains F	M	Rural Hills F	M	Rural Terai F	M	Urban Hills F	M	Urban Terai F	M
Ultra Poor										
6-9 yrs	4.39	3.05	3.86	2.23	3.21	2.22	2.83	-	-	-
10-14 yrs	7.7	4.39	8.43	4.82	5.59	2.46	7.01	0.5	-	-
Poor										
6-9 yrs	4.26	2.71	3.26	1.96	3.12	1.86	2.58	0.84	2.84	1.78
10-14 yrs	7.28	4.21	6.82	3.78	6.53	3.78	5.6	2.11	5.67	2.67
Non-Poor										
6-9 yrs	4.28	4.17	3.19	1.7	2.21	1.34	1.2	0.44	1.99	0.79
10-14 yrs	7.93	4.77	7.66	4.41	5.37	2.84	3.63	1.53	4.37	2.23

Source : Based on NRB/MPHBS, 1984/85.

Note : Using the Nepal Rastra Bank/Multi-Purpose Household Budget Survey (NRB/MPHBS) data, the Work Bank recently classified the absolute poor in Nepal into the Ultra Poor (those below the Ultra Poverty Level (UPL) and with per capita monthly income between Rs. 50-80) and the Poor (those above the UPL but below the Poverty Level) (PL) and with per capita monthly income between Rs. 100-145). The Non-Poor are those just above the PL and have a per capita monthly income of Rs. 220-250.

In the 10-14 year age group household chores such as cleaning and washing, constitute the major share of domestic work. The third most important set of of tasks includes fetching water and fuel and fodder collection (for the hazards of water fatching, see Box 17.1).

Results of the RIDA survey study on the situation of the girl child in Nepal demonstrated a similar pottern of findings. The results of the time use pattern investigation were based on amalgamated data from 400 households in 8 ethnic groups. In addition to showing that girls work more than boys and that their workload increases with age, the findings showed that out-of-school children work twice or thrice as long as their school going peers (see Table 17.3) on domestic work, and subsistence and conventional economic activities.

> **How Water Fetching Affects Health** Box. 17.1
>
> Carrying water is one of the most arduours of tasks in the rural areas of developing coutries; a task which is usually carried out by women and children. Carrying water on the head requires strength in the neck and considerable skill, a skill often acquired at around nine years old (*sic*). The task of carrying heavy loads over long distances requires a great deal of energy, which comes from metabolized food. The longer the distance and the more difficult the terrain, the greater the quantity of food needed. Women [and children] carrying water are frequently exposed to malnutrition, anaemia and water related diseases.
>
> A major problem arising from carrying water is the early ageing of the vertebal columns. Where children are concerned, the main problem associated with carrying heavy loads of water is the effect on the growth of bones. When children begin to carry water, they are still growing and a deformity known as scoliosis of the verterbral column may occur, particularly when water is carried on the hip or shoulder. Carrring water on the hip may also cause deformed pelvic bones in children. Poeple carrying water on their backs with a head strap [this is a common method in Nepal] exhibit a marked cranial depression, and many suffer from severe headaches. Also, because of the development of the neck muscles, they may have problems with the thyroid gland. Other problems include fractures, slipped discs and damage to the knees.
>
> Providing more appropriate means of transport and sitting water supplies within a reasonable distance may lessen the health problems of women and children. One of the aims of the Water Decade is to reduce health problems by providing safe water close to the houses. By reducing energy requirements, women [and children] will be less vulnerable to malnutrition; by providing safe water the incidence of water related diseases will decrease; by reducing walking distances the skeleton will not suffer as much, and one of women's [and children's] many carrying tasks will be considerably reduced.
>
> * Excerpted from "Women carrying water: how it affects their health" by Annie Dufaut, *Waterlines*, 6(3), January 1988, pp. 23-5.

Wage Labour in the Informal Sector : The Case of Girls in the Current Industry

It is estimated that children (below 14 years) and minors (14-18 years) form 33.11 per cent and 19 per cent of the carpet industry workers respectively (UNICEF, 1991). Few data exist on the situation of girls in the carpet weaving industry, and the exact number of children involved in it is not really known. According to one study there are 526 registered carpet factories in the Kathmandu valley alone, with a total labour force of 17,435 of which a large number are children. In the RIDA survey 3 factories were covered. A total of 51 children, 26 girls and 25 boys in the age group 10-18 were interviewed to gain insights into the conditions in which children weave carpets. It was observed that sometimes children as youngs 9 years of age are inducted into the carpet weaving industry. Some of the important findings with regard to girls were as follows :

Few data exist on girl wage workers in the informal sector

* most girls came from agricultural homes; some came from homes where either the father or mother or both were involved in carpet weaving;
* about 69 per cent (or 18) of the girls were illiterate; others had obtained between 1 and 4 years of schooling;
* none of the girls were attending school currently, though all except two expressed a desire to be educated.
* poverty was the most commonly stated reason for working; other reasons were death of a parent, lack of educational facilities, maltreatment at home and expectation of a better life in the city.

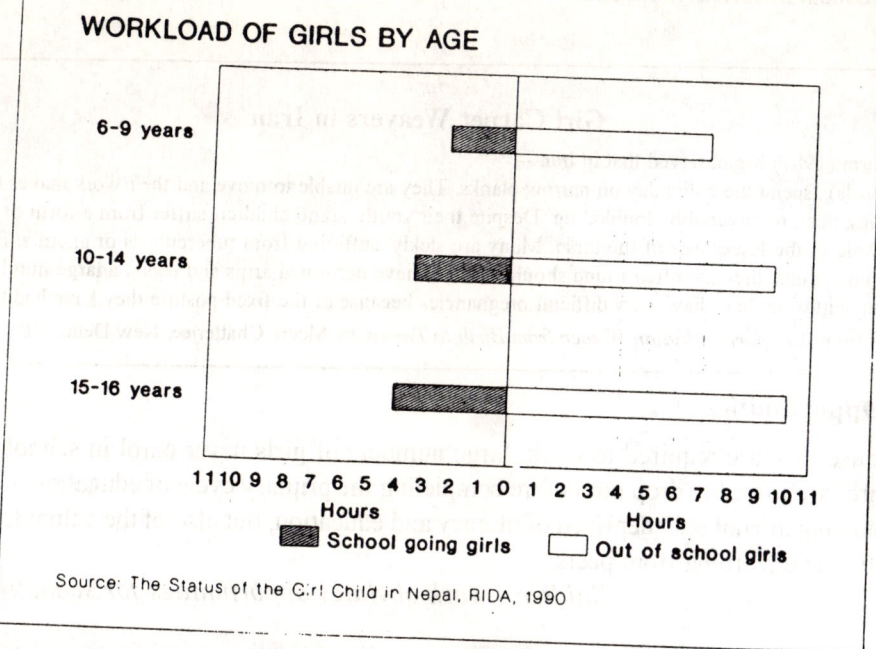

WORKLOAD OF GIRLS BY AGE

[Bar chart showing workload hours for school going girls and out of school girls across age groups 6-9 years, 10-14 years, and 15-16 years.]

Source: The Status of the Girl Child in Nepal, RIDA, 1990

* most girls and boys (60 per cent) did not complain about the conditions in their place of work;
* girls worked for an averge of 12 hours a day at the loom and were willing to work longer;
* twenty-one of the 51 children had health complaints which were not necessarily related to carpet weaving; 32 children felt that the work was hazardous.
* on average a child earned Rs. 37 (about US$ 1) per day and in most cases wages were surrendered to the parents or guardians;
* sixty-eight per cent of the girls were seprated from their immediate families and came from the eastern, central hill and mountain regions of the country.

Table 17.3 : Gender Differences in the Workload of School Going and Out of School Children

Age Group	School Going Girls	School Going Boys	Out of School Girls	Out of School Boys	Total Girls	Total Boys
6-9	2.32	1.82	7.04	4.39	3.98	2.42
10-14	3.50	2.23	9.54	9.55	5.79	2.95
15-16	4.13	3.11	10.13	7.92	7.13	3.59
Total	3.18	2.20	8.94	6.19	5.44	2.81

Source : The Status of the Girl Child in Nepal–A Survey Report, RIDA, December 1990.

The study does not provide and qualitative information about the working conditions in the carpet weaving industry. It can however be surmised that conditions are not very different from those in other developing nations (see Box 17.2).

> **Box 17.2**
>
> ### Girl Carpet Weavers in Iran
>
> Burra (1987) has observed that in Iran—
> "(girls)...spend the entire day on narrow planks. They are unable to move and their work makes them adopt a squattting posture, invariably doubled up. Despite their youth, some children suffer from a form of anykylosis of the whole of the lower part of the torso. Many are sickly, suffering from tuberculosis or anemia. By the time they become adults, they are often round shouldered and have deformed arms and legs... a large number of them are subsequently sterile or have very difficult pregnancies because of the fixed posture they have had to adopt".
>
> * Quoted from *A Report on Indian Women from Birth to Twenty* by Meera Chatterjee, New Delhi: NIPCCD, 1990.

Missed Opportunities

Because they are required to work, large numbers of girls never enrol in school. Even those who do enrol are forced to drop out before completing the primary cycle of education. Girls who are denied schooling are not only deprived of literacy and education, but also of the valuable opportunity of interacting and learning from peers.

Children's work obviates opportunities for schooling and play

Play is an essential part of any child's physical, motor cognitive, social and emotional development. Through play children learn to be creative, practive their language skills, participate in group activities, learn to cooperate, and cope with distress. Mechanical and repetitive work can be boring and stultify the young mind and body—indeed rob it of its childhood.

Constitutional and Legislative Safeguards

The UN Convention on the Rights of the Child enjoins State Parties to:
1. ...recognise the right of the child to be protected from economic exploitation and from performing any work that is likely to be hazardous or to interfere with the child's education, or to be harmful to the child's health or physical, mental, spiritual, moral or social development.
2. ...take legislative, administrative, social and educational measures to ensure the implementation of this article. To this end, and having regard to the relevant provisions of other international instruments, State Parties shall in particular:
    (a) provide for a minimum age or minimum ages for admission to employment,
    (b) provide for appropriate regulation of the hours and conditions of employment; and,
    (c) provide for appropriate penalties or other sanctions ensure the effective enforcement of this article.

Child labour in factories, mines and other hazardous industries is forbidden by Article 20 of the Constitution. Section 14 of the Nepal Civil Rights Act prohibits employment of children who are under the age of 14 years as does Section 17 of the Factory Act. While these provisions exist, there is no comprehensive legislation against child labour in Nepal. The Nepal Law Reform Commision has prepared a draft Children's Act which when promulgated will afford children a variety of protective measures.

It is debatable whether the enactment of appropriate laws against child labour will produce the desired deterrent effect: In fact, experience in other developing countries shows that wherever such laws exist they are grossly violated. This is primarily so because a large proportion of children's work is invisible and because, at the best of times, the informal sector (in which most wage earning children are located) is, by its every nature, impossible to control or regulate. Moreover, poverty forces children to be "willing victims"—they will endure pitiful working conditions rather than risk losing source of income.

Is legislation against child labour the answer?

Protection From Exploitation : The Need for A Coordinated Approach

At the same time as child labour results from poverty, through denying children opportunities for education and training, it perpetuates the low skill-low income-poverty-exploitation cycle. The eradication of exploitative child labour must be our guiding goal. However, given the slow pace of change in the socio-economic environment of the country, it will take a while to reach it. In the short-term it is necessary to take measures to ensure that the work burden of young girls is lessened, that they receive at least some education and training, and that the working conditions in child labour intensive industries are regulated.

Lessening Young Girl's Work Burden

* Given that a large proportion of young girl's time is taken up in caring for younger siblings, it is recommended that *early child care centres* are established in conjunction with primary schools, so that girls may attend school. If such an arrangement is not feasible, the formation of Community Groups which will provide child minding facilities during school hours should be encouraged.
* It is recommended that the strain on young girls to collect fuel and fodder and to fetch water is reduced by :
    — transferring *appropriate technology* to the villages, such as the use of solar energy and bio-gas, fuel production from waste and the growing of fuel trees;
    — provision of *drinking water* in all habitations;
* Additionally, the technology of *smokeles chullashs* which reduces drastically the health hazards associated with cooking on traditional hearths, should be introduced in villages, in order to protect the health of all members of the family, including girls and women who do almost all the cooking.
* Importantly, all families should be encouraged to promote more *equitable work sharing* among boys and girls at home.

Opportunities for Education

Alongside efforts to make communities appreciate the importance of educating girls, certain measures will have to be taken within the educational system to afford girls the opportunity to obtain some of the benefits of schooling.

Non-formal Education

The *Cheli Beti* programme has been received positively. Through evening classes girls are trained in literacy and numeracy. The programme should be expanded and enriched. At the same time the effort should be to try and intergrate girls, who have attended *Cheli Beti* classes and achieved some amount of competence in literacy, into the formal school system.

Formal Education

The formal school system should allow for lateral and multi-point entry in order to accommodate girls who have had some education.

In order to attract and retain girls, school timings should be fixed according to the convenience of the majority of girls and boys in the catchment area. Schools should also be responsive to seasonal demands for child labour and every effort should be made to make the summer holidays coincide with the harvesting season, or shorten or lengthen the school day according to the demands on children's time. This kind of flexibility should be available in at least the primary school years.

Legislation

Even though it is appreciated that law without accompanying public opinion is of limited value, the enactment of suitable legislation would reffirm the State's commitment to protect children from abuse and exploitation. Such legislation would also empower social organizations working for children to ensure that young labourers are not exploited in the workplace and that unscrupulous employers are appropriately penalized. Of course, girl's labour inside the home and other forms of household related work would continue to stay outside the ambit of such legislation. Programmes to universalize education and alleviate poverty would probably be the only means of reducing girl's domestic drudgery.

The Need for Information

Both qualitative and quantitative data are required to inform efforts aimed at relasing young girls from work that restricts their development. Data that demonstrate the negative effects of certain forms of work on girls health and development need to be gathered in order to corroborate theoretical claims. Regional date which analyse different work patterns also need to be collected. In this context the work burden and needs of urban girls must be identified.

References

Chatterjee, M. (1990). *A Report on Indian Women from Birth to Twenty,* New Delhi : NIPCCD.

RIDA (1990). *The Status of the Girl Child in Nepal—A Survey Report,* Kathmandu : RIDA, (draft mimeo.).

Singh, S.L. (1990). *Work Burden of Girl Child in Nepal—An Analysis by Poverty Levels,* Kathmandu : Ministry of Labour and Sociel Welfare/HMG.

The United Nations Convention on the Rights of the Child (1989).

UNICEF (1991). *Children and Women in Nepal—A situation Analysis,* Kathmandu : UNICEF (draft mimeo).

18

CHILD LABOUR IN NORTH AMERICA

Introduction

To a greater or lesser extent, children in every type of human society have always taken part and still do take part in those economic activities which are necessary if the group to which they belong is to survive. However, the notion that child labour is a social problem, a phenomenon hindering the harmonious physical and mental development of the child, is a relatively recent development. This interpretation of child labour and the accompanying idea that the child should be protected against it, came to the fore when paid child labour (that is the systematic exploitation of children by employers outside the child's family) become common.

The nature of adolescence in American society has undergone a dramatic change over the past forty years. In increasing numbers, schools age adolescents have entered the work-place, holding part time jobs after school that consume substantial portions of their afternoon school, nights and weekends. The large teenage, part time labour force that staffs the counters of fast food establishments, waits on customers in retail stores, assembles parts in industrial setting, and cleans motel rooms and office buildings has become such a familiar part of our social landscape that we may fail to note its unique character or to ponder its larger social significance. In those western notions which are today the most economically advanced countries in the world, it was taken for granted in the past that children would work alongside their parents in the fields or in the home. However, when the change over to manufacturing industry took place neither changed the circumjstances. Thus in the nineteenth century it became common for children to work in factories, especially textile mills, from the age of 6 years onwards, in abysmal working conditions involving a daily stint of some 14 hours and with almost no mean of protection against the risk of accidents. Even as recently as the beginning of the twentieth century, some western children were still being employed in coal mines or were kept busy at home on work sent out to them by manufacturers. Happily, in most developed countries economic, moral and legal progress has relegated exploitation of this kind to the past. This is not to say, however, that child labour in these countries, despite its being illegal, has completely disappeared, as we shall see late. In the developing countries and in Southern Europe the exploitation of children has not been eliminated and is still prevalent or fairly widespread in many places.

According to a recent ILO estimate, the number of working children between the ages of 5 and 14 in developing countries is 250 million, of whom some 120 million work full time. Africa, the poorest region, has the highest incidence of child workers-some 40 per cent. The figure for Asia and Latin America is about

20 per cent. In absolute figures, Asia has the largest number of child workers. Approximately 61 per cent of child workers are in Asia, 32 per cent in Africa and 7 per cent in Latin America.

Child labour still exists in industrialised countries. In South European countries, a large number of children are found in paid employment, especially in activities of a seasonal nature, street trades, small workshops or in the context of home work. Child labour has not completely disappeared either in other parts of Europe. It has increased in Central and Eastern European countries as a result of the difficulties faced by large sectors of the population due to the transition from a centrally planned to a market economy. Elsewhere, in the United States, the number of young people between the ages of 12 and 17 who work is put at 5.5 million, or 27 per cent of the total of children in this age group. To this figure must be added that many children under the age of 12 illegally employed in various activities for example, in urban garment-manufacturing workshops, as street traders and especially as seasonal and migrant workers on large farms.

Facts and Figures

Though reliable statistics are rare, available information suggests that the number of working children remains extremely high. No region of the world today is entirely free of child labour.

Although the internationally recommended minimum age for work is 15 years (ILO Convention No. 138) and the number of child workers under the age of 10 is far from negligible, almost all the data available on child labour concerns the 10 to 14 age group.

Combining various official sources, the ILO estimates that more than 73 million children in that age group alone were economically active in 1995, representing 13.2 per cent of all 10 to 14 year olds around the world.

- The greatest numbers were found in Asia 44.6 million (13 per cent) followed by Africa 23.6 million (by far the highest rate at 26.3 per cent) and Latin America 5.1 million (9.8 per cent).
- Estimates by country showed the following rates of economic activity among children 10 to 14: Bangladesh (30.1 per cent), China (11.6), India (14.4), Pakistan (17.7), Turkey (24); Cote d'Ivoire (20.5), Egypt (11.2), Kenya (41.3), Nigeria (25.8), Senegal (31.4); Argentina (4.5), Brazil (16.1), Mexico (6.7); Italy (0.4), Portugal (1.8).

"But this is only part of the picture", says Assefa Bequele, departmental Director and child labour specialist at the ILO. "No reliable figures on workers under 10 are available though their numbers, we know, are significant. The same is true of children between 14 and 15 on whom few reports exist. If all of these could be counted and if proper account were taken of the domestic work performed full-time by girls, the total number of child workers around the world today might well be in the hundreds of millions."

Though mostly prevalent in the developing regions, child labour also exists in richer industrialised countries. "In southern Europe, there have always been relatively large numbers of children working for pay, in particular in seasonal activities, street trades, small workshops or in a home setting".

In central and eastern Europe, the difficulties connected with the transition from a centrally planned to a market economy has led to a substantial increase in child labour. The ILO report points out that "the same is true of the United States, where the growth of the service sector, the rapid increase in the supply of part-time jobs and the search for a more flexible workforce have contributed to the expansion of the child labour market."

Estimated percentages of economically active children between 10 and 14 years of age, 1995 (Selected countries and territories)

Africa (%)
    Algeria 1.63
    Burkina Faso 51.05
    Burundi 48.97
    Cameroon 25.25
    Cote d'Ivoire 20.46
    Egypt 11.23
    Ethiopia 42.30
    Ghana 13.27
    Kenya 41.27
    Mali 54.53
    Morocco 5.61
    Niger 45.17
    Nigeria 25.75
    Senegal 31.36
    South Africa 0.00
    Tunisia 0.00
    Uganda 45.31
    Zambia 16.27
    Zimbabwe 29.44

Asia (%)
    Bangladesh 30.12
    Bhutan 55.10
    China 11.55
    East Timor 45.39
    Hong Kong 0.00
    India 14.37
    Indonesia 9.55
    Iran 4.71
    Iraq 2.95
    Japan 0.00
    Jordan 0.68
    Malaysia 3.16
    Nepal 45.18
    Pakistan 17.67
    Philippines 8.04
    Saudia Arabia 0.00
    Syrian Arab Rep. 5.78

Turkey 24.00
Thailand 16.22
Viet Nam 9.12
Yemen 20.15

Europe (%)
Albania 1.11
Hungary 0.17
Italy 0.38
Portugal 1.76
Romania 0.17

Latin America (%)
Argentina 4.53
Bolivia 14.36
Brazil 16.09
Chile 0.00
Colombia 6.62
Costa Rica 5.48
Cuba 0.00
Dominican Rep. 16.06
Guatemala 16.22
Haiti 25.30
Mexico 6.73
Nicaragua 14.05
Paraguay 7.87
Peru 2.48
Uruguay 2.08
Venezuela 0.95

Oceania (%)
Papua New Guinea 19.31
Solomon Islands 28.89
Polynesia 3.67

Percent of Total World Child Labour

Region	1980	1985	1990
Africa	17.0	8.0	21.3
Americas	4.7	5.6	na
Asia	77.8	75.9	72.3
Europe	0.3	0.2	0.1
Oceania	0.2	0.2	0.2

Source: ILO 1993. Note: na...not available

Comparison of Labour Force Participation Rates of Children and Adults by Region (per cent)

Region	15 years and over	10-14 years
Africa	65.2	22.0
Americas	61.8	7.9
Asia	68.1	15.3
Europe	54.5	0.3
Oceania	62.7	6.9

Source: ILO 1993.

Social, Economic and Cultural Background

If we are to understand why child labour today takes the form that it does, the phenomenon must be set against its social background. Broadly speaking, we may say that child labour persists in inverse relation to the degree of economic advancements of a society, country or region. The exploitation of children is one result of the complex, unchanging nature of society, not only in most of the developing countries but also in some regions of the developed world. The notion of child labour is rooted in the traditions and attitudes of the regions where it is practiced, as a remnant of the past, a form of resistance to change. As an illustration of this, we may mention the belief very widely held in the developing countries, that the more children here are in a family, the more hands there are to help to increase the family income. Whether this belief be justified or not, it is merely a tradition, handed down from generation to generation . Again, in the developing countries the idea that a child who is no longer a baby should be maintained without working is uncommon. This idea stems not so much from poverty as from the traditional belief that there is no point in making any plans beyond those for satisfying the family's immediate basic needs. It is an idea that betrays and attitude devoid of any impulse or evolution and change. Following the same train of thought, reference is sometimes made to an age old educational principle that is base only on the need for survival: that if one does not work one has the option of starving or of stealing. This principle if applied from a very early age. In fact, when the need for survival and the social function of traditional behaviour converge, long-term planning becomes irrelevant: today's meagre incomes, out of which any savings are impossible, cannot be sacrificed in the hope that tomorrow's incomes and other benefits might be greater.

In such a social setting, whenever a child decides or agrees to work in order to earn his living he thinks he is taking the decision himself. The truth of the matter is that this decision has in effect already been taken for him, through the attitude of his parents and through the influence of the entire social environment in which he lives: that is, he accepts a role which turns him into both the victim and the involuntary accomplice of an unjust situation. Once this kind of thinking is accepted, it is clear that the parents who benefit directly or indirectly from the exploitation of their children do not consider that they are deliberately acting in a despotic and inhuman manner; rather, they believe that they have a natural right to take advantage of (not to exploit) all the family's resources, which generally amount to little more than the number of hands it has at its disposal. Furthermore, the parents consider that, as in the family undertaking of former times, the child is learning a job that will be of value to him in the future; without their being aware of the harmful effects that certain forms of work at an early age can have on child. It is not the family that should carry the blame for the fact that the child has to work, since the courses of action open to the family are few in number; it is society as a whole that is at fault. Like all social problems, child labour is not an isolated phenomenon, nor can it ever be so.

The Role of Legislation

Custom and the law usually hold that the work that children do alongside their parents is distinct from the exploitation to which they may be subjected when they work for third parties. Indeed, this is generally so, since parents usually look after their children's welfare; nevertheless, however much the physical effort, the hours of work and the boredom inflicted on the child may be reduced and however satisfactory his working environment may be, he will invitably be concerned in the smooth running of the family undertaking and will inevitable share, with his parents, problems, pre-occupation's and uncertainties which are not usually the concern of children of his age.

It was in the more developed countries that people first became aware of the harmfulness of child labour and of the need to introduce compulsory education and to give children the necessary opportunities for recreation, and legal and practical measures where gradually introduced to this end. It does seem, however, as though these measures were not always inspired purely by humanitarian motives, they were also designed to protect the employment and wages of adult workers. In fact, it is known that children who enter the labour force carry out work that would very well be done by an adult-that is, they usually deprive an adult of the job in question. Moreover, the child does the job for a much lower wage than would have to be paid to and adult. For this reason many employers prefer to engage children, knowing that they can pay them lower wages than if the same type of job were to go to an adult. There is in fact a vicious circle here: on the one hand, child labour increases unemployment amount adults and reduces their income; and on the other, the unemployment among adults and reduces their income; and on the other, the unemployment and low wages of adults force them to put their children to work in order to boost the family income. Thus child labour simultaneously increase and reduces the family income I but, as is clear, it reduces rather than increases that income.

What is Child Labour

The abuse and misuse of children at work is called child labour. It is work that exploits children. In very nation in all times, employers have exploited children and continue to do so. Such exploitation comes in many forms. Some employers pay low wages or no wages at all. Others force children to work excessive hours or fail to provide them with a safe, healthy working environment. If the exploitation is severe enough, permanent physical, psychological, intellectual, social, and moral damage-even death-can result. The work of the young English chimney sweeps was child labour.

Today no society anywhere in the would advocates child labour. Indeed most nations have laws outlawing it. Yet child labour continues and, according to a United Nations report, is a growing evil. True, children don't sweep chimneys anymore, but they do work at a many other, sometimes more dangerous, unhealthy jobs.

Youth employment as opposed to child labour is the employment of children at appropriate jobs with considerate employers, under healthy conditions and at fair wages.

CHILD LABOUR IN THE PAST
Problem and its History

During the middle ages, from about 476 to the late 1400 in some societies, parents believed that they owned their children and therefor treated them like property. Rich and poor parents alike used their children for economic gain. Among the poor, parents needing money might choose to cell or apprentice one or more of their children to keep the rest of the family from starving. The working child, whether apprenticed or sold, was in a vulnerable position, for whether the master was kind or cruel, the child had to work not under the supervision of a parent but under the rule of a stranger. The master alone determined the hours and the condition, so the hours were usually long and the work hard. Children generally accepted their lot in life as everyone expected children of the poor to work.

Industrial Revolution

Three hundred years later, in eighteen century England, new discovery in science and technology initiated a major tread that would change the face of society forever: replacing some human power with energy derived from sources like water and coal, and using new machines to do what humans had done in the past. Thus began the Industrial Revolution.

The inventions during the Industrial Revolution transformed the world from a peasant society to an industrial one, and in this new society child labour was used extensively, the first industry to become industrialised was the textile industry. Each new invention inspired other inventions and together they changed the way people lived, worked, and did business. As a result of the Industrial Revolution the major workplace shifted from the farm and home to the factory. England quickly became the industrial leader of the world. Entrepreneurs with money to invest began building factories to house the new machinery. This construction soon required some workers to build the factories grew, so did the number of people required to tend them. A labour shortage resulted, and employers turned to children. Since children, especially the children of the poor, were abundant and replaceable if one child died, he or she could easily be replaced by another, condition were ripe for exploitation. Employers went to work houses, collected children, then transported them in crowds, sometimes for many hundreds of miles, to work all day and often during the whole right in factories.

At first the general population believed that employing children was beneficial to both the child and the community. Work kept youngsters out of trouble, gave them early self-reliance, and provided extra money for their families. However, employing children created new family hardships because as more and more children went to work, unemployment grew among the heads of households. Employerrs replaced adults with children since children could be hired for less money. As unemployment among adults grew, families began starving. In turn, more children began working, and so the cycle continued and enlarge. The earnings of children simultaneously helped and hurt families. Naturally, it was the children of the poor who suffered. The children of the rich did not have to work in factories.

The average age at which children went to work was very young. It was not un-common in the 1700s and 1800s for seven year old to work in mills and mines. They worked eighteen hours or more a day and grew up illiterate because they did not go to school. Their parents encouraged them to work and even found jobs for them, because the choice was to work or starve. Because of child labour, children were crippled by industrial accidents became chronically ill because they lacked proper exercise and clean air, and were prone to other diseases because of improper diets, Many died.

Working conditions in the mills and mines were so bad that adults in England began coming to the aid of children. In 1796 a group of physicians in Manchester became so alarmed at the declining health of children working in cotton factories that they formed a Board of Health and appealed to Parliament, the British legislature, to stop the social evils that were killing children. Dr. Thomas Percival, one of the members of the group, wrote in a report that "children and others who work in the large factories, are peculiarly disposed to be affected by the contagion of fever,... the close confinement,... (the) effects of hot or impure air, and... the want of the active exercise... The untimely labour of the night, and the protracted labour of the day, with respect to the children, not only tends to diminish future expectations as to the general sum of life and industry by impairing the strength and destroying the vital stamina of the rising generation, but it too often gives encouragement to idleness, extravagance and profligacy in the parents who, contrary to the order of nature, subsist by the appression of their offspring ." Dr. Percival, then, blamed not only the employers for the harsh life of children, but also the parents.

Around 1800 a growing number of enlightened people in England began speaking out against the injustice of child labour. In 1802, Parliament passed the first law regulation child labour. However, the law was not enforced and applied only to children dependent upon charity. In the following decades famous authors like Elizabeth Barrett Browining and Charles Dickens used their pens to bring the problem to the attention of the public. It was hard for the middle class and the affluent to believe the effect industrialisation was having upon children.

In 1833 Parliament passed stronger measures to protect children. Although these laws helped, they were not enough. Charles Dickens once again explored the problem, this time in Oliver Twist, the story of poor orphan boy drawn into the criminal world of London. Dickens pointed out the greed, cruelty, and selfishness of adults and their effect upon young children pushed too young into the work force.

It was common at the time for factories to have whipping rooms for children who misbehaved, worked too slowly, or fell asleep during working hours, it was not unusual for employers to chain children to equipment so they could not run away. As bad as these working conditions were, what shocked the public more than anything else was the revelation in 1842 of the barbaric working conditions in the coal mines. Examiners found children "chained, belted, harnessed like dogs in a go-cart, black, saturated with wet, and more than half naked-crawling upon their hands and feet, and dragging their heavy loads behind them- (the children)...present and appearance indescribably disgusting and unnatural."

When the information reached the more well to do public, they were outraged and pressured the government to pass laws protecting working children. However, not until the end of the nineteenth century, when economic and social conditions changed in the united kingdom as a whole, did life improve for the working children.

The United States and the United Kingdom share a common history. As early as in 1700, in order to meet a labour shortage in the colonies, British and American employers recruited large number of poor British children to work alongside American born children. All of these children were as overworked and mistreated in the colonies as in England. The conflict over the issue of industrialisation was one of the causes of the American Revolution. After the revolution the mother country no longer had the power to set limits on the former colonies and so industry expanded rapidly. As mechanisation increased, so did the need for workers, including child workers. The children were as young as ten and worked twelve to thirteen hours a day. Corporal punishment was not unusual and was sometimes done in special whipping rooms. For a long time the only opposition to employment of children in the U. S. came from visiting English and French travellers. As in England the more the children worked, the more they depressed their parent's wages, making their employment more necessary. While some people did try to protect the children, the few laws written were, as one historian put it, "so many dead letters". And so the vicious circle existing in England became established in America.

America Accepts Child Labour

Why did America accept child labour? For one thing, most people had little knowledge of what was going on the government did not record national statistics on working children. For another, children were treated better than in England. Although the general public accepted the whipping rooms, believing that punishment kept the devil out of the child, the beating were not as brutal as those in England. Furthermore, there were no American girls dragging loaded coal wagons deep underground in coal mines.

Another reason for accepting child labour was that many people believed working children kept parents from becoming dependent upon public charity. In addition, working children kept production costs down, and this made the nation competitive abroad.

Finally, people believed that children benefited morally from their work. It was an established belief that idleness was a sin and industry a virtue. From the earliest colonial days, the long standing belief was that work was good for children. It built character and taught responsibility and thrift. While these may indeed result from work, in fact the employer benefited far more than the employee.

For example, throughout the nineteenth century, manufacturers in Connecticut, Southern and western Massachusetts, and Rhode Island commonly hired and entire family but paid only one wage, called a "family wage". In this arrangement a man, his wife, and their children worked in the same factory but the employer paid only the man. He added a bit extra to the man's usual pay for his family's help. Everyone, including the children, was encouraged-sometimes forced to work long hours and at night. There was not time for school, and men with large, growing families were in greater demand than single men or men with small families.

The major concern of early nineteenth century liberal was not the treatment of young workers, but rather their lack of education, illiterates could not read the Bible. In 1813 Connecticut passed a law requiring manufacturers to provide young workers with instruction in reading, writing and arithmetic, however, the state did not enforce the law. Legislators, however, were ambivalent perhaps hypocritical about whether the best interests of the nation lay in cheap child labour or in the educated children. This pattern was typical throughout the country in the nineteenth century. Work conflicted with school, America seemed unsure which to limit. In 1830 a labour union member in Philadelphia lamented that the product of work was uneducated young people. He protested that the workers in cotton factories were primarily boys and girls from six to seventeen years old who worked from daylight until dark. In

1836, Massachusetts passed a law requiring children to be in school three months each year. No where, however were the laws enforced and children continued to work long hours. In Lowell Massachusetts, major textile centre, witnesses reported that "little mites of ten were on duty nearly fourteen hours a day and then did household tasks and went to evening school." Industrialisation in the U.S. proceeded slowly until after the Civil War, when economic conditions changed rapidly and both the North and the South greatly expanded their industry. The combination of a critical labour shortage (there were simply not enough people to run the machines) and the preference employers had for cheap labour encouraged the nation as a whole to continue accepting child labour and its evils. By 1900, 25,000 children under the age of fifteen were working in southern factories. Ninety per cent of these were in North and South Carolina, Georgia and Alabama. These states had neither compulsory education laws nor child labour laws and the illiteracy rate was three times higher than any other state.

If working conditions were bad in the United States, they were worse in other parts of the world. Between 1881 and 1890, 5.2 million people migrated to the U.S These new immigrants entered the labour market in large numbers. They came from European farms and villages and moved into overcrowded, filthy tenements. They were poor and mostly uneducated, and few could speak English. Immigrant children went to work in the same factories and mills as adults, creating surplus of workers. The new immigrants were willing to work harder for less money than the native born just in order to survive. Desperate parents encouraged their little ones to begin work early instead of going to school. Children frequently worked "off the books" that is, employers did not keep work records, so children either would not be paid at all or would be paid far fewer hours than were actually worked. The 1900 concensus did not include working children under ten or those who worked "off the books" or the many children who earned money by selling merchandise on the streets, so the figures were greatly understated.

The newly arrived children joined other economically disadvantaged children in what where termed the "street trades". Children working the street were in a particularly defenceless position. At first neither the parents nor anyone else acknowledged that street children had a problem. These working children were the subject of romantic stories. The public readily accepted this idealised version of reality. In truth street children worked long hours in the worst kinds of weather. Boys and girls sold apples and other fruits, peanuts, flowers, coal, ice and wood. Others collected or stole junk to sell. Street work brought illness and even death to the young workers. Financial pressures forced many who ere in School to leave or miss class so frequently that they might as well have not been enrolled.

Sweetshop

Working children who were not outside on the streets, were inside in factories, many of which were sweetshops. There were two kinds of sweetshops. One kind comprised small manufacturing establishments in rundown buildings where people worked under unsanitary conditions for wages that were so low that even when an entire family worked all day and into the night, they still did not earn enough money to buy food, clothing, shelter, and proper medial care. Hunger was common. Many died in fires because they were unable to escape from the locked rooms in which they laboured long hours. Sweetshop employers paid the workers by the article assembled or constructed instead of by the number of hours required to complete the task. Sometimes the worker would make only the sleeves on a garment. Sometimes they would only sew buttons or assemble part of a larger object. Such work was called piecework.

The second kind of sweatshop was the home itself. Many people lived and worked in tenements-crowded apartment buildings poorly heated, inadequately ventilated, and insufficiently lit. Like the factories, they were often firetraps. Manufacturers often gave piecework to women and children to do at home, turning the home into a sweatshop. While home industry in the form of craft work had always been a part of life, now it was different. Piecework was not creative, and the working conditions were no longer under the worker's control. A worker had to complete the work at the speed and in the manner determined by the employer.

In the early twentieth century, piecework manufacturing was an important part of the production process. The task was often simple and monotonous. It consisted of one process constantly repeated, hour after hour, day after day. The women and children who did this work were mainly immigrants.

Many children worked at home at a variety of tasks such as carding snaps (attaching dress fasteners to cardboard rectangles), making jewellery, sewing buttons, stringing tags, drawing threads on lace, linking and wiring beads, setting stones, and finishing underwear. Even if some children did attend school, their parents frequently kept them home to complete a work assignment. Tenement houses were not healthy workplaces. They were firetraps and infested with vermin, often dirty, and poorly ventilated. Children easily got sick in such and environment and often communicated their diseases to others. The latter quarter of nineteenth century saw enormous changes in the American economy and an entrenchment and expansion of the worst practices associated with child labour, led to the beginnings of a child labour reform movement in America.

CHILD LABOUR TODAY

In the developed countries the overwhelming majority of children who work do so in agriculture, in family or no family undertakings, during the school holidays and outside school hours, but above all at harvest and sowing time, on a wide range of jobs which may at times be heavy and dangerous. The minority who work in urban centres are employed in the sales or distribution sector (delivering papers, milk, etc.), in hotels and restaurants, especially in holiday resorts and during the school holidays, and in some light and occasional jobs such as baby sitting.

Today child labour is defined as the illegal employment of children when the children are under the legal minimum age, when they work longer hours than allowed by law, when their compensation is unfair, illegal, or non-existent, or when the working conditions endanger their health.

Changing Adolescent Work Place

In order to understand the impact of work on adolescent's development, it is necessary to look closely at the nature of the work they do and at the circumstances surrounding their employment. Under which circumstances is working likely to benefit youngsters, and under which circumtances is it likely to interfere with their healthy growth and development? In our view, three dimensions are crucial: whether the work experience imparts skills or knowledge valuable for adult work life (the educational context of the experience); whether the work is performed in order to fill a financial need of the youngster's family or the community, or out of a sense of the youngster's future financial needs (its economic context); and whether the work brings young people into contact with adults who have a stake in preparing them for adulthood (its social context).

Over the last century, the conditions surrounding work for American adolescents have moved steadily away from the positive pole of each of these three dimensions. Whereas work at one time served a valuable educational purpose for young people, performed an essential economic service to the family and community, and facilitated the development of relationships between young people and nonfamilial adults, during the past one hundred years early work experience has declined in its educational value, in its economic significance, and in the degree to which it fosters meaningful intergenerational contact. Moreover, during the last quarter century, we believe, much of the work available for young people has shifted from neutral positions on each of these dimensions to negative ones. And for this reason, over the course of the last century, the impact of early work on young people's development has become less positive.

This sort of continuity between the knowledge and skills acquired through early work and those needed for adulthood has not been limited to life in traditional societies. Prior to industrialisation, it also was common for young people's early work experience to be directly linked to the work they eventually would perform as adults. In the United States and in much of western Europe at least up until the end of the nineteenth century many young people were socialised into adult work roles through apprenticeships, both formal and informal, in which they were paired with adult workers in order to learn a specific craft or trade. In many cases, especially in those where the apprentice boarded with his or her employer, the relationship between the two was expected to serve a social as well as an economic function: the adult was charged with the socialisation and education of the youngster: the youngster was expected to treat the mentor dutifully and respectfully. Indeed, as historian John Gillis (1981) points out, the householder the employer of the young person was called *pater families*, "because he should have fatherly care over his servants, as if they were his children".

During the last quarter of the nineteenth century, increased industrialisation, the erosion of opportunities within the skilled trades, and the rise of secondary education together led to the disappearance of apprenticeships. Sinking opportunities for adult craftsperson led to the zealous guarding of opportunities in the skilled and semiskilled trades by unions (Kett 1977). According to one study of British youth, by the turn of the century only about 15 per cent of out of school employed teenagers were working in the skilled trades (Gillis 1981).

The declining number of apprenticeship opportunities during the closing decades of the nineteenth century led to quire different outcomes for youngsters from different social and economic backgrounds. Adolescents form affluent families who is the past might have had desirable apprenticeships arranged through family connection-instead where enrolled in school. These teenagers did not seek employment until their schooling was completed, often after a prolonged professional education.

Youngsters from poorer families reaped no such benefits of industrialisation. Adolescents whose families were dependent on their children's earnings could not afford to continue in school. Rather they were forced to work in whatever jobs were available, typically, in dead end, "boy labour" jobs created by industrialisation, such as errand runners of street vendors-jobs that were unlikely to provide opportunities for advancement.

In the highly technological, highly specialised, and rapidly changing job market of contemporary

America, however, adolescent work has become, for many irrelevant to adult careers.

A decline in adolescent factory work took place several decades later. Thus whereas during the first part of the twentieth century many adolescents were employed as factory workers-largely in cotton mills and canneries these jobs gradually disappeared as the child protection movement gained momentum, more stringent child labour laws were enacted, and compulsory schooling became more widespread.

Percentage of 16 and 17 year old workers (students and nonstudents combined) Employed as Skilled Labourers (Crafts and Trades), Factory workers, and Farm Workers, 1940-1980.

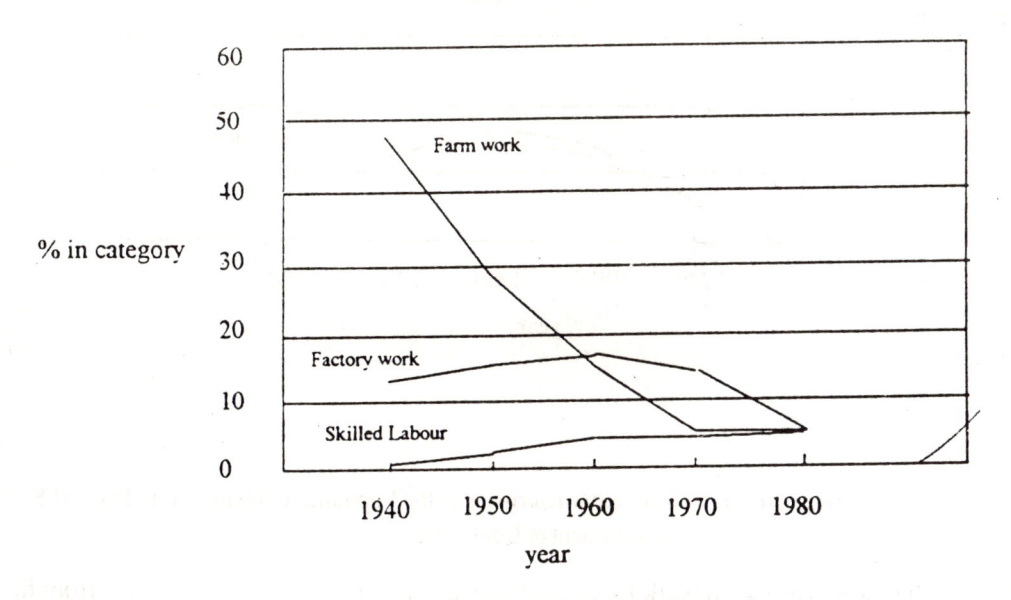

Source: U.S. Bureau of the Census, Characteristics of the Population (Washington. D.C., U.S. Department of Commerce)

In contrast to the decline of crafts, factories, and farm work during this period, the employment of the young people in retail and service position expanded rapidly. In 1940 service worker (including private household workers) accounted for only 3% of employed 14 and 15 year olds and only 6% of employed 16 and 17 year olds. Sales workers accounted for approximately 9% and 7% respectively.

The flow of adolescent workers into sales and service work-perhaps a more tidal wave than a flow-was especially strong among students workers, for whom the part time, flexibly scheduled positions in resturants and shops appeared tailor made. By 1980 teenagers were employed in a substantially "new" adolescent workplace. Together, jobs in the retail and service sectors accounted for 56% of all employed 16 to 17 year olds-nearly half of all male 16 and 17 year old workers and over two-thirds of all female workers of this age. The "old" adolescent workplace of crafts, factory, and farm positions, today accounts for only 14% of 16 and 17 year old workers.

Percentage of 16 and 17 year old workers (students and nonstudents combined) Employed as Service Workers (Excluding Private Household Workers) and Sales Workers, 1940-1980.

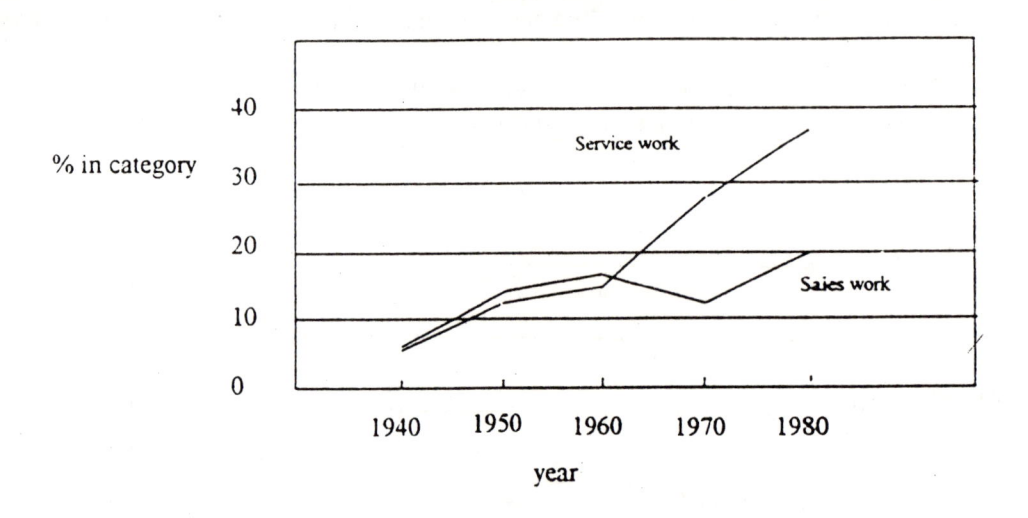

Source: U.S. Bureau of the Census, Characteristics of the Population (Washington, D.C., U.S. Department of Commerce)

Although the entire American work force had been moving in this direction, the shift from farm, factory, and crafts work to retail and service work was far more rapid among teenagers than among adult workers.

Child Labour in Cities and Towns

The law states that children between fourteen and sixteen years of age may not work more than forty hours in any one week when school is not in session or more that eighteen hours in any one week when school is in session. Furthermore, children may not work more than eight hours in any one day when school is not in session, nor more than three hours in any one day when school is in session. In addition children may not begin work before 7:00 A.M. or work after 7:00 P.M.

Sixteen and seventeen year olds may work at any time for unlimited hours in all jobs not declared hazardous by Secretary of Labour.

Today there are two main groups of working children: the children of the poor and the children of the middle class. (Rich children may work too, but they constitute a smaller group than the middle class). Children are motivated to work for the same reasons adults work, and when given the opportunity most American teenagers, like adults, choose to work. Two thirds of graduating high school seniors will have worked at some time during their ten years.

Percentage of 16 and 17 year old workers (students and nonstudents combined) Employed in the "New" (Service and Sales) Versus the "Old" (Crafts, Factories, and Farms) Adolescent Workplace, 1940-1980.

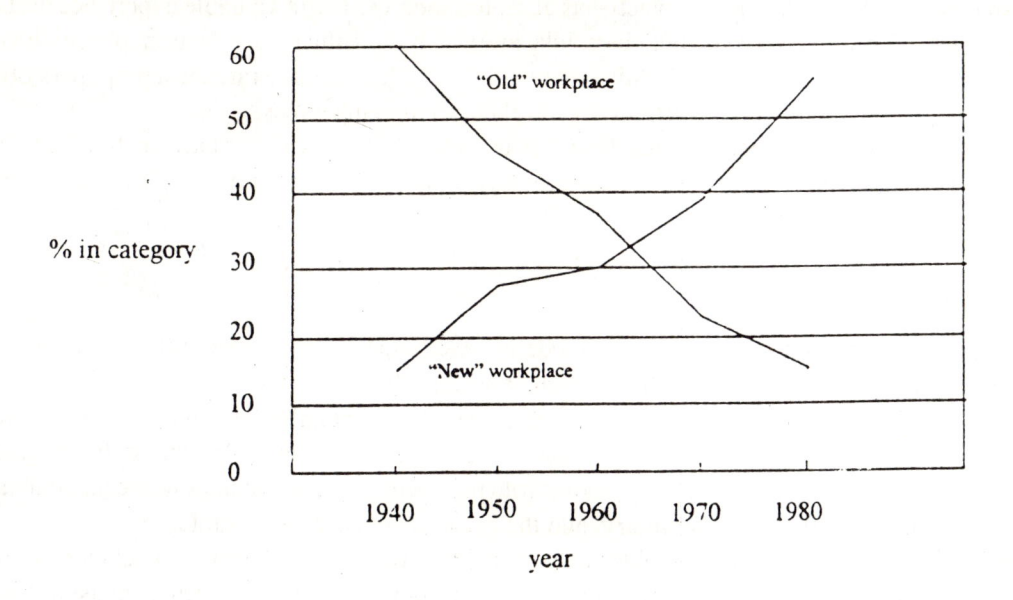

Source: U.S. Bureau of the Census, Characteristics of the Population (Washington, D.C., U.S. Department of Commerce)

The racial and ethnic imbalance between children who work and those who do not, mirrors the imbalance amount the full time adult labour force. That is, white children are more likely to have jobs than black or Hispanic students although black and Hispanic families tend to be poorer on average than white families. Like adult employment rates, teen employment figures are the lowest for the poorest teenagers.

Among the poorest working children are recent immigrants from Asia, Mexico, and Latin America. Many of these children cannot speak English, and their parents are illiterate in any language. Many of these teens labour in sweatshops under conditions similar to those of the earlier European immigrant children. As in earlier times, these children are often too young to work, but their families are so poor that they must. Many of them show little desire to attend school and are frequently truant.

The second group of working children are from the middle class. They are the majority of the working teens. They work for their own material gain, motivated by materialism and consumerism, not poverty. They work no to eat but to have spending money and by themselves luxurious like stylish clothes, cars, and electronic equipment. A few save money for college, and few help their parents in family business. Among these teenagers the amount of time they work is unrelated to family income, parental education, or parental occupation.

Street Work

Children still sell newspapers before and after school and on weekends. They usually do this in their own neighbourhood. American society has accepted such work as a valuable experience despite the hours (early morning) and risks (muggings, bike injuries, bad weather, etc.). Newspaper employers hire paper boys and girls because few adults are willing to work at the pay rate the newspapers offer. Some newspaper offer scholarships or bonuses to their young employees.

Candy selling is a another street trade that involves children. While selling candy can be a ligitimate job for children (numerous non-profit organisations have children selling candy as a fund raise), some employers are less than honest.

Sweetshops

Children still work in sweatshops. A "modern" sweetshop is any business that routinely and repeatedly violates wage, hour, and child labour laws and disregards the health and safety of its employees. The Fair Labour Standards Act and later the Occupational Safety and Health Act were intended to outlaw such businesses. Yet the practice persists, particularly in the Northeast. Investigators have found children working in overcrowded rooms with poor ventilation in buildings where the stairways were in disrepair, the bathrooms unsanitary, and the fire extinguishers inoperable.

Investigators saw fourteen year olds working for low wages on dangerous machinery in belt and garment factories, although the law prohibits children below the age of eighteen from using power driven machinery. Children as young as five passing garments between women working on sewing machines, and such children, of course, were not paid. Their mothers were paid not by the number of hours they worked but by the number of pieces they completed. Since the women could produce more when their children helped, they encouraged their children to work with them. Children sometimes stayed time from school in order to work. In one garment sweatshop, a twelve year old was working in an environment where the toilets malfunctioned, where the workers prepared their food next to machines that were in operation, and where at lunch time people ate form plates on the littered workshops floor.

Experts agree that the number of sweatshops has been increasing in recent years. how many actually exist is not known, since it is impossible to look into every home or building to search for such activity. Sweetshop employers hire children, cut adult wages, and pay not overtime, but when an investigating agent walks into a sweetshop. The news spreads quickly and the children are "squeezed out the door" before the investigator can talk to them. If the investigator asks about working children, "everyone dummies up."

Sales and Food Service

More youths work in sales or food services than in any other field. Nearly 50 per cent of working teens work in sales and nearly 46 per cent in food service. A great many teen work in stores, including grocery sores, drug stores, variety stores, clothing stores, and music stores. Anything that has been sold in a stores has probably at one time or another been sold by a teenager. In addition to selling, a teenager working in a store may be asked to perform any number of other duties such as opening or closing the shop or helping with cleanup, inventory, packing and unpacking, shelving, and pricing. Working in a store is generally not dangerous, but the hours a young person works often exceed the legal restrictions.

The General Accounting Office of the United States government surveyed the directors of state labour departments and found that in New York alone, half of the 5, 000 restaurants "met the criteria for sweetshops." Fast food restaurants rouetinely kept children working beyond midnight on school nights an subsequently paid less than minimum wage with no overtime. In addition, restaurants often violated fire codes by blocking exit doors, overloading electric circuits, and handling combustible materials improperly. In Milwaukee, Wisconsin, Terence Falk, a high school English and speech teacher, worried about his students to investigate why they were falling asleep in class and generally lagging in academic performance. He wondered what they were doing outside of school and learned about the work schedule of several of them. For example, he found that one boy, a high school junior, worked everyday until after midnight at a *McDonald's* and that a sophomore girl worked at a *Taco Bell* six days a week until at least 10:00 p.m. The academic performance of both these students had slipped. The girl's grades came down a grade and the boy was in danger of failing. A third student usually worked until 3:00 a.m. at *Burger King*. He often did not report to school the next day and talked occasionally about dropping out of school entirely. Falk found the same pattern repeated not only in his class but in different schools throughout the city.

Acting

Children also work in the entertainment industry. More than 5,000 children under the age of nineteen were members of the Screen Actors Guild. The organisation is affiliated with the AFLCIL labour union, and its purposes is to protect the interests of actors and actresses who make commercials or work in the film and television industries. The assumption is that working actors and actresses need and intermediary between themselves and their employers. People also assume that parents will not exploit their children.

In order to get just one job, a child may have to have as many seventy auditions. Agents who help children find jobs and negotiate contracts for them tell stories about overanxious parents who "exploit their children physically, emotionally, and financially as they drive their children from one audition to the next, hoping for the big break.

In California, a gathering place for child actors and actresses, the law does not require parents to set aside most of a child actor's earnings into a special savings account belonging to the child alone. One the average, only 25 per cent of what a child earns is actually saved for the child's future. Child actors and actresses are sometimes placed in a position of supporting their families.

On the Farm

Hired children may be white, black, Hispanic or Asian. Many of them are migrant labourers. Migrant labours move from state to state picking fruits and vegetables as they ripen.

Farm children may work in groups with other children or with their parents in the hot sun or chilling rain. Picking crops is backbreaking an repetitive, and the hours are long. Children too young to pick may fetch empty containers for their parents, bring water or lunch, or haul full containers to the ends of rows. Picking is a kind of agricultural piecework. Pickers are paid by the basket they fill, not the hours they work. Adult wages are so low that children have to work in order to help support their families. Judging by the volume picked, a ten year olds child does not pick very much; nevertheless the earnings are important.

Many farm owners would prefer not to hire children, however, some families are so desperate for money that if an owner won't permit the children to help out in the field, the family may choose another farm. Owners desperate for pickers will bend the law or look the other way and permit children to work.

Illiteracy and Poverty

Picking families are mostly poor. They stay in a community only long enough to complete a harvest. Many children either do not attend school at all, or if they attend irregularly and switch schools frequently. Authorities rarely enforce compulsory school attendance. Generally the children can't keep up with their peer group, and they fall behind in their studies.

Many migrant children prefer not to go to school because they are embarrassed by the clothes they wear and the free lunches they receive. Poverty often means no magazines or books in the house, few toys, and illiterate parents. They temporary "homes" may lack electricity or a quit place to read. For all these reasons children quit school.

Poverty means children live in shacks and sometimes old buses. They may have to share a kitchen with several families and use an outdoor privy built too close to the drinking water supply. The children are often sick.

Pesticides and Illness

Farm children are frequently exposed to dangerous pesticides as they work. The children get the pesticides on their skin when they brush against the treated leaves and breathe the poisons in as they work. Young children ingest the poisons when they put their fingers in their mouths. Also though it is illegal to spray on a field where people are working, it is not illegal to spray in the adjacent field. The wind carries pesticides form field to field, and the children inhale the poisons as they breathe. Some children are born deformed because their parents were exposed to toxic pesticides. Farm poisonings are a regular part of farm work. It is commonly known that children under the age of ten are working in the fields during school hours, and are working twelve hour days and exposed to pesticides with no access to field sanitation.

Accidents

Serious injury as a result of farm accidents is another problem common to farm children. In September 1989, the Wall Street Journal on its front page reported a "farming injury epidemic" among children, with 300 deaths and 20,000 injuries annually in farm accidents.

Farm accidents have many causes. One is that the children operate sophisticated farm machinery they are too small and too young to handle safely. They routinely operate drive tractors, wagons, and power takeoffs. Another is that frequently the equipment itself is unsafe.

Work List

Giving you a graphic idea of surprising number and variety of operations that used children in industry, agriculture, and trade here is a partial list, drawn from a 1990's study of child labour, of the task boys and girls were called on to do.

- **Cotton Textile Mills**
  Quilt boy, battery girl, helper in weave room, clerk, doffer sweeper, spinner, spare hand spinner, Bobbin boy, office boy, button holder, marks roving, spooler, spare hand in weaven room, assistant cloth inspector.
  - *Food Factories*
  Apprentice, grader (pickles), bottler (pickles), pitting dates, packing, weighing, general helper.
  - *Candy factories*
  Packing, wrapper, floor girl.
  - *Paper Mills*
  Sorting waste or rags, machine tender, handwork, edger, cut and tie tapes, packer.
  - *Shoe Factories*
  Helper (cobbler's shop), hand work or table work, lacing shoes, general helper, cementing.
  - *Foundry*
  Cleaning moulded parts, helper to crane operater, coremaking.
  - *Machine Shop*
  Helper.
  - *Cosmetics Factories*
  Labelling perfumes, putting stoppers in bottles, filling bottles.
  - *Laboratory Supplies and chemicals*
  Assembling, packing bottles.
  - *Lumber*
  Pole peeling, logging.
  - *Paper Box Factories*
  Turning in lidding up, bending, covering, shaping, packing, gluing off, wrapping.
  - *Street Trades*
  Selling newspapers, delivering newspapers, shoe shinning, pedding.
  - *Industrial Homework*
  Children help in work on men's, women's and children's clothing, neckwear, artificial flowers, feathers, trimming, novelties, stationery, lamp shades, jewellery, lace, dolls, toys, folding and pasting cellophane envelops, sorting waste and rags, (sometimes before they are washed).
  - *Clerical Work*
  Unskilled, in stores, banks, telephone and telegraph companies, offices of factories, and other offices of all sorts and kinds. Occasionally bill clerks, helpers in shipping departments, fibres, bookkeepers, etc.
  - *Grocery Stores*
  Delivery boy and clerk, driver of delivery wagon, selling clerk.
  - *Bakeries Retail*
  Baker's helper, general helper, delivery boy, helper sales.

- *Meat and Fish Markets*
  Bundle boy, fish cutter, butcher's helper.
- *Communications and Trade*
  Helper on wagon for junk, Dealer, messenger for taxi company, labourer, hauling on truck, messenger for printing company, messenger for telegraph company, helper on milkman's truck, helper on moving on company truck.
- *Labourers*
  Manufacturing industries, (In 1990 many boys and girls of 14 and 15, and few under 14, were listed as "labourers" in all the different industries.
- *Domestic Service*
  Mother's helper, housework.
- *Laundries*
  Folder, shaker, wrapper.
- *Tea Rooms, Restaurants, etc.*
  Curb coy, waitress, preparing fruits, cashier, selling clerk.
- *Hotels*
  Bellboy.
- *Other Personal Services*
  Kitchen helper in clinic, hospital waitress, seamstress, cleaning, apprentice in beauty parlour, apprentice in barbershop, usher in movie theatre, general helper in pottery works, auto polisher in garage, printing machine worker.
- *Canneries*
  Can boys, can girls, peeling tomatoes, snipping beans, shucking and cleaning come, inspecting vegetables and berries or tables or at moving belts, shucking oysters, peeling or picking shrimp, and other processes of a miscellaneous kind.
- *Grain Regions*
  Hoeing, picking up potatoes, picking and husking corn, shocking grain, hauling of all kinds, herding cattle, helping to butcher, cleaning seeds, clearing fields of stones and thistles, preparing manure for fuel, helping with sheep shearing, plowing.
- *Cranberry Bogs*
  Picking.

The Current Debate

Today, many children work, some because they have to and other because they want to. Sometimes the work seems harmless enough, while other times it doesn't. As in the past, some people believe that youth employment is beneficial and others that it is not. Sometimes the needs and agendas of the various parities involved children, employers, parents, educators, reformers are in conflict.

Should Children Work Even Under Ideal Conditions?

Assuming "Perfect" working conditions, there are many good reasons for children to work. Youth employment brings income to those who need it. The right kind of labour has the potential of helping young people learn how to handle money, take more responsibility, manage time, work as part of a team, and meet the obligations set by a boss. Work contributes to personal growth and self worth. It can be bridge between childhood and adulthood.

Work exposes teenagers to new experiences, such as putting them in contact with people they would not ordinarily meet, and helps them to learn first hand what it's like to participate in our free enterprise system. Youth employment may boost the economy as a whole because it encourages spending and increases the amount of money in circulation. Those who favour youth employment believe, also that unemployed children tend to get into trouble.

On the flip side is another set of arguments criticising youth employment as it exists today. By working, children reduce the time available to study. Learning, opponents of youth employment say, should be a child's first priority. Students who work long hours are often too tired to perform well in school. When this happens they limit their opportunities to acquire the education they will need to earn a good living in a highly technical society. Reformers argue that while business and the national economy may benefit from youth employment in the short run, in the long run the nation needs a well educated work force. It's bad enough that students who work the legal numbers of hours are deviating from their main task; it's even worse for children who work over the legal maximum number of hours. In addition, studies show that working teens tend to use more drugs, alcohol, and tobacco then teens who do not work simply because the working teens have the money to do so.

Teen years are an important time in life for intellectual and emotional growth, a time to develop family relations and personal relationships, but that student who work have little time for this.

Students, like adults, are divided on the issue. Ryan, a seventeen year old high school junior who works at a Burger King, speaks for may working youths when he says. "If I want to work, their should be no law against it." And Karen, a fifteen year old sophomore, feels that working less would not automatically mean her grades would get better. "I could study my whole life and I'd probably still never get A's".

On the other hand, when Geoff was seventeen year old high school senior he quit his job when his grades started to go down. He realised he needed good grades to get into a good college. "At school I was just doing the minimum to get by. I am glad I quit. It to off the pressure and my grades went up. But when I quit, my boss really yelled at me and said it was my obligation to find a replacement." After graduating high school, going on to college, getting a degree, and landing a good hob, he has decided to return to college for additional education. The job market is very competitive.

Are Their Violations?

Both sides agree that violations do exist. Disagreement rises over the nature of the violations.

Working Hours

Employers say that on the rare occasions when there are child labour violations, they are unintentional and are not as bad as they appear to be. Violations, say employers, are often caused by the complexity of the laws. Some employers find it difficult to figure out what kind of work the law permits and what kind it does not. For example, the law allows fourteen and fifteen year olds to perform "kitchen work and other work involved in preparing and serving food and beverages" but prohibits "cooking and baking." What fifteen year olds are permitted to do at lunch counters, they are not permitted to do elsewhere. In addition, different compliance officers in different regions interpret the law differently. Furthermore, these people say, laws are also ignored and deliberately broken. Reformers cite government reports and Operation Child Watch as proof of widespread violation of the parent child labour laws. For example, the New York State Labour Department estimates that about 4,500 sweetshops in apparel industry firms operate in New York City alone, many of them illegally employing children.

Hazards and Injuries

"Every year in this country, hundreds of children and teenagers are killed while working. Thousands more are mained or seriously injured. Many reports on individual on the job incidents are available. A seventeen year old in Pennsylvania, for example, was killed while operating a compactor balling machine in a grocery store, a fifteen year old also from Pennsylvania was killed cleaning out a dough mixing machine, and thirteen year old Maryland boy lost his leg in a laundry extractor. A fifteen year old in Alabama was killed while engaged in wrecking and demolition work, a sixteen year old in Texas was injured while operating hoisting equipment, a seventeen year old in Georgia was killed while removing the top of a hickory tree.

Although no one wants to see children injured or killed on the job, interestingly, some parents are unconcerned about the possibility.

Should Restrictions Be Increased or Reduced?

Most teenagers after spending a full day in school are unlikely to go home and immediately begin studying and doing homework. Students need time to rest eat, and hand out. Educators argue that there is a difference between staying up late to participate in musical programme, a theatrical performance, or a sporting event, and staying up late to clean tables and wrap hamburgers. School activities, they say, offer intellectual, social, cultural, and physical growth opportunities that youth employment does not. Reformers add that meeting the needs of restaurant dinner crowds or shortening check out lines in stores is not the responsibility of teenagers.

Reformers argue that without good laws, youth employment would quickly degenerate into child labour, with all the abuses and horrors of the past. Protection, they say comes through laws and their enforcement. If the laws can't be enforced, then perhaps youth employment should be banned entirely. Otherwise, enforcement needs to be stepped up and made stricter.

A good example is the many child labour violations that continue to exist especially in modern sweetshops. Here recent immigrant children work under conditions similar to those of a hundred years ago. Many people believe that if the laws were more restrictive and penalties large enough, such abuses would not occur.

The Child Labour Coalition, a group that includes such organisations as the American Academy of Paediatrics, American Federation of Teachers, Consumer Federation of America, General Federation of Women's clubs, National Education Association, Children's Defence Fund, and various labour unions wants Congress to enlarge the number of prohibited teenage occupation and work activities, reduce the number of hours children work, and vigorously enforce the laws with higher fines.

Reformers want to prohibit anyone under eighteen from selling door to door, driving school buses, or using power tools. They say that teens engaged in these activities are getting hurt and the government has the obligation there is a labour shortage and young people are needed to fill these positions; if fines are increased, some businesses will no longer be able to afford to hire children.

Taking Responsibility

Since youth employment is probably here to stay and violations will never completely disappear, it is up to everyone involved to make the experience of youth employment a positive one. And although adults are still ultimately responsible for enforcing or breaking the laws, underage students can still take responsibility for making sure they are not abused or put into dangerous condition.

Teenagers who choose to work can do a great deal to protect themselves in the work environment. They can inform themselves about child labour laws in their own state and find out what occupations and specific kinds of equipment they are not permitted to use. They can refuse to work "off the books" or more hours than the law allows. It would also help if students remember that they have more of an obligation to themselves and their own future than they have to their employers. Indeed, employers need the work of young people, as much if not more than the young people need the jobs. Students who know the law and stand up for their legal rights can wield the power to help stop child labour.

CHILD LABOUR LAW

The World of Young Workers

To most people, child labour laws are a quaint idea, thought of as an historical landmark in this century's fight for labour rights, unionisation, and industrial safety standards—that is, when they are thought of at all. Most people think that the exploitation and endangerment of working minors is no longer a societal problem, and thus, that legal restrictions on their labour are either minimal or non-existent. Many of us might even think that whatever regulation there is must amount to needless government interference. This is definitely one of those cases when most people would most definitely be wrong.

We do have federal and state child labour laws, and they are quite extensive and comprehensive. The reason for the continuation and expansion of these laws is simple. Today, more teenagers are working at more types of jobs, during more weeks of the year for longer weekly hours than has ever been true in the past. The 1990 Census documented over 20 million young people aged 12 through 17. At any given time during the year, it is estimated that some 5 1/2 million of them are working, and that does not include those under 12 year-old who are working illegally. Over half of the 16 and 17 year-olds and more than a quarter of all 15 year-old are part of the nation's workforce.

These high school students aren't just stopping by Mom and Dad's hardware store after classes to put in two hours behind the counter before they start their homework. Those 15 year-old average 17 hours of work per week, while the 16 and 17 year-old average 21 hours of work per week. These figures reflect only the reported incidence of child labour. We know that in the vast underground economy and even in the legitimate sector, millions of additional young people are hired in illegal jobs, exactly because they are less experienced, less costly, and less complaining employees.

And what jobs do these young workers typically perform? The Bureau of Labour Statistics of the US Department of Labour reports that almost four out of five young workers aged 16 through 19 are concentrated in just three types of employment: om retail sales and service work (particularly in food service), as administrative support staff, and as labourers and handlers.

And are these jobs wholesome, safe activities for developing youngsters? Occupationally related accidents and injuries have been soaring in the past few years. The National Institute of Occupational Safety and Health estimates that each year over 64,000 teens are treated in emergency rooms for their occupational injuries, exclusive of agricultural injuries. In fact, adolescents suffer an estimated occupational injury rate of up to 16 per 100 full-time employees, compared to the adult rate of less than 9 per 100 full-time employees. Cuts and lacerations, usually of the hands and fingers, are the most common youth employment injuries, followed by bruises and contusions and strains and sprains. These injuries arise from the inexperience of young workers, not their age or development level. An extremely large proportion of workplace injuries, some 40 per cent, occur to workers in their first year of work, regardless of their age.

Given the high level of employment activity among youngsters, we need to understand the legal restrictions that have been enacted for their protection. Although the School-to-Work Opportunities Act of 1994 did not detail the legal compliance needed by its state-funded agencies, its requirement of adherence to all federal, state, and local laws most prominently includes the application of child labour laws to the wide variety of work and training programmes authorised by the Act. In fact, it is clear in the School-to-Work Opportunities Act that the federal and state child labour laws will apply to its employment and employment-related programmes, and that compliance with these restrictions is mandatory. It is crucial that those involved in implementing the Act fully understand, appreciate, and support these rules as the reasonable response to the risks of child exploitation and endangerment that they represent.

The Federal Fair Labour Standards Act (FLSA)

Except where there are specific exemptions, the employment of workers under age 18 is regulated by the FLSA. But the FLSA applies only to employees engaged in commerce. This means that volunteer work, such as fund-raising and non-profit charities, as well as school activities that meet the technical criteria constituting bona fide educational training experiences (as distinct from providing labour), are not covered by federal child labour laws.

Occupational Provisions
Under Age 14

If an employment relationship exists, the only non-agricultural work activities lawfully permitted to those under age 14 are those that are exempt and therefore not covered by the the FLSA. These include working for one's parents in occupations other than manufacturing, mining, or Hazardous Occupations. Those employed as domestic labourers in and around their employer's homes, as well as actors or performers in movies, theatres, radio or television productions and children who deliver newspapers to the consumer are also exempt.

Ages 14 and 15

The next particularly significant group of occupational provisions are those restricting the work of 14 and 15 year-olds. The first rule to note is that whatever is not specifically prohibited is, in fact, a lawful work activity for this age group. There is, however, also a list of work activities that are explicitly permitted, although usually with some limitations, and always limited to their performance of such activities in retail, food service, or gasoline service establishments. If they are performed at another type of business, they are not permitted for 14 and 15 year-olds. Thus, they are permitted to be employed at the following work activities, at one of the three permitted work sites, with the stated limitations on their actual duties.

They can be employed in office and clerical work, including operating office machines, but only operating such power-driven machines, not repairing, oiling, adjusting or assisting on such activities. They can cashier, sell, model, produce art work and work in advertising departments, window trimming and comparative shopping. They can also price, mark, and tag, by machine or by hand, as well as assemble, order, pack and shelve.

They can also bag and carry out customer's orders. They can do errand and delivery work by foot, bicycle or public transportation. Clearly, errand and delivery work by motor vehicle would not be permitted. They can perform clean-up work and grounds maintenance and use a vacuum cleaner of floor waxer in their duties, but not a power-driven mower or cutter. This last prohibition on operating lawn and other types of mowers and hedge and other types of grounds maintenance cutters frequently arises in municipal youth employment programme placements. The rule is clear. Under federal law, this equipment cannot be used lawfully until the worker is 16 year-old, and only in connection with employment at a retail, food service, orr gasoline service establishment. Also, some states restrict the use of power mowers and cutters even further, not permitting their use by youngsters until they turn 18.

With some exceptions, kitchen work and other work involved in food and beverage preparation and service are permitted for 14 and 15 year-old, including the operation of machines and devices used for such work, such as dishwashers, dumbwaiters, toasters, popcorn poppers, milk shake blenders and coffee grinders. Cooking and baking, however, are not permitted.

Certain restrictions concerning cooking and baking and food preparation are so commonly involved in young people's work and so detailed that a separate discussion of their actual meaning is required. Although there is a ban on 14 and 15 year-old working as cooks and bakers, in fact this restriction does not include those types of cooking and baking usually performed in fast food establishments. This is because this prohibition does not apply to cooking and baking at "soda fountains, lunch counters, snack bars or cafeteria serving counters," which were the fast-food establishments of the 1940s when these prohibitions were written. The U.S. Department of Labour has applied this exception to the ban on cooking and baking to fast food establishments, ruling that one of the crucial elements of a work site that must be present to come within this exceptions and thereby permit such activity, is that the cooking and baking must be able to be seen from the front service counter.

As a result of the years of enforcement by the U.S. Department of Labour and the integration of these rules with the H.O.s that restrict the labour of all those under 18 years old, 14 and 15 year-old can use food preparation equipment only if it is of the domestic variety in size, power, and complexity.

Specifically, for instance, the ban on minors operation of bakery equipment has meant that 14 and 15 year-old are not permitted to operate, repair, adjust, oil or perform similar activities on dough mixers, which are frequently used in mass volume pizza-making restaurants. The generally permitted activity of "kitchen work" has another barred activity for this age group—meat processing. This common food preparation activity at the deli departments of large supermarkets and at certain types of fast types of fast food restaurants is barred as a Hazardous Occupation. Since the use of the electric slicer is not permitted until the age of 18, that restriction is relevant when interpreting the apparent permission of every type of kitchen work for 14 and 15 year-old.

Also, no. 14 or 15 year-old may operate, set up, adjust, clean, oil or repair power-driven food slicers and grinders, choopers and cutters, and bakery-type mixers. This prohibition controls all work activities at retail and food service businesses for 14 and 15 year-olds and must therefore be understood as the significant limitation on food preparation, cooking and baking that is intended.

Another work activity that 14 and 15 year-olds can perform is cleaning vegetables and fruits and wrapping, sealing, labelling, weighing, pricing and stocking goods. However, such work can only be performed in areas that are physically separate from those where meat is prepared for sale or at outside freezers or meat coolers. These restrictions would bar a youngster under 16 year-old from wrapping, sealing, labelling weighing or pricing goods in the meat cutting, trimming, and preparation areas of supermarkets and butcher shops, for example.

Working in connection with cars and trucks is permitted this age group, as long as it is limited to dispensing gas and oil, providing courtesy service at a service station and cleaning, washing and polishing cars. Specifically excluded activities for 14 and 15 year-olds in this field included work involving the use of pits, racks of lifting apparatus or involving the inflation of any tire mounted on a rim with a removable retaining ring, as is most frequently used in tire repair.

In addition to the permitted work activities at retail, food service and gas service businesses, there are also specific jobs at those locations that are barred for workers under age 16. For example, they may not perform any duties in or around a boiler or engine room. And they are not permitted to maintain or repair the retail, food service or gas service station work premises nor its machines or equipment. They cannot use ladders, scaffolds or the like, nor work from window sills, washing outside windows. They may not work in freezers or meat coolers or in meat preparation, although, as previously discussed, they may wrap, seal, label, weigh, price and stock foods, including meat, when not performed in the prohibited areas. They may not load or unload goods from trucks, railroad cars or conveyors. This last restriction is most commonly applicable to food processing occupations in fruit, vegetable and seafood operations, where conveyored foodstuffs are scanned and selected. They also may not work in warehouses, except for office and clerical work off the warehouse floor.

We now turn our attention to the employment of 14 and 15 year-olds at non-agricultural locations other than retail, food service and gasoline service establishments. Again, this discussion is amplified by the rule that they may also be employed in any occupation except those that are specifically prohibited. Those specifically excluded occupations bar many workplaces as well as actual occupations.

For example, and most prominently, 14 and 15 year-olds may not be employed in any manufacturing, mining or processing occupation. The restriction on "processing" has been defined to include any work that transforms materials or goods in any way, such as folding freshly laundered shirts. It also includes more obvious applications of the word, such as fish filleting, poultry dressing, nut cracking and commercial laundering and dry cleaning (unless it is in a retail, food service, or gas service site in one of the occupations specifically permitted to 14 and 15 year-olds in the previous discussion). They also cannot be employed at any duties that take place in workrooms or workplaces where goods are manufactured, mined or processed, again except for those permitted duties in retail, food service and gas service businesses.

Other prohibited activities include operating or tending any power-driven machinery of whatever sort and hoisting apparatus, other than the office machines and other machines specifically permitted for operation by 14 and 15 year-olds in retail, food service and gas service establishments. They also cannot be employed in occupations in connection with transporting persons or property by any means, warehousing and storage, communications and utilities and construction, including repair, unless the occupation is in office or sales work and is not performed on the transportation media involved or at the actual construction site. And of course, they can perform no Hazardous Occupations, since those are barred for all workers under 18 years old.

All of these restrictions on the non-agricultural labour of 14 and 15 year-olds are subject to some exceptions for Work Experience and Career Exploration Programmes (WECEP). Students who are WECEP participants may be excepted from some of these occupational restrictions pursuant to an agreement between the U.S. Department of Labour's Wage & Hour Division and a State's Educational Agency. Youth programme administrators need to check with their local educational authority to learn what exceptions are permitted in their area.

As to the agricultural employment of 14 and 15 year-olds, the federal child labour law specifies particular machines and activities that are not permitted for their vocational use, unless the worker is a certified student learner of 4 H or vocational agriculture training programme certificate holder. Again, programme administrators need to check with their local educational authority to establish which agricultural work activities are excepted in their community.

Ages 16 and 17

The only occupational restrictions for 16 and 17 year-olds are the 17 Hazardous Occupations. They apply either on an industry-wide basis, with exceptions for specific occupations, or on an occupational basis, regardless of the industry in which the occupations are found. There are no exceptions to ten of the H.O.s, while seven of them, which will be noted, do permit 16 and 17 year-olds to engage in the activity if they are bona fide student learners or apprentices. Only those H.O.s which are most frequently violated or pose special interpretation problems will be discussed in detail here, although all will be listed.

There are no exceptions to the following ten H.O.s, which means that they are prohibited for all 16 and 17 year-olds.
* Manufacturing and storing explosives.
* Motor vehicle driver and outside helper. However, this restriction does not bar 16 and 17 year-olds from car and small (under 6,000 pounds) truck driving, when it is "occasional and incidental" to the youth's employment, and then only during daylight hours, and not including any towing of vehicles. This eliminates all jobs that require either driving for deliveries, errands,

and pick-ups, and all jobs as the assistant for such activities, even if the young worker never takes the wheel. The law (and the documented experience of a very high rate of adolescent injuries) considers a job consisting of pulling over on public roads, clogged urban streets, or at transportation bays to load and unload from delivery trucks or driving for perhaps a ten-hour day, to be an extremely hazardous activity, quite different in kind and in result from young people's recreational use of their own cars.

* Coal mining.
* Mining other than coal mining.
* Logging and sawmilling, although 16 and 17 year-olds may work in the offices or in repair or maintenance shops or logging camps of such operations.
* Jobs involving exposure to radioactive substances and ionizing radiation's.
* Operating, riding or assisting on power-driven hoisting apparatus, including elevators and work that involves riding on a manlift or on an unattended freight elevator, except that operating an unattended automatic passenger elevator is permitted.
* Operating, assisting, setting up, adjusting, repairing or cleaning power-driven bakery machines, including dough mixers, most commonly used in commercial pizza restaurants, as was previously discussed.
* Manufacturing brick, tile or like product, except for work in the offices of such an establishment.
* Wrecking, demolition, and shipbreaking, including cleanup and salvage work (and also including all such activities at the site of a total or partial razing), demolishing or dismantling of a building, structure, ship, or any other vessel. This bars 16 and 17 years-olds from working on the site of construction activities that involve wrecking or demolition, but not from otherwise permitted jobs at construction sites in general.
* The next group of H.O.s permit 16 and 17 year-olds certified student learners and enrolled apprentices to perform the activity, but all other 16 and 17 year-olds are restricted.
* Operating, setting up, adjusting, repairing or cleaning power-driven woodworking machines, including bearing or removing any material or refuse directly from a saw table or the point of operation.
* Operating, assisting, setting up, adjusting, repairing or cleaning power-driven metal forming, punching or shearing machines, which does not however, include machine tools, whose use is permitted to this age group.
* Most jobs involved in slaughtering and meat packing, processing or rendering, or in such plants or such wholesale, retail, or service establishments, and all jobs involved with operating, feeding, setting up, adjusting, preparing or cleaning power-driven meat processing machines. These meat processing and preparation activities are also prohibited at supermarkets, delis restaurants or at any other location.
* Operating, assisting, setting up, adjusting, repairing or cleaning power-driven paper product machines, including paper balers. Also barred by this H.O. is all work that involves starting or stopping such machines or placing materials into or removing them from such machines.

Paper balers are usually found at supermarkets and other large retail operations, where they are used to break down paper boxes. This activity leads to frequent serious injuries.

* Operating, assisting, setting up, adjusting, repairing or cleaning power-driven circular or band saws and guillotine shears, unless they are equipped with fully automatic feed and ejection. This prohibition includes starting or stopping the machine or placing materials into or removing them from the machine.
* All jobs in roofing operations, except for such related activities as gutter and downspout work, installing air conditioners, exhaust, ventilating and similar appliances attached to roofs.
* Excavation work, including working in incomplete tunnels and shafts.

Hours Provisions

Ages 14 and 15

The federally permitted hours for 14 and 15 year-olds vary during the year, depending upon the seasonal changes of school sessions. Except for enrolees in the Work Experience and Career Exploration Programme (WECEP), 14 and 15 year-olds are not permitted to work during school hours when school is in session, whether or not they are attending school.

During school days, 14 and 15 year-olds may work up to 3 hours; during weeks when school is in session they may work up to 18 hours per week, unless they are WECEP participants, in which case they may work up to 23 hours per school week. At the times during the school year when school is not in session, such as Christmas vacation periods, they may work 40 hours per week; on weekend days during the school year, they may work 8 hours.

Permissible times of day are also regulated for 14 and 15 year-olds. From the day after Labour Day through May 31, they may work only between the hours of 7 a.m. and 7 p.m. From June 1 through Labour Day the permitted evening hour is extended, allowing them to work between 7 a.m. and 9 p.m. The night-hour limitation requires that young workers utterly complete their jobs by that hour; therefore to ensure that all required work is completed by the restricted hour, those under 16 years old should work only until 30 minutes prior to the permitted night-hour limit, thus leaving some time for the unexpected delays and added duties that may occur at the last minute in many occupations.

Ages 16 and 17

There are no federal hours restrictions on the work of 16 and 17 year-olds, but, as will be discussed shortly, there are some states laws that apply to the working hours of this age group.

Age Certificates

The FLSA does not provide for the issuance of Age or Employment Certificates, but will accept state-mandated certificates as proof of the age of a young worker. Employers who keep these on file can protect themselves from unintentionally violating federal or state child labour laws.

This completes the discussion of the FLSA's child labour law provisions. Other relevant issues, such as employment certificates, theatrical employment, alcohol beverage service abd newspaper delivery are matters of state law only.

State Child Labour Laws

For an accurate portrait of the actual laws and regulations that govern each area, state child labour laws must be integrated into the FLSA provisions. Programme administrators should check their states child labour laws by calling the nearest State Labour Department office, Wage & Hour of Labour Standards Division, usually located in major cities. Upon request, most states offer an explanatory brochure, suitable for programme administrators, employers and parents. Many states are also pleased to send someone from their Labour Department to speak to interested groups to explain their law and answer specific questions.

Although the variation among the states child labour provisions is wide, there are certain commonalties. An Employment Certificate is required by most states for most types of work and it is the employer's responsibility to ensure that it has been issued. The employer must keep it on file at the employment site. The certificate is issued by the local school authority upon the submission of such required documentation as the child's proof of age, employer's statement of the work to be performed and its hours, parental consent and proof of worker's physical fitness. Most states provide for several types of certificates. They most typically have an employment certificate for student's part-time work during the school year. They may also have a full time employment certificate for summer work or for those who are no longer in school.

Also, occupation-specific certificates are usually required for such work as theatrical and modelling activities, street trades, newspaper delivery and agricultural work. Some states require a new employment certificate application and issuance with each new employment or for each year. Others permit the right to work by issuing certificates that are valid until the young worker turns 18 years old. Two states require adequate school performance or attendance as the prerequisite to certificate issuance. All states can revoke their permission, under a variety of circumstances.

Other elements that are exclusively under state law include rules concerning theatrical employment, newspaper delivery work and handling, serving, or manufacturing alcoholic beverages. In the case of theatrical work (which frequently includes modelling as well as entertainment jobs in all media), most states have multiple restrictions, varying the types and hours of permitted work according to the age of the performer. These provisions also usually address the educational arrangements that must be made in order to employ a young theatrical worker. Frequently, as noted above, a special theatrical employment certificate or permit is required, with a variety of qualifications demanded by the different states. In states with large entertainment industries, these permits are usually issued by a separate unit of the educational or labour departments.

For newspaper delivery, in addition to age and hours limitations, there is frequently a provision requiring a specialised newspaper delivery permit, distinct from the usual employment certificate. Most commonly, the deliverer's school issues such permits.

Employment involving alcoholic beverages, whether as a server, cashier, sales clerk or manufacturer, is also exclusively governed by state law. Most commonly, young workers must be 21 years-old in order to sell, serve or manufacture alcoholic beverages, although some states permit it at age 20. Most of these state laws bar young workers under 18 from any role involving the sale, service or manufacture of alcoholic beverages, although some states allow youngsters to cashier beer purchases at grocery stores at age 16. These strict limitations mainly affect young worker's employability at full-service restaurants where liquor is sold and served. In most states the rules concerning the employment of minors at these occupations are under the jurisdiction of the state Alcohol Beverage Control Commission (or equivalent).

Another area under exclusive state rule is any limitation on the hours of work of 16 and 17 year-olds. About one-third of all the states have some restriction on their permitted night-hour, total weekly or daily hours.

In addition to child labour laws, there are some other areas of law with age-specific provisions relevant to young workers. For example, workers compensation laws in many states have separate provisions for child labourers. Frequently, they penalise employers of illegally hired minors by doubling or trebling the compensation due such an injured worker. State workers compensation boards (or the equivalent) should be checked for the rules governing minors.

Finally, all education rules that affect child labour are solely a function of state law. These rules address such work-related issues as compulsory school requirements (affecting, for example, which young people may be legally available for full-time work), the availability and requirements for vocational education, exceptions to the usual work restrictions and special work permits issued to educationally or physically handicapped youth. The local district would be the first place to check on these regulations, although for state-wide issues, a call to the state educational department would also be appropriate.

If should also be noted that states have their own enforcement personnel as well as their own code of violations and penalties. But the states vary widely in their commitment of resources and political will to police child labour. Maryland, for example, has had no child labour law enforcement for several years and refers all complaints and inquiries to federal labour enforcement offices in their state. New York is at the other end of the spectrum, with over 100 labour investigators, many of them assigned to specialised units dedicated to ferreting out child labour violations in the garment industry, agriculture or retail trades. The most universal form of enforcement is the "complaint method" where in state labour investigators respond to complaints they receive by telephone or letter.

Our youngest workers need and deserve our assistance in insuring that their working lives, whether part of their school curriculum or not, are safe, healthy and legal. The cost of our neglect, in injured bodies and exhausted minds, is too high for our sons and daughters to pay. (27)

PREVENTING DEATHS AND INJURIES OF ADOLESCENT WORKERS

Each year, approximately 70 adolescents die from injuries at work. Hundreds more are hospitalised, and tens of thousands require treatment in hospital emergency rooms.

The National Institute for Occupational Safety and Health (NIOSH) request assistance in preventing deaths and injuries among adolescents at work. In 1993, 68 adolescents under age 18 died from work-related injuries, and an estimated 64,000 required treatment in hospital emergency rooms. Adolescents have a high risk for work-related injury compared with adults.

This Alert summarises available information about work-related injuries among adolescents, identifies work that is especially hazardous, and offers recommendations for prevention.

NIOSH requests that the information in this Alert be brought to the attention of employers and parents of adolescents, educators, and adolescents. NIOSH request special assistance from safety and health officials and professionals, departments and boards of education, parent-teacher associations,

Risk of Work-Related Injuries Among Adolescents
Deaths

The U.S. Bureau of Labour Statistics identified 136 work-related deaths of adolescents under age 18 in 1992 and 1993 (68 deaths each year) [Derstine 1994; Toscano and Windau 1994]. Agricultural businesses and retail trade accounted for the most deaths (Table-1). Many of the deaths of adolescents under age 16 occurred in family-owned businesses.

Adolescent and adult workers have similar risks of fatal occupational injuries. NIOSH has determined that in 1980-89, the risk of injury death for workers aged 16 and 17 was 5.1 per 100,000 full-time equivalent workers compared with 6.0 for adult workers aged 18 and older [Castillo et al. 1994]. This similarity in risk in cause for concern because adolescents are employed less frequently in especially hazardous jobs. The rate of fatal injuries among adolescents should therefore be much lower than for adults.

Table-1 : Fatal Work-Related Injury Deaths of U.S. Adolescents by Industry and Age, 1992-93

Age of worker and industry	Number of deaths
Workers under age 14	
Agriculture, forestry and fishing	21 (16 in family businesses)
other	6
Total	27
(1)	(2)
Workers age 14 and 15	
Agriculture, forestry and fishing	12 (7 in family businesses)
Retail trade	6
Services	3
Other	8
Total	29
(1)	(2)
Workers aged 16 and 17	
Retail trade	25 (3 in family businesses)
Agriculture, forestry and fishing	20 (5 in family businesses)
Construction	11
Services	10
Wholesale trade	5
Manufacturing	4
Other	5
Total	80

Source: Derstine (1994).

Nonfatal Injuries

NIOSH estimates that 64,000 adolescents required treatment in hospital emergency rooms for work-related injuries in 1992 [Layne et al. 1994]. However, research indicates that only one-third of work-related injuries are seen in emergancy rooms [CDC 1983]. NIOSH therefore estimates that nearly 200, 000 adolescents suffer work-related injuries each year. A substantial number of injured adolescents require hospitalisation. From July through December 1992, an estimated 950 adolescents were hospitalised for their injuries (Layne et al. 1994).

Compared with adult workers, adolescents have a high risk of work-related injuries requiring treatment in hospital emergency rooms. Nearly 6 of every 100 full-time equivalent adolescent workers obtain treatment in hospital emergency rooms each year [Layne et al. 1994]. Data from a 1982 study that collected data for workers of all ages suggest that workers under age 18 have higher injury rates than adult workers [CDC 1983].

Sixty-eight per cent of occupationally injured 14 to 16 year-olds experienced limitations in their normal activities (including work, school, and play) for at least 1 day, and 25% experienced limitation in their normal activities for more than a week [Knight et al. 1995]. More than half of these adolescents reported that they had not received any training in how to prevent the injury they sustained. A supervisor was present at the time of the injury in only about 20% of the cases.(29)

Work Associated With Large Numbers of Deaths and Serious Injuries

Federal child labour laws prohibit some work associated with large numbers of deaths and serious injuries such as driving a motor vehicle and operating a forklift. Other hazardous activities, such as working alone in retail businesses and cooking, are typically permitted.

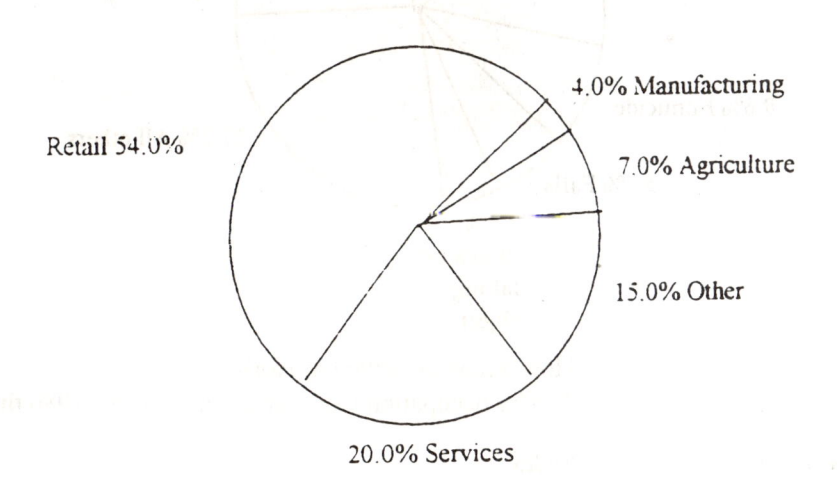

- Retail 54.0%
- 4.0% Manufacturing
- 7.0% Agriculture
- 15.0% Other
- 20.0% Services

Where Teens are Injured at work
(Based on 1992 data of adolescents (14-17 years old) treated in emergency rooms.)

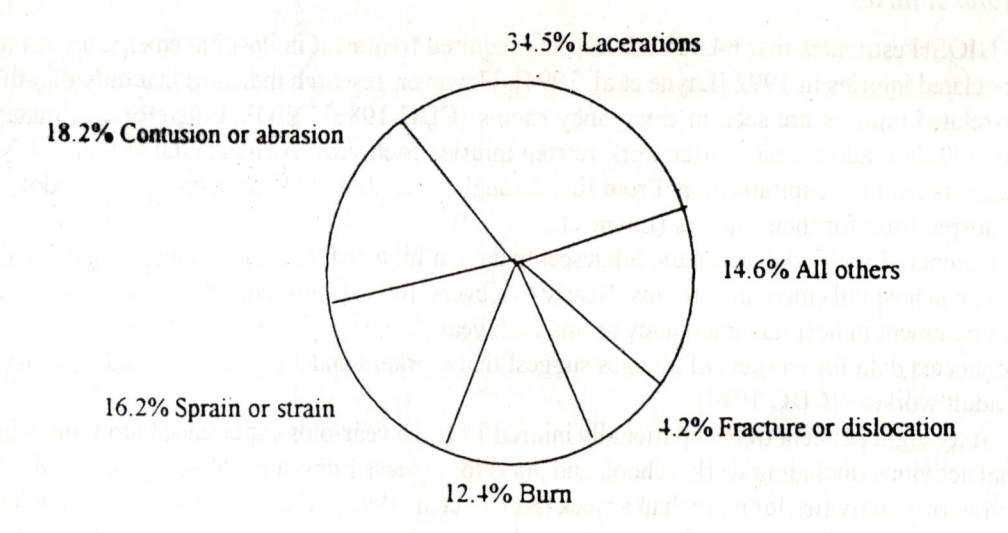

How Teens are Injured at work

- 34.5% Lacerations
- 18.2% Contusion or abrasion
- 16.2% Sprain or strain
- 12.4% Burn
- 4.2% Fracture or dislocation
- 14.6% All others

(Estimated number of adolescents (14-17 years old) occupation injuries in U.S., July through Dec. 1992.)

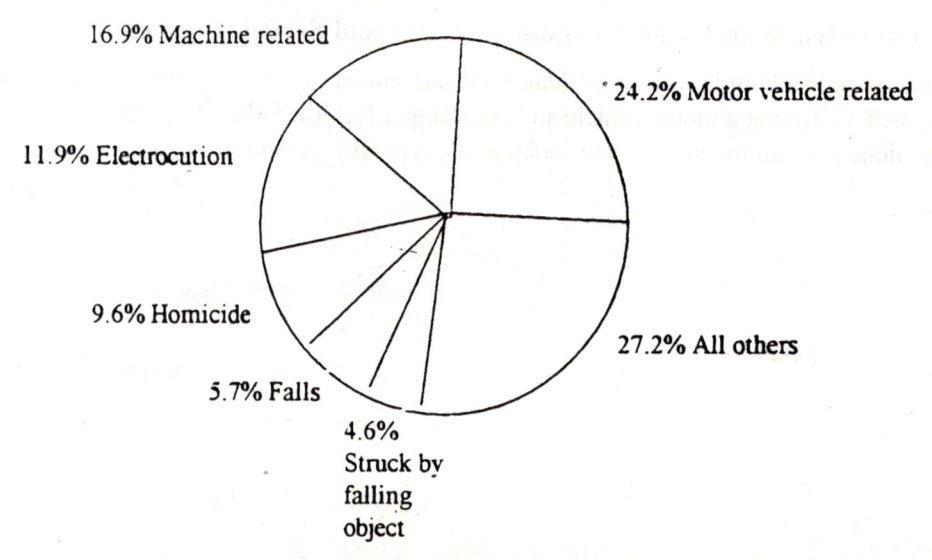

How Teens are killed at work

- 24.2% Motor vehicle related
- 16.9% Machine related
- 11.9% Electrocution
- 9.6% Homicide
- 5.7% Falls
- 4.6% Struck by falling object
- 27.2% All others

(Number of 16 and 17 year-olds killed by occupation injury death in the U.S., 1980 through 1989.)

Working In or Around Motor Vehicles

Motor-vehicle-related deaths accounted for nearly one-fourth of the work-related injury deaths of 16 and 17 year-olds during the period 1980-89 [Castillo et al. 1994]. These deaths include those of workers who were drivers and passengers in motor vehicles, pedestrians, and bicyclists involved in crashes with motor vehicles.

The following jobs are examples of work that may be associated with motor-vehicle-related deaths and injuries:
* Delivery of passengers or goods (**such** as furniture, appliances, parcels, messages, newspapers, pizzas, groceries, and pharmaceuticals)
* Services that require routine travel to provide home-based service such as cable television installation and repair, appliance repair, and landscaping services
* Residential trash pickup
* Road maintenance (such as operation of sweepers)
* Work at road construction sites (including flagpersons)
* Work at gas stations, truck stops and auto repair shops

Operating Tractors and Other Heavy Equipment

Machine-related deaths were the second leading cause of work-related injury death for 16 and 17 year-olds for the years 1980-89 [Castillo et al. 1994]. Tractors alone accounted for 44% of the machine-related deaths.

The following lists examples of heavy equipment associated with deaths:
* Tractors used in farm settings and nonfarm settings such as construction
* Forklifts
* Excavating machinery such as backhoes, bulldozers, steam and power shovels, and trenchers
* Loaders such as bucket loaders, end loaders, and front-end loaders
* Road grading and surfacing machinery such as asphalt and mortar spreaders, graders, levelers, planers, scrapers, road linemarking machinery, steam rollers, and road pavers

Working Near Electrical Hazards

Electrocution was the third leading cause of work-related injury death among 16 and 17 year-olds for the years 1980-89 [Castillo et al. 1994]. Electrocutions accounted for a greater proportion of work-related injury deaths in adolescents than in adults (12% versus 7%). Contact with an energised power line caused more than 50% of the electrocutions.

The following types of work pose an increased risk for electroduction:
* Using poles, pipes, and ladders near overhead power lines during construction work, painting, and pool cleaning
* Working on roofs to perform jobs such as roofing, roof maintenance, cleaning of rain gutters, installation and repair of heating and cooling equipment, installation and repair of television antennas, and cleaning of chimneys and smoke stacks
* Operating or contacting boomed vehicles, such as bucket trucks, telescopic forklifts, and telescopic cranes
* Using grain augers and moving grain elevators and irrigation pipes near power lines
* Tree trimming
* Wiring of electrical circuits and other work involving exposure to electrical circuitry, including work performed by electrician's helpers

Working at Jobs with a High Risk for Homicide

In 1993, assaults and violent acts accounted for about one-fourth of all work-related injury deaths of adolescents [Toscano and Windau 1994]. Most work-related homicides are associated with robbery (75% in 1993).

The following types of jobs involve increased risk for work-related homicide :
* Working alone or in small numbers in businesses where money is exchanged with the public and the risk for robbery-related homicide is high—for example, in convenience stores, gas stations, restaurants, hotels, and motels
* Working alone in contact with large numbers of people where there may be opportunities for uninterrupted assaults for example, working in motel housekeeping, delivery of passengers or goods, and door-to-door sales.

Working with Fall Hazards

Falls were the fifth leading cause of work-related injury death for 16 and 17 year-olds during the years 1980-89 [Castillo et al. 1994]; they accounted for 8% of these deaths in 1993 [Toscano and Windau 1994]. Forty per cent of fatal falls were from or out of a building or other structure [Castillo et al. 1994]. Fatal falls were documented for distances ranging from 10 feet to 14 floors.

The following types of jobs are associated with work-related falls:
* Using ladders and scaffolds to work at heights–such as, in building construction, building maintenance (brick cleaning and and window washing), painting, and harvesting fruit trees
* Working on structures or near openings in building construction
* Working on roofs
* Tree trimming

Cooking and Working Around Cooking Appliances

Severe burns are a risk for adolescents involved in cooking. An estimated 5,200 adolescents sought emergency-room treatment for work-related burns associated with cooking or working in a place where food was prepared during the 18 month period from july 1992 through December 1993 [NIOSH 1994].

The following types of work involve burn hazards associated with cooking :
* Cooking in restaurants and other commercial settings
* Servicing cooking equipment–adding, filtering, and removing hot grease from fryers, and cleaning grills and fryers and their associated vents
* Working near cooking appliances where workers may slip into or against equipment

Hazardous Manual Lifting

From July 1992 through December 1993, overexertion accounted for approximately 4,500 work-related injuries of adolescents treated in hospital emergency rooms; about 2,500 of these injuries were attributed to lifting [NIOSH 1994]. These estimates are conservative, since sprains and strains that result from repeated stress on the body (as opposed to a single injurious event) are often not treated in emergency rooms but by private physicians or clinics. Sprains and strains associated with lifting are frequently severe [Parker et al. 1994]. Although an individual's ability to safely lift objects varies, work for adolescents should not generally require them to lift objects weighing greater than 15 pounds more than once per minute or to lift objects weighing greater than 30 pounds; tasks involving continuous lifting should never last more than 2 hours [NIOSH 1994].

The following types of work may involve hazardous manual lifting:
* Working in warehouses
* Delivering furniture and appliances
* Retrieving, carrying, or stocking shelves with relatively heavy items
* Working in health care settings where patients are lifted and moved
* Installing or removing carpet or tile
* Baling hay

Other Hazardous Work

Other particularly hazardous work that is not typically prohibited by Federal child labour laws includes work in petroleum and gas extraction, Commercial fishing, many jobs that require use of respirators, work in sewage treatment plants or sewers, work on industrial conveyors, many uses of compressed air or pneumatic tools such as nail guns, farm work using all-terrain vehicles, and work around many types of machines with power take-offs or similarly rotating drivelines [NIOSH 1994].

Although work can have many benefits for the development of adolescents and may be financially necessary, the potential for serious injury and death must be recognised and addressed. Large numbers of adolescents are killed and seriously injured at work each year. Employers and parents of adolescents, school counsellors and teachers, and adolescent workers may be unaware of the risks and circumstances of work-related injuries to adolescents. Information in this Alert can help those involved make informed decisions about safe work for adolescents and prepare adolescent workers to recognise hazards on the job. (30)

Recommendations (31)

Employers

NIOSH recommends that employers take the following steps to protect adolescent workers:
* Know and comply with child labour laws and occupational safety and health regulations that apply to your business. Post these regulations for workers to read.
* Assess and eliminate the potential for injury or illness associated with tasks required of adolescents.
* Provide training to ensure that adolescents recognise hazards and are competent in safe work practices.
* Routinely verify that the adolescents continue to recognise hazards and employ safe work practices.
* Evaluate equipment that adolescents are required to operate to ensure that it is both legal and safe for use by adolescents.

* Ensure that adolescents are appropriately supervised to prevent injuries and hazardous exposures.
* Involve supervisors and experienced workers in developing and injury and illness prevention programme and in identifying and solving safety and health problems.

Parents

Parents should take the following steps to protect adolescent workers:
* Take an active role in the employment decisions of your children.
* Discuss the types of work involved and the training and supervision provided by tghe employer.

Educators

Educators should take the following steps to protect adolesecent workers:
* If your are responsible for signing work permits, know the State and Federal child labour laws.
* Talk to students about safety and health hazards in the workplace and student's rights and responsibilities as workers.
* Ensure that school-based work experience programmes (such as vocational education programmes and School-to-Work programmes) provide students with work experience in safe and healthful environments free of recognised hazards.
* Ensure that school-based work experience programmes incorporate information about worker's legal rights and responsibilities and training in hazard recognition and safe work practices.
* Consider incorporating information about worker's rights and responsibilities and occupational safety and health into high school and junior high curricula to prepare students for the world of work.

Adolescents

Adolescent workers should take the following steps to protect themselves:
* Be aware that you have the right to work in a safe and healthful work environment free of recognised hazards and that you have the right to refuse unsafe work tasks and conditions.
* Know that you have the right to file complaints with the U.S. Department of Labour when you feel your rights have been violated or your safety has been jeopardised.
* Remember that adolescent workers are entitled to worker's compensation in the event of work injury or illness.
* Obtain information about your rights and responsibilities as workers from school counsellors and State labour departments.
* Participate in any training programmes offered by your employer, or request training if none is offered.

* Recognise the potential for injury at work and seek information about safe work practices from employers and State labour departments.
* Follow safe work practices.

WHAT YOU NEED TO KNOW ABOUT TEENAGE JOBS

Remember: A part-time job is just that, because children's most important job is their education. An education will help prepare them for better and higher-paying work as an adult. If you are a teenager and want to work, then you, your parents, and your teachers should know what the laws are governing young workers, and what your rights are. Child labour laws regulate the types of jobs young people can have and the hours that can be worked. Here are some questions and answeres designed to help the working teenager.

How Old Must I Be Before I Work?

In most cases, you need to be at least fourteen to have a job. There are some exceptions to this minimum age requirement for such jobs as newspaper delivery and farm work.

How Many Hours Should I Work?

A Child Labour Provision section of the Fair Labour Standards Act sets the following rules for minors :
* There are no specific federal hourly limitations for children thirteen and younger, since the occupations permitted are restricted to domestic service, newspaper delivery, and nonhazardous work for their parents. Specific hours for these jobs are regulated by the states.
* When school is in session, fourteen and fifteen year-olds may work, but not during school hours and no more than three hours a day, eighteen hours a week. When school is not in session, work may not exceed eight hours a day, forty hours a week. These teens are prohibited from working before seven A.M. and after seven P.M., except during summers, when they can work until nine P.M. The types of work are also restricted.
* There are not hourly restrictions for sixteen and seventeen year-olds. However, there are numerous jobs involving hazardous equipment that are prohibited to them.
* There are no child labour restrictions (wage or hour) for young people working on farms owned or operated by their parents.

Remember: If you work too much, your health, your grades, and your social life may well suffer.

How Late Should I Work?

Teenagers should never work past ten p.m. on a night before school. Unfortunately, many laws are unclear about this. Problems do arise when teenagers work too late into the night. In most states, there are hour limitations that require students not to work past a designated time. These laws are meant to protect the student worker.

Will My Job Be Dangerous?

Nowadays far more teenagers are likely to work in a fast food outlet than at any other job. A 1991 government study shows that young people working in the fast food industry have a much higher likelihood of being hurt than workers in many other industries.

Here are some of the common workplaces where teen get hurt, as well as the applicable Child Labour provisions of the Fair Labour Standards Act:

* *Restaurants* : Fourteen and fifteen year-olds may not cook, bake, or be involved in any occupations that involve setting up, operating, adjusting, cleaning, oiling, or repairing power driven food slicers and grinders, food choppers and cutters, and bakery-type mixers.
* *Grocery Stores* : Youths under eighteen may not operate, assist in operating, set up, repair, oil, or clean any power driven paper product machines.
* *Pizza Deliveries* : Youths under eighteen may not be hired for the sole purpose of making deliveries by car.
* *Car Wash* : Children thirteen years and younger may not, under federal law, work in car washes.
* *Agriculture/Commercial Farm* : Children under the age of twelve are prohibited from working on any farm unless it is owned by their own family.
* *Driving* : No minor may work as a motor vehicle driver on any public road or highway; in or about any mine, including open pit mines or quarries; or at places where logging or sawmill operations are in progress. There is an exception for occasional driving of a car or light truck, as long as such driving is restricted to daylight hours and is only "occasional and incidental."
* *Bakeries* : No minor may operate, assist in operating, set up, adjust, repair, oil, or clean any dough mixer; batter, mixer; bread dividing, rounding, or moulding machine; or certain power driven bakery machines, or set up or adjust cookie or cracker machines.
* *Roofing* : No minor shall work in roofing, including work in applying weather proofing materials such as tar, tile, slate, metal and shingles to roofs of buildings or other structure. No minor may work in related metal work, such as flashing, or work on alterations, additions, maintenance, or repair of existing roofs

Remember this list does not cover everything you might possible run into. If in doubt about whether to operate a machine or how to operate it and keep yourself safe, ask your supervisor. Refuse to operate anything that you do no understand or that you consider potentially dangerous.

What Should I Do If I Am Injured?

First, you should get immediate medical attention. Second, the costs, associated with any job-related injury are your employer's responsibility. Your employer should have worker's compensation insurance to pay for nay medical costs. If you lose pay because of your injury, then you may be entitled to a worker's compensation payment. Be sure to notify your boss and your parents of any work related injuries.

Will A Job Hurt My Grades?

Work can be a positive experience. It can teach useful skills, discipline, money management, and human values. But teenagers who work too long or too late at night see their grades decline. Sometimes, in order to work, many teenagers take less difficult subjects rather than the math or sciences that can help them get better jobs as adults.

Remember : While a German or Japanese teenager is home studying calculus and chemistry, a U.S. teenager is often working. (33)

Can Something Be Done?

If we lived an ideal worked, we wouldn't worry about the harm that can be done to children who work. Just think: if all young people grew up in economically secure families; if their families were loving and supportive if they went to schools that challenged their minds, encouraged their growth, developed their talents and skills; if after completing their studies they were assured of entry level jobs and opportunities for advancements, without regard to age, sex, national origin, or colour...if all these were true, it would be the best of all possible worlds. But that is not the world we live in.

The real America is a nation where :

* The richest 1 per cent of families control more wealth than the bottom 90 percent.
* The wealth of the top one fifth of households rose by 14 per cent since 1980, while the bottom four fifths fell by 23 per cent, according to the 1990 census report.
* It is mostly the comfortable, well off people who vote and have political influence.
* More and more Americans feel they are outside the system.
* The climb out of poverty has become harder in the last twenty years.
* The economy has been less welcoming to the young, the unskilled, and the less educated.
* Racism has become America's most persistent disease.
* The income gap between black and white Americans continues to increase.
* Young families with children has significantly less money than such families did a generation ago, a trend especially true for young black and Hispanic families and for those families with little education.
* Increase numbers of the poor, one in four, are children.
* Nearly six million children under the age of twelve or one out of every eight go hungry each year.
* One is four homeless people in cities is a child.
* Half of America's seventeen year-old do not have reading, math, and science skills that would allow them to perform tasks required in many kinds of jobs.
* In sum, people fear that something has gone terribly wrong and that their future and their children's future are in real trouble.

What's unequal, what's unfair, are hard facts of life. It's important to know these things but to do more than remember them. We must think about what could be done to remedy the inequities of life in our society. No political or economic programme would remove all inequities not in a year, not in the four years of any president's term in office. Because programmes don't work miracles. The problems we are aware of are too deep rooted for that. Yet what can be done would make a significant difference in the lives of young people and their families. [34]

The Reasons Why Children Work

Within this social framework in which a centuries old traditions impels the child to work from an early age, the most pressing reason for him to seek work is the need to reduce to the greatest extent possible the poverty in which he is living and thus to help him to satisfy his basic needs. Even the smallest payments in cash or in kind are welcome in the poverty stricken home in which, as a rule, he lives. Moreover, the child is led to believe that he must work from an early age through solidarity with the family group, so as to compensate as much as possible for the economic burden that the represents and to share in the maintenance of his family, which is usually very large one.

Children may also feel obliged to work because they are doing badly at school and because there is no other alternative. If the parents ae able to let the child go to school for only a few years, it is likely that he will encounter more difficulties during his years at school than a child from a better off family. However, in many cases the parents prefer to send the child out to work rather than to school, either because there is no school with in reasonable distance of the family home or because they cannot do without income the working child brings, in or because they cannot need the cost of sending the child to the school, or again beacuse they cannot see what use schooling would be to him.

Another direct cause of child employment is the situation at home. There may be tension and uncertainty, provoked or increased by poverty, the father may have left home, the mother may be alone, the father or the mother, or both, may fall ill, or become physically unfit, or die. However, the argument that the children are obliged to work because of the disappearance of the bread winner is often fallacious, because it is generally the head of the family himself who sees to it his children go out to work.

Again, when rural family migrates to the town, the adults are straight away faced with new and unkown environmental and labour situation. As a result of the instability and insecurity that this causes, the children are often set to work so that the family may survive.

In developing countries the driving force behind every case of child labour is, of course, poverty, but the basic cause is usually a combination of some of the factor that have just been mentioned.

In the developed countries that picture is completely different, since in those countries children do not work in order to meet their basic needs or because they are following traditions but in order to earn a little extra money, and the parents do not put pressure on their children to get paid job during the years when they should legally be going to school. Moreover, far fewer children go out to work, and if they do, the work is in any case done outside school hours. [35]

INTERNATIONAL CO-OPERATION

There has in recent years been increased attention to the problem of child labour in various international foray. The work of UNICEF and the United Nations Commission on Human Rights are well known and do not need elaboration. Regional intergovernmental organisations have also addressed aspects of problem, such as the adoption by the Committee of Ministers of the Council of Europe of Recommendation No. R(91)11, 1991, concerning sexual exploitation pornography and prostitution of, trafficking in, children and young adults.

The International Confederation of Free Trade Unions (ICFTU), one of the very early campaigners against child labour, launched a global campaign for the elimination of child labour in 1994 and continues to be active in advocacy and research on behalf of working children. An important development among the ILO's social partners is the emerging interest of international employers' organisations in child labour. The General Council of the International Organisation of Employers (IOE) passed a resolution in June 1996 on child labour which makes a number of basic recommendations to employers and their organisations. The resolution calls, inter alia, for putting an immediate end to slave-like, bonded and dangerous forms of child labour, and for developing action plans at the international, national industry and enterprise levels. It calls on the Executive Committee to follow up the resolution with a proactive programme of work by the IOE.

There are many other less known organisations which were active in the child labour area but whose work is of fundamental significance to the campaign against child labour. For example, the main actors in the tourist trade, such as tourist agencies, hotels and air carriers, are beginning to take direct action to fight against sex tourism. The Universal Federation of Travel Agents' Associations (UFTAA) adopted in December 1994 a Child and Travel Agent Charter, committing itself to the fight against child sex tourism. Futher, in August 1996, in Stockholm, the World Tourism Organisation (WTO) announced that it was forming a joint public-private sector task force of tourism groups to tackle the problem of organised sex tourism and child prostitution. The task force, the Tourism and Child Prostitiution Watch, aims to encourage self-regulation in the tourism industry by increasing awareness of the problems of sexual exploitation in tourism, and collecting information on sex tourism and measures that have been successful in stopping it.

The International Criminal Police Organisation, Interpol, estabilshed in 1992 a Standing Working Party on Offences against Minors to assist its member countries in combating sexual exploitation of children, including, in particular, child pornography and the activities of paedophiles. It bases its work on a resolution on offences committed against minors which was adopted by the Interpol General Assembly in 1992. This important resolution deals with the measures required to combat the sexual exploitation of children, including the seeting up of an international register of paedophiles.

Most recently, a World Congress on Commercial Sexual Exploitation of Children was held in Stockholm, Sweden, in August 1996. The conference adopted a Programme of Action which should contribute to the global effort to suppress this very serious problem. Other similar international events are planned. The Government of the Netherlands organised an international conference in Amsterdam in February 1997 in co-operation with the ILO on the most intolerable forms of child labour. Rpresentatives were invited from industrialised and developing countries that have laready taken steps to eliminate abusive child labour. The purpose of the conference was to exchange views and experiences and to promote international co-operation in this area. A similar meeting will be convened by the Government of Norway in Oslo in 1997, in collaboration with the ILO. [36]

CONCLUSION

Information and Awareness-Raising

Public awareness-raising is a vital tool to create an appropriate political and social climate against child labour and a demand for policy reforms. Exploitative child labour tends to be hidden from view. Children, their parents, employers, adult workers and the public at large are often not aware of the dangers of premature work for children. For too long child labour, even its degrading and particularly hideous forms, has been tolerated as an inevitable part of the life of the poor.

Creating a Broad Social Alliance Against Child Labour

The importance of raising the level of social concern cannot be overstated, for experience over many years and from around the world clearly demonstrates that significant public pressure is often required to make progress on the child labour issue politically possible. Both the public and private sectors can play an important role in public awareness-raising. Historically, this has been an activity in which the independence and single-minded commitment of non-governmental organisations have made them the crucial element. But there is ample room for both the public and private sector to act in complementary and co-operative ways. In fact, it is difficult to envisage a successful campaign against labour in general, and against hazardous work in particular, without ample participation by both governmental and non-governmental organisations. These should act in collaboration even though their particular roles may be different. Each has its strengths and weaknesses. What is required is to arrive at a formula-clearly suited to national conditions—which can reinforced and build on their respective strengths.

Non-governmental organisations can, for example, be effective in advocacy, organising communities and implementing local projects. Governments can focus on the establishment of an appropriate legislative and policy climate, the provision of universal compulsory education, increasing the access of poor households to employment and income, and ensuring strict adherence to certain minimum labour standards such as the prohibition of work in exploitative and hazardous occupations or activities, and of work before the completion of primary school.

Governments

This said, the attitude of governments towards the needs and rights of children is decisive for their protection and the promotion of their welfare. This is especially so in developing countries where the presence of the State is strongly felt in practically all aspects of national life. Thus, government policy is crucial for eliminating child labour, particularly its most intolerable forms. It represents the official commitment of government to the protection of children from economic exploitation and, when vigorously pursued, places the authority of the State behind this objective. Furthermore, it can exert a powerful influence on national values an public opinion, mobilising financial and institutional resources on a scale unattainable by the private sector and community organisations. The role of government is so central that the mere absence of a national policy, or even a sign of ambivalence towards the protection of working children tends to be interpreted as tacit consent to their exploitation.

Employers and Their Organisation

Progressive and far-sighted employers have often perceived the evils of child labour, and have lent their support to its control and abolition. It could not have been so dramatically reduced in the formal sector without their concurrence. As key contributes to the economic development of their countries and communities, employers need to be aware of their effect on human resource development. According to the labour practices they follow, they can either delay or advance the development of human capacities for the future. By abandoning dependence on child labour, and by carefully protecting the development of children who do work, employers can benefit their society and the long-term health of business and industry.

Employers' organisations can encourage progressive child labour practices by making employers in the formal and informal sectors sensitive to the special needs of children, informing them about child labour laws, educating them about the greater long-term benefits of non-exploitative personnel management approaches, and assuming leadership in working with governmental and non-governmental organisations to reduce violations of child labour law.

Workers and Their Organisation

Workers' organisations are increasingly involved in child labour issues, and that participation should be increased. Some have issued public statements against child labour. Others are directly defending children's rights through action programmes of protection and prevention. Rising to the defence of working children would be consistent with the social ideals underlying the origins of most labour movements, lifting their vision beyond the pocketbook interests of their membership. Workers' organisations could be especially useful in documenting child labour abuses monitoring the effectiveness of enforcement mechanisms, educating working children about their rights and how to exercise them, and receiving and referring complaints about violations of child labour law. They could also successfully undertake to organise children, homework's, domestic servants and other exploited workers much in need of protection.

Non-Governmental Organisations and Voluntary Groups

NGOs and voluntary groups have always played an essential role in the protection of child workers by advocating effective laws and enforcement mechanisms, and by pressing government to implement those laws effectively. Determined "watchdog" groups can aggressively investigate both abuses of children in the workplace and official dereliction of duty in containing those abuses. They can also take critical issues to the courts, and have an important role to play in organising children, their parents and communities in taking a stand against child labour.

Unfortunately, many countries with significant child labour problems do not have the benefit of strong, organised advocacy groups. There is thus an urgent need for the establishment of such groups where they do not exist, and for technical and financial support to them where they do. The international NGOs, drawing on experience and human resources the world over, could be especially useful in promoting, training supporting national groups of young and adult citizens dedicated to the protection of working children and the abolition of child labour.

Other Segments of Society

Other members of civil society have an extremely important contribution to make in the fight against child labour. Professional media organisations have a special responsibility in informing the public about child labour issues. Universities are also valuable allies, particularly for researching specific aspects of the child labour problem, training the staff involved in field activities and assessing the impact of pilot action programmes undertaken on behalf of working children. Because political resolve is essential in order to tackle child labour problems, parliamentarians are also important partners. Last, but not least, are the millions teachers and educators, and health, population and other extension workers, who can be motivated to participate in the prevention of child labour at the local and national levels. Their role in efforts to combat child labour has been little explored, and air potential for being mobilised in the campaig against this scourge is only beginning to be tapped. The integration of child labour issues into the school curriculum, for instance, concerning the dangers of specific types of work, the alternatives to work, the rights afforded to working children under national law, and the means of defending them can prevant many children from entering work. Teachers can influence the community by informing families about the costs and dangers of child labour; acting as child labour monitors to help survey the extent of school non-attendance and its relationship to child labour in the community; and supporting community participation in planning formal and non-formal education programmes to ensure that all child workers and potential child workers are reached. Last but not least, former working children are a powerful tool in convincing other children and society at large of the need to fight child labour. Their experience should be used and their potential harnessed in designing and implementing strategies against it. [37]

BIBLIOGRAPHY

1. Lela B. Costine : Child Welfare : Polices and Practice (New York, McGraw Hill, 1972).
2. ILO : Child Labour : A Global Challenge (Amesterdam Child Labour Conference, Feb. 1997).
3. Armando Cocco : "Lavoro Minorile Apprendistato Scuola". In Formazione Domainim Jan. 2985, p.51.
4. Elias Mendelievich, Children at Work (Cambridge, England : Polity Press, 1989).
5. J. Aiken and Ho Boyden : Combating Child Labour (Geneva : International Labour Office, 1988).
6. "Resolutions for the consideration of the Manchester Board of Health presented by Dr. Percival to the Manchester Board of Health, Han 25, 1796," in Abbott.p.107-108.
7. Walter I, Trattner, Crusade for the Children : A History of the National Child Labour Committee and Child Labour Reform in America (Chicago : Quadrangle Books, 1980), p.27.
8. Quoted in ibid., p.23.
9. Walter I, Trattner, Crusade for the children : A instrument for whipping children as and "eighteen inch leather strap with tacks driven through the strinking end", (Chicago : Quadrangle Books, 1983), p.30.
10. Ibid., pp. 30-35.
11. Edith Abbott : "A study of the Early History of Child Labour in America". American Journal of Sociology, Vol. 14, July 1980, p.37
12. Nettie P. McGill, Child workers on City Streets, (Washington, D,C : U.S. Government printing office, United State Department of Labour, Children's Bureau, 1988), p.3.
13. Grace Abbott, The Child and the State : Legal Status in Family, Apprenticeship, and Child Labour : Selected Document with Introductory Notes, Vol. 1 (Chicago : University of Chicago Press, 1988) pp.398-404.
14. Ellen Greenberger and Laurence Steinberg, When Teenagers Work : The Psychological and social costs of Adolescent Employment (New York : Basic Books, 1986), p.11.
15. Ibid., pp.18-20.
16. Ibid., p.179.
17. Ibid., pp. 34-37.

18. United States General Accounting Office, "Sweetshops" in New York City : A Local Example of Nationwide Problem, (Washington, D.C. : U.S. Govt. Printing Office, June 1989), pp.8-23.
19. Kendall J. Willis, "Garment Sweetshops are Spreading", New York Times, Sep. 6, 1987, Section 1, p.38
20. Los Angles Times, May 1, 1989, Section 4, p. 5.
21. Wall Street Journal, Sep. 5, 1989, Part A, p.1.
22. Rosalind Wright. "The Hidden Cost of Child Labour". Family Circle, March 12, 1991, pp.83-85.
23. Ellen Greenberger and Laurence and Steinberg, When Teenagers Work : The Psychological and Social Costs of Adolescent Employment (New York : Basic Books, 1986), pp.90-155.
24. General Accounting Office, "Sweetshops" in New York City : A Local Example of Nationwide Problem, (Washington, D.C. : U.S. Govt. Printing Office, 1990), p.2.
25. General Accounting Office, Child Labour : Increases In Detected Child Labour Violations Throughout the United States (Washington, D.C. : U.S. Govt. Printing Office, 1990), pp.45-51.
26. "Sweetshops" In New York City, pp. 8-10.
27. Dorianne Beyer : Child Labour Laws and STW Transition, Understanding and Applying Child Labour Laws to Today's School-to-work Transition Programmes, Centre Focus Number 8, April 1995.
28. NIOSH, Request for assistance in Preventing deaths and injuries of adolescent workers, Cincinnati : US Department of Health and Human Services, Public Health Service, CDC, 1995 : DHHS publication no. (NIOSH) 95-125.
29. Ibid. 1995, DHHS publication no. (NIOSH = National Institute for Occupational Safety and Health) 95-125.
30. Parker DL, Carl WR, French LR, Martin FB (1994). Work Associated with Large Number of Death and Serious Injuries, Minnesota Department of Labour and Industry U.S., 1994.
31. Derstine B (1994). Youth worker at risk of fatal injuries. Paper presented at the 122nd Annual Meeting of the American Public Health Association, Oct. 30, 1994, Washington, DC.
32. NIOSH, Request for assistance in Preventing deaths and injuries of adolescent workers, US Department of Labour, 1997.
33. Rudolph A. Oswald : Cheap Raw Material : Young American Worker's Bill of Rights, 1990, p.5
34. The State of the World's Children 1991 (New York : Oxford University Press, for UNICEF), p.42.
35. Elias Mendelievich, Children at Work (Cambridge, England : Polity Press, 1989).
36. During 16th World Congress on Child Labour in Brussels, 25-29 June 1996, the ICFTU (International Confedration of Free Trade Unions) adopted its most recent Satement on eradicating child labour.
37. ILO : Combating the Most Intolerable Forms of Child Labour : A Global Challenge, Amesterdam Child Labour Conference, Geneva, Feb. 1997.

19

THE CHILD GEM POLISHERS OF JAIPUR

At least 50 per cent of children working in the gem polishing industry are completely illiterate. Some of them have been educated up to the third standard and others dropped out even earlier. Since the education they had received was so meagre, whatever they learnt in the early years has been forgotten and today they are completely illiterate. Surprisingly, this is one industry where the need for education for upward mobility is seen as an absolute necessity by all those involved in the industry.

The Gem Polishing Industry of Jaipur, Rajastan : Past and Present

The gem industry of jaipur is as old as the city itself. Jaipur is the capital of the State of Rajasthan and a few hours away from New Delhi by road. In AD1727, when Jaipur was built, Maharaja Jai Singh invited a number of jewellers from Delhi, Agra and Benaras and gave them royal patronage to start the gem industry in Jaipur. The tradition of royal patronage was continued by Maharaja Ram Singh who ordered the principal market of Jaipur city to be named 'Johari Bazaar' or the market of jewellers the main city square to be known as 'Manak Chowk' or Ruby Square.

Jaipur is well known for its coloured gem stone industry just as Surat in Gujarat is the main diamond-cutting centre in India. Coloured gem stones can be either precious or semi-precious. The gems are sapphires, rubies and emeralds. The range of semi-precious stones is much larger and includes, amongst others, lapis lazuli, turquoise, corals, garnets, amethysts and topaz. Ninety-five per cent of all coloured gem stones in India are polished in Jaipur. The other centres of gem polishing are Cambay in Gujarat where agate is polished, Bombay, Hyderabad, Karwar, Trichur, Coimbatore, Nellore, Cuttack and Calcutta. While there are serveral processes in the coloured gem processing industry will be explained later, the different processes are usually collectively referred to as gem polishing. Henceforth in this report, the term gem polishing will be used for the sake of consistency. It must also be mentioned here that the gems polished in Jaipur are not only made for use as jewellery but are also carved for decorative purposes. Carving is also done for jewellery though the processes are slightly different. The carving of gems is also considered to be a part of the gem polishing industry.

Under royal patronage, the jewellery business thrived and since Jaipur was strategically located on the imperial route between Delhi and the South, the traders were able to get raw material and unsold gems very easily. They reshaped, polished and set the gem stones in gold and silver ornaments which became famous in the courts. In earlier days, the gems cut and polished for the royal families were very large. Today, the gem industry caters to the international market. The easy availability of cheap labour here makes it lucrative business. The other main gem polihing centers in the world are Israel, West Germany, Thailand, Sri Lanka and Taiwan. According to Shekhar Vashisht, a gemologist based in Jaipur, the main buyers of Indian gem stones are the USA, France, Hong Kong, Italy, Japan, Kuwait, Saudi Arabia, Singapore, Switzerland, UK and West Germany. The USA is the biggest buyer of emeralds. India earns about Rs 1400 *crores* (1 *crore* is equal to 10,000,000) per annum from the export of gems.

Though the gem polishing industry is the single laregest employer in Jaipur city, there has never been any census or survey of gem artisans and workers. Conversations with those in the gem trade suggested that there sy least 60,000 workers engaged in it. Of these, it was learnt, 51,000 (85 per cent) are Muslims and 9000 (15 per cent) are Hindus. Hindu workers are ethnicaly either Marwari or Gujarati, I was told that there are about 12,500 women and female children amongst the Muslim Workers, accounting for about 25 per cent of the work-force of that community. The Gurpadaswamy Committee Report of 1979 (GOI 1981: 9) came to conclusion that there were at least 10,000 Children in the gem industry. Investigations in Jaipur point to there being at least 13,000 Muslim children (over 25 per cent of the Muslim work-force) and over 600 Hindu children (about 7 per cent of the Hindu work-force). It can safety be assumed that over 13,000 children below the age of fourteen years (or over 20 per cent of all workers) are involved in the gem industry. If one were to include children between the ages of fifteen years, the percentage share of children in the total work-force would probably go up to a figure of about forty. The estimates of working children given above are likely to be on the lower side. (Burra 1987b)

The gem polishing industry, as mentioned earlier, is as old as the city of Jaipur and to that extent it is a traditional occupation of most workers in Jaipur blonging to the Muslim community. Children learnt the craft from their fathers and both girls and women participated in the activity. *Bindai ka kaam* (the work of making holes in beads), was traditionally done by women and even today, is done by them. However, as the international demand for gems increased, the ultrasonic machine for drilling holes was introduced and now this work is done by unskilled adult males. As a result production, and consequently wages, have risen too. Women have been displaced from the gem industry as the technology of gem polishing improved. Girls work at the home because of the tradition of *purdah* (the selusion of women).

The great influx of child labour into the industry is a relatively recent phenomenon because the international demand for gems has risen sharply and parents see this industry as a means of upward mobility for their children. Earlier, children worked with their parents but they combined school with learning the craft. In many families tradition of gem polishing has been kept alive through several generations. It required a certain amount of knowledge about trade and the outside world, for which some education was essential. Since the demand for gems was not very high, child labour was not very widely prevalent. Today, the need for cheap child labour is closely linked to the international demand for and competitive prices of gems.

It was widely accepted in Jaipur that the official figures regarding the export of polished gem stones do not account for even a third of what is illegally exported out of the country. It is therefore very difficult to assess the total production of polished gem stones in Jaipur. The only available figure is that 90 per cent of the total production of gem stones is exported. I visited more than 500 units where work of gem polishing was being carried out. I also visited about twenty homes where the work of gem polishing was being done with the help of family labour and a few *bavelis* (mansions) where the master craftsmen were getting work done on a lot basis, for traders, in their own homes. I spent twenty days in the field and was able to interview nearly a 100 children below the age of fourteen years in their schools. Wide-ranging discussions were held with different segments of the gem polishing industry: fifty workers, ten traders, three master craftsmen, three exporters and several government officials.

Processes in the Gem Industry

The cutting and polishing of gems in Jaipur is done by simple machines which do not cost more than Rs 1000 or so. The rough stones are imported from all over the world.

The first process is to sort out the raw material and then cut them in required facets or sides. Gem stones are first slit by means of thin disc of relatively soft metal whose edges are slightly indented. The cut stone or *ghat* (rough cut sotne) is then cemented to a wodden stick for rough shaping against an emery of carborundum wheel.

The artisan uses a stone lap; whild sitting on the floor, he turns the *jindra* (lap) by means of a *kabana* (bow), the string of which is the driving device. By this side is a bowl containing emery, the onsistency of which is adjusted by mixing it with water before it is used for grinding. In his left hand, he holds the stones that he is manipulating and in the other, the bow which makes the grinding stone rotate. After charging the lap with the appropriate abrasive, the lapidary first grinds the table facets. The other facets and angles are dependent on the deign.

After the stone has been given a rough shape, the master craftsman takes over and corrects the slight irregulariteies left by the cutter. Once the shape and facets are cut and polished, the work is given to children to do the final polishing by using oxides which give the stones their lustre.

The chief forms of cutting stones are the 'brilliant cut' and 'the step cut'. Transparent stones like emeralds, rubies and sapphires are facet cut and translucent stones like turquoise, corals, opals and star stones are cut in cabochons and do not have sides. A simple cabochon has a carved top and a flat base.

The processes mentioned above are the most basic ones used in the gem polishing industry. The machines used very according to the type of stone being polished. Thus, while ruby beads are made by hand because rubies are precious stones, granet—a very cheap stone—is mechanically polished in drums. Precious stones are processed by hand and the semi-precious by machines to cut down the cost of production and increase supply.

Children are engaged in large numbers in making of *ghats*, facting and polishing of semi-precious stones but in the precious stones industry, children are largely engaged in the final polishing of the gems with oxides where there is absolutely no danger of any damage to the finished product. In the final polishing of gems with oxides, the enitre labour force consists of children below the age of fourteen years.

Structure of the Gem Industry

The term commonly used for commission agents and brokers ins *dalal* (middlemen/broker). These people are merely go-betweens the workers and the trader.

Amongst artisans, there are two or three types of people. Most artisans usually referred to as *ustads* (masters) because they impart training. But for greater clarity, a distinction is made here between the *ustad* and the master craftsman who gets work on 2 contract but who generally does not employ children below the age of fourteen either because the quality of work he does requires skills a child does not possess or because the child below the age of fourteen is likely to cause damage.

At the next level are people referred to later as *ustad* contractors. These are adults who have learnt the work from master craftsman and who have set up their workdhops and mainly employ children below the age of fourteen. They use children because they are a source of cheap labour recruited under the guise of apprenticeship.

At the third level are the workers, who work either for master craftsmen, *ustad* contractors, traders and exporters or are self-employed. More than 80 per cent of all fall in this category.

The gem industry is a multi-tiered industry. At the top of the pyramid is the exporter/ trader/ manufacturer. The entire industry funcions through *dalals*.

There is no unidformity in the structure of othe gem plolishing industry. In the big export houses and trading units, the work is supervised by supervisors who come in the category of management are the trusted lieutenants of the exproter. There are different categories of employees, first is the person who grades the raw material. Once it is graded, each piece is marked with pencil showing the place where the stone is to be cut. The person in charge of grading and marking the raw material is called a *marking karnewala* or *nishan laganewala*. After the pieces have marked with a pencil, each stone is sliced and given a rough shape known as *ghat*. The person who makes this rough shape is called a *ghat bananewala*. Once the *ghat* is ready, then it is sent for various types of polishing.

Many different kinds or arranements exist in the gem polishing industry. For instance, the *ghat* machines may belong to the worker but the premises to the exporter. Sometimes, both the premises and the machines blong to the exporter and all the workers are paid employees of the exporter or trader.

There is another kind of structure, where the master craftsman sets up his own workshop and the trader brings the raw material to the craftaman who employs twenty-five or thirty workers in his *haveli* (mansion) and uses children in the polishing of gems with oxides. If the work-load is too much, he may in turn pass on the work to other workers who have been trained by him and have their own workshops—The *ustad* contractors. These *ustad* contractors in turn employ both adults and children and also work themselves.

There is a third structure that exists where the worker may own a machine at home—usually to process semi-precious gems—and where the small-time trader, who does not want to be burdened with regular employees, gives the raw material and the worker uses his family labour, the women and children, and gives the finished goods back to the trader. This petty trader may be a wholesale dealer or even an exporter and he deals directly with the artisan at home and thus saves the commission he would otherwise have to pay the *dalal*.

A fourth system is where the worker has his own machines, buys the raw material, processes the stones and then sells them directly to the dealer. These may be finished or semi-finished products. A common sight is the gathering of workers—both adults and children—at Ghat every evening between 5.30 p.m. and 7.30 p.m. The workers carry small packets of gems to sell to *dalals* who buy the goods directly from the workers and sell to other brokers who in turn exporters/ manufacturers.

The *dalal* is crucial to the gem trade and acts as an intermediary between the worker and the dealer. He is paid a 4 per cent commission by the worker to sell the goods to the trader. He knows where and who is making what and it is his job to provide the goods to the trader on time. The worker is in no position to look for contract with the trader directly because this is too time consuming.

At Gopalji Ka Rasta in Johari Bazaar, the *dalals* meet every evening carrying shopping bags to precious and semi-precious gems which they from the workers and sell to the traders. The commission agent is vital for the worker, the small dealer and the artisan. He not only sells on behalf of the worker in the local market also helps the small-time artisan-turned-dearler in exporter his goods.

The most common arrangment is one where the worker is employed on a monthly wage. He may be employed by the master craftsman, the exporter, the trader or the *ustad* contractor. The number of people who are self-employed is relatively small. However, since the gem polishing equipment is not very expensive. several workers try and save their money and invest in a machine so that they can buy raw mateiral from their savings and sell the finished products to the *dalals*. This ensures an added income and is one ways which, in a small way, the worker gets to make money.

Thus, at the very top is exporter who may have his own manufacturing unit or may contract the work to a master craftsman, who has his own labour force. By and large, I was told, master craftsmen do not become traders themselves because traders would then entertain suspicions about whether the master craftsmen had misused or interchanged the raw stones given to them for their own purposes. Therefore, traders discourage master craftsmen from getting into business and are willing to pay very high prices for the work done.

Child labour is most widespread in the semi-precious stone industry where children are engaged in almost all the processes. In the precious stone industry, they are engaged in fewer processes such as cementing roughly-shaped stones on sticks and finally polishing gems with oxides.

Adult and Their Wages

The Marwaris and Gujaratis comprise 15 per cent of the total labour force engaged in the processing of semi-precious and precious gem stones but control 95 per cent of the market. The Marwaris, who start working in the actual fahioning of gems, are usually adults in the age range of twenty to thirty years and have at least a BA degree. They state as workers only because their ambitions are either to get top management jobs or to start their own business. They get paid high salaries of at least Rs 2000 a month and work a few years in order to gain experience on the job. The Gujarati workers have less education, are usually within the age range of fifteen to twenty years and are paid between Rs 1000-1500. The Muslims who control less than 5 per cent of the business provide 85 per cent of the work-force. An average worker gets paid 20-25 a day or Rs 500-650 a month. By and large, the workers are illiterate or semi-literate.

The methods of paying wages in the gem industry are varied and there is no uniformity in the wage structure. The highly-skilled *ghat bananewala* gets an average monthly salary ranging betweens

Rs 1000 and 5000 a month depending upon the value of the stones he is fashioning. Such are the wages paid to highly-skilled workers in the precious stone industry. The worker does not earn anything on days when he is ill or the workshop is closed.

Most master craftsmen, who also work as *ustad* contractors, get paid by gross weight for faceting and making beads. Thus the raw material is first weighed and labour charges given by carat weight to the master craftsman who shares it with the workers. If the weight of the raw material is reduced in the process of faceting or of making beads or if there is any breakage, it is not the responsibility of the labour.

In the case of cabochons and carving of gems into figure, payment is made according to the weight of the finished produce. The trader wants the carved peice to weigh less so that he can pay less and craftsman wants the piece to weigh more because his payment is dependent on the weight of the finished stone. The rate of these jobs is higher so that the artisan is not tempted to make a bulky piece just to get more money.

At every level, the trader's/ exporter's main attempt is to concel from the worker—be it the master craftsman or the artisan or the low-level worker—where and for whom the product is being made. The higher the stakes, the greater the subterfuge. Thus for example, if the exporter has an order for a chess set in a precious stone, he will not give all the work to one artisan but pretend that he has only an order for two kinghts. Once those are complete, he may ask the artisan to make him two bishops and perhaps give another pair to another artisan. By the time the artisan realizes that he is in fact making a chees set for which the trader is probably going to make a thousand per cent profit, it is too late for him to raise his labour charges. A shrewd artisan, if he knows that the need of the trader is great, can command very good labour fees; but to do so he needs to be educated and to be able to understand the demands of market forces and the wily ways of the trader whose main aim is to make a quick buck and somehow keep the profits with himself. The role of education in upward mobility will be discussed later.

In Jaipur, the gem polishing industry is considered to be the best employer because the wages are relatively high and the prospects very good. All around, people see their contemporaries who have risen from being mere workers to dealers and show-room owners. Everywhere one goes, one finds people trying to make a fast buck by either buying cheaply and selling at a premium or starting a side business. Many low-level functionaries run small businesses in their spare time and involve other members of the family.

People talked in awe and envy of those who had made a lot of money in the business. The big exporters had their own show-rooms in New York and owned houses and real estate. Those who were not in the same league hoped to reach it in another generation. Jewellers were always referred to as (multi-millionaires). There were many exporters who had recently reached the top and made their millions. At every level, the person aimed and aspired to reach the next. Thus, the worker wanted to become an *ustad* contractor and the *ustad* contractor and wanted to become a dealer. A dealer hoped to set up a show-room on Mizra Ismali Road, the main business area. And everyone wanted to become and exporter.

But while were examples of upward mobility amongst those who had gone into business, there was not much evidence of this process amongst workers. The bulk of workforce remained artistans, dependent upon their wages. Every now and then, a worker would save a little money, buy raw material, finish the goods and sell to a *dalal* and, if he was lucky, make a neat profit. But examples of such success stories amongst workers were rare. This fact, however, did not prevent people from trying.

The chances of upward mobility are also very real so it is not inconceivable that a person raises his econonmic status within a few years. The main was to assess the situation and to play one's cards well. There were people who were not gem plolishers but were trying to enter industry by sending their own children to work at a young age. The gem industry of Jaipur is seen as the main avenue for upward mobility.

Work, Apprenticeship and the exploatation of Children

There are who categories of working children in the gem polishing industy. The first category is made up of those who work full-time form 8 a.m. to 6 p.m. and belong to families of manual lahbourers: they are lowest in the economic hierachy. These children are in the age-range of six to ten and are completely illiterate.

In the second category are children of families who have a fairlyy steady income: some parents are involved in gem polishing but others hold occupations as government servants, tailors, barbers, etc. Their children go to schools—mainly government schools—and work for about hours a day after school. Their age-range is ten to fourteen years.

The children of master craftsmen or good artisans who earn more than Rs 1000 a month do not work even though gem polishing is done at home. They enter the gem polishing industry but usually after they have completed their schooling and certainly not before the age of fifteen years. The reasons for this state afairs will be explained later.

While an attempt has been made to distinguish between different categories of children involved in the gem polishing industry, some children do not fall within this scheme. Some children of artisans may be working full-time and some children of manual labourers may be going to school. But by large, the categories described earlier would hold good for the bulk of the child labour force in the Muslim community.

Child labour is recruited under the guise of apprenticeship training by master craftsmen, *ustad* contractors, exporters and traders. While child labour is very visible in the walled city of Jaipur and particularly in workshop run by the *ustad* contractors, children also work in *havelis* in Johari Bazar, but they are fewer in number and less visible. It is also very difficult to link a worker to his employer and therefore to say which big exporters are exploiting children is not easy. This statement is clarified elsewhere. In what follows, the exploitation of children by *ustad* contractors will be described.

Children in the gem polishing industry are engaged ostensibly as apprentices, but in fact provide cheap labour. The learning process takes anything up to five or even seven years and the child begins work usually at the age of six or seven. During this period, the child does not get paid regular wages, but is occasionally given a few rupees so that he continues to be interested in the work.

The general pattern for children who work from 8 a.m. to 6 p.m. is that in the first one and a half years, the child gets no wages—not even in kind—and he works for at least ten hours a day. During the first year, he learns to attach unpolished gems on sticks for polishing, fetches and carries for his master, does domestic work, cleans the premoses and so on. By getting a child to do this work, the *ustad*, the contractor saves on a domestic servant and wages of an adult worker. By engaging a child to do all the running around, and some unskilled work, he saves around Rs 150-200 a month.

In the second stage, when the child has worked for a year and a half or so, he is shown how it grind one facet on a stone besides continuing to do domestic work. This goes on for three or four months and sometimes, the *ustad* contractor stretches this period to a year without wages. After two years, the *ustad* contractor starts paying the child Rs 50 a month occasionally gives him some old clothes, tea and sometimes even food. In the second stage, the child does work worth Rs 250-300 a month, at the very least. Every now and then, when the child becomes restless and wants to learn more and there is danger that the child may leave, the *ustad* contractor increases the wages and as the wages increase, the child given more directly productive work and less domestic work. The *ustad* contractor does not want to pay wages and make the child do domestic work when there is a ready supply of younger children who can be engaged without wages.

Once the child has spent three or four years and has started learning to make facets, he is worth at least 300-400 to the *ustad* contractor. By this time, he may get Rs 100 month and old clothes, tea and food. By the time the child is fourteen of fifteen years old, he has learnt most of the finer polishing techniques and would be earning about 150-200 a month whereas an adult would get Rs 500-600 for the same job.

It is at this stage that the *ustad* contractor finds it difficult to hold on to the child on the pretext of training. At the age of fifteen or sixteen, a child who has learnt some skills can do about 30 per cent more work than adults, I was told, and it is at this stage, that the *ustad* contractor is really interested in hanging on to the child. He may marginally increase the wages of the child and promise to teach him some more, thereby retaining him for a couple of years more. Beyond five or six years, it is impossible to keep the child because by then there is also community pressure to release him. The parents of the child are also interested in shifting the child to another contractor so that the child can be bring in a regular wage.

It must be mentioned that this system of exploitation under the guise of apprenticeship training is not cofined to *ustad* contractors but it is not visible elsewhere. while this category of high-visibility children, who work full-time, is made up of the off-spring of casual labourers, one finds that often artisans also bring their children to master craftamen with the hope that if the child pleases the master craftsmen, his future will be assured. These children work almost the same hours but may not be as young. The children I had an opportunity to see were in the twelve to fourteen age-group. But I did not get an opportunity to talk to those, who were either very young or did not wish to speak in front of their master.

The children who went to school in the morning and worked later were more accessible and I was able to interview sixty-four children in five different schools, all below the age of fourteen years. Out of these sixty-four children, only five said they got a holiday on Sundays as well as half-day on Fridays for prayers. All the others got time off from work only on Fridays and worked the full day on Sundays. The children said that they got no wages although they worked four to five hours a day, six days a week. All of them said that they got money on festival days from the *ustad*. Only three boys had got 15 on festival occasions. The others got Rs 10 or less.

This money they gave their parents. Sometimes, the parents gave the child half the money and sometimes only a rupee or two. Only one child who drilled holes in beads on his father's machine got paid Rs 2.50 for drilling holes in a hundered beads. He said that the market rate was Rs 5.00 for this work. He had opened an account with the State Bank of Bikaner and Jaipur. Five boys saved the money with their mothers. The others liked to spend the money on eating out. I asked the children whether they knew how the money they earned was spent. Shamim, a twelve-year old said: *'Hamare upar he kharacb ho jata hein'* (The money gets spent on us.)

It is difficult to make an accurate assessment about the number of children in these two categoies and their proportions in the labour force. At Galta Gate, on one occasion in the afternoon, I had counted fifty-seven children below the age of fourten years in thirty units. But on a morning visit, I could count impression that a large number of children were in fact going to school and working later.

In Zia-ud-din ka Mohalla at char Darwaza, I countered eighty children below the age of fouteen years, the *ustad* contractors for whom the children were working said that these children were full-time workers and did not go school. At Baba ka Tibba in Ramganj Bazaar also, counted twenty children who were working full-time. On Kalyan Ji Ka Rasta, all the twenty-five children were full-time workers.

In many of the units I visited, the children were not sitting at the machines but were engaged outside the unit, either carrying a jug of water of fanning a coal *chulha* or stove or just standing around. I was told by Aminbhai that all the children gathered around were working full-time. In Ramganj Bazaar, child labour is widely used. One dealer in gems has an album with coloured photographs of children working. He said that his foreign clients were very impressed that small children could be made to work and this was used to profit in his sales strategy. The myth of a traditional occupation coming down from father to son also repeatedly used to good effect!

How Exporters Child Labour

It is not just the *ustad* contractor who exploits child labour but owing to the way in which the industry is organized, it is very difficult to link the exporter with his workers. The really big exporters dealing with precious stones get workers to work in their *havelis*. Behind the locked doors of Johari Bazaar in Gopal Ji Ka Rasta and in Haldion Ka Rasta, workers are cutting faceting and polishing gems for exports and do not come under any kind of labour legislation. And child labour is engaged as well. In the evenings, it is possible to see young boys of ten and twelve years wearing *the hmats/lungis* (a long cloth worn by men) with their faces, hands and clothes streaked with green colour—chromium oxide—the agent used for polishing emeralds which are largely exported to the United States.

When asked, government officials, traders, brokers,contractors, local people and tourist drivers, all deny that the work of gem polishing is done anywhere other than in the walled city where the Muslims live. This is factually incorrect. Exporters and big-time traders directly engage workers including children but it is very difficult to assess the number of children employed in the precious stone industry. According to the Labour Commissioner of Rajasthan, there are approximately 2000 children employed in the precious stone industry but this figure is based more upon speculation than hard data. In fact, any attempt to research the gem industry is fraught with difficulty. The standard reply if one asks to see how gems are cut and polished is that exporters do not want people to come and visit their units because they are afraid that trade secrets will be stolen. This explanation, however is blatantly untrue and only means of preventing any kind of inspection from taking place. The atmosphere here is uncanny. No one knows who is doing what behind closed doors. A veil of secrecy covers the entire place. It is impossible to get what might seem to be even a simple piece of information. One is deliberately misled. Even structurally, the layout is like a maze and it is quite impossible for someone to go back to the same place unaided. I however, was fortunate to be able to see the manufacturing process organized by one of the major gem exporters in Jaipur.

Through a local contact, I was asked to come to Johari Bazaar and then taken to *haveli*, which was like a maze. We went through various narrow corridors and everywhere four or five workers were either cutting or making *ghats* under the strict supervision of the management. In several rooms, a *munim* (accountant) could be seen sitting by the hour and his main job was to shield his master. If any official came to enquire too closely about the activities of the exporter or wanted to meet him, the standard reply was : *party ko milne gaye hein* (he has gone to meet buyers). In fact behind most of these rooms. precious gems are being polished but no one knows who is doing what. From the second floor of the *Delhiwale ki Haveli*, I could look into several other *havelis* and everywhere there were workers polishing gems. In many places I could see children but it was difficult to count them as I was accompanied by the work supervisor of the export agency. All the *havelis* seemed to be connected for we entered from one side street and come out through another, and I had lost track of direction.

I was then taken to Badi Chaupar, where we stopped in front of wholesale market in which poor-quality wheat was being stored. The man took me inside. It was a horizontally layered building. In the first quadrangle. there some flour-grinding machines. In the second quadrangle, there were just some gunny bags stacked up in piles. In the third quadrangle, on the second floor, emeralds of very high quality were being polished. There were deep niches in the walls which opened into a courtyard so that natural light was avaiable and in every niche, there were four or five workers directly employed by the exporter on a montly salary but without any protection under labour legislation. It so happened that I had visited the area previously. But when I asked the local shopkeepers if there was any gem polishing going on, I was categorically told that I was in the wrong locality! People are generally afraid ot give any information about the gem polishing industry because of the clout of exporter/trader/manufacturer. The stakes are so high that no one wants to unnecessarily part with any information.

The some work supervisor took me to semi-precious stones units in *Char Darwaza*. I asked whether the machines and the premises belonged to the *ustad* contractor but was told that both belonged to the exporter. This was a cutting unit where children were working. The arrangement was very neat. The work supervisor engaged a labourer whom he trusted and who was paid the same wages as other workers. But this labourer was also given an *inam* (gift) because it was his responsibility to see that nothing was pilfered and also because he paid the wages of the other workers, who were paid a monthly wage. Since children were also working here, I was told quite openly: 'Why engage an adult for Rs 500 to do a job that a child is willing to do Rs 50?'

Big-time exporters do not pay or have any direct dealing with the lower category of workers but engage manufacturing supervisors to do the dirty job. This arrangement persists in most units where the work of carving, faceting, grinding and polishing is being done for the particular exporter and where the labour is not doing work in their spare time for other exporters. The child can be made to work for Rs 5 day while an adult will demand at least Rs 25 for the same job. The man who recruits the labour is given an incentive to recruit cheap labour for his employers to boost their profits and cheapest labour is child labour. Behind closed doors and veils of secrecy, children toil and exporters prosper!

Why Parents Send Their Children to Work

It is quite clear from what has gone before that all employers—whether exporters, master craftsmen or *ustad* contractor—are interested in child labour because it is the cheapest from of labour available. The only redeeming feature of the situation if it can be called that, is that the children live with their parents in the same neighbourhood and, therefore, at least they have a home to go to. As one master craftsman said:

> It makes me mad to see how children are being exploited both by the parents and the employers. The employers are like blood-suckers, draining the man and taking advantage of his helplessness. It would have been better if these children had never been born for the life children lead is one of sheer misery.

To a question as to whether the child actually learning on the job, his answere was:

> A child of six or seven has neither the physical nor the mental ability to absorb the work. The child who starts working at age of six or seven years can never become an artisan; he will only be a worker and he will end up by sending his own children to work at an early age. A child of fifteen is another matter, particularly if he is educated. He can learn in a year or two what a child of seven cannot in five years. Apprenticeship training should start at fifteen years and not before. These children are not being trained, they are being used.

If it is easy to see why employers employ children, the parents also have a point of view. Employers of children felt that it was the irresponsibility of the parents that resulted in their children working. Rashidbhai, an *ustad* contractor said:

> 80 per cent of the parents live off earnings of their children and sit around gambling and drinking. There is nothing the government can do for such useless people. Their greed and laziness is their main problem.

But conversations with working children told a different tale of exploitation, Hameedbhai is fifty years old. After working for forty years he was able to save Rs 10,000. He decided to buy raw material—uncut emeralds— and worked for fifteen days with the help of his family members. Once the emeralds were processed, he took them to the *dalal* to sell directly thinking that thereby he would be able to keep the commission he would normally have to pay to an intermediary. On his first day in the market, He asked for Rs 15,000 for the goods but the *dalal* bargained for a lower figure. The day I met Hamidbhai, he had been beaten down to rs 11,000. Hamidbhai could not wait my longer and said to me:

> The *dalal* knows how little staying power the worker has and how to apply pressure. They know our desperation and from just looking at our wait patiently like vultures. The *dalal* knows that I can't wait any longer and tomorrow I may not even recover the money I spent on the raw material. I used my whole family to finish the goods and we will not be able to get even the minimum labour charges.

Hamidbhai's story is not unique in the gem polishing industry. Other adult workers said that *dalal* would not pay them for days on end. I witnessed an interesting tableau at Ghat Gate one evening where I was told that workeres, both adults and children, come to sell what they have produced. The dealer who had taken me there said that if one wanted to make a quick buck on a deal, Ghat Gate was the place to do so. I was besieged by workers with little *pudias* (packets containng gems). The dealers were waiting across the road on the other side. One by one, they would cross the road and wait. While the labourers start gathering from about 5.30 p.m. onwards, the dealers move in for the kill around 6.30 p.m. The negotiations start only around 7 p.m. By that time, the worker is desperate. If he does not sell his goods that evening, there may not be an evening meal. The dealer or the *dalal* knows his plight so he waits. The smaller dealers buy from Ghat Gate and sell to big-time dearlers at Gopal Ji ka Rasta in Johari Bazaar. The big-time dealers supply to agents of exporters and the product that was bought in one evning for Rs 25 from the worker may ultimately end up selling for Rs 250 at the very least.

A *dalal*, who is also a small-time exporter, told me that the only way to make money was to be *'chatur and chaukn'*('clver and alert'). The *dalal* waits to see how he can get: *'Ek rupaiye ka maal, aath anne mein* (To be able to buy goods worth one ruppe for eight annas). *Dalals* proudly say that the time to buy is just before Id and Muharram, important religious occasions for Muslims, when the worker needs money. At that time, if you are shrewd, you can buy gems for a pittance: *'Ek rupaiye ka maal, char anne mein* (Goods worth one rupee for four annas). Shrewd *dalals* stock up at that time and it is also then that workers get indebted. It is not for nothing as Sajuddin Mian said: 'The rich are becoming richer and the poor are becoming poorer.'

While intially one gets the impression that working children are children primarily of artisans, on deeper investigation, I found that this was not so. In fact, there is a clear-cut hierarchy and the status of a man can be judged from whether he sends his child to work or to school. There is also a distinction between those who send their children to private schools and those who send them to government schools. There are three categories of parents. In the first category are master craftsmen and some less-skilled artisans who can earn up to Rs 100 a day. They generally send their children to private schools. Even artisans who earn less often prefer to send their children to private schools. Bade Main is one of the most talented master craftsmen in Jaipur. He earns staggering sums because he is one of the few craftsmen who can copy antiques. particularly in jade. He has two sons, ten and twelve, who go to school. Bade Mian said:

> Even during the summer vacation, I do not let the boys come to the workshop. Once a child starts making money or hearing conversation about money, he is tempted to work and his mind gets distracted from his studies.

Jabbarbhai, another master craftsman, said the same thing:

> There is plenty of time for a child to pick up the job. If he wants to succeed in this competitive world, he must be educated.

I was told that the children who work full-time from 8 a.m. to 6 p.m. are children of *paldaras* (casual labourers). Bade Mian was of the view that 80 per cent of working children were children of rickshaw-pullers, bakery workers, barbers and the like. This was also confirmed by Jabbarbhai. The explanation proffered was that manual work is vey hard and parents of these children do not want their children to end up doing the same job. They much prefer to send their children to the *ustad* contractor even without wages in the hope that the child will eventually be trained in an occupation which is more remunerative. This was confirmed to me by sveral other people like an auto-rickshaw owner-cum-driver, an adult worker-cum-supervisor who worked for Bade Mian, a cycle-repairer and several casual labourers I had opportunity to interview.

I asked a school teacher why some parents, though keen to send their children to school, do not do so and was told:

> Primary education is virtually free and the school are Rs 5 for the whole year for classes III to V and Rs 30 a year for classes VI to VIII.

There are also special conessions for Scheduled Castes and Scheduled Tribes but the parents still have to spend at least Rs 150-200 a year on books and uniforms. It is those people who cannot even bear this additional expense who send their children to work.

Quraishi, a young contractor who is about twenty-five years old said:

> Of course, a child who gets education is smarter, he can grasp things more easily and will learn much faster. He will also earn a lot of money. But in this trade, even an illiterate fellow after a few years of training, can earn 20 a day, and earn it with dignity. If your father has been rulling rickshaws or hauling sacks on his back, this is clearly better.

I was told that no-one whose *khandani pesha* (traditional occupation) was gem polishing sent their children to work at a very young age. If an artisan was good at his job, the chances would be that his children would be at school. Most people said that more than 80 per cent of children who worked full-time had loans taken by their parents against the security of their labour but the loans did not generally exceed Rs 500.

It seems that about 50 per cent of the total child labour force in the gem polishing industry consists of children whose parents have either an uncertain income or a very hard life or both. These parents send their children to work in the fond hope that the child, if he is able to get into gem industry, will be saved from working as a *coolie* (porter), cycle-richshaw puller, *hathgadi* (hand-cart) Puller, etc.

Behind Indira Market is Kalyan Ji ka Rasta. It is an area, I was told, where most of the working children belonging to families of casual labourers work. I saw eighteen workshops where gems were being polished. In most of them, two or three very little children below the age of eight were working. Some people had set up a makeshift arrangement on the road-side where a *charpai* (bed) was being used to give shelter from the sun. Three children were sitting under the shade of bed, polishing gems. The children in the area were much younger than children I had seen elsewhere and I was told that all these childrenn's fathers were manual labourers. Inside the *mohalla* in an open space, ten children were playing. They looked as if they had been working from the state of their hands and clothes. In one workshop three children, who could not have been more than six years old, were bent over a small coal *sigri* (stove). Their faces were not even six inches from the coal which they were blowing upon to keep the embers alive. They would blow into the embers, warm it and then fix the uncut gem stone on it. They had to do this repeatedly so that the stone was firmly stuck in the right position: it could then be sent for further grinding and polishing. These three boys were being supervised by an adolescent. I tried to talk to these children but they refused to respond and in fact did not even look up while I was talking. A crowd of about seven or eight people gathered around. The contractor, whose workshop it was, looked slightly aggressive and did not like my asking so many questions. He told me that in this area all the working children belonged to labourers' families. Their parents were in no position to send their children to school because they could not afford the expense of books and uniforms. I asked the adolescent boy if he had been educated. He could apparently only sign his name and do some simple accounts. He had started working at the age of six. An elerly man came up and said that he was the father of the adolescent boy and worked as a *khula mazdoor* (casual labourer) himself. He had two sons and three daughters and he had put them to work on gem polishing when they were six or seven. He said:

> I am *khula mazdoor,* working in shops loading and unloading goods. I sent this boy to school for a year or two but then decided that it was better to get the boys to learn a decent craft. So I brought them to the *ustad.* Even if they don't earn anything in the intial years, they will earn enough later to make a decent living after or six years. My son has been spared the indignity of manual labour.

There or four people were also *mazdoors* said the same thing. It was the ambition of every *mazdoor* to get his child to become a *nagine ka karigar* (a gem stone artisan). Hafizbhai, father of one of the working children, said:

> If a man like one only lives on tea because I can't really afford too much food, what do you expect will happen? Most of us get T.B. and we can't afford to get any treatment. How can I afford to send my child to school? Even if my child gets no wages today, in a few years he will start earning a decent living.

I interviewed a cycle-repair man who had worked for twenty-five years on the footpath. He belonged to the casted of roof-thatchers. He had four daughters and two sons. He had four brothers who were carrying on their traditional occupations but all the children in the next generation were gem polishers. He took me to the unit where his eight-year old son worked. He said:

> I drop him off to work at 8 a.m. before I set up shop under this tree. The first I ask my wife when I get home is whether Bablu has come home. All the time I am worried. I want him to leran the trade but such a small child away from home can easily get into company. This is the greatest danger faced by young children.

Mohammad Ali had sent his boy to school for a couple of years but withdrew him in favour of the gem industry. He said:

> My wife was keen that the child learn to work rather than study. She sould point to all the other families where children were working and not going to school. So I agreed to send him to work. After all, Babu is never going to become an officer. If he can be spared taking up our traditional occupation, that's good enough

I interveiwed a richshaw-puller at the bus stand who had three daughters and four sons. All the boys were engaged in the gem industy. The younger ones, at twelve and thirteen years, went to school and also worked in the afternoon. He said:

> Life as a cycle-rickshaw-puller is rough. I started as a millworker but the mill closed down and so for the last fifteen years, I have been pulling rickshaws. This work is very hard and although I can earn Rs 25 or Rs 30 a day, it is exhausting and uncertain. At least in the gem polishing industry, one can sit in a quiet, cool and work rather than sweat and toil in the heat.

In the last category are some parents who send their children to work even when they can afford to send their children to school. Rafiqbhai is in this mid-thirties and is an auto-rickshaw owner-cum-driiver. His whole family is involved in the gem industry. His wife and daughters drill holes in the beads and string them into necklaces. His two boys work for the *ustad.* Although he earns about Rs 50 a day on the average and can afford to send his children to school, he said:

Why send the child to school when you can get him to learn a trade? After all, educated or uneducated, he will be in this line. There are no great advantages in education. But if the child starts learning young, he will start earning young.

Educational Status of Working Child

Suprisingly even though education is seen as a must for upward mobility in this industry 50 per cent of all children working in the gem polishing industry are completely illiterate. As mentioned earlier, even those who were educated up to the third standard learned so little that whatever they had picked up had been totally forgotten. *Dalals*, contractors, master craftsmen, workers and artisans felt strongly that education was an absolute must for all children. I met and has the opportunity of talking to several adults involved in the industry and everyone of them felt that education was a must for all children below the age of fifteen years. Some cases are recounted below which indicate the depth of feeling about the role of education in the struggle for upward mobility.

Bade Mian as mentioned earlier is one of the most talented master craftsmen in Jaipur. He earns *lakhs* (Rs 1 Lakh is equivalent to Rs 100,000) of rupees a year as an artisan because he is one of the few craftsmen who can copy antiques. He showed Me a Chinese jade bowl, which he was working on, for which he was going to get Rs 30,000. He said:

Let me tell you the story (showing me a half-carved jade bowl) of this Chinese jade bowl for which I am going to get Rs 30,000. A dealer came to me with a catalogue and asked me to carve the bowl from the design. One look at the design and I realized that the man had got an unsuspecting American to buy the bowl saying it was of the Shah Jahan period. I knew what the game was because not only am I educated but I have also gone to art school and I know that leaves turned this way on jade are only found in antiques of that period. This man knows that I can carve an exact duplicate. I know that antiques or goods that can passed off as antiques sell at a permium abroad and therefore I could demand this price. I know that the dealer will make at least a *lakh* of rupees on this transaction; otherwise, he would not be willing to pay such a high labour fee.

Bade Mian is totally against the use of child labour. He himself only trains children above the age of fifteen years. He had only one young boy working for him but he insists that children first go to school and then come to him. Rehman is a twelve year old boy who goes to the local school from 7 a.m. to 12 noon. He gets home, has lunch and then goes to Bade Mian's to work till 5 p.m. He was asked by Bade Mian to show me the units where children working. I asked him whether children liked to go to school or to work. He whispered to me that children of his age hated to work all day because it was tiring and boring and their eyes hurt because they were glued to the gem. He himself did not mind learning from Bade Mian because he wanted to become a craftsman. He also did not go regularly. He took me to his father's unit. His father, Samirbhai is a self-styled *ustad* contractor who told me that his *ustad* was also Bade Mian. In his unit, where there were seven children, the youngest— he proudly told me—was not quite five years of age! They were polishing cut gem stones. The workshop was absolutely dark and running exclusively on child labour. All the children were illiterate.

Bade Mian is a staunch believer in education for all children. He sometimes has a couple of children who come to learn from him but he insists that the continue his education for part of the day or at least complete the fifth standard. His own four children are all at school but he wants to get a higher education. He will only teach them after their education is over. Said Bade Mian:

Without education, you are finished. You can easily be cheated by trader. You can never hope to expand your business because you won't be able to speak or understand the language you need. You will never be able to communicate with the foreigners who are the real buyers.

This master craftsman went on to say that education develops the mind and ability to grasp ideas increases. He said:

Let me give you an example. When I started working there were fifty other with me, but I was one of the few educated boys. After five years of training, I left and started my own business and many of my former colleagues came to work for me. They were uneducated and till this day work merely as wage workers. There has been no change in their economic status. In my Thirty years of experience, I can say one thing and that is: an illiterate child can never become an artisan.

In zia-ud-din ki Gali I counted seventy children at work, all between the ages of six and ten years. I talked at length to the *ustad* contractor who was running his whole unit using child labour. He told me that his own children, inculding two daughters, were at school. He pointed to one of older children woking for him, who was about forteen years and his own son and said:

My father was constable turned *dalal*. When I finished my matriculation exam, my father put me to work to learn the job of polishing gems. All my five children are studying. This boy (pointing ot his fourteen-year old son), was in school till very recently but now I have withdrawn him from school because he does not really have an aptitude for studies. I want my children to be educated so that they can keep accounts, deal with traders and, if later we expand our business, they will be able to deal foreign byers.

Jalaluddin employs six children in a small room for polishing gems. He works along with them and also supervises the work. Three of the six children had no education at all. One child had only been educated up to first standard and the other up to the third standard. He said that more than 80 per cent of working children had no education at all. He blamed the shortsightedness of the parents for this state of affairs. He said:

I am slightly better off than the parents of some of these children but I had made up my mind that I would starve and, if necessary, even let my children starve but would not put them to work at an early age. I would educate them. In any case, just because a child is going to school, it doesn't mean that he can't learn to work for a few hours. But if a parent wants to make money on the child, then education is out of the question.

Jalaluddin, of course, offers loans to the parents of these children and effectively binds to him while his own children go to school!

I interviewed sixty-four school-going children in government schools between the age of ten and fourteen years. The idea was to find out what their socio-economic background was. Interestingly, more than 85 per cent of children who worked after school were not childern of artisans. Their fathers were either in government service or employed as barbers, tailors, bakers, masons and a few even as casual labourers. In some homes, the mothers were doing *bindai ka kaam* and in others, ultra-sonic drilling machines for piercing holes in beads had been installed; but these were not families of tradtional craftamen.

In a private school, I interviewed thirty-four children and more than 50 per cent of them came from families of gem artisans, though less than 10 per cent worked after school. But the children said that while they themselves did not work, other children did. My interviews with *ustad* contractors had also revealed the same trend. *Ustad* normally did not allow their own children to work but employed other children to do the work.

Children who work full-time are obviously the most deprived. But those who go to school and work afterwards as well also have a very tough schedule. In the gem polishing industry, the child does not need to work at a young age because everyone recognizes the need for education. Yet a large number of children do work. Part of the problem has to do, as sixteen year-old Jamal explained, with how parents feel: 'If we have too much time on our hands, we are likely to get into bad company and start abusing out sisters and mothers.' Or as Zakir, ten years old said; 'Our parents think that if we play we will become vagabonds and get into company. They, therefore wants us to work.'

Interviews With School Teachers

I interviewed six school teachers. They said that the strain on children who studied and went to work was enormous but, in spite of everything, they did not falter in their home-work. One teacher said that despite their best efforts, these children did not do well academically and then the parents would blame the government schools for the child's poor performance. This was one of the reasons why children dropped out without finishing their education:

> 'How can a child study and work day in and day out for twelve hours without it having some adverse effect? After all, a child too is human!'

Another teacher said that sometimes the children did not find time and had to do their home-work during the P.T. or games period. Working children were considered to be very conscientious but their ability to grasp was not as good as those children who did not have to work. The teachers started discussing the relative intelligence of working and non-working children. They were of the opinion that working children were not as intelligent though out of six teachers present, one admitted that the problem was not that they were less intelligent but that the stresses and strains of going to school and then working took their toll and working child was usually exhausted even after a night of sleep. Another teacher than said:

> There has to be difference in the academic standard of children who can devote time to their studies and those who go straight to work. If child gomes to school at 7 a.m. and after a brief lunch, works til six in the evening and then does home-work at night, what can you expect? But one thing must be said of working children, they try very hard.

Labour Laws And Their Implementation

Surprisingly, while the gem polishing industry is the largest single employer in Jaipur and polished coloured gem stones net the Government of India foreign exchange to the tune of Rs 1400 *crores* a year, no labour laws apply to this industry. Informed sources in the industry say that one of the main reason why India is able to compete in international market in spite of not getting best quality raw material is that India has cheap labour. In the international gem market, India holds the fourth position with respect to the export od emeralds, which are mainly sent to the United States of America. In the export of rubies and sapphires, India holds and fifth position. India supplies he world market with the cheapest emeralds. The main competitors for India are Switzerland, Israel and Hong Kong where the labour charges are much higher.

The idea that the Factories Act should be made applicable to the gem industry was considered ridiculous when mooted. Informed sources said that the political clout of gem traders was such that attempts to the bring this industry under the Factories Act had been abandoned. Some said that while the government was interested in the welfare of workers at one level, the need for earning foreign exchange was paramount and so production would therefore always have an edge over labour welfare.

Mt visits to several manufacturing units of exporters, described earlier, suggested that inspections would be impossible and it would be very hard to prove that a particular exporter is employing a particular number of workers. It is only when one is not a government official that exporters tell you proudly that they have fifty workers under them or 500 employed directly by them on salaries. Since the workers are working in verandas, sheds and places difficult of access and there are no name-plates anywhere, it is difficult to say who is working for whom. In fact, most of the big traders/ exporters/ manufacturers have their own permanent employees who are permanent only in the sense that they have been working for severeal years; they are not permanent according to the provisions of the Factories Act and do not get paid for days they may be ill or when there in no work. They are not entitled to any benefits under the Factories Act because these units do not fall within the definition of what constitutes a factory: in one *haveli,* while there may be forty workers employed, they would be working in several rooms and verandas.

ANNEXURE

Table 1 : Number of workers by type, industrial category, residence, age group and sex in India, 1981

Sl. No.	Industrial category	Residence	Age group (Years)	Main Workers Person	Main Workers Male	Main Workers Female	Marginal workers Person	Marginal workers Male	Marginal workers Female
1	2	3	4	5	6	7	8	9	10
	All categories	All	All ages	2,22,517	1,77,544	44973	22,089	3,537	18,552
			0-14	11,169	7,413	3,756	2,424	684	1,740
		Rural	All ages	1,76,434	1,36,831	39,603	20,875	3,090	17,785
			0-14	10,191	6,681	3,510	2,363	658	1,705
		Urban	All ages	46,083	40,713	5,370	1,214	447	767
			0-14	978	732	246	61	26	35
1.	Cultivators	All	All ages	92,523	77,591	14,932	10m362	1,474	8,888
			0-14	4,013	2,912	1,101	1,183	352	831
		Rural	All ages	90,157	75,475	14,682	10,119	1,406	8,713
			0-14	3,961	2,869	1,092	1.174	349	825
		Urban	All ages	2,365	2,115	250	243	68	175
			0-14	52	43	9	9	3	6
2.	Agricultural labourers	All	All ages	55,500	34,732	20,768	8,864	1.178	7,686
			0-14	4,774	2,783	1,991	1,007	240	767
		Rural	All ages	52,713	32,835	19,878	8,637	1,125	7,512
			0-14	4,629	2,694	1,935	993	236	757
		Urban	All ages	2,787	1,897	890	227	53	174
			0-14	144	89	55	14	4	10
3.	Livestock, forestry fishing, hunting and plantations orchards and allied activites	All	All ages	4,992	4,160	832	435	130	305
			0-14	704	563	141	67	34	33
		Rural	All ages	4,155	3,422	733	405	116	289
			0-14	674	537	137	65	32	33
		urban	All ages	838	738	100	30	14	16
			0-14	30	26	4	3	2	1
4.	Mining and Quarrying	All	All ages	1,264	1,101	163	19	8	11
			0-14	27	16	11	3	1	2
		Rural	All ages	810	676	134	17	6	11
			0-14	25	14	3	3	1	2
		Urban	All ages	454	425	29	2	2	-
			0-14	3	2	1	-	-	-
5.	Manufacturing Processing, servicing and repairs (a) Household Industry	All	All ages	7,711	5,647	2,064	862	107	755
			0-14	424	229	195	69	17	52
		Rural	All ages	5,433	3,932	1,501	681	82	599
			0-14	324	171	153	57	14	43

1	2	3	4	5	6	7	8	9	10
		Urban	All ages	2,279	1,716	563	182	25	157
			0-14	101	58	43	11	3	8
	(b) Other than household industry	All	All ages	17,432	15,834	1598	587	189	393
			0-14	541	400	141	40	14	26
		Rural	All ages	6,059	5,229	830	406	103	303
			0-14	259	170	89	30	9	21
		Urban	All ages	11,373	10,605	768	181	86	95
			0-14	282	230	52	10	6	4
6.	Construction	All	All ages	3,565	3,207	358	141	69	72
			0-14	80	52	28	11	1	7
		Rural	All ages	1,729	1,528	201	97	38	59
			0-14	48	28	20	9	3	6
		Urban	All ages	1,836	1,679	157	43	30	13
			0-14	32	24	8	2	1	8
7.	Trade and commerce	All	All ages	13,929	13,012	917	365	172	193
			0-14	245	224	21	20	13	7
		Rural	All ages	4,918	4,480	438	238	98	140
			0-14	98	84	14	14	8	6
		Urban	All ages	9,012	8,533	479	127	74	53
			0-14	147	140	7	5	4	1
8.	Transport, storage and communications	All	All ages	6,069	5,899	170	73	61	12
			0-14	34	31	3	1	1	-
		Rural	All ages	1,923	1,876	47	37	30	7
			0-14	9	8	1	1	1	-
		Urban	All ages	4,146	4,023	123	34	30	4
			0-14	23	22	1	1	1	-
9.	Other services	All	All ages	19,530	16,360	3,170	381	149	232
			0-14	327	204	123	24	9	15
		Rural	All ages	8,536	7,377	1,159	238	86	152
			0-14	163	105	58	17	6	11
		Urban	All ages	10,995	8,983	2,012	143	64	79
			0-14	163	98	65	7	3	4

Source : Census of India 1981, Series, 1, India, Part II, Special Report & Tables Based on 5 per cent sample Data, 1984.

Table 2 : Workforce Participation Rates by Gender and Residence and Sex Ratio of Workers, India, 1971-91

Residence	Year	Total Males	Females	Main workers Males	Females	Marginal Workers Males	Females	All workers	Main workers	Marginal workers
1	2	3		4		5		6		7
Total	1971	52.5	11.9	-	-	-	-	210	-	-
	1981	52.7	19.8	51.6	14.0	1.0	.58	351	253	5,245
	1991	51.6	22.3	50.9	15.9	0.6	6.3	400	290	9,424
Rural	1971	53.5	13.1	-	-	-	-	232	-	-
	1981	53.8	23.2	52.6	16.0	1.2	7.2	410	289	5,756
	1991	52.5	26.7	51.8	18.6	0.7	8.1	477	337	10,600
Urban	1971	48.8	6.6	-	-	-	-	116	-	-
	1981	49.1	8.3	48.5	7.3	0.5	1.0	149	132	1,715
	1991	48.9	9.2	48.6	8.1	0.4	1.0	167	150	2,648

Source : Proceeding of the First National Workshop on Improvement of Statistics on Gender Issues, C.S.O., Deptt. of Statistics, Ministry of Planning, Programme & Implementation, April 1994, p. 90.

Table 3 : Usual Status Worker Population Ratio by Age (5-9, 10-14 and All Ages), Sex and Residence in India, 1983 and 1987-88

Age group (Years)	Residence	1983 Male PS worker	All worker	Female PS worker	All worker	1987-88 Male PS worker	All worker	Female PS worker	All worker
5-9	Rural	20	26	18	25	7	23	6	24
	Urban	5	8	5	7	5	5	3	3
10-14	Rural	213	253	170	240	145	190	126	182
	Urban	93	113	54	70	73	85	45	65
All ages	Rural	613	635	287	373	517	539	245	323
	Urban	568	581	138	173	496	506	118	152

Source : Fourth Quinquennial Survey on Employment and Unemployment (NSSO 43rd round) Special Report No. 1 Key Results of Employment and Unemployment Survey, All India (Part-1), January 1990.

Table 4 : Workforce Participation Rates in the Age Groups 5-9 and 10-14 as Per Current Weekly Status in Various NSS Round

Age Groups	Male 1977-1978	1983	1987-1988	1989-1990	Female 1977-1978	1983	1987-1988	1989-1990
5-6	-	0.5	0.5	1.0	-	0.6	0.3	0.6
	(5.5)	(5.2)	(3.9)	(1.3)	(3.6)	(3.0)	(2.4)	(2.4)
19-14	-	9.8	7.5	8.9	-	5.4	4.6	4.5
5+	55.5	55.9	55.6	56.4	14.2	13.5	13.5	13.8

Notes: 1. The figures for the year 1983 (38th round) are from Sarvekshana April 1988 (Vol 11, No.4 issue 35) and are different from those reported in Sarvekshana April 1986 (Vol. 9, No.4), covering only two sub-rounds.

2. The figures within brackets are for the age group of 0-14 years.

Source : National Sample Survey Organization.

Table 5 : Percentage Distribution of Children (Age 5-9 and 10-14 Years) by Principal Usual Activity Status, Sex and Redidence in India, 1987-88

Usual Activity (Principal) Status		Rural Male 5-9	10-14	Rural Female 5-9	10-14	Urban Male 5-9	10-14	Urban Female 5-9	10-14
1	2	3	4	5	6	7	8	9	10
A.	Working (or Employed)								
	(1) Worked (Self employed or as helper) in household enterprises	0.5	9.0	0.4	7.2	0.3	3.1	0.2	2.0
	(2) Worked as regular salaried/wage employee	0.1	1.6	-	0.5	0.1	2.3	0.1	1.2
	(3) Woked as casual wage labourer in public works	-	0.1	-	0.1	-	-	-	-
	(4) Worked as causal wage labourer in other types of work	0.1	3.8	0.1	4.8	0.1	1.9	0.1	1.3
	Total employed	0.7	14.5	0.6	12.6	0.5	7.3	0.3	4.5
B.	Not working but sought work	-	0.5	-	0.4	-	0.8	-	0.2
C.	Neither working nor available for work								

1	2	3	4	5	6	7	8	9	10
	(1) Attended educational Institutions	27.6	67.0	23.5	12.3	72.6	81.3	67.7	72.4
	(2) Attended domestic duties only	-	0.8	0.5	11.4	0.2	0.6	0.6	9.5
	(3) Attended domestic duties free and was also engaged tailoring weaving, etc., in collection of goods for household use	0.1	1.1	0.5	10.9	0.1	0.2	0.1	2.9
	(4) Not able to work due to disabillity	-	0.2	-	0.1	0.1	0.2	0.1	0.2
	(5) Beggars etc.	-	0.1	-	0.1	-	-	-	-
	(6) Others	71.6	15.8	74.9	22.2	26.5	9.6	31.1	10.3
	Total not in labour force	99.3	85.0	99.4	87.0	99.5	91.9	99.6	95.3
	Total	100	100	100	100	100	100	100	100

Source : Based on Fouth Quinquennial survey in Employment and unemployment (NSS 43rd Round) Special Report No.1 Key Results for Employment and Unemployment Survey, All India (Part-1) January 1990.

Table 6 : Percentage Distribution of Labour Force as Per Current Weekly Status Acrosss Employment Categories in Age Group 5-9 and 10-14 Years 1989-90

Employment categories	Male 5-9	Male 10-14	Female 5-9	Female 10-14
Self employed persons				
a. Agriculture	9.1	6.3	28.6	15.6
b. Non-Agriculture	36.4	48.4	28.6	48.9
Regular/ Salaried Workers				
a. Agriculture	0.0	0.0	0.0	0.0
b. Non-Agriculture	0.0	16.8	14.3	17.8
Casual Workers				
a. Agriculture	0.0	2.1	0.0	4.4
b. Non-Agriculture	45.4	20.0	14.3	13.3
Unemployed persons	9.1	6.3	14.3	0.0

Source : Sarvekshana (45th Round of NSS).

Table 7 : Unemployment Rates in The Age-groups 5-9 and 10-14 as Per Usual Status (Principal Workers Only) in Different NSS Rounds

Age Groups	Male 1977-1978	1983	1987-1988	1989-1990	Female 1977-1978	1983	1987-1988	1989-1990
5-9	–	5.3	0.0	10.0	-	0.0	0.0	0.0
	(7.7)	(10.7)	(9.8)	(11.1)	(9.7)	(2.0)	(4.2)	(0.0)
10-14	–	11.0	9.9	11.3	–	2.5	4.3	0.0
5+	6.5	5.9	6.1	4.3	17.8	6.9	8.8	3.5

Note: The figure within brackets are for the age group of 5-14 years.
Source: National Sample Survey Organization.

Table 8 : Unemployment Rates in the Age-groups 5-9 and 10-14 as Per current Weekly Status in Different NSS Rounds

Age Groups	Male 1977-1978	1983	1987-1988	1989-1990	Female 1977-1978	1983	1987-1988	1989-1990
5-6	–	3.5	0.0	9.1	–	6.6	0.0	14.3
	(7.0)	(10.0)	(10.4)	(6.6)	(4.3)	(3.8)	(4.1)	(2.7)
10-14	–	10.3	10.7	6.3	–	3.5	4.2	0.0
5+	7.1	6.7	6.6	4.6	10.6	7.5	8.9	3.9

Note: Figures in brackets are for the age group of 5-14 years.
Source: National Sample Survey Organization.

Table 9 : Average Wage Earnings (Rs. 0.0) Per Day Received by Casual Wage Labouers by Age Group and Industry in Urban Areas 1987-88

Age Group	Gender	0	1	2	3	4	5	6	7	8	9	1-9
5-14	M	8.36	–	6.03	7.50	–	14.68	7.42	10.47	8.57	9.37	8.77
	F	6.74	600	4.57	7.27	–	12.00	–	–	--	5.71	5.81
15-59	M	13.08	17.46	18.04	17.13	16.91	19.47	15.47	17.73	17.51	17.15	17.89
	F	7.63	11.73	8.28	8.91	10.55	11.90	8.57	15.11	18.63	9.38	9.65
60 & above	M	10.75	12.73	18.64	18.08	–	20.96	18.64	17.66	10.75	13.37	17.70
	F	6.95	–	4.93	5.00	–	10.87	6.65	–	5.00	7.07	7.01
All ages	M	12.82	17.38	17.46	16.78	16.91	19.41	15.00	17.63	16.86	16.55	17.54
	F	7.57	11.23	7.86	8.67	10.55	11.87	8.44	14.98	16.85	8.87	9.23

Source: Sarvekshna Sept., (1990).

Table 10 : Per 1000 Distribution of Unemployed Persons by Current Weekly Activity in the Age-groups 5-9 and 10-14 Years

Age Group (yrs)	Residence	1990-91 Male	1990-91 Female	1991-92 Male	1991-92 Female
5-9	Rural	1	2	–	–
	Urban	–	–	–	–
10-14	Rural	2	–	3	2
	Urban	9	–	9	4

Source : National Sample Survey Organisation.

Table 11 Per 1000 Distribution of Unemployed Persons by Principal Usual Activity Category in the Age-groups 5-9 and 10-14 Years

Age Group (yrs)	Residence	1990-91 Male	1990-91 Female	1991-92 Male	1991-92 Female
5-9	Rural	2	2	–	1
	Urban	1	–	1	2
10-14	Rural	4	2	2	1
	Urban	10	2	12	7

Source : National Survey organisation.

Glossary

Main Workers	:	One who has worked for the major part of the year preceding the date of enumeration *i.e.*, those who were engaged in any economically productive activity for 183 days or six months or more during the year.
Marginal Workers	:	Those who worked time at all in the year preceding the date of enumeration but did not work for the major part of year i.e. those who worked for less than 183 days or six months.
Non-Workers	:	Those who have not worked any time at all in the year preceding date of enumeration.
Usually Employed	:	Those worked for a relatively longer period of a reference of period of 365 days preceding the date of survey.
Prinicpal Status Worker	:	A person categorised as 'worker' on the basis of his/ her principal status.
Subsidiary Status Worker	:	A 'non worker' who pursued some gainful activity in a subsidiary capacity.
All Workers	:	Include principal status workers and subsidiary status workers.
Workere Population Ratio	:	The number of persons usually employed in a particular age group per 1000 persons in the age group.
Work Participation Rate	:	Percentage of workers to the total population.
Current Weekly Status	:	A person is considered to be employed if he/she pursues any one or more of the gainful activity for at least one hour on any day of the previous week.

Industry (Division) :

Agriculture, hunting, forestry & fishing	0
Mining and quarrying	1
Manufacturng	2 or 3
Electricity, gas and water	4
Construction	5
Wholesale and retail trade the restaurants and hotels	6
Transport, storage and communication	7
Financing, insurance, real estate and business service	8
Community, social and personal services	9

❏❏❏